JOHN CHARLES FRÉMONT

❖

John Charles Frémont, painted by Thomas Hicks, probably based upon an 1856 photograph by Matthew Brady. The year before, Brady had stopped using daguerreotypes and thereafter adopted the wet-plate method of photography upon which modern photographs are based. That process resulted in a better model from which artists could paint portraits. Hicks painted portraits of many famous Americans, including President Abraham Lincoln. (Reproduced by permission of the Huntington Library, San Marino, California)

JOHN CHARLES FRÉMONT

❖

Character as Destiny

By Andrew Rolle

UNIVERSITY OF OKLAHOMA PRESS : NORMAN AND LONDON

Some Other Books by Andrew Rolle

An American in California; The Biography of William Heath Davis, 1822–1909
(1956, 1981)
The Road to Virginia City: The Diary of James Knox Polk Miller (ed.) (1960, 1989)
California: A History (1963, 1969, 1978, 1987)
The Golden State: A History of California (coauthor) (1965, 1979, 1990)
The Lost Cause: Confederate Exiles in Mexico (1965)
*The Immigrant Upraised: Italian Adventurers and Colonists in an Expanding
America* (1970)
The Italian Americans: Their History and Culture (1972)
The Italian Americans: Troubled Roots (1980, 1984)
Los Angeles: From Pueblo to City of the Future (1981)
Occidental College: A Centennial History (Los Angeles, 1987)

Rolle, Andrew F.
    John Charles Frémont : character as destiny / by Andrew Rolle.—
1st ed.
        p.   cm.
    Includes bibliographical references (p.   ) and index.
    ISBN 0-8061-2380-X (alk. paper)
    1. Frémont, John Charles, 1813–1890. 2. Explorers—United States—
Biography. 3. Generals—United States—Biography. 4. Presidential
candidates—United States—Biography. I. Title.
E415.9.F8R65   1991
973.6′092—dc20
[B]   91-50305
                                                                                          CIP

Text and jacket designed by Sue Hollingsworth

The paper in this book meets the guidelines for permanence and durability of the
Committee on Production Guidelines for Book Longevity of the Council on Library
Resources, Inc. ♾

For Myra
who helped put it all together

He must blaze a nation's way.

—Rudyard Kipling, *The Foreloper*

A century and a half ago a heady and enigmatic young adventurer, John Charles Frémont, sought to chart the wild and unknown reaches of America's farthest west. His five dramatic expeditions made "the Pathfinder" the nation's best-known explorer-hero. Today he continues to receive credit for opening up much of its far western frontier regions.

Frémont's years of exploration were indeed remarkable. He covered more ground than any other government explorer, including Meriwether Lewis and William Clark. Clad in buckskin, like the heroes of James Fenimore Cooper's *Leatherstocking Tales,* Frémont and his men confronted dangerous natives and an untamed wilderness. He was at his best while riding at the head of his faithful Delaware scouts, hunting buffalo and deer, describing fauna and flora, observing tribal celebrations, or trading with the Klamaths for salmon. His scientific reports helped to dispel the myth that the western plains were the "Great American Desert." Frémont correctly forecast that water, hidden underground, could transform the aridity of the continent's vast intermountain region.

Frémont's life spanned the nation's transition from canoes and buckskins into the age of steam and machinery, from wilderness to industrial empire. He was not only a major explorer of the American West, but also a disputed conqueror of California, one of its two first senators, a Civil War general, a developer of mines and railroad lines, the first Republican presidential candidate, and governor of Arizona Territory.

Frémont's career flourished in an America that loved adventure and excitement. His spectacular exploits encouraged a legendary image. So did his blunders. At almost every step he seemed poised on the verge of greatness, which he sometimes transformed into failure through unpredictable decisions. He commingled inconsistency with pretentiousness, igniting contention and controversy.

But Frémont also possessed splendid capacities, although they were marred by such serious faults of character. His soft voice and outwardly modest gentility are difficult to balance against his unremitting grudges and his volcanic passions. Frémont's behavior fits that view of human nature according to which a leader becomes his own worst enemy. Yet hardened mountain men repeatedly accompanied him on dangerous expeditions. In adversity and misery, as during the

1844 midwinter crossing of the Sierra Nevada, or even on the disastrous fourth expedition into northern New Mexico and Colorado, a coterie of followers found reassurance in his leadership.

There is no need to deprive Frémont of his complex human dimensions. We need to portray both strengths and weaknesses. There is no reason, moreover, either to defend or to condemn him. This book, using a relatively cautious psychiatric approach, will seek to show that Frémont's illegitimate birth and strange parentage—which has so long remained in deep shadow—influenced a compensatory development of his personality. The very name of his father was a pseudonym, and his roots were not French, as every biographer has maintained, but French Canadian.

Biographers and historians alike have idealized Frémont or damned him. They have called him "A Man Unafraid," and "The West's Greatest Adventurer." Some, less generously, have even changed his sobriquet, "the Pathfinder," to "follower of other men's trails." His contradictory life has perplexed all of his interpreters. They could not explain his obdurate behavior and poor judgment.[1]

Frémont shrugged off the reprimands of two presidents, defying superior officers both in the midst of battle and on the frontier, where he could best escape conformity. Thus, he usually acted out his impulses outside the circle of important public figures who either hated or supported him. Although he had the backing of a powerful father-in-law, Senator Thomas Hart Benton of Missouri, Frémont did little to avoid being court-martialed or accused of abandoning his men during acts of folly. He exposed himself to charges of cannibalism in the wilderness, womanizing, and even opium consumption. Frémont did not help his cause, for his own memoirs masked his inner feelings. Instead, he said blandly that he would confine himself to those "events and incidents that make up daily life."[2]

Most modern interpreters do not separate standard historical events from the personalities that help to shape their times. Sometimes motives are difficult to unearth. Nevertheless, Leon Edel, the biographer of Henry James, urges us to seek out "the figure under the carpet, the evidence in the reverse of the tapestry." For beneath the outer shell there lies "the secret self, the inner myth" about a person's life.[3]

I have used psychiatric techniques, for the most part, when supported by the evidence, not so much to search for Frémont's personal secrets but rather to seek a better understanding of the man. As one slowly follows the calendar of his life, some unique personal characteristics do tend to unravel themselves. While it is tempting to single out key events or personalities that produced trauma in Frémont's career, one should also allow his interactions with numerous persons to point the way. He himself was a highly defended person, obscuring the origins of his many controversial decisions. Yet he repeatedly acted out or displaced his anxieties onto others, never looking clearly into the mirror of his flawed ambition.

Whether my approach will convince general readers as well as historians and psychoanalysts is another matter. Opposition to such a biographical technique usually divides into that voiced by critics who object to any sort of psychological inquiry and that of those for whom interpretations of a person's life are either never analytic enough or too sweeping. Often the quotations of contemporaries tell the story best. By using their evaluations, readers can make up their own minds about key controversies in Frémont's life.

Ideally, biography should be a shared discovery. Psychology aside, it involves inferential reconstruction of human conduct from historical traces. This book is no exception. It reexamines the influence of Frémont's long-misunderstood parentage, his involvement with the Benton family into which he married, the controversies surrounding his five expeditions, his alleged conquest of California, his court-martial, and his stormy Civil War disputes with President Lincoln, the influential Blair family, and a bevy of West Point generals. It also examines Frémont's incessant financial scrapes, including legal indictments in France and England.[4]

There have been other enigmatic leaders in America's history, among them Aaron Burr and, in recent times, Generals George Patton and Douglas MacArthur. But none of them, including Frémont's derring-do contemporary General George Armstrong Custer, ever aroused quite such public dispute. While not as flamboyant as Custer, Frémont too was capable of temperamental flareups and notorious precipitate acts. Careless of consequences, he also used the money and power of others to advance his own ambitions. Testing personal as well as geographic boundaries, he repeatedly refused to accept blame for the disasters he caused, always preferring the role of hero.[5]

Whenever such daredevils come to grief, controversy about them commences. In addition to Custer, at least three other contentious historical figures are guaranteed to start an argument among biographers: Mary Queen of Scots, the English monarch Richard III, and, at a different level, John Charles Frémont.

Frémont's career provides us not only with a window onto an expanding America. It also presents an opportunity to unravel a psychodrama of major intensity. New as well as overlooked material from Canada, Great Britain, and Virginia; manuscripts at the Library of Congress and the Huntington, Bancroft, Princeton, and Columbia libraries; and diaries and letters printed in recent years were unknown to previous writers. What has emerged from these sources is a complex and grandiose personality enmeshed in constant turmoil throughout a long, controversial life.[6]

Finally, a note about style: Frémont's name is accented throughout the book, as he himself signed it. In the notes the first names of all writers of manuscript material are shown by their initials only in order to save space.

ANDREW ROLLE

ACKNOWLEDGMENTS

❖

I decided to write my own biography of John Charles Frémont in 1967, when the late Allan Nevins asked me to prepare a new sketch of Frémont for the *Encyclopaedia Britannica*. Grants from the National Endowment for the Humanities and from the American Philosophical Society have supported the writing of this book. I also thank the Southern California Psychoanalytic Institute and the Cedars-Sinai Medical Center at Los Angeles, where I received training in psychoanalysis and psychiatry. Over the years the Henry E. Huntington Library has provided space and time in which to write as well as intellectual companionship.

I have benefited, as with my last book, from the suggestions of Myra Moss Rolle. Others who have been of help include Martin Ridge, Robin Winks, Jacob Cooke, David Danelski, Peter Olch, Sandra Myres, Mary Lee Spence, Werner Marti, David Weber, Norris Hundley, Jr., Christina Bozza, Iris Engstrand, Karen Lystra, George Brockway, Donald Lamm, Hal Barron, Charles Royster, Judson Grenier, Frances Squires Rolle, Luisa Reyes, Grace Allen, James Clark, and Aida Donald as well as the late Ray Allen Billington and Fawn Brodie.

A version of this book appeared in my article "Exploring an Explorer: Psychohistory and John Charles Frémont," *Pacific Historical Review*, May, 1982, pp. 135–63. Finally, it is appropriate that the leading American publisher of our country's explorational history should be bringing out this biography. I wish to give special acknowledgment to the managerial and editorial skills of John Drayton, Sarah Morrison, and their consultant, Noel Parsons.

JOHN CHARLES FRÉMONT

❖

John Charles Frémont's emotional complexities are not easy to trace, rooted as they are in a strange parentage. Over many years, only one version of his clouded past has persisted.

Frémont's mother, Anne Beverly Whiting, was the youngest of twelve children of Colonel Thomas Whiting, a large landowner in Gloucester County, Virginia, and a leading member of its House of Burgesses. Whiting had died during Anne's childhood, and her mother had subsequently married a man who dissipated the estate. The family married Anne off on October 13, 1796, at age seventeen, to Major John Pryor, a Revolutionary War veteran forty-five years her senior. Pryor, who could have been her grandfather, was described as stuffy, short, fat as butter, and very rich and very gouty. For a time he was military agent for the commonwealth of Virginia and also operated a resort, Pryor's Haymarket Garden, in Richmond, where he and Anne lived. She later told her son that she had "dragged out twelve long years of wedded misery" with Major Pryor, during which "she became melancholy" and "shunned the gay society and habits of life to which her husband was addicted."[1]

In 1808 one Charles Frémon (no *t*) arrived in Richmond. Of French background, he passed himself off as a royalist émigré and for the next two years taught the city's affluent young ladies foreign languages and painted wall and ceiling frescoes in their homes. He also taught swordsmanship to young Virginia gentlemen and did "occasional upholstering." For a time he became a "French professor" in a "female academy" run by Louis H. Girardin, the joint author with John D. Burk of *A History of Virginia* (1816).

By June 1810, Frémon had so insinuated himself into the Pryor household that Anne's husband allowed him the use of a cottage on the grounds of his recreation park. There Frémon began to teach Anne French. When, before long, the major learned he had been cuckolded, he angrily vowed retribution. Anne wrote to a brother-in-law that Pryor, in fact, had turned her "out of doors at night and in an approaching storm" and that he threatened her with "the most cruel and violent treatment."[2] The ensuing scandal was impossible to conceal. A petition of December 7, 1811, speaks of "criminal intercourse" between Frémon and Anne. The last notice from the infuriated Pryor appeared in an 1811 Richmond newspaper, in which he stated that his wife had abandoned his home and had run off with Frémon:

> Whereas my wife Anne has totally alienated her affections from me by the vile and invidious machinations of an execrable monster of baseness and depravity, with whom I have recently discovered she has for some time past indulged in criminal intercourse, and has in consequence thereof abandoned my bed and board for the protection of her seducer, with whom I have reason to believe she has gone off, therefore forfeiting all claim to my support.[3]

According to the generally accepted version, John Charles Frémont's father was a native of Lyons, an exile from the French Revolution who was en route to the West Indies when his ship was captured by an English cruiser. Plausible Canadian sources offer a quite different version of Frémont's parental origins that has been overlooked. These sources tell us that his father was actually Louis-René Frémont (with the *t*), born at Quebec City on December 8, 1768, to Jean Louis and Catherine Reine (née Boucher de Boucherville) Frémont. Frémont's grandfather had come to Canada from Saint-Germain-en-Laye in France. In 1800, Louis-René ran for a seat in Quebec's Chambre de l'Assemblée. In an appeal for votes in the *Gazette de Québec* on June 17, he pointed out to prospective backers that he had been born and raised among them, had engaged in commerce, and knew their wishes well. Suddenly, and unexplainably, however, he withdrew from the campaign in favor of another candidate, who subsequently won a seat in the province's parliament.[4]

On an uncertain date, Louis René Frémont left Canada for the Caribbean island country of Saint-Domingue (or Santo Domingo), now the Dominican Republic, where he planned to join an aunt who lived in its French colony. But the French vessel on which he sailed was captured by an English frigate. After several years of imprisonment at an unknown place, he escaped to Norfolk, Virginia, where he called himself Charles Frémon, hoping to elude recognition.

Unable to find work in Norfolk, Frémon next went on to Richmond. By 1811, his last known employer there, Girardin, prodded by the irate Major Pryor, published a notice in the *Virginia Patriot* that described Frémon's elopement with Anne as an "improper intrigue." Girardin added: "I ceased to employ C. F. about two years ago." Meanwhile, "Frémon had taken a house on the Hill and lived publically with a common prostitute!!!" When so accused, he answered: 'I will do as I please now. I will not be here long.' " Frémont's future mother, as a result of her illicit affair, was no longer considered a prominent married woman. In the view of Richmond society, Frémon was no longer "a fit person to give instructions to young ladies."[5]

Anne and her foreign lover thus fled first to Williamsburg, then to Norfolk, taking along with them several Negro servants whom she had inherited as slaves. Among them was "Black Hannah," who would become John Charles's nursemaid. It is impossible to say what early warmth he received from her that disposed him to act so favorably toward blacks for the rest of his life. In the summer of 1811 they moved to Savannah, Georgia. There, at 563 Bay Street, Anne ran a boardinghouse in which she gave birth to her first son. Frémon also found employment there, teaching dancing and French at J. B. Le Roy's Academy. Soon after the birth of John Charles on January 21, 1813, the little family began to travel again.[6]

John Charles's earliest memories were of the faint smell of smoke from Indian encampments. His nomadic parents traveled "with their own carriage, horses, and servants, stopping where convenience of towns and dwellings required, and not infrequently passing the night in Indian villages or by camp-fire" because of inadequate funds to lodge their retinue.[7] Rattling across the landscape in a noisy carriage, they never tarried long in any one place. Each night they firmly tethered the horses that would carry them as far west as Tennessee. One could, thus, say that Fremont was born with rambling in his blood. His life would itself be an extraordinary journey of discovery.

In Nashville, on September 4, 1814, boisterous frontier realities burst in on the one-year-old John Charles's family. That night a bullet blasted its way through the room in which the child was sleeping at Clayton Talbot's Tavern. Remarkably, the pistol shots were fired by the toddler's future father-in-law, Thomas Hart Benton, who with his brother Jesse had found himself at the same hostelry as Frémon's group. Also at the tavern, and wounded by one of Benton's bullets, was the argumentative Andrew Jackson, who one day would become president of the United States. Although the shooting was circumstantial, John Charles thus experienced an early and rude introduction to frontier society. A fierce manliness permeated life throughout the wooded Appalachians, the world of Andrew Jackson and Davy Crockett, of coonskin caps with raccoon tails, of buckskin raiment, tomahawks, and flintlock muskets.[8]

On the very day of the upsetting, haphazard shooting, Anne had given birth to a daughter named after herself. By the next year the family was back in Norfolk; Elizabeth was born there in 1815, as was Thomas Archibald (called Frank) two years later. By 1818, Frémon died, depriving the five-year-old John Charles of his father just before that father planned to emigrate to France or to return to Canada.[9]

During all this time, Anne had remained legally married to Major Pryor. At age seventy-six, the abandoned Pryor had married (presumably after divorcing Anne) his young housekeeper, and he outlived his wife's seducer by five years, dying on March 23, 1823. Pryor's comfortable life lends credibility to the criticisms of the French traveler Hector Saint-John de Crèvecoeur that such southern propertied men were addicted to foolish pleasures supported by the slave system. Gentlemen merchants and planters who lived along the shores of the low country styled themselves "the Chivalry." These landed gentry mostly left it to the ladies of the Tidewater to set household standards. In the social world that Anne had left, household blacks were treated much like members of a family. This superficial paternalism featured ties with black nannies, who virtually became members of the affluent and respectable families of Tidewater society. Anne had turned her back on that world. Her foreign lover now dead, she would pay the consequences of her attempted escape from it. And so would her son.

Some southern women owned little or no property unless, like Anne Pryor, they had inherited slaves. But maintenance of even a servant or two was expensive, for they had to be supported. And Anne, who now began to call herself Mrs. Frémont (with the *t*), owned no land, the real basis of southern prestige and power. Her lover had left behind nothing of value whatsoever except useless memories.

These disadvantages would haunt John Charles throughout his life. He certainly would not grow up under the affluent circumstances that his mother had known. And his struggle for self-validation was different from hers. During the 1856 presidential campaign he would desperately seek evidence of his father's Quebec origins and of the possible marriage of his parents. But he himself was then accused, in addition to being a bastard, of hiding his foreign birth. If this charge had been substantiated, it would have disqualified him as a candidate for the American presidency. Although Frémont was actually born in the United States, no birth certificate has ever been found for him.[10] More important for the development of his self-image, the boy thought of himself as illegitimate, with a mysterious and stormy past. Such was the parentage of John Charles Frémont at an age that the Freudians perceive to be the classic period of Oedipal development.

In 1819 the young lad put down his first roots in Charleston, South Carolina, where his mother had moved. Along its cobblestone and brick roads were dozens of porticoed and pillared white mansions built in the early 1700s. The town was protected from the sea by cannon aimed from the East Battery toward the confluence of the Cooper and Ashley rivers. Gardenlike Charleston was a place of great beauty, surrounded by lakes, lush magnolias, and jet-black cypresses.[11] Peacocks sauntered down meandering paths amid a panoply of flowers. In the hinterlands, up the Ashley River, indigo and rice plantations had been carved out of Indian lands. A wilderness of swamps, marshlands, tall cypresses, and live oaks stretched out beyond plantation mansions.

John Charles loved to saunter down the stretch of Church Street known as Cabbage Row. Beyond it was the marketplace where slaves were auctioned off as if they were pieces of furniture. Blacks were not allowed to follow military units, to bathe horses in public, or to walk on the Battery. He watched them by the hour and saw them arrested, and sometimes beaten, for fighting or being out after the warning tattoo sounded. Runaways were turned over to their master for punishment; others met stiff retribution by the local courts. In short, John Charles experienced racial repression everywhere about him in Charleston. And this would affect his future behavior, too.

Like that of the blacks, his own status was precarious. In the antebellum South, illegitimacy was scandalous. Its society remained patriarchal to the core. Lineage, wealth in the form of land, and outwardly circumspect behavior were the prerequisites of prestige and power.

As for Anne Pryor, at age thirty-four, widowed and shunned by Tidewater society, she was poor and alone, with three illegitimate children to rear. Not surprisingly, her son remembered her at that time "as a woman of most extraordinary grace and beauty, of gentle, captivating manners, with a sweet but singularly melancholy disposition"—the word *melancholy* being the nineteenth-century term for depression.[12] There is a close relationship between mourning, melancholia, and loss; underlying all three is malaise. John Charles's mother may have fastened upon the boy her own sad realizations that it would be impossible to hold together her miserably declined family clan. Indeed, death and the escape of her children did ultimately prove inevitable.[13]

After its founding in 1670, Charleston had attracted a notable French colony, but its clannish members offered Anne's family no support. She herself was not of Gallic background. Catholics, furthermore, condemned illegitimacy as much as did Anglo Protestants. Yet the French influence remained intangibly in her son's past—as did his lack of a proper lineage and legitimate good name. With no father and no property, Frémont had little exposure to traditional family ideals—French or southern. He could not look forward to the traditional division of family property. On the other hand, unlike the sons of Charleston's best families, the boy never saw its patriarchal life as "a school for subordination." He never had "to negotiate the transition from subordination to dominance."[14] When he eventually struck out on his own, he would do so without fear of a father's wrath or punishment.

In the homes of Charleston's rich, circumstances were entirely different.

The slightest slip in conduct could tarnish an entire family. One father advised his son: "Render yourself as accomplished as you can & endeavor to fix yourself in the station of a respectable independent Gentleman, & that station you will certainly find the happiest in the world." Even after his son's marriage, this father paid the young man's bills. But such sons had to avoid "any slur on any of us," as one contemporary put it. John Charles thus did not have to spend years in that "perfect idleness" so characteristic of his rich contemporaries. Nor was he bound to a parental orbit of loyalty from which escape was impossible and rebellion a crime that led to disinheritance.[15]

During 1826, to supplement his mother's meager finances, John Charles clerked for Charleston lawyer John W. Mitchell, who had taken a keen interest in him. His job as a clerk gave the lad "the first rudiments of his education at Dinwiddie Court House." Then only thirteen years old, he already was observing nature's wonders. An acute observer of streams, mountains, flora, and fauna, the boy put his knowledge to good use for his employer. Mitchell noted the "scientific skill and neatness" with which Frémont "carefully and accurately surveyed" the legal boundaries of a rice field in a dangerously malarial locality that experienced surveyors had refused to enter.[16]

Lawyer Mitchell suggested that Frémont should go to John Roberton's preparatory school and agreed to underwrite the tuition. "Mr. Mitchell," the schoolmaster later recalled, "had resolved to place him under my care for the purpose of learning Greek, Latin, and Mathematics sufficient to enter Charleston College." Roberton, a shrewd Scotsman, saw that

> he was no common youth, as intelligence beamed in his dark eyes, and shone brightly. I should call him handsome, of a keen, piercing eye, and a noble forehead. . . . I at once put him in the highest class, just beginning to read Caesar's Commentaries. . . . He began Greek at the same time and read with some who had been long at it. . . . Whatever he read he retained.

Within a year Roberton's "beloved and favorite pupil" had read Caesar, Nepos, Sallust, the six books of Virgil, much of Horace, two books of Livy, the *Graeca Minora*, part of *Graeca Majorca* and four books of Homer's *Iliad*.[17]

At age sixteen, the youth was confirmed at Saint Philip's Episcopal Church. Its records list him as "Charles Frémont." For a time his mother hoped he would become a clergyman. Roberton, however, recalled: "When I contemplated his bold, fearless disposition, his powerful inventive genius, his admiration of warlike exploits, and his love of heroic and adventurous deeds, I did not think it likely he would be a minister of the Gospel."[18] Fascinated by heroic exploits, young Frémont read Roberton's own translation of Xenophon's *Anabasis*, which told of the ten thousand Greek mercenaries who went on a military expedition to the land of the Persian king Cyrus in Asia Minor to combat Kurdish tribesmen and suffered a disastrous military defeat there. The "Upcountry March," carried out against great adversity, strongly impressed the young man who would one day head a series of his own expeditions.

His teacher continued to praise him: "I could not help loving him," Roberton recalled, "so much did he captivate me. . . . It was easy to see he would one day rise to eminence." Years later, Frémont wrote of his old professor: "I am very far from either forgetting you or neglecting you, or in any way losing the old regard I had for you. There is no time to which I go back with more pleasure than that spent with you. . . . I remember nothing so well, and so distinctly as what I acquired with you."[19]

So rapid was his progress in Greek, Latin, and mathematics that in May, 1829, he was admitted to the junior class of the College of Charleston on a charity scholarship established by Reverend Christopher Gadsden, later bishop of the local Episcopal diocese. His new teachers found Frémont mannerly but restless. He clearly disliked the headmaster, the Reverend Jasper Adams, who presided over compulsory daily prayer at the struggling college of sixty-two students and required a full seven hours of daily instruction.[20]

One biographer portrays Frémont's school years as ones in which he was "superficially curious rather than profound," making the young man out to be a vagabond who sought triumph through adventure. With dark hair, olive skin, a quick mind, and a lean body, Frémont displayed "a singular simplicity and courtesy" but "made freedom a religion." Soon disciplinary problems grew out of his love of the outdoors and the excitement of truancy.[21]

Instead of studying, John Charles could often be found sporting on the green of Charleston's meadows and exploring salt marshes, streams, and limestone ridges. "I know I was a transgressor," he recalled almost gleefully:

> I had my compensation. The college authorities had wrapped themselves in their dignity and reluctantly but sternly inflicted on me condign punishment. To me this came like a summer wind. . . . I smiled to myself while I listened to words about the disappointment of friends, and the broken career. I was living in a charmed atmosphere and the edict only gave me complete freedom.[22]

Frémont was developing a knack for disguising his animosity toward people and institutions. But in his memoirs he preferred to focus on his early love of adventure: "This is an autobiography and it would not be true to itself if I left out the bit of sunshine that made the glory of my youth. . . . There will be enough hereafter of grave and hard conflict and dissension, violence and injury and fraud; but none of these things were known to us, that little circle of sworn friends." He had frequented a small group, mostly French-speaking children of political refugees. One of them was a young Creole girl named Cecilia, the eldest daughter of a family that had escaped from the island of Saint-Domingue during a local revolt. She was captivated by his dark, wavy hair, olive skin, and blue eyes beneath full black brows. He, too, still only seventeen, recalled that he "was passionately in love" with her. This schoolboy infatuation was also at the expense of his studies, except for mastery of French, which he spoke incessantly with her.[23]

A classmate, later a clergyman, derisively recalled Frémont's carousing at Charleston's Tivoli Gardens, a haunt for "lowlifes." There he belonged to a thespian club that met every Saturday night, when "he trod the mimic stage to the admiration of the groundlings and wound up with a drunken revel, which was often continued through Sunday. No wonder the Pierian Spring offered him no charms on Monday."[24] On that day he was always absent from classes. Yet in later life Frémont prided himself upon never swearing or imbibing spirits, and after those early accounts there is no further mention of his drinking to excess. Unlike other boys, he did not experiment with smoking.

Bright and quick, despite his truancy, young Frémont achieved high marks in his classes, learning almost too rapidly. But he hated school life, especially its meager rations. Early in 1830, John Charles was granted leave to become a tutor in the household of a wealthy planter. Paradoxically, he also taught mathematics at John Wotten's private school and did more surveying for lawyer Mitchell. Returning to college classes only intermittently, he was warned repeatedly by Dr. Adams that he might not graduate. He never again settled down to his studies.

On February 5, 1831, only a few months before commencement exercises, Adams dismissed him from the college for "habitual irregularity and incorrigible negligence."[25] Despite his truancy, in 1836 the faculty granted him a college degree. Nowhere in his memoirs is there a hint of gratitude for it. He repeatedly veiled his disdain for higher authority by a soft-spoken tone of voice and exterior courtesy. Underneath lay a continuing need to alleviate restlessness by further escapades.

Physically, Frémont was as handsome as Lord Byron and as adventurous as Sir Richard Burton. Throughout these years he loved to sail "dangerously near the breakers on the bar" amid the choppy waters of Charleston Bay. Although he read by the hour the chronicles "of men who had made themselves famous by brave and noble deeds, or infamous by cruel and base acts,"[26] he could also be captivated by a volume on practical astronomy, over which he pored for hours on end. He remembered that two books influenced him in a significant way: one was a chronicle of men who had achieved great fame; the other offered a challenge to the creativity and precision that lay dormant within his enigmatic nature. These two kinds of works seemed to symbolize the two earliest unstructured parts of his nature—adulation of the heroic versus love of learning. He would use both traits to overcome family disasters.

Another of these tragedies occurred in 1832 when his sister Elizabeth died at the age of seventeen. He acted as though his younger brother, Frank, did not really exist, recalling in his memoirs: "We were only two, my mother and I. We had lost my sister. My brother was away. . . . I was unwilling to leave my mother. Circumstances had more than usually endeared us to each other and I knew that her life would be solitary without me."[27] Subsequent events would prove how disingenuous was this memory of his.

His mother had done the best she could to encourage his education while he deserted school to play Robinson Crusoe in the woods. Although he would be separated from her most of his life, he idealized his mother. And he experienced continuing wonderment about his father, for the international escapee Charles Frémon, no ordinary father, had been "deeply interested in studying the character and condition of the North American Indians, and spent the last years of his life in visiting the many tribes."[28] His father's fascination with the American wilderness thus formed memory traces going back to John Charles's first imitative moves toward exploration and Indians. Attempting to come to terms with his father, the son forged a powerful link to nature, with its truly exciting challenges. Furthermore, he could overcome nature's dangers on his own without having to rely on other persons who might again let him down.[29]

One of his defenses was to distance himself from intimacy with others. More and more he hid his true feelings underneath a mask of stoicism. But this distancing was not allowing him to leave his disrupted childhood fully behind, for John Charles remained emotionally in the shadow of his mysterious but absent father. He did not regain whatever trust he had once felt for a parent who disappeared from his life at age five. One result was a series of mixed signals from the past.

Frémont also developed what psychoanalysts call a "grandiose selfhood" as both buffer and shield against further disappointments. By acting out his anxieties he could avoid added painful losses of persons and causes as well. But the price was to be an unmodified developmental pattern repeated throughout his life.

Another coping mechanism was to wall off sadness over the loss of a father who yet remained present in his life but as a painful memory. In all his writings he did not once mention his father, and certainly not his mother's scandalous union with him. (Similarly, Charles Darwin, who lost his mother at age eight, left only two sentences behind regarding her.) Such silence has its own meaning as early wounds continue to hurt. Some leaders, among them Andrew Jackson, do emerge from fatherless homes relatively unscathed. But others do not. For these, the original memory of loss is sometimes so painful that it must be avoided at all costs.[30]

Frémont's adolescence coincided with a sense of national urgency to open up the American West. Since the time John Charles was born, a second war with

England had ended. Leaders in Washington were debating how to manage an expanding, newly confident United States. During his boyhood, Frémont heard echoes of Jefferson's wish to prevent France from regaining those western territories acquired by the Louisiana Purchase—that vast region above New Orleans in the south and well beyond Saint Louis to the west. The new frontier symbolized the nation's promising future. The West would, in fact, help to shape a personal self-image as well as that of the nation he served. As Congress spoke of opening up the continent to ultimate settlement, a great opportunity lay ahead for so bright and ambitious a lad.

With the first part of his life's voyage over, Frémont would expatriate himself permanently from the South by escaping to the West. Although his frustrations appeared to sink out of sight, like an underground stream below the prairies he would traverse, they reappeared in repeated wilderness adventures that lay ahead. He would live as though he could, through repeated defiant adventures, validate himself and become a legitimate leader of men.[31] ❖

Young Manhood

At age twenty, Frémont, full of vigor and energy, luckily found another model for his still rudderless ambitions. Joel Poinsett, the most renowned figure in South Carolina, befriended him, as he put it, when "the outlook for my future was vague" and provided "kindly aid and counsel" that was "often valuable to me, then and afterward." The affluent and powerful Poinsett was a trustee of Charleston College and a fellow parishioner of Saint Philip's Church. He became minister to Mexico and then President Martin Van Buren's secretary of war, but he was best known, in Frémont's own words, "by the scarlet Poinsettia which he contributed to botany."[1] The study of plants and flowers would likewise become a major interest of John Charles. Also, the two men shared Unionist views about the future role of the South at a time when leaders such as John C. Calhoun had begun to stress "states' rights" over those of the national government.

Poinsett, attracted by Frémont's intelligence, secured an appointment for him on May 8, 1833, as a teacher of mathematics aboard the naval sloop-of-war *Natchez*. As there was no naval academy yet, midshipmen received instruction in navigation, algebra, and trigonometry aboard ship.

On board with Frémont was the future Admiral David Farragut, then a lieutenant. Both men would hold high commands during the Civil War. Their cruise was to last two and one-half years. At Rio de Janeiro a midshipman actually lost his life in a duel. When Frémont was asked to act as a second in yet another duel, he and the opponent's second, Decatur Hurst, averted disaster by loading the guns with powder but no lead. The two seconds took great satisfaction in accompanying "our men triumphantly back to the ship, nobody hurt and nobody wiser."[2] Paradoxically, Hurst was himself later killed in a duel.

After the *Natchez* landed in Argentina, there was also a new romance for Frémont—the first since his infatuation with the Creole girl Cecilia. An obscure diary, written years later, records a chance meeting with a Captain Crabbe, "formerly in the Marines and [who] was in the same ship at Buenos Ayres in which Frémont was Capt's Clerk." Crabbe reported "that he [Frémont] was desperately in love with Miss Palmer, the daughter of the American Consul there."[3] Frémont never mentioned this involvement to anyone.

Upon his return to Charleston on October 31, 1835, a college classmate,

Charles Axson, met Frémont on one of its streets: "I stopped and inquired what he was doing. To my surprise he replied that he was a chaplain in the United States Navy. . . . He got the pay of chaplain but was really a teacher of mathematics. . . . 'When there is nothing to do, the captain makes me read prayers' [he said]."[4]

Early in 1836, after requesting service in the Mediterranean on the frigate *United States*, Frémont prepared for an examination as a permanent mathematics instructor in the navy. He passed, was appointed, and was ordered to duty instead aboard the *Independence*. But in the intervening eighteen months he grew bored and decided to accept another offer as an assistant army engineer under Captain W. G. Williams, who planned to survey a railway line from Charleston to Cincinnati through the Carolina mountains. Into April of 1838, Frémont (at a salary of $1,200 per annum), helped Williams map lands in South Carolina's Indian territory, from which the Cherokees would be removed as new settlers filtered westward. It was important for both soldiers and explorers to win the good will of these natives either by gift-giving or intimidation. Ideally, Indian lands were to be kept free of white encroachment until they were surveyed and tribal treaties were drawn up. Initially, Frémont showed much sympathy for Indians, as he had demonstrated for the plight of Charleston's Negro slaves.

Frémont was already keeping a barrier between himself and others. Robert F. Livingston, a trail companion during this 1837-38 expedition, describes him as serious, guarded, and having no close friends. Livingston (who may have edited his original journal for election purposes in 1856) also wrote: "I am mystified with regard to the character of my companion, Frémont. The most taciturn, modest man I ever met . . . not readily drawn into conversation, looking at times as if he were resolving some difficult problem in Euclid . . . a genius, a diamond of the first water, a person of no ordinary capacity." Livingston also noted Frémont's "indomitable perseverance," his "determination to surmount every obstacle," and his capacity for "patient investigation unsurpassed." The diarist concluded: "He is loved, respected, and admired by us all. First impressions of persons are generally the best. It is mine that Frémont will, at some future day, be distinguished; such energy; such perseverance; such application and talent cannot escape notice."[5]

Young Frémont, placed in command of a squad of surveyors, candidly told them about the genuine dangers they all faced together. Only up to a point did he, however, listen to the counsels of Captain Williams's scouts, sometimes suddenly darting off in a direction opposite to that which they had advised. Yet Frémont's uncanny alertness to his wilderness surroundings would repeatedly help, now and in the future, to keep his men alive.

As if reborn in nature, Frémont (like two other illegitimate children of genius, John Audubon and Leonardo da Vinci) immersed himself in describing plants and animals as well as measuring the wonders of the earth. Such quests fitted the Victorian mythology that inquiring and strong-hearted heroes were always victorious. The Latin roots of the word *explore* are related to the synonyms *delve*, *fathom*, *scout*, and *investigate*. While in search of his own selfhood, Frémont melded into the nineteenth-century conviction that explorers could defeat not only their enemies but also nature itself, even against staggering odds. Heroes of their age, Frémont and his wandering English counterparts, Sir Richard Burton and General Charles ("Chinese") Gordon, epitomized the fearless adventurers extolled in the highly popular novels of Sir Walter Scott. Each demonstrated an ability to project an image partly based upon showmanship.

Frémont, like Burton, possessed a striking physical appearance. Repeatedly, observers commented upon the riveting effect of his eyes:

> Nature had fitted Frémont out physically as a hero. Sir Philip Sydney was demeaned . . . by his lean, big-jointed figure and pimpled skin. But the American Sydney had the carriage of a soldier and the face of a poet. At first sight of him, the boy who blacked his boots, or the woman who was his laundress, felt vaguely that he was unlike other men— something bigger and finer, made for some great purpose.

The same writer spoke of his "singular simplicity and courtesy in talk and manner," which made him especially seductive to women.[6]

So handsome a young man would have little trouble meeting women. His treatment of them, however, according to another contemporary, was hardly that of a noble hero. This jealous observer depicted the youthful bachelor as "steering through life like a Portuguese man-of-war over the crests of the waves . . . in love already again."[7] Later, during Frémont's 1856 presidential campaign, strange bits of gossip about his dalliances in the 1830s surfaced. According to one probably prejudiced witness, he had won over and then abandoned a girl whom he called his fiancée:

> I had every opportunity of seeing the *love* exhibited by the couple, on very many occasions. . . . He was engaged to her, and deserted her without cause, and the family was very much distressed. . . . When the Louisville and Cincinnati Railroad was being surveyed about 1838, John C. Frémont was one of the Engineers, and a

gay, buxom chap, and spent a great deal of time in Greenville Village, and became acquainted with a very pretty girl in moderate circumstances. . . . She lived in front of the house I occupied. . . . I have witnessed the intimacy myself, and the facts are notorious in our town.[8]

Other versions of the same story appeared in the *Saint Louis Leader* and the *Charleston Courier* during 1856. Both repeated the charge that Frémont had abandoned a fiancée, a Catholic milliner, with whom he had "repeatedly attended church services."[9] He treated all his female entanglements as passing flirtations, always to be kept secret. He may, however, have duped each of the women involved into thinking that he would marry them.

Actually, his mind remained focused upon carving out some sort of professional future. On July 7, 1838, Poinsett, as secretary of war, got President Van Buren to appoint Frémont a second lieutenant in the Corps of Topographical Engineers, a select branch of the army whose roster then consisted of only thirty-six officers. Headed by Poinsett's old friend Colonel John J. Abert, the corps was charged with laying out new national borders as well as charting wagon trails and future railroad routes to the West.

As Frémont was still only twenty-five years old, this appointment represented an important turning point in his career. In 1838 it led, furthermore, to yet another significant personal contact and to friendship as well. While posted to duty at the nation's capital, he met Joseph Nicola Nicollet—astronomer, cartographer, and member of the French Academy of Science. Nicollet, trained at the famed Paris Observatory, had been driven out of France by the Revolution of 1830. At age forty-six, he had emigrated to the United States. By 1832 he had begun astronomical observations in the White House garden at Washington D.C.

Also charting the West's mineral resources and watersheds, Nicollet was, by the mid-1830s, the first explorer in America to use astronomical instruments and chronometers. He also pioneered the use of the barometer to measure altitudes. Nicollet became the first systematic modern cartographer, mapping the enormous geographical triangle between the upper Mississippi and Missouri rivers. He planned to extend his surveys west and north of Saint Louis, terminus of both East and West, which sat between the headwaters of the Mississippi and that river's mouth on the Gulf of Mexico. But by the time Frémont met him, Nicollet had begun an eleven-year losing battle with cancer. By 1838 he sorely needed an assistant who could assume charge of the daily routine of what was to become his last expedition.

Frémont was truly fortunate to be in the company of so respected a naturalist, one who also possessed an exquisite sensitivity for the land and ethnography of the West. Nicollet personally feared for the ultimate destruction of the natives, whom he called "redmen." He influenced Frémont, at least temporarily, concerning their plight. Both men realized that these proud and colorful tribesmen of ancient ancestry were still as much a mystery to the invading white world as they had been to Frémont's own nomadic father. By the hour John Charles watched the natives standing near their tepees, blanketed and gaudily painted. Living among them were the French-speaking hunters and trappers with whom he would spend half a lifetime.

Frémont, fluent in French, adventurous, and ambitious, was an excellent choice as Nicollet's adjutant, although he did not relish having to keep straight the accounts of the expedition.[10] During his brief stint in the navy, however, he had learned to keep a log and even began to refer to his expeditions as "voyages." For his services Nicollet agreed to pay him four dollars per day plus a few expenses.

In Saint Louis, founded by French fur trappers in 1764, Nicollet introduced Frémont to his circle of French friends. The Chouteaus, Sarpis, and other trading families were enriching themselves while transforming the town's log huts into brick and stone buildings. Contact with the French helped to reestablish the young man's bond with his father's kinsmen.[11] At this time Frémont began to accent his name. The Viscount de Montmort and a "Monsieur" J. Eugene Flandin (only seventeen years old) would also accompany this 1838 expedition, as did another Frenchman, Captain Gaspard de Belligny, and some sixty French Canadian métis, or mixed-bloods, who served as trained scouts and hunters.

On April 4, 1838, its roster complete, Nicollet's party set off northwestward out of Saint Louis. They planned to map relatively obscure territory between the Mississippi and Missouri rivers. Although this triangle of land was as yet unmapped, it had been crisscrossed by whites as early as 1738, when Pierre Gaultier de Varennes, sieur de la Vérendrye, and his son Louis made forays out of Montreal as far west as present-day South Dakota.

Nicollet and Frémont's wooden vessel experienced the annual spring rise on the streams and rivers they encountered. This was caused by the melting of the snows of the faraway Rocky Mountains. The craft fought its way upstream against menacing snags and sandbars. Beyond a fringe of small towns that lined the river's western bank lay the unexplored American West, which would absorb the energies of several generations of explorers.

By summer, Nicollet and Frémont were at the Saint Anthony Falls, named in the late seventeenth century by Louis Hennepin, a mendicant French friar. At Fort Snelling, built a dozen years earlier near the muddy junction of the Mississippi and Minnesota rivers, they obtained from its French sutler (the frontier term for merchant) some pork, flour, flints, and tobacco.

The new faces and the places Frémont was encountering reinforced his dormant ties to his Gallic lineage. This is a significant aspect of his story that has been overlooked. Yet French Canadian trappers and explorers, called voyageurs or coureurs de bois, were everywhere in the West, seeming to live perpetually in the wilderness. The young mixed-bloods who took Indian wives were called *bois brûlés*, or "burnt woods," further reminding Frémont of his paternal origins. He was to favor those *hommes des montagnes*, or "mountain men," whom he and Nicollet employed as hunters and trappers.

The very country through which he and they moved had been named by the French: the Traverse des Sioux was a major prairie and river valley; the Coteau des Prairies was yet another landmark separating the waters of the Missouri and Mississippi. Beyond lay the Lac qui Parle, or "Talking Lake." The game of lacrosse, played by the Indians, was named by the French. Buffaloes were called *les vaches*; the camp kettles of the voyageurs were *chaudières*. In this environment, Frémont became even more fluent in his father's native tongue.

During this expedition, long before he met the guides Jim Bridger and Kit Carson, Frémont initially received firsthand instruction about surviving in the wilderness from French Canadian mountain men, especially the illiterate Etienne Provost. On his own expeditions he would repeatedly take along such seasoned *engagés*. During lonely nights around the campfire, he listened attentively to the patois of Alexis Godey, Basil Lajeunesse, and Antoine Robidoux, three loyal favorites. He showed a deeply felt respect for his métis helpers: "They are good shots and good riders, and have a prairie-wide reputation for skill in hunting and bravery in fighting."[12]

Each evening Frémont had to provide Nicollet with careful cartographic observations. This routine instilled in him a lifelong discipline. He reported his respect for his French mentor in letters to his mother and to Poinsett. He was deeply thrilled when the great explorer insisted that a Minnesota lake, and a plant, too, be named after him. Frémont did not then imagine that he would himself be naming far more geographical sites than almost any other American.[13]

Late in 1839 the Nicollet party returned to Saint Louis. The expedition was at an end. Upon his reentry into Washington, Frémont was confronted with sad family news. His younger brother, Frank, had died, reportedly from "an accidental gunshot wound" that might actually have been suicide; this term is still frequently employed to cover such an event. Frank had left home at age fifteen to seek a career as an actor. Poverty, homelessness, and humiliation were too often the ingredients of a thespian life. He died before the birth of his daughter, Nina, who thereupon became the ward of John Charles. Later, John Charles was to name a son (born in 1854) Frank Preston Frémont.[14]

In order to attend Frank's funeral in Charleston, Lieutenant Frémont received a short leave of absence from the Topographical Corps. There was precious little left of his family life. After his brother's death, with his sisters also gone, he said that his mother became totally his own. But he and his mother did not actually seem to have enjoyed a close relationship. The bond with his mother, as did that later with his future wife, became ambivalent. For he did not give full commitment to either woman, spending much time away from both of them.

His mother virtually faded out of his life after she became involved with a third male companion, marrying a man named Hale. In 1838 her son addressed a letter to her as Mrs. Anne Beverly Whiting Pryor Hale. He could not use his own name—Frémont—in writing her, painful proof that she had never married his father. Nothing is known about Hale or the date of their marriage or even what happened to him. By 1844, Frémont's wife, Jessie Benton Frémont, referred to her mother-in-law as a widow living alone.[15]

Following his brother's funeral, Frémont returned to the South only for emergencies. He and Nicollet carried on their cartographic work at the Coast Survey Building near Capitol Hill in Washington. Overlooking the Potomac, at the center of American geographical knowledge, they helped to plan further penetration of the West.

Young Frémont would remain in the capital for the next several years. He much enjoyed its stimulus, although the Washington of that day, said writer Nathaniel Hawthorne, was a crude rural place, a settlement of "marble and mud." Long before the wings of the capitol building were extended and its dome enlarged, rude houses sat in the inhospitable provincial backwater, which was cursed with a beastly climate, unpaved roads, little sanitation, and a dreaded slave market. Yet Washington was becoming a center that would be significant in Frémont's life, with legislators pouring in from throughout the country. As office buildings, lawns, and fancy tailor shops lifted the city out of its crudity, it also offered unique contacts and a chance for widening his political horizons.

Nicollet and Frémont's 1838–39 expedition had produced the most accurate contemporary map of the Mississippi from Natchez northward to its headwaters in Minnesota. Their account, entitled *A Report Intended to Illustrate a Map of the Hydrographical Basin of the Upper Mississippi River*, was published by the government in 1843. No document had ever before been based upon ninety thousand readings of latitude and longitude and upon measurements of altitudes above sea level, carried out by the first successful use of barometers for mapmaking. This achievement earned Nicollet and Frémont the praise of President Van Buren and of Secretary of War Poinsett.

Nicollet had introduced Frémont to a variety of new approaches to cartography and exploration. The most novel of these involved astronomy. The government's observatory was located on the top floor of the residence of yet another foreign professional, Ferdinand R. Hassler, Swiss-born head of the United States Coast and Geodetic Survey. This close friend of Nicollet, with whom Frémont came to reside, was to provide further modeling for the young lieutenant.

However, another Hassler apprentice, the naval officer Charles Wilkes, well educated and of good family background, would become a rival. Both men clamored to make their reputations—one at sea, the other on land. One day they would clash over the cartography of the Pacific Coast. Both were deeply ambitious, and each was fated to undergo court-martial proceedings.

In Washington, Hassler, their common mentor, replaced the severely ill Nicollet in Frémont's life. Hassler's mapmaking staff on Capitol Hill was much sought after by those who urged penetration of the trans-Mississippi West. He ended up serving as a second model and a fourth counselor for Frémont. Unlike the tactful and benign Nicollet, however, Hassler tended to be imperious, even cantankerous on occasion. But he directed no personal rancor toward Frémont. Indeed, Hassler generously made available a large library as well as his geodetic instruments and mathematical expertise, amassed when he was the government's superintendent of weights and measures. In the supportive atmosphere of Hassler's study, Frémont pored over the newest maps and findings about the farthest west. With reference books open to selected pages, he exulted in studying by himself, reading for hours on end.

Both Nicollet and Hassler belonged to the eighteenth-century scientific European tradition established by naturalists such as Georges-Louis Buffon. These enthusiasts all sought to unravel the mysteries of nature in an America not yet fully explored. Their detailed descriptions and drawings of its exotic birds, snakes, insects, and geological phenomena were at the very edge of systematic knowledge about the natural world. Topography and draftsmanship, whether in portraying landscapes, flora, or fauna, were captivating a worldwide audience.

While Frémont developed these skills, Poinsett's support also continued to be crucial. An ardent expansionist, he attracted not only Frémont but also other promising young leaders, among them Edward McCrady and C. G. Memminger. As Frémont wished to remain within Poinsett's coterie, he tried to show his appreciation by sending Poinsett's wife a bearskin rug left over from the Nicollet expedition. He later gave some smoked buffalo tongues for her 1840 New Year's dinner, to which she fortunately invited him.[16]

In Washington's cordial social environment, Frémont's new backers posed no personal threat. His first competitive problems with older men would begin only after Poinsett introduced him to his future father-in-law, Senator Thomas Hart Benton of Missouri. He would become repeatedly angered at being bossed about by his elders, but not *all* of them. For the present, his affable earlier sponsors—Roberton, Poinsett, Nicollet, and Hassler—encouraged him to move forward with his career. They were surrogate "significant others," to use psychiatrist Harry Stack Sullivan's term, inspiring both trust and security. Each provided valuable modeling. Albeit temporarily, they served as substitute figures for Frémont's absent father. Their dictates and expectations sometimes ran counter to his wishes, but with society just beginning to reward Frémont, he was not yet in any position to show resentment of authority.[17]

Both Nicollet and Hassler encouraged Frémont's questioning of all aspects of nature. But the early loss of his father, and lack of an extended bloodline family with whom to practice working out sensitive emotional issues, deprived Frémont of the ability to trust others. This distrust was, in turn, linked to his inability to attain full commitment to anyone, even in marriage. For such narcissists "trust goes inside." One important consequence of his mistrust of others was to spark an overblown determination to succeed, whatever the price.[18]

For Frémont, as it did for his father, wandering became a way of life. The child, once moved frequently from place to place with little attachment to any one home, became intoxicated by rainbows, butterflies, and the wilderness. As if fleeing from each disappointment, he defined exploration as "the true Greek joy in existence, in the gladness of living." His surveys, investigating the immensity of vast spaces, afforded him a convenient self-absorption as he challenged high mountains in the winter and forbidding deserts in the summer. Forever escaping the restraints of city life, Frémont was able, in his own words, to go "out into excitement of strange scenes and occurrences. . . . Forced out of myself . . . [I] for long intervals could forget what I left behind."[19]

Repeatedly he also showed the ill effects of an unpredictable early environment by his reluctance to conform and disregard of what others thought. Although loss of a parent is a traumatic experience, children can be more private about their losses than adults realize. Isolated, a child may find it impossible to express sad, conflicting feelings, which remain unspoken. Otto Rank has described how a son, unable to deal with early loss of a father, may take secret revenge upon this absent figure by striving to surpass him with extraordinary achievements. In this way the "child-man" gains a strange personal victory. In the wilderness, neither father, mother, nor wife was necessary for survival. John Bakeless has described the connection between rejection by such explorers of their "love objects" and risk-taking: "What, after all, is a woman, compared to solitude in the wilderness, Indians, the bright face of danger, the high adventure of the Rockies, canoes in foaming rapids, a grizzly hunt, or sword blades flashing in the sun, a flag that flutters over steel-tipped columns . . . and polished brass and bugles, calling, calling."[20]

Like Frémont, other young explorers of the wilderness, too, have typically fled into primitive areas, perhaps influenced by a confused parentage. Like Frémont, Henry Stanley, Kit Carson, Jim Bridger, and Meriwether Lewis were left fatherless from an early age. Stanley, like Frémont, lost his father at the age of five, and a stepfather thereafter as well. There are other similarities between these two particular men. Both Frémont and Stanley were born out of wedlock.

Stanley, called the toughest man that ever lived, remained deeply driven, concocting pathetic lies about himself, through a life full of honors.[21]

Did the energetic explorers who swarmed over the American West and Africa compensate for their disabilities by nurturing an immense curiosity about nature? Each seemed more in love with the wilderness than with anything else in life. Or were their early losses merely coincidental? Adventure offered them all a different way of mastering the world around them, and with public applause, too. These celebrated men lived in an age that worshiped explorers as much as ours caters to rock stars.

Nicollet predicted that if Frémont lived long enough, he would "carve out for himself a distinguished position among the *savans* of the age." The young officer would leave Poinsett, Nicollet, and Hassler behind as he tried to establish himself within the Corps of Topographical Engineers. But that government agency was still tiny and fragile, and his contacts within it were mostly with West Pointers, who resented a politically appointed outsider. Between the War of 1812 and the creation in 1818 of the Topographical Corps, or Bureau, some 10 percent of West Point graduates were trained as topographical engineers. Against these clannish stalwarts, Frémont sorely needed support from a new source.[22]

While he tried to find a way to achieve greater personal power, his thoughts were increasingly upon universal themes. As he put it: "My mind had been quick to see a larger field and differing and greater results. It would travel over a part of the unknown countries known; and the study without books—the learning at first hand from nature itself; the drinking first at her unknown springs—became a source of never-ending delight to me."[23] Another important phase of his life was about to begin. As the poet Robert Frost might have put it, this choice of a path to follow would make all the difference. ❖

As Frémont's career slowly moved toward center stage, two crucial figures entered his life: Thomas Hart Benton, chairman of the Senate Committee on Territories, and the senator's vivacious and intelligent daughter Jessie. Known on the Senate floor as "the Old Thunderer," Benton, six feet four inches in height and full of pomp and authority, flinched at nothing. As Missouri's first senator, he cut a striking figure with heavy black hair and imposing side-whiskers. Like Frémont, he had experienced personal loss at an early age. When only eight, Benton became virtual head of his family after the death of his father. He and his mother, however, inherited a vast acreage following further deaths of five of his seven brothers and sisters.[1]

Both Benton and Frémont were deeply influenced by the expansionist views of Thomas Jefferson, who in 1803 had acquired the vast Louisiana Territory. A personal friend of Benton, that visionary president had initiated an era of continental exploration that Benton and his future son-in-law came to equate with freedom and adventure. Jefferson was the chief sponsor of the expedition on which, between May 1804 and September 1806, Meriwether Lewis and William Clark followed the Missouri to its source, found a way across the Rocky Mountains, descended the Columbia River to its mouth, and returned to Saint Louis.

In 1806 another government party, headed by Lieutenant Zebulon Montgomery Pike, had set out to explore the headwaters of the Arkansas and Red Rivers and also to observe "with great circumspection" Spanish settlements in New Mexico. Pike had moved southwestward as far as the Rio Grande, which he believed to be the elusive Red River. Although he traveled across parts of present-day Texas, Kansas, and Nebraska and as far west as Colorado, where he named Pike's Peak, his reports were bleak and incomplete. Clearly, the topography of the Far West still remained to be mapped definitively. Benton and Frémont would soon tackle this task together.

The War of 1812 with the British, during which Pike was killed, had temporarily interrupted further exploration. Not until the year 1819 did the American government authorize Major Stephen Long to head an expedition to the Rocky Mountains. Long's report, like Pike's, was even less favorable regarding prospects for settlement of the area between the Missouri, Arkansas, and Platte rivers. But by 1819, Benton had emerged as America's strongest advocate of western expansion. As editor of the *Saint Louis Enquirer*, he used that newspaper as a forum to urge development of all the land west of Missouri. Pike and Long had been mere forerunners of national leadership in exploration.

In 1824 Benton held a last touching meeting with the aging Jefferson, during which they discussed the need for further expeditions to the farthest West. Eighteen years had passed since Lewis and Clark returned with their valuable account of its mineral, plant, and animal life. A new generation of explorers was about to appear on the scene, aided by Benton, who headed up a congressional group committed to examining the unknown riches of America's West. He sorely needed an experienced cartographer like Frémont to act as his eyes and ears in the wilderness.[2]

Before that cooperation could occur, however, Frémont and Jessie Benton had to meet. They did so because of the death of a president. On April 9, 1841, the Benton family accepted an invitation from the Corps of Topographical Engineers to view the Washington funeral cortege of William Henry Harrison from the windows of offices leased for the government's mapping activities. The handsome Frémont acted as host for the occasion. Dressed in his newest uniform, he tended a cozy fire and graciously served coffee and ices from a daintily set table. With somewhat reckless extravagance for one on a junior officer's salary, he had decorated the premises with plants and cut flowers. In this arboreal setting the twenty-eight-year-old lieutenant and the sixteen-year-old daughter of the senator were immediately attracted to each other.

Jessie, the second of five Benton children and one of four daughters, was born on May 31, 1824, at Cherry Grove, the home of her maternal grandfather, Colonel James McDowell, near Lexington, Virginia. The McDowells were one of Virginia's leading families, along with the Randolphs and the Wyeths. Mrs. Benton's aunt had married a Madison.

Jessie spent her childhood and adolescence in both Washington and Saint Louis. The aura of the West pervaded every timber of their Missouri home, where both William Clark and Meriwether Lewis were frequent visitors. In Washington she was especially proud that when she was a girl President Andrew Jackson's bony fingers had played with the soft strands of her hair as he talked with her father. Indeed, Benton's nickname, "Old Bullion," referred to his cooperation with Jackson, as his spokesman in the Senate, to win their fight against the United States Bank. In the Benton house on C Street the guests frequently included Chief Justices John Marshall and Roger Taney as well as the widows of Alexander Hamilton and President James Madison. On occasion the Martin Van Burens also dropped by to visit.

Jessie was thought to be an attractive little girl by older friends of the family. Dressed often in a pink frock, her bright auburn hair cascading around her shoulders, and with deep, reflective eyes, she exuded self-confidence beyond her years. She was hardly the touching little creature that a parent might put in crinolines, tea-cozy dresses, and fluffy bonnets. She was, instead, so at ease with adults that she even seemed able on occasion to handle her imperious father. Later in life the frontier scout Kit Carson called her plucky and proud. Others saw her as high-spirited and willful. In her teens Jessie was slender of waist, with her hair parted in the middle and drawn tight behind her head in mid-nineteenth-century style. Only in later years did she become heavy, corseted, and bosomy.

To Jessie, her mother, Elizabeth Preston McDowell Benton, was a somewhat remote figure. According to one account, Mrs. Benton "could not wholly escape from the grim Scotch Puritan atmosphere that had dominated her home. Like all the McDowell women, she was a rather high-minded abolitionist. Jessie recalled that while her mother had "grown up among slaves who could object to nothing, and though our own servants were free born, and some had been set free by my parents, yet the idea of claiming equal rights to rest or religion did not occur to them—but it did to my mother."[3] Sunday dinners in the Benton household were always cold, out of sympathy for the kitchen help. Eventually Mrs. Benton employed only white servants. The senator begrudgingly came to share his wife's racial attitudes. And Jessie would transmit these feelings to John Charles, who, having been raised by Black Hannah and other slaves belonging to his mother, also came to hate slavery, the South's dominant institution.

Jessie and her father appeared to Frémont to be deeply devoted to each other. About this she herself boasted, "I came into my Father's life like a breath of his own compelling nature; strong, resolute, but open to all tender and gracious influences, and above all, loving him."[4] Daughter and father were inseparable. Benton had carefully sheltered his adored Jessie well into her teens, planning and supervising her studies, aided by a splendid classical library collected by Grandfather Benton. Her parents sent her to the best and most fashionable private academy, located in Georgetown; there she would presumably be safe from all suitors. For they intended that she should marry well, strengthening their dynasty's security, always a great source of pride in the South.

Threatening all these glowing hopes for Jessie's future there now loomed a menacing outsider. This bastard son of an émigré of unknown origins was ineligible to enter southern society, despite her infatuation with his good looks and obvious charm.

Shortly after President Harrison's fateful funeral, in a transparent effort to enhance his standing, Frémont sent Mrs. Benton the potted plants and flowers that had adorned the government office where he had met her. Then a contest of wills began. Jessie remained captivated by young Frémont's keen blue eyes, dark curly hair, and clean-cut features. Though small of stature, he was strongly built and vigorous. John Charles was equally attracted by her gaiety and a hint of fire underneath. An alarmed Mrs. Benton—who years before had forced the senator to sever his own connections with the army—warned Jessie about the itinerant life that an ill-paid junior officer's wife would have to lead; Frémont had no proper family, no money, and no prospects for rapid promotion. When Jessie continued to hint about marriage, her mother sent her off to attend a Virginia cousin's wedding, which involved weeks of activity. She also tried to break up the couple by means of the influence of Mrs. Poinsett, wife of the secretary of war. Meanwhile, Jessie, forced to part from her lieutenant, nursed her anger. The Bentons thought separation would end their daughter's relationship with Frémont. Hers was surely but a transient girlish adoration of a handsome young devil in uniform.

Although Jessie at age seventeen was likened to a rose, and to a beautiful picture as well, she was hardly a quavering school girl, even while attending Mrs. English's Female Seminary in Georgetown. Because of Jessie's strong will, it would take a radical act to separate her from a new-found love.

Senator Benton suddenly arranged through Secretary Poinsett for War Department orders directing Frémont to head a survey party to the lower Des Moines River in Iowa Territory. Frémont and Nicollet had earlier charted its headwaters, but Colonel Abert and Poinsett wanted its course plotted to its mouth. On June 4, Abert ordered the lieutenant to "repair without delay to the mouth of the Racoon Fork of the Des Moines."[5]

Once again in the field, Frémont savored an affectionate note from Nicollet: "No day passes when I do not accompany you in heart and thought in all your moves." The Frenchman suspected, "Il y a quelque diablerie là-dedans," an ulterior motive for the sudden government orders. Nicollet's caring message also contained a veiled reference to the goings-on within Senator Benton's household. Nicollet reassured John Charles that the young explorer was deeply missed by a distraught Jessie, and he closed with words of encouragement: "I await you with open arms to embrace and to congratulate you."[6] He was doing all he could to set matters straight between her parents and John Charles. Desperately ill, but regarding Frémont as his cartographic heir, he knew that the Benton name could gain his protégé entrance to power at Saint Louis, gateway to the West, as well as in Washington.

This painting of a youthful Jessie Benton, by T. Buchanan Reid, was a favorite of hers. In old age she proudly displayed it on the wall above her desk in the Frémont home at Los Angeles. (Courtesy of the Southwest Museum, Los Angeles, California, N. 30665)

Early in September of 1841, Frémont returned to Washington from his Des Moines River expedition—and in triumph. He emerged from the wilderness with thirteen new maps of that watercourse. A flurry of newspaper accounts applauded his achievement. Instead of sidelining the young officer, Senator Benton had unwittingly brought him into the national limelight.

Jessie's beau also proved that he knew how to court, flatter, and pursue her. Benton therefore had no further recourse but to command the couple to postpone any further thought of marriage. So they began to meet in secret, then decided to elope. There were other suitors waiting with their proposals of marriage to Jessie. Even Martin Van Buren, who became president in 1836, was interested in her. Because "Little Van" and her father had been thrown into close association with Andrew Jackson, Benton was also a Van Buren adherent.

Jessie coldly spurned all outstanding marriage prospects. But once she decided to wed Frémont, Washington's Lutheran, Methodist, and Presbyterian ministers all refused to marry the couple without Benton's consent. Finally, the young couple found a Catholic priest, Father Joseph Van Horseigh of Saint Peter's Church, who agreed to marry them clandestinely, on October 19, 1841.[7] Fifteen years later, when Frémont ran for the presidency, his opponents cited marriage by a priest as evidence that he was a closet Catholic.

After her marriage, Jessie returned to live with her parents, awaiting an auspicious moment to break the news to them. A month later, the rapidly declining Nicollet counseled the couple to tell the senator about the wedding before he died. Nicollet ended his days in the care of French clerics at Saint Mary's College in Baltimore. After Jessie and John Charles slipped away by train for a last bedside visit with him there, the glow of their happiness revived Nicollet temporarily. But he was fading fast. The couple's only real advocate died on July 17, 1843.

When Jessie finally told her father they had secretly married, Benton flew into a rage and ordered Frémont out of his house. Jessie, standing close to her husband, looked into her father's eyes and defiantly repeated the biblical pledge of Ruth: "Whither thou goest, I will go. Where thou lodgest, I will lodge."[8] Rather than lose so resolute a daughter, the senator underwent a change of mind and told his new son-in-law to gather up his belongings stored elsewhere, prior to moving into the Benton house. Meanwhile, Benton would prepare his wife to receive this shocking news. Eventually the couple joined the Bentons in their large house on C Street. The senator had been bested by his favorite child. Only because loss of all control over her was at stake did he capitulate.

Frémont did not yet realize how remarkable was his new wife's heritage. The two foci of Jessie's life had been the nation's capital and her parents' Missouri home. The family regularly commuted between Washington and Saint Louis by rail, steamboat, and coach, a bulbous yellow carriage that Jessie called "Cinderella's Pumpkin." Jessie and John Charles also would spend a good deal of time aboard this contraption to and from Saint Louis, the Benton western power base.

Until Frémont could be assigned command of another expedition, the couple stayed mostly in Washington. Jessie was fond of stating that its very political life "revolved about my father." She boasted that the War Department was run either from the Benton library in Saint Louis or from her father's Washington committee room. For twenty years Benton was chairman of several powerful Senate committees that involved things military. He was also, in Jessie's words, "practically the Secretary of War . . . for he was a fixture while a Secretary is only a political accident."[9]

Benton, first elected U.S. senator from Missouri in 1821, retained that office for three decades, becoming a colorul political figure. He was admired even by his enemies. When, in February 1855 his Washington home burned down, both houses of Congress adjourned out of sympathy, and President Franklin Pierce himself called on the Bentons to express his regrets.[10]

But Benton's relationship with Frémont remained an ambivalent one. At first the senator actually favored another son-in-law, the lawyer William Carey Jones, and the Benton-Frémont family fusion for which Jessie hoped was never truly complete. Each man possessed too insistent a will. Jessie once politely observed that "neither Mr. Frémont nor my Father were of natures to compromise with a wrong," though she really meant that they could hardly accommodate each other. Jessie saw herself as "a connecting link between my father's thought" and what Frémont placed into action. As Jessie put it, "So the two minds and wills became one, and step by step their work was accomplished," or so she hoped.[11] But the contrast between them was especially evident in public, where portly old Benton frequently dispensed authoritative orotundities. Compared to him, Frémont was shy, tending to fall embarrassingly silent in the presence of strangers.

Over time, however, largely because of Benton's commitment to national expansion, he begrudgingly backed Frémont as an explorer. The senator's cabal of expansionists in the government was especially anxious to map the route to Oregon "scientifically," to describe South Pass and other landmarks carefully, to assess the navigability of streams, to find the best places to build forts, and to establish the West's true latitudes and longitudes. Benton would see to it that Frémont's later geographical reports went on public sale, partly at his own expense. He would even subsidize a brochure entitled the *Thrilling Sketch of the Life of Col. J. C. Frémont*, for circulation in England in connection with the showing of Skirving's Moving Panorama, in order to publicize Frémont's exploits. He even dared to believe he could pass on the Benton family mantle to Frémont. After the death of the senator's son, Randolph, in 1852, Benton was left without a male heir. Although Benton thus promoted his son-in-law's image in the press, he would oppose him on other occasions, including Frémont's bid for the presidency in 1856. Their closeness was superficial.

To his father-in-law, Frémont appeared at turns bland and at other times erratic. Benton was a calculating man who thought out matters in advance. Frémont often did the opposite. Although Frémont was given to understatement, he was also proved to be touchy about small issues. And he was surprisingly impulsive as well. Although Benton would sometimes be unsuccessful in running interference for his son-in-law, Frémont's reliance on his political muscle made him less judicious than he might have been.

The younger man found it difficult to move in high circles in the company of so wily an ally as Benton. At first awed by the senator, he had to square his recently acquired standing within one of the most powerful political families in the country with his still tentative role in the military establishment, where jealousy of him was to be expected. Although the young officer had gained a new set of allies through his wife's contacts, there were disabilities both for himself and Jessie. Caught between Frémont and her famous father, she was not to have an easy task in her roles as mediator, daughter, wife, and mother.

Jessie had Frémont's drive and ambition, but her intellectuality was different from that of her husband. His was a scientific bent; hers, literary and artistic. She deferred to his training and general knowledge in seeking to prove to Senator Benton that she had not married a second-rater.

Jessie's continuing dedication to her father resembled obeisance to a god-like figure. Their relationship, similar to that of a father with a son, was at times almost subversive to her marriage. One of her favorite quotations was Portia's speech from Shakespeare's *Julius Caesar*: "My father gave me early the place a son would have had. I grant I am a woman but . . . think you I am no stronger than my sex, being so father'd and so husbanded?" Jessie, of all Benton's children, most closely resembled her father in drive, flare for the dramatic, and a character that one contemporary labeled as almost masculine: "She no more had a woman's mind than she had a man's. It was simply a *great* mind. . . . Clear, logical, unhesitant, fearless, it grasped whole whatever matters came before it, digested them promptly, and drew from them sound and certain conclusions."[12] Disallowed a public image in her own right, she used her talents to promote her husband's, all the while trying hard to fuse her identity with his. She dutifully would nurture his image as a romantic knight of the plains and high peaks who suffered numbing cold and parched deserts in order to tame America's wilderness.

Publicly she called Frémont not by name but, after he attained the stipulated ranks, "the Colonel" or "the General." She also respectfully capitalized the word "Father," whether referring to her husband before their children or to Senator Benton. Although she skillfully concealed her anger toward her father whenever he thwarted her husband's wishes, Jessie was implacable against any person or decision perceived as threatening to Frémont's well-being.

Jessie's emotional strength became legendary. She cultivated a capacity to endure grief and misfortune almost cheerfully when both struck, which was quite often. She once said she was like a deep-built ship that drove best under a stormy wind that also unfurled her husband's sails. Though they shared a mutual, if unstated, need for fame, she would not be the senior partner in its pursuit, but her will became merged with his. Anyone whose life touched her husband's was of interest to her. She was a real presence whom others could not push far. She opened his mail and anticipated his answers. They seemed to be as one in work and career. Jessie would learn, however, that there were limits to her influence over John Charles. The outside world scarcely knew how much he guarded his inward self whenever she became bossy or absurdly self-inflating.

Until he met Jessie, the concept of family had played virtually no role in Frémont's life. He had lived as a wanderer. Once married, she appeared to settle him down while he was not in the field. Outwardly, the couple seemed a perfect fit, convex to concave—she the lively mistress of social repartee, he the reserved but thoughtful husband who presumably listened to her counsel. But this harmony lay mainly on the surface. Their marriage left him free to pursue his many interests while she patiently tried to dwell in the shadows of his career.

Jessie secretly defied the Victorian inclination to make women the property of men, with no outlets of their own and with few useful skills. She would not be an unused ornament. Although without official power, she would exercise her influence at the very least by trying to mediate between the two men in her life, and with others as well on her father's and husband's behalf. Jessie's accomplishments extended far beyond those of homemaker.[13]

Although he sometimes disregarded her advice, John Charles usually came to trust Jessie's judgment as if it were his own. But as their common interests became fused in one another, she did little to rein in his worst judgments. Though she was generally steadier than her husband in decision making, Jessie could on occasion also act hastily and without enough reflection—unlike her father. The couple too often responded to higher authority by defiance, even toward presidents.

At times Jessie would push her husband well beyond his abilities to perform. By encouraging an exaggerated sense of destiny in him, she mythologized his exploits and made them seem more original than they really were. But because she was bound to grow restless in her supporting role, she sometimes emerged as a pushy manager of him.

As Mrs. Benton had predicted, the Frémonts were often to be separated. He was in the field five of the first eight years of their marriage. During those intervals a lonely Jessie lived in one of her parents' two houses. Although she

Theodore Roosevelt used this imposing portrait of Thomas Hart Benton as the frontispiece of his biography of the senator, which was published in Boston in 1899. Benton is shown here, at the peak of his powers, with a reading glass on a black silk ribbon. Frémont, his son-in-law, thought him a formidable figure, indeed.

never became reconciled to her husband's long absences and waited passionately for his return, Jessie also remained close to her father, but in altered ways. She dined at his table every day whenever her husband was away. And when the senator himself was absent, she wrote him each night "so that even though distance separated them, they were always one at nightfall."[14] Many husbands could have felt threatened by a wife's persistent attachment to her father. Benton had gone so far as to insist that when the wedding was finally announced in the newspapers, Jessie's name be placed ahead of his son-in-law's. Given Frémont's chaotic childhood, his fear of engulfment was almost inevitable, however much he may have desired the love of the Bentons. His western expeditions would therefore place him well beyond Jessie's or her family's reach, both physically and emotionally.

Although, as a result, their union would eventually suffer, only after thirty-five years of marriage did she show signs of disappointment in her husband. For sometimes the odds against the Frémonts were high. For Jessie, especially, there were the disappointments shared by many strong-willed army wives forced to appropriate the personas of their husbands. In that role, both Jessie and Elizabeth ("Libbie") Custer shared some illuminating spousal similarities, which were revealed in their writing.[15]

Frémont and Custer were leaders who lived in a private world. While protecting their mythologies, Libbie and Jessie learned to share gratifications that flowed partly from the flickering influence they exerted over their idolized spouses. On occasion both women provided parenting for their proud, solitary, and sometimes adolescent marriage partners.[16]

If Jessie ever suspected that her John Charles was what the French call a *génie manqué*, or failed genius, she gave no public hint of it. Instead, whenever adversity loomed, she reminded him of a favorite phrase taken out of his Gallic past: "Le bon temps viendra," or "The good times will come." Jessie made this their secretly shared motto. During long winter nights when he was off on his expeditions, she had to provide her own upbeat reassurances. ❖

First Expedition

On his expeditions, Frémont pursued "the flower and the rock," as he would put it later in life.[1] For him, nature in its nobility stood in supreme contrast to the untrustworthiness of all opponents. Though physically dangerous, both the mountains and plains were forever. Only flowers and rocks were truly dependable as he fled from the troubled South of his childhood toward the West's prairies and peaks.

Clad in fringed buckskins, rifles slung over the pommels of their saddles, Frémont and his men would repeatedly ride into the wilderness. But unlike other explorers, he became embroiled in controversies that resembled the intrigues and escapades of Sir Richard Burton. These arguments ran the gamut from unrealistic decisions made on the trail—usually on the spur of the moment—to public disputes and private quarrels. Even in his youth he could not abide the role of underdog. But sometimes Frémont lost control of events. A risk-taker cannot always thwart the forces of nature or the wishes of other men. He repeatedly tried to do both.

In mid-1842, while still only twenty-nine years old, Frémont had a spectacular opportunity to lead his own government-backed expedition—the first of three that would gain him a national reputation. His orders were to survey strategic lines of travel along which military posts might be established from the Missouri to Fort Laramie, South Pass, and the Wind River Range. To bolster this assignment, Senator Benton and and his close colleague, Senator Lewis Linn, also of Missouri, pushed an appropriation bill for thirty thousand dollars through Congress.

Jefferson Barracks in Saint Louis was the center from which military parties left for the West. There Frémont came to feel the true power of his father-in-law and the hold that the senator had over the French population. Benton was known in Saint Louis as *l'ami des Français*, or "friend of the French." The little "Paris of America" lay on the edge of an immense frontier that the French explorers had left untapped. Jessie described the local women as looking like transplanted French peasants with "their thick white caps, sabots and full red petticoats." She herself had learned to speak French from Parisian maids and governesses.[2]

On May 2, 1842, Frémont left his pregnant young wife and headed westward from Saint Louis. Not until the following October would he return. In her

Souvenirs of My Time (1887) Jessie likened her long waits for him to the loneliness endured by the wives of Nantucket whalers. Staying behind was not easy, especially when rumors reached her of Indian attacks or of her husband's "desperate suffering from snows and starvation."[3] It was her fear of the unknown that caused Jessie the most anxiety.

Frémont took along Benton's twelve-year-old son, Randolph, and the senator's great-nephew Henry Brant. Together they planned to chart the Platte River along the trail to Oregon by way of South Pass. Although the first lap of each expedition was by tradition a short march, Frémont thereafter stepped up the daily pace. But mud holes and rain cut down the party's movement to only a few miles per day. Sometimes the turf was so soggy that wheeled vehicles sank down to their hubs and had to be unloaded before the men could dig them out of the sod. The group traveled with eight carts drawn by two mules each, accompanied also by horses and oxen. For a time a milk cow and her calf trailed along across "the ocean of prairie."[4] Wildlife was abundant, and skilled bison hunters had little trouble supplying the camp with fresh meat.

On the overland trail, which took most parties at least four months to traverse, Frémont had the company of twenty-one of those greatest of survivalists, the mountain men; among them were "creole and Canadian voyageurs." These seasoned companions, whom he had recruited at Saint Louis, had already traveled throughout most of the West without compasses or maps. They had given its plains, mountains, and rivers their first names. They knew how to find birds' nests; what berries to pick and eat; where the best honeybee hives were; how to skin and stretch hides; and how to make rope, sandals, soap, and even needle and thread from western plants. They could throw an axe with deadly accuracy and catch fish with their hands as the Indians did, and they knew where to find nonpoisonous water holes. Under their guidance, Frémont's tenderfeet became expert at bridling horses and packing mules as well as adjusting saddles and gear each morning.

Although Frémont won the adherence of the frontiersmen Kit Carson, Basil Lajeunesse, and Alexis Godey, less admiring was Charles Preuss, the red-haired and moody German mapmaker who secretly kept the only diary (in German) written during the first expedition. The diary, published only in 1958, provided

Preuss with a personal safety valve. He was ten years older than Frémont and had studied geodesy in Prussia. Preuss was irritable and often depressed. On the third day out he labeled Frémont "childish" and "a foolish lieutenant." Preuss wished "with all my heart" that he "had stayed in Washington. Not because of the hardships, but because of that simpleton Frémont."[5]

Preuss feared the medical dangers that abounded along the route of march. Scurvy, cholera, and Rocky Mountain spotted fever were serious hazards. As the streams grew drier and scarcer, underground rivulets spewed forth rusty-colored liquids that smelled like rotten eggs. Cholera, caused by impure water, reached epidemic proportions in the 1840s. It was the most lethal gastrointestinal disease the expedition faced, and certainly the most dramatic. A sudden onset might be followed by death in twelve to twenty-four hours. Alkaline and bacterially contaminated water and food also caused frequent bouts of diarrhea. Frémont hardly knew how to guard against typhoid fever and dysentery, which were so debilitating.

Life in the wilderness also resulted in accidental gunshot wounds, lacerations, and bone fractures. Grizzly bears posed a real danger. Because the cause of scurvy (a deficiency of vitamin C) was still unknown, Frémont dispensed calomel, epsom salts, and arrowroot tea. His vouchers from a Saint Louis pharmacist also list quicksilver, camphor, nitric acid, laudanum, purgative pills, and emetics. He carried along surgical instruments as well, using them on one occasion to reset the broken nose of Delaware Charley, an Indian guide.[6]

Despite all these hazards, Frémont would repeatedly attract followers willing to escape into nature with him, sharing the odyssey of travel over ravines and treacherous rivers and amid thundering herds of buffalo, droves of wild horses, and menacing Indian parties. There were also the many inconveniences of the trail. At night, when one had to relieve himself, it was painful to leave the warmth of a campfire, set in a sheltering grove of cottonwoods, to step out onto the cold vastness of the prairie. Usually a serpentine path led to a makeshift slit-trench latrine that was sometimes located near the pointed leaves of yucca or surrounded by brittle sagebrush and impenetrable clusters of tumbleweed.

The group also hid its private terrors, which Preuss recorded. His diary provides a more realistic counterweight to Jessie's romanticizing of her husband's reports. Frémont tolerated the grouchy Preuss only because of the German's superb drafting skills. Preuss could, however, be inaccurate, as he was in describing some "distant woods" that turned out to be a herd of buffalo. After accompanying the hero-explorer on his first, second, and third expeditions, Preuss returned to Washington, D.C., where, melancholy and morose, he hanged himself from a tree. Like Meriwether Lewis and other western trail followers, he simply gave way to despondency.[7]

Frémont never knew of Preuss's carefully concealed diary, even after the German's suicide. Frémont had ordered that no personal records be kept, for army policy forbade diaries in "enemy territory." The full intent of his government expeditions was, furthermore, always veiled. "I'll do my own writing," he warned. He wished only his story to emerge.[8]

Also, he detested private grumbling, although he indulged in it himself on occasion. Frémont's men could not complain about how he had equipped the party, for his ledgers show that he carried along thousands of dollars' worth of food and equipment. He dispensed these as would a modern military post exchange. His men could sign vouchers and pay later for tobacco, wool caps, mitts, or needles and thread. The government supplied their white canvas tents.

On this first expedition the army charged Frémont $78.25 for experimental daguerreotype equipment, but the pictures he took with it were a failure. He also toted along a three-foot, six-inch astronomical telescope (worth $220.00) as well as compasses, thermometers, and a mercury barometer. A collapsible India rubber boat with airtight compartments (later lost) cost him $200.00. A Harrison wagon (also lost) was carried on his books at $115.00. Frémont bought horses along the Platte River Trail at prices ranging from $21.98 to $100.00 each. Mules cost about $30.00 apiece and were sold in pairs. Other supplies included soldering irons, copper kettles, saws, axes, a goatskin trunk, and tomahawks manufactured in Saint Louis. A notation in his ledger book states that he also bought bunting "to make a flag, which is necessary among the Indians."[9]

Some items were vital. Each night Frémont's four cooks started their fires with flint and steel. After dark they baked "Bannock bread" in fire pits atop frying pans, using swamp corn. The party was expected to live off the countryside as much as possible. The mules fed on the cottonwoods along the rivers while hunters foraged daily for game and firewood. Whenever wood grew scarce, the men gathered dried *bois de vache*, or buffalo chips. Their leader was not bothered by constant meals of salt pork or buffalo—fried, roasted, or broiled. Occasionally the cooks served trout. There had also been rare feasts proffered by friendly Indians. About one of these, consisting of glutinous puppy meat, Frémont wrote: "Fortunately I am not of delicate nerves, and continued to fill my platter."[10]

Proud of the harmony that he kept while in camp, he boasted that he used neither spirits nor tobacco, yet in the field he called his pipe "this true friend of mine in every emergency." He did, however, ration snuff and tobacco. When his cooks had no more salt, they used gunpowder, though bitter, as a substitute. The saltpeter in the powder was thought to act as a sexual depressant. Only on rare occasions did Frémont pass out rations of brandy and wine. He tried to bar hard liquor of any sort and strongly opposed bartering it with the Indians. A keg of liquor, he angrily observed, "will purchase from an Indian everything he possesses—his furs, his lodge, his horses, and even his wife and children—and any vagabond who has money enough to purchase a mule can go into a village and trade."[11]

Without liquor or women, he asked his men to cover about fifteen miles per day, either on horseback or afoot. By evening they sometimes ended up in water-soaked tents and blankets, harassed by mosquitoes and vermin. For food his expedition was mostly dependent upon what was supplied by hunters. Climate was a perennial problem. At times chunks of ice floated on the rivers they crossed. Or when they traveled between streams, the wind howled and whined through their camp as dust parched their throats, fraying the nerves of even the steadiest of the men.

The Platte baffled even the most experienced travelers. Flowing roughly from west to east, the river was known to be too thick to drink and too thin to plow. Most of its width was filled with sandy islands, bars, rocks, and tree stumps. Although the stream bed was normally shallow, it was difficult to ford. Too muddy for bathing, its waters left an unpleasant taste in one's mouth. Travelers called the Platte a moving mass of sand. Yet in the spring its south fork became a raging torrent, with thousands of sandhill cranes flying high above it.

At the Platte's forks Frémont divided his group. The main body was to proceed over the Oregon Trail to Fort Laramie. That route, with which overland parties had been familiar since the early 1840s, followed the North Platte through what is now Nebraska and southeastern Wyoming to the fort, then continued westward to South Pass, the continental divide, and beyond. Frémont personally led four men toward Fort Laramie by way of the South Platte and Fort Saint Vrain. When the two parties converged at Fort Laramie, Jim Bridger, just returned from further west, warned them that bands of young Blackfeet, Cheyennes, and Sioux were on the warpath.

The commander at Fort Laramie suggested that the party temporarily remain within the fort for protection. But Frémont decided to press westward, one of his orders being to survey locations for future forts to protect settlers against marauding tribes. Hostile natives had declared war on everything west of the Red Buttes, already a famous sandstone landmark. The country swarmed with scattered war parties. Old Indians encountered on the way west also spoke of young hotheads on the warpath.

Refusing to back off in the face of these warnings by the chiefs, Frémont told them he had been sent by the Great White Father. He reiterated his "fixed determination to proceed to the end of the enterprise on which I had been sent." Frémont informed the natives that his aims were peaceful. Yet he was ambivalent about Indians. Though, like other distrustful frontier travelers, he kept his ammunition ready for instant protection, he actually pitied them: "We have taken from them their property and means of support and are bound to a corresponding obligation." Preuss complained in his diary: "We are no military expedition to fight the Indians. It would be ridiculous to risk the lives of twenty-five people just to determine a few longitudes and latitudes. . . . The men are not all inclined to continue without reinforcements."[12]

Frémont later recalled that some of his men "were disposed to cowardice, and anxious to return. They had but to come forward at once, and state their desire," he said, "and they would be discharged." In the midst of a wilderness filled with natives, only one man, however, decided to return eastward. Frémont was oblivious to the dangers that this returnee would face: "I asked him some questions, in order to expose him to the ridicule of the men, and then let him go." In the times of danger a commander is within his rights to suppress any sign of hesitation or shirking among his men. They will not ordinarily follow a leader who tolerates fear. Francis Grierson once heard a Frémont scout say, "There ain't a bullet can touch him. That man's got what they call a charmed life." Grierson himself was convinced that "of all the public men of that time, who led adventuresome and romantic lives, Frémont was the most daring and the most original.[13]

Out on the trail, the explorer found special solace when surrounded by willows, grass, and prickly greasewood. Yet he was an official invader, and his government-sponsored surveys would help put an end to the very freedom that he, the free trappers, and the roaming tribes enjoyed. The high point of the Rocky Mountain fur trade occurred from 1825 to 1845, years during which greedy trappers had devastated the beaver. Some of the mountain men whose services he used, among them Jim Bridger and the Chouteau family, established trading posts, settling down to a life as "sutlers" or provisioners of overland parties. For years Bridger and Carson also acted as guides for the Topographical Engineers.

Kit Carson, born on the frontier four years before Frémont, had also left home at an early age. When only sixteen he began his long career as trapper and guide. Frémont, who first met Carson in 1842 on the deck of a riverboat steaming up the Missouri toward Chouteau's Landing, paid him one hundred dollars per month as a guide—three times what Carson had received as a hunter at William Bent's fort. Carson became devoted and dependable. Unable to read or write, he was impressed by his new, educated commander. Carson would be useful to Frémont for many years, especially among the Indians. Although he had an Arapaho "wife," Carson had experienced gruesome encounters with Indians and did not hesitate to chastise natives who took vengeance on white parties. Yet he served as go-between with the tribes whose dialects he spoke. The process of making Carson into a legend would have been impossible without Frémont's backing.[14]

Not all of Frémont's mountain men stirred up such adulation. Some were braggarts who passed on their tall tales canonically. Jim Bridger, a guide on the first expedition, typified their carefree descriptions of the lay of the land. His comments about Frémont resembled those of the cartographer Preuss. Bridger would one day arrogantly refute Frémont's official reports with the disparaging comment that the explorer knew nothing about the country he mapped. Although weather-beaten trappers had first described the distant valleys that lay over the Great Divide, Frémont and his scouts were preparing the way for the West's ultimate conquerors, the three hundred thousand pioneers whose wagon trains would furrow the overland trails from 1840 to 1869.

In addition to Carson and Bridger, Frémont's 1842 expedition included half a dozen seasoned scouts, among them the Irishman Thomas ("Broken Hand") Fitzpatrick, also known as "White Hair," and Jim Beckwourth. Both were listed as voyageurs. Whereas Carson received $2.50 per day, Fitzpatrick drew $3.33 daily. Most of the men received $0.45 per day plus rations. Preuss, on Frémont's roster as "topographical assistant," received $4.00 per day plus travel expenses from Washington, D.C., to the Missouri frontier at $0.10 per mile. Frémont's own pay was only $33.00 per month, but he was entitled to allowances for "responsibility," including rations, clothing, quarters, and servants.[15]

Beyond Fort Laramie, as the expedition traveled through hostile country, Carson and Bridger urged special precautions. Frémont had to halt the expedition an hour or so before sunset. Campfires had to be extinguished by dark in order not to attract passing natives. Except for guards, no guns were to remain loaded in camp lest they go off accidentally. The illiterate Carson considered the situation serious enough to make an oral will before Frémont. Fortunately, no hostilities occurred.

Nevertheless, the danger posed by the Indians—beyond their begging and stealing—remained uppermost in Frémont's mind. A good native bowman could get off six arrows in sixty seconds. The idea of scalping, too, sent a shudder down many a man's spine. The leader took care to counter those fears: "I had always been careful of my men . . . so far as the nature of our exposed life permitted, for in case of accident, as we had no surgeon, I was myself the only resource. . . . I loved to have my camp cheerful and took care for the health and comfort which carry good temper with them."[16]

Autumn approached. They were moving into the high country. Cold blasts of air howled in from the north off the Wind River Range. Clouds leaden with snow hovered over the party's thin tents. Hands froze and ears turned numb. Frémont estimated elevation by taking the temperature at which water would boil.

Although Charles Preuss faithfully sketched the peaks that loomed up ahead, he was disappointed by their appearance. Comparing the western mountains with the Alps, he found them wanting. Perhaps because the Wind River Range did not suddenly soar up before them, as did the Matterhorn, his drawings tended to exaggerate the jaggedness of each summit. Most foreign travelers into the West, and Frémont himself, did not share Preuss's dourness about its highest peaks. For the Englishman Fitz Hugh Ludlow, for example, the Rockies were like "the stairs of heaven after the last soul has ascended [from] earth."[17]

Frémont, fascinated by the mountains he saw along the route, suddenly decided to ascend one of them, which he mistakenly called "the loftiest peak of the Rocky Mountains." Frémont Peak, which he named after himself (possibly today's Gannett Peak, 13,730 feet high), is located in Wyoming's Wind River Range. This mountain had already been scaled in 1835 by Captain B. L. E. Bonneville. After maneuvering icy slopes, Frémont and five companions reached its snowcapped summit. Sensing the opportunity for reportage in every major newspaper, Frémont unfurled a hand-sewn flag with thirteen red stripes flanked by a triumphant eagle clasping a bundle of arrows and an Indian pipe of peace in its claws. In its background was a field of twenty-six blue stars. Frémont wrote in his journal: "We had climbed the loftiest peak of the Rocky Mountains and looked down upon the snow a thousand feet below; and standing where never human foot had stood before, felt the exultation of first explorers." From that spot one could see all the lakes and streams that flowed toward the Green River of the Colorado, which the Indians called the Seedskadee. Visible too were the forested flanks of the Wind River valley, the streams of which fed into the headwaters of the Yellowstone and Missouri rivers. The date was August 15, 1842.

As he rested on the peak, a bumblebee appeared out of nowhere, lighting on Frémont's knee. He considered that bee a fellow pioneer crossing a common mountain barrier. But the insect did not escape, for Frémont placed it within a book alongside flowers he had collected for Jessie on his ascent. She would sentimentally commemorate this gift to her by having the figure of a bee stamped onto her personal stationery.

With this sentimental reverie behind him, the explorer descended Frémont Peak and pressed on toward another promontory, Independence Rock—an outcropping of stones located in the Sweetwater River valley one hundred miles from that much higher mountain. He incised a large cross on the rock, which was later to be called a "register of the plains." Countless overland pioneers would chisel or even paint their names on its bulbous surface. While camping near its base, Frémont planned the expedition's return trip to Saint Louis.

The expedition had reconnoitered territory as far as the headwaters of the Green River. But Frémont needed to survey the Platte more closely, for it seemed likely that its "mile wide and inch deep" stream bed would become a major travel artery for future migrant parties. At flood time, however, this seemingly tranquil stream could be treacherous. After returning to the Platte, he ordered the men to break out and to inflate the collapsible rubber boat. Before leaving Washington he had stored the boat in the Benton house. The Bentons had been delighted to get rid of its awful stench; to eliminate the smell they had caused the house to be fumigated.

Frémont now proceeded, at the confluence of the Sweetwater and Platte rivers, to take a calculated but dangerous risk with this experimental craft. Though he found the wild Platte swollen, he would attempt to shoot a series of rock-lined rapids on the badly flooded river. The elastic boat, twenty feet long and five feet wide, paddled by three men, quickly capsized. Lost were six guns, several pistols, ammunition, blankets, one of Frémont's journals, the group's sextant and circle (surveying instruments), and a telescope. "Carts, barrels, boxes, and bales were in a moment floating down the current." Two men who could not swim were luckily saved from drowning after catapulting over a rolling cataract. A precious 150-pound bag of coffee, sugar, and other provisions also floated downstream. "I don't know how we could have gotten boat and baggage across the rocks," Preuss wrote in his diary. "It was certainly stupid of the young chief to be so foolhardy where the terrain was absolutely unknown."[18]

This rubber boat accident was to cost Frémont personally. Although he billed the government for some losses, most charges were disallowed. Among them was Basil Lajeunesse's loss of an overcoat ($5.00), which Frémont reported as "in the service of the United States." Frémont also later wrote: "I am at this time a defendant in a suit brought by another man for a gem lost" during the boat mishap.[19]

Although Frémont was usually reined in by past training, one senses in his impetuous mishandling of the rubber boat a forecast of future irresponsibility, a momentary triumph of excitement and the courting of danger over good sense. His rashness might well "have destroyed completely the records of his expedition."[20] He had, indeed, placed himself in harm's way.

After the boat episode was over, he was, fortunately, able to repair his precious barometer, which had been smashed against a rock, by using a powder horn scraped to translucency and glue made from buffalo tendons. To take the place of the rubber skiff, Frémont ordered his men to sew together a buffalo-skin bull boat eight feet long and five feet wide. Such fur-trade boats were fashioned of hides stitched together, stretched over a willow or cottonwood frame, and caulked with tallow. Both ends were pointed, an improvement over the circular, unnavigable Indian bull boats. Nevertheless, Frémont's second boat also proved unwieldy and had to be abandoned, as Preuss had predicted in his diary: "Frémont has crazy notions in his head again. Tomorrow he wants to rig up a raft and try to navigate down the Platte. . . . The river is more than a mile wide and in many places, I believe, hardly navigable for a large wash tub."[21]

It was late in the year as the expedition picked its way homeward through greasewood, boulders, and stubble. They traveled eastward by way of Grand

Island toward Chouteau's Landing in Kansas—all except Carson, who instead headed toward Taos to winter at that New Mexican pueblo. Near the end of September, Frémont's men had traversed two thousand miles of territory. Before long the expedition would reenter Saint Louis. But Frémont still needed a boat with which to descend the Missouri River with his heavy specimens and equipment. Fortunately, he encountered the trader Peter Sarpy, whom he commissioned to quickly build a navigable craft.

Finally, on the morning of October 1, Frémont arose from his cot, left his tent, and heard "the tinkling of cow-bells at the settlements on the opposite side of the Missouri."[22] On October 17, as autumn rains began to fall, his party reentered Saint Louis, and only twelve days later they would be in Washington. Frémont had been gone four long months.

Never knowing when he would return, Jessie had set a place for him every night at the supper table, even at her parents' home. After his return from this expedition, Jessie gave birth to their first child, Elizabeth. The day she was born (November 13, 1842) Frémont presented baby and mother with the hand-made flag he had unfurled atop the summit of the Wind River Range. The flag's symbolic triumph over the dangers of the frontier paralleled Jessie's private victory in producing this first offspring. Although she called herself a "water-drinker by training and preference," Jessie toasted with champagne both her husband's triumphant return and the little child who lay beside them in its wooden crib.

Jessie almost felt a motherly pride in her husband's many achievements. They were both prepared conveniently to forget that there were few corners of the West where one could set down an exploratory boot for the first time. Senator Benton could always argue that Frémont was uncovering unique information. He had, indeed, made sixty-eight separate observations of latitude and longitude. Although he had repeated troubles with his chronometer, he was only five miles off in calculating the vast distance between Chouteau Station in Missouri and South Pass in today's Wyoming. He had also taken six hundred meteorological readings, all of which reified knowledge about overland trails, soil conditions, and water resources. Added to the findings of Lewis and Clark, this information would prove vital to later overland parties.

Frémont's report would confirm that the plains between the Missouri River and the Rocky Mountains were not completely arid. Once the Indian threat had been contained, settlers could homestead millions of acres of government land west of the Missouri for dry farming. The Platte River valley could also be relied upon as a new water resource. Settlers moving relentlessly in prairie schooners toward the tier of states beyond the Mississippi added pressure for a greater assertion of American rights in Oregon Territory (today's Washington, Oregon, and Idaho), which was at that time held by the British and the United States in a kind of joint tenancy. The British had extended their power across an entire continent to the Pacific. Token garrisons and Hudson's Bay Company clerks manned outlying posts that enforced English rule.

The nation that put the largest number of settlers in the northwest first would emerge as its possessor. But this depended upon opening at least a dirt pathway westward that unskilled wagoners could follow with confidence. In 1843, Senator Linn, Benton's close colleague in Missouri, sponsored legislation to extend American homesteading into Oregon and the entire northwest in order to extinguish British claims to the area.

Benton, the major prophet of expansionism and proponent of the North-west Passage to India, deliberately buried mention of the shallow, muddy, and sluggishly unnavigable streams that could never be great avenues of commerce. Partly because of the lies he concocted, the Indians would be subdued, the buffalo would be hunted to virtual extinction, and the legend of a verdant West would blossom.

Frémont's activities thus were at the heart of full opening of the West. As liegeman of Senator Benton's expansionists, he now had to settle down to sorting out piles of specimens that would form the data from which his 210-page report could be assembled. Colonel Abert ordered him to Washington, where he might best do the job. He had to transform a ledger of daily field notes into a chronicle that could be read by all.

At that time, however, he was experiencing some puzzling hemorrhages of the nose, so he cajoled Jessie into helping put together the manuscript. She was accustomed to copying out her father's speeches with a Perry-point steel pen on sheets of satin-finish foolscap, even editing various drafts. She would do the same for her husband, turning over their baby girl, Elizabeth, to a wet nurse in order to share his writing desk. Jessie not only transcribed dictation, but also, because he detested the boredom of writing, did more and more of it for him. Little did he know how much she would affect its influence, for she enlivened his prose, although it is too high-flown for most modern readers. Above all, she relished being helpful to him.[23]

Some have promoted Jessie to the status of a ghost writer and reduced her husband to a mouthpiece of Senator Benton. Both extremes are unfortunate. Each partner contributed to and took great pride in the 1843 report. With Jessie's embroidering, however, his recollections emerged as larger than life. She sentimentally portrayed her husband as rhapsodic about such matters as wild roses and bees encountered along the route of march. Jessie tried to relive vicariously each step of his expeditions. The invisible traveler sought to experience even the sights and sounds her husband had seen and heard in the wilderness. She left behind an unpublished description of their close collaboration:

Often he would dictate in the mornings, pausing only for a more fitting word, for the whole of the four hours walking about. The freedom of movement was essential to his freedom of expression. It was my great reward to be told that but for me the work could not be done.

        Sometimes an observation would need verifying and Mr. Frémont would sleep with the alarm clock under his pillow. . . . These broken sleeps made no harm to me. I was only twenty and I loved my work.[24]

One interpreter, overlooking the teamwork between the Frémonts, tells us that his scientific papers were overly picturesque, "as though he had caught himself day dreaming." Had his reports not been altered by Jessie, they would never have appealed to such large nineteenth-century audiences. The Indian spears and shields he brought back with him, as well as buffalo robes, she converted figuratively into a prose that spoke of vivid reminders of "the days of chivalry." Actually Frémont had usually watched his men hunt buffalo through a scientific telescope. It was Jessie who pictorialized descriptions of dangerous old bulls bearing down on his party, making his "heart beat quicker." She reported such scenes as literary landscapes that produced "a kind of dreamy effect."[25] Left alone, Frémont would have portrayed himself, if not modestly, primarily as a scientific observer, certainly not the glory hunter about whom Preuss continually complained.

None of Frémont's fellow topographical engineers was more aware of phenomena encountered on the trail. Every sound, rustling in the shrubbery, or change in the weather was noticed by a cartographer skilled in classifying both fauna and flora. Each evening he ordered the expedition to pitch tents early so that he could gather botanical and geological specimens before nightfall set in. His science was never suspect, for he was the personification of mapmaking no longer based upon rumors, guesses, and estimates that could be inaccurate by hundreds of miles. Nightly star sightings, frequent sketches, and detailed study of the landscape often produced accuracy to within a few hundred feet.

But instead of the tedium and duress of such observations, Jessie saw to it that Frémont's reports strongly featured adventure. In them he is made to boast: "My holster pistols were a hair-trigger pair, and old companions which I like for that, and because they were true as a rifle." At another point he remarked: "It would have been dull work if it had been a plod over a safe country and here and there to correct some error." About the routine, he also observed that "it is surprising how a long day's march dwindles away to a few miles when it comes to be laid down between the rigorous astronomical stations" he had to establish.[26]

With the expedition at an end, his memories were of precautions and fears. To prepare his men for any eventuality, he had ordered them to engage in regular target practice. They were also to scare stray buffalo away from campsites.

Lightning and thunder might otherwise cause the group to be trampled to death by a stampeding herd as they slept. Other dangers included whole villages of prairie dogs, which dug holes into which horsemen could easily stumble while chasing away buffalo. It was such practical matters that had really occupied him. All that he had seen and done, indeed, provides us with insights not only into himself but also about how the West then looked to its invaders, whether explorers or pioneers.

The 1843 report, and his later recollections as well, stressed the privations his men had endured. He repeatedly sympathized with their complaints, whether about body lice, ticks, gnats, or the clouds of mosquitoes that made sleeping at night almost impossible.

Despite all inconveniences, the mapping of the West was as central to Frémont's generation as the space age has been to ours. His 1843 report was both a geographical and political document. It called for new forts and trading posts to support settlement beyond the Rockies. Frémont's observations to the War Department were transmitted to Senator Linn, who put forth a resolution that Frémont's findings immediately be published by the government. Linn, as did Benton, continued to oppose joint occupation of Oregon by England and the United States. Ultimately Britain would bow to the inevitable, accepting the line that today separates the United States and Canada.

Much of this expansion of national boundaries was possible because of Frémont's reports. Exciting and graphic, as well as cartographically reliable, they do not quite resemble those of other American explorers. Even the great Lewis and Clark expedition had taken along no scientific observers. While Frémont's writings are technical, their grace best resembles Washington Irving's *Adventures of Captain Bonneville* (1837) and his *The Rocky Mountains* (1847). Both books are based upon the exploits of Bonneville. But, unlike Frémont, Bonneville had sought beaver furs as much as he had engaged in exploration. The business of trappers was furs, not maps. Furthermore, they guarded jealously such information as the location of their favorite water holes. Frémont did the opposite. He purveyed the latest information about the West, which had been disparate at best.

This publication of information would further encourage the stream of emigration to Oregon and California. Meanwhile, the buffalo on the High Plains would dwindle away, depriving a large wandering Indian population who depended upon these animals for sustenance. Soon the natives would themselves be ruled from scattered military posts and debased with the whiskey peddled by itinerant traders. But subsequent overland parties would make their journeys with a greater feeling of security because of Frémont's reports.[27]

The Pathfinder was to be hailed by a number of luminaries of his century, domestic and foreign. Ralph Waldo Emerson extolled such men who "traversed the nervous, rocky west," while the English writer Rudyard Kipling, in his *The Foreloper*, praised the role of "the Explorer" who risks death to find an unknown world "lost beyond the ranges":

> He shall desire loneliness, and his desire shall bring
> Hard on his heels a thousand wheels, a people and a king. . . .
> For he must blaze a nation's way, with hatchet and with brand,
> Till on his last-won wilderness an empire's bulwark stand.

In ages past, another explorer of genius, Leonardo da Vinci, like Frémont also illegitimate, had written about any discoverer of the unknown in celestial terms: "He turns not back who is bound to a star." Frémont, soon to be hailed as a Columbus of the Plains, would become America's new frontier virtuoso. ❖

On to California, the Second Expedition

In 1842, while Frémont waited in Washington for a new assignment, a dramatic event took place in the Pacific that would ultimately affect his future. Commodore Thomas Ap Catesby Jones, commander of the American squadron there, heard a rumor from a passing ship that war had broken out with Mexico. He instantly headed for Monterey in California, where he captured the town and hoisted the American flag. When the report proved false, he withdrew and apologized. But his embarrassing attempted coup reflected Washington's aggressive policy on the Pacific Coast.

Frémont's early expeditions accompanied an expansionist frenzy at a time when there were only about ten thousand Mexican citizens living in California. Because this distant province of a politically weak Mexico was, in fact, defenseless, he learned that official Washington feared Great Britain or some other power might seize California.

During 1843, he socialized with key members of the government. While the Frémonts dined at the table of Secretary of State Daniel Webster, they heard that Webster had been trying to purchase Upper California. But the American minister at Mexico City had reported that the Mexicans refused his offer. Webster persisted in the belief that the United States should somehow at least obtain San Francisco Bay and all of its surrounding territory. Before long, Frémont received quick authorization to mount a second expedition, supposedly to map the area between Saint Louis and the farthest West.[1]

"I have the honor to acknowledge . . . your letter . . . and to thank you for your suggestions in reference to the survey now required in the vicinity of the Rocky Mountains," his superior, Colonel Abert, wrote Senator Benton in mid-March of 1843. "Be assured that they will receive the greatest attention," Abert half-resentfully concluded, knowing that Benton strongly backed his son-in-law for the government's next winter expedition. But other explorers also vied for funds for exploration. Among them was the navy's Captain Charles Wilkes, already on the Pacific Coast, with whom Frémont might eventually rendezvous.[2]

Frémont was actually in the midst of what the historian William Goetzmann has depicted as the second great phase of America's history of exploration. Under government auspices a number of expeditions would proceed to map the continent. Whereas his first venture had a limited purpose, taking Frémont up the Platte to Fort Laramie, South Pass, and the Wind River Range, his second would evolve into something more ambitious. Initially he was ordered to chart the route from the Arkansas River through South Pass to the Great Salt Lake. He again would cross the Rockies at their lowest point. But this time he headed for Oregon Territory, descending the Walla Walla and Columbia rivers to the Pacific Coast. He would then move southward past Klamath Lake into today's western Nevada. Then he would make a controversial decision to cross the Sierra Nevada into California.

At Saint Louis, Frémont recruited a number of former trappers not yet willing to settle down to a life of trading. His party numbered thirty-nine men, including two Delawares engaged as hunters and guides. These Indians came from a reservation near today's Kansas City, having been displaced westward by population pressures and tribal rivalries. Reduced to purveying fish and game to that city's residents, they were grateful for Frémont's employment of them as scouts and hunters. He was partial to them because of their trustworthiness. Once again he picked up Thomas Fitzpatrick as the expedition's guide. He also recruited for the second time the hunter and scout Kit Carson. The explorer took along as his personal valet Jacob Dodson, "a free colored man." Formerly Benton's manservant, Dodson had volunteered to go west. Also on the expedition's roster was Frederick Dwight, en route to the Sandwich Islands and China, who was to leave the party at Fort Boise. Lucien Maxwell, later the largest landowner in New Mexico, became chief hunter at $1.665 per day. Finally there was William Gilpin, editor of the *Saint Louis Argus* and future governor of Colorado.[3]

From Colonel Stephen Watts Kearny, then commander of the federal arsenal at Saint Louis, Frémont obtained some Hall carbines and a twelve-pound brass howitzer. This heavy armament aroused doubts in the minds of his men about the group's peaceful intentions. On May 10 they finally left Chouteau's trading post.

As the party made its first camp only four miles outside Saint Louis, Jessie, who was then in the town, received a dispatch from her husband's superior, Colonel Abert, in Washington. Abert requested that Frémont explain why he was taking along such an oversized and menacing weapon on a nonmilitary venture. Jessie, still only in her teens, but a senator's daughter, knew that Abert's query might delay, if not cancel, the expedition that her husband had meticulously planned. The general's communication could be construed as an order for her husband to return to Washington in order to explain the controversial cannon. So Jessie held back Abert's letter.

From the start of their marriage there had been political as well as personal connivance between Jessie and her husband. This collusion, sometimes against regular army officers, often verged upon insubordination. Jessie's warning note to John Charles read:

> Dear Charles:
> Do not delay in Camp one minute longer. Trust me, and move westward at once.
>
> Jessie

This was only the first of many such interventions by the dutiful Jessie. Frémont's reply to his wife's warning message was: "Goodbye, I trust, and go."[4]

In an article that she wrote for *Century Magazine* in 1891, Jessie recalled: "I wrote Mr. Frémont that he must not ask why. . . . The animals could rest and fatten at Bent's Fort. Only GO." Meanwhile, she explained to Frémont's superiors at the Topographical Bureau in Washington, "the country of the Blackfeet and other fierce tribes knew nothing of the rights of science, but fought all whites. . . . [T]herefore the howitzer was necessary."[5] Only upon Frémont's return did he learn of the full content of Abert's letter and thank the dutiful Jessie for her act.

Frémont later recalled: "She did not hesitate to suppress the order, and write me the letter which caused me to make an immediate start. She did not communicate this proceeding to Colonel Abert until I was far beyond the reach of recall. Mr. Benton was not in Saint Louis, and she took council with no one." Although Frémont had been placed under Abert's command by presidential order, at this point Abert had nothing against the young officer personally. Indeed, he once reprimanded Lieutenant John Pope for disparaging Frémont's cartographic work. But through Senator Benton, Abert now had to deliver an implied reprimand to Frémont: "Now as the equipment of his party contemplated a serious change in the character of the expedition under his command, one that might involve the Government in Indian hostility, I have no doubt you will admit it to have been a negligence deserving some reproach. . . . The Department might have prohibited the expedition."[6]

Jessie cynically interpreted Abert's instructions as nothing more than an "excuse for breaking up the expedition."[7] But there was good reason for the government to forbid Frémont his howitzer. Relations with both Great Britain and Mexico were uneasy, and the howitzer was unsuited to any exploring expedition

A contemporary cartoon pokes fun at the U.S. Army Corps of Topographical Engineers, of which Frémont was a member. From George Horatio Derby, *Phoenixiana; or, Sketches and Burlesques* (New York, 1856).

entering disputed territory. But Benton resented even Colonel Abert's slight reprimand. President Tyler and his secretary of war, John C. Spencer, seemed uninformed of how much pressure Benton was placing upon his son-in-law.

Frémont had actually ignored higher authority, unusual conduct for an officer still so young. Benton's backing of him would furthermore promote anger among his fellow topographical engineers, over 85 percent of whom were West Pointers. His competitors for rank and promotion within the corps were quick to perceive that his personality and mannerisms did not quite fit the military mold. He seemed to pursue his own visions of reality, and his impetuousness was threatening.

Meanwhile, Frémont's second expedition proceeded westward at a snail's pace. At dusk each day he told his men to take great care in unpacking scientific instruments carried by a dozen mule-drawn carts. Group members complained that women and children alike would reach the Oregon country more rapidly that year than did their expedition. Each morning every cart had to be reloaded, tents struck, horses saddled, and mules hitched to their harnesses. Occasionally a horse broke loose and ran away, which further delayed travel. The balky mules, too, had to be brought into line, no easy task during repeated river crossings.

At Elm Grove, thirty miles out of today's Westport, Frémont ran into the Missouri party of Joseph B. Chiles, on his second trip to California. Well equipped and knowledgeable, Chiles's men had just shot some wild turkeys and two deer. They offered meat to Frémont, who promptly took two choice hindquarters of venison. About this incident Chiles's son recalled: "My father and his bunch were so mad they left Frémont" behind without further contact with him. On the frontier it was the hunter who bagged a buck that ate the best parts of the animal. Not so with Frémont.[8]

The cumbersome fieldpiece, to which Frémont had become stubbornly attached, further slowed the party's march westward. The three men needed to operate it hated to lug it along. Their commander, Louis Zindel, a Berliner, had first met Frémont on Nicollet's 1839 expedition. Zindel had been trained in the Prussian army as an artillery expert, and he also knew how to make rockets. Once when the gun carriage broke down, Preuss confided in his diary: "I must report that the chief orders the cannon to be moved in front of his tent every night." Although the weapon repeatedly alarmed the Indians, Frémont claimed it was the U.S. flag that upset the natives. Partly because of the beastly cannon, as even Frémont had to admit, the Snake River "proved impracticable for us, the water [temporarily] sweeping away the howitzer and nearly drowning the mules, which we were obliged to extricate by cutting them out of the harness." While fording the Columbia, "the howitzer was occasionally several feet under water." When other streams had to be crossed, "the gun-carriage was unlimbered and separately descended by hand."[9] Because Frémont's party was well armed, he did not really need the howitzer. But he still remained ambivalent about the dangers of Indian attacks.

Benton had suggested that gaudy presents for the Indians would be his best defense: "It is indispensable that the officer who carries the flag of the U. States into these remote regions, should carry presents. All savages respect them. They even demand them; and they feel contempt & resentment if disappointed." Repeatedly Frémont issued orders against natives who menaced his camp. Later, his son Frank interpreted his father's unusual precautions as wholly necessary: "He was slow to anger, but when aroused there was nothing that would stop his appropriate action. In his frontier experience he would willingly kill to enforce orders necessary for the security of the men under his care. . . . He would not shade duty to save himself from enmity."[10]

Once, while the party was drying buffalo meat, a clutch of Arapahos and Cheyennes charged the camp by mistake, thinking they were attacking other nearby Indians. On another occasion, Osages ran off some of the expedition's horses, which had to be painfully recaptured. Frémont felt especially vulnerable when his men, divided and temporarily lost, struggled into camp days late. Charles Preuss recorded in his diary that this group had "split into three parties." He believed that Carson, to whom Frémont usually listened carefully, was stirring up a panic over the Indian menace "in order to make himself feel important."

Preuss also, as during the first expedition, thought his leader distracted by too many trivial matters: "Frémont became angry when my horse urinated. He whipped its tail when it had only half relieved nature."[11]

The party proceeded westward along the Kansas River instead of the Platte, which Frémont had used on his first expedition. He hoped to go up the Kansas to the headwaters of the Arkansas River, then to move toward central Colorado in search of a new pass through the Rockies, south of where most emigrants then traveled westward. After crossing the shallow Republican River, northwestward through arid and broken terrain, they eventually reached the headwaters of the Cache la Poudre, going toward the Laramie Plain. Fighting off mosquitoes and gnats, Frémont's expedition had to cross the swollen north fork of the Cache la Poudre as many as nine times per day until they reached the Laramie River in today's Wyoming. Most crossings had to be bridged, and the guides sought to avoid putrid streams used as buffalo wallows. Evidence of farming or human habitation had last been seen back on the Kansas, where women were "engaged in digging prairie potatoes."[12] Short on rations, the men were glad to put together dinners of stewed skunk and tea made from bitter wild cherries.

Their trail wound close to the northern Rockies by way of the Sweetwater River toward today's western Wyoming. The route had fairly dependable water sources and some grazing for animals. Its slope was preferable to a sparser southern overland route by way of the Rio Grande valley and the Gila River into the scorching Mojave Desert. Frémont's party next crossed South Pass, which would become the best gateway to western America. Subsequently the mystique grew that he was its discoverer, but Robert Stuart in 1812 and Thomas Fitzpatrick and Jedediah Smith in 1824 had all used the pass. Frémont did not actually consider his own crossing a momentous occasion and described South Pass as no harder to climb than Washington's Capitol Hill. The continental divide was, nevertheless, ten thousand feet high nearby.

The government considered it vital to keep the entire Oregon Trail free from Indian attack. This "fortunate avenue to the West" would soon be traversed by thousands of lumbering covered wagons and heavy-gaited oxen. West of Fort Laramie they would wear a track five feet deep into the sandstone ridges—a track still visible today. Frémont's primary mission was to stake out the route beyond Fort Laramie where other military posts might be established. He believed that "a show of military force in this country is absolutely necessary" in order to "keep the Oregon road through the valley of the Sweet Water and the South Pass of the mountains constantly open."[13]

There were suddenly so many overlanders that Chiles recalled seeing "trains of wagons . . . almost constantly in sight." These "pulverized the dusty trails," raising clouds that almost blotted out the sun. Pioneers with their wagons heavily overloaded found the journey toward Oregon and California a long one.

The Chiles party carried along farm implements and even machinery for a sawmill. But most groups were not nearly so well equipped as Frémont's government-sponsored venture. At some campsites the wagons queued up, grateful indeed to find brackish and alkaline water. Furniture discarded on the trail alongside the bones of their horses and mules would soon mar the trail. Its rock and sand wore down animals and humans alike, smashing wagon wheels in clouds of heavy dust under the burning sun in this land of sagebrush, scarce game, and potentially menacing Indians.

At night Frémont's men sat around the campfire telling stories about a "terrible whirlpool" whose waters "found their way to the ocean by some subterranean communication." This was the mythical Buenaventura River, which supposedly flowed "from the Rocky Mountains to the bay of San Francisco." Explorers had long sought a waterway that would lead to the shores of distant Cathay. But the quest for the Buenaventura, alas, would evaporate in the desert interior of the Great Basin—the last large area of North America still uncharted by explorers. Although the maps of Albert Gallatin (1836) and of Captain B. L. E. Bonneville (1837) dismissed as apocryphal the existence of the Buenaventura River, or "Great River of the West," Frémont persisted in searching for it. He should have known that Jedediah Smith, and later Walker and Joseph Chiles, en route to California, had found no trace of such a river. In 1841, Captain Wilkes had determined that only the Sacramento River's headwaters lay in the Sierra Nevada. Not until Frémont reached Sutter's Fort did he finally admit that the Buenaventura did not exist. Had he read Washington Irving's book about Captain Bonneville, he would have given up looking for it earlier than that.[14]

Frémont was, however, able to clear up other tales of wonderment repeated by trappers since the earliest days of exploration. Whereas they had often followed the trails of migrating animals, he used the new science of mapmaking by astronomical observation. Each night his cartographers engaged in star sighting. As a result, future wagon masters could follow Frémont's newly surveyed trails, the maps of which were usually accurate to within a few hundred feet.

Moving on the Oregon Trail, they followed it northwestward along the Bear River, before veering southward toward the Great Salt Lake. They had heard of a trapper myth which concerned some springs which Frémont's party reached on August 25, 1843. This was Beer Springs. Its strange gases were said to produce "a sensation of giddiness and nausea." He did a chemical analysis of these springs and of Steamboat Springs, in today's north central Colorado, and determined that their sulphurous waters, though effervescent, were merely mineral in content, no different from countless other such underground springs. Frémont said he named Steamboat Springs, but it had probably been called that by previous visitors, for the waters gave off a sound like a steamboat whistle. His men greatly enjoyed drinking the effervescent soda water, which tasted a bit like frothy lager.

Their heady hilarity ceased after they found an enormous rotted frog in Steamboat Springs.

On September 6, 1843, after descending the western slopes of the Wasatch Range, Frémont was perhaps the first explorer to discern that the Great Salt Lake had an interior drainage. A rumor to the contrary was begun back in 1824 by Jim Bridger, probably the first white man to see that body of water. Upon tasting its brine, he reputedly shouted: "Hell, we're on the shores of the Pacific!" Other trappers, too, thought the lake to be an arm of that ocean. Frémont applied the term "Great Basin" to this "inland sea stretching in still and solitary grandeur far beyond the limit of our vision." The spectacle stirred him so that he expressed doubt "that the followers of Balboa felt more enthusiasm when, from the heights of the Andes, they saw for the first time the great Western ocean."[15]

Frémont later gave the Mormons their first description of a promised land in Utah. Brigham Young acknowledged that the young officer's report persuaded him to start the major Mormon settlement there.[16]

Frémont named a few Utah landmarks after himself, but not Frémont Island, located in the middle of the lake. As his men swam naked in the lake, he again used an India-rubber boat to explore it. With rubber buckets and leather bottles the expedition systematically gathered water samples, also probing birds' nests along the shoreline.

On September 12, Frémont left the Great Basin behind in order to move toward the Snake River country. An early winter had set in, and he almost lost his cannon in the Snake's rising waters. By September 19, snow began to fall. The party was short of game, though Carson shot some gulls, which were supplemented by killing a sick horse. They did manage to acquire an antelope from an Indian in exchange for some powder and lead shot before they reached the British post at Fort Hall.

At Fort Hall, Frémont was able to buy badly needed store goods along with five oxen. He also decided to rid himself of men who continually grumbled about the weather and lack of provisions. As if to test their courage, he picked the middle of a blizzard to state that the expedition would have to return homeward later than expected. He then allowed eleven men who wished to return to Saint Louis to do so immediately.

With winter approaching, Frémont wanted no shirkers in his crew. A member of the party, Thomas Salathiel Martin, tells us that the leader imposed stricter discipline for the rest of the trip and that "martial law was read." The explorer, however, did allow occasional recreation, including a shooting match, the first of which Martin, an experienced backwoodsman, won. Frémont put up as prizes "7 fine rifles made at Louisville, Ky."[17]

He knew that competing males, interacting under stressful conditions, make it necessary for a leader to settle disputes promptly, all the while staying above such personal storms. Otherwise a sudden loss of morale could easily result. Small rifts can crop up even from resentment over routine tasks. Short rations, bad weather, face-to-face contact for too long—all of these create stress. The leader of an exploratory party must go to great lengths to maintain emotional balance. If a group was too heterogeneous, Frémont found that stronger personalities within it sought to take over, destroying the consensus he wanted.[18]

On one hand, he could take good care of his men, as he boasted in his memoirs. On the other, as he did during the fourth expedition, he could virtually abandon them, a paradox that metaphorically resembled his father's abandonment so long ago.[19] Frémont dealt with younger men without any feeling of threat—an attitude he did not have toward superiors. On rare occasions he almost acted like a surrogate father to those who were junior in age. Conversely, officers of greater experience whom he outranked were almost always critical of Frémont. Preuss, his cartographer, never really liked him. Nor did Isaac Cooper. Yet Frémont's managerial qualities on the trail, for the most part, inspired loyalty, or his men would not have accompanied him on five expeditions. His control within small parties, however, was far more successful than his command of larger units during the Civil War.

On September 23, 1843, the lieutenant took his remaining men into the Snake River valley. Early in October the group reached Fort Boise, a Hudson's Bay Company post, then they moved on to the Waiilatpu mission of Dr. Marcus Whitman, 130 miles east of The Dalles. As early as 1836 this Protestant physician-turned-missionary and his wife, Narcissa, had set up their way station on the Walla Walla River twenty miles upstream from the Columbia River. At Whitman's, Frémont was grateful to trade a mule for potatoes, and there he met pioneer parties that broke up their wagons as rafts to float down the Columbia from Wallula toward the Pacific. But icy torrents could spell disaster for the inexperienced. Frémont's men had to lower themselves on ropes alongside plunging waterfalls and deep pools. Upon reaching clear water, Frémont, Preuss, and two companions descended the river by Indian canoes.

Colonel Abert had ordered Frémont, in a letter of March 10, 1843, to confer with Lieutenant Charles Wilkes, whose naval expedition along the Pacific Coast had anchored up the Columbia at Fort Vancouver, today's Vancouver, Washington. Their joint surveys, which were to connect, would complete the last transect of mapping operations in North America shared by the topographical corps and the navy. We do not know whether the two rival explorers actually met in the field, but as we shall see, Wilkes would become an implacable enemy after Frémont ridiculed the naval officer's cartography, which conflicted with his own findings. It was a mistake for anyone to criticize either man. Each never forgave a perceived insult. And both had a perfect knack for starting quarrels.

Next, Frémont sought out Dr. John McLoughlin, head of Hudson's Bay

Company operations in the Northwest. McLoughlin was friendly enough, considering that Frémont's party had entered his sphere of influence, wherein his company monopolized all commerce. By 1840, McLoughlin had built a chain of twenty forts and trading posts, creating a veritable fur-trade empire in a land of green forests and grassy meadows. This reigning patriarch of the Oregon country, with his great shock of white hair, now provided the young explorer from a rival country with food and shelter. McLoughlin even invited the party to dinner.

That occasion led to renewed tension with Preuss, because Frémont wanted him to cut off his beard to make him more "presentable" to McLoughlin—"Just for the privilege of a few dinner invitations," Preuss wrote in his diary. The disgruntled German refused and had dinner with some Indians in his own tent. According to a note in the Preuss diaries, inserted years later by Mrs. Preuss, "Frémont became so mad that he wanted to challenge Carl to a pistol duel. The rascal . . . found that he was too stupid to continue the work." Preuss also recorded in his diary: "If I were unmarried, I should have immediately accepted Frémont's offer [to stay behind]."[20]

More charitable toward Frémont was Peter Burnett, later California's first American governor, who traveled with the explorer back up the Columbia to The Dalles, where Frémont's main party remained bivouacked. They used three dugout canoes manned by Indians from Fort Vancouver. Only because the weather was freezing, according to Burnett, did Frémont push the natives. When they were too slow with their loading and unloading chores, he went so far as to "put out their fires." Thus "finding it necessary to work or shiver, they preferred to work." Burnett heartily approved of Frémont's severity.[21]

On November 21, 1843, after ten days of heavy travel, they reached the encampment at The Dalles. Frémont's men rejoiced that he brought them flour, beans, and other sundries obtained from the Hudson's Bay Company. Burnett's recollection of the leader was quite favorable:

> He was then about thirty years old, modest in appearance, and calm and gentle in manner. His men all loved him intensely. He gave his orders with great mildness and simplicity, but they had to be obeyed. There was no shrinking from duty. He was like a father to those under his command. . . . I thought I could endure as much hardship as most men, especially a small, slender man like . . . Frémont, but I was wholly mistaken.

Burnett also recorded that Frémont could sleep for nights on end in wet and uncomfortable clothing, wearing only "a thin calf-skin boot, and yet he could endure more cold than I could with heavy boots on. I never traveled with a more pleasant companion. . . . His bearing toward me was as kind as a brother."[22]

Frémont had originally planned an eight-month expedition. It had taken six to reach Fort Vancouver. Three months' more travel lay ahead. Instead of heading back eastward to Saint Louis, he now decided to move toward the southern border of today's Oregon, taking along new horses, mules, and even cattle, also purchased from McLoughlin's Canadians. Moving along the Cascade Range, the party recorded the eruption of Mount Saint Helens. They also mistook Klamath Marsh for Klamath Lake,[23] and they made other cartographic errors west of what Frémont called Summer Lake. A stream that he thought to be the headwaters of the Sacramento was actually the Sycan, which runs into the Klamath. This mistake became embedded in his official report and accompanying map. Though these were relatively minor errors, they misled at least one later overland party seeking the Pacific. No wonder the area's major stream came to be called the Lost River. Today, some of these rivers have become disconnected ponds.

It was all too easy to err while surveying hundreds of miles of terrain that had never been mapped. Furthermore, delicate scientific paraphernalia was jarringly carried along in a canvas-covered Jersey wagon equipped with springs that easily broke. Frémont's glass barometers were so fragile and imprecise that he resorted to measuring elevations by reading the boiling point of water. He also used what Theodore Talbot, an assistant, called an "astronomical and meteorological instrument," with which they determined longitude by the position of the moon. Each day there were new plants and trees to name as well. Among them was the yellow-flowered *Frémontia vermicularis*, which grew near lush fields of wild flax, and a fragrant sage called artemisia.[24]

Preuss rumbled along in the wagon, angered each time Frémont made a last-minute change in their route, He sarcastically expressed his emotions in his secret diary and continued to complain about leadership: "What a life in such weather, such a country, and such management!" On another occasion: "Frémont changes his mind every day as usual."[25]

The party moved southward toward modern-day Reno in Nevada. Suddenly, off to their right, the sharp eastern scarp of the Sierra Nevada loomed up. Frémont ostensibly had no firm plans to cross the mountains into California, although Preuss's diary mentions that possibility, as do the homebound letters of Talbot. Such an endeavor would present a test of great endurance for a party that had already traveled so far and that had encountered so much discomfort. Frémont's remaining twenty-five men were tired and footsore. Some were clearly anxious to return eastward to Saint Louis.

But upon first viewing the crest of the Sierra Nevada, Frémont was transfixed by the sight of peaks close to nine thousand feet in elevation. Intrigued by the prospect of crossing the seemingly uncharted range that lay before him, he spoke of its heights as "more lofty than the Rocky Mountains."

Although the explorer was about to enter forbidden Mexican territory, he had an understanding with Senator Benton to feel out the strength of California's military forces. Though his official orders called only for a survey of the Oregon Trail westward to the Pacific, he had the capacity to rationalize even the worst of decisions and then to believe his own deceptions.

Historians have treated Frémont's midwinter crossing of the Sierra Nevada as irrational. In his memoirs, however, he maintained that the decision not to return eastward was made in part because of the poor condition of his animals. The horseshoes were falling off the hooves of his ponies, and there were no nails to replace them. According to him, his men, though they had been on the trail for eight months, reacted favorably: "My decision was heard with joy by the people, and diffused new life throughout the camp," with "cheerful obedience." A few may have actually wished to enter California, that forbidden and fascinating province of Mexico. Kit Carson said: "We were nearly out of provisions and cross the mountains we must, let the consequences be what they may."[26]

The party might have wintered in today's Reno–Carson Sink area in relative safety. In the mountains the snow drifts were forty feet deep. One account described "a number of Indians" coming into Frémont's camp, telling him "by means of signs, that it would be sure destruction to attempt the passage." The Indians, equipped with snowshoes, offered to trade pine nuts and rabbits for cloth, but at first they refused to become guides. Several natives, beguiled by some green army blankets, finally succumbed.[27]

As the year 1843 receded into history, the young Lochinvar began to give up hope of being able to return eastward without facing the wintry plains. On January 18 he decided, instead, to take his men westward across the Sierra range. With the frost sparkling on the slippery grasses above the Carson Sink, Frémont impetuously took his men up the sharp slope near Carson Pass toward California. The Washoe and Paiute Indians he had encountered along the Truckee River in today's Nevada estimated a trek of only four days to reach Lake Tahoe, which was located on the crest of the Sierra. Skirting remote passes for which no maps existed, he started to cross the "range of light" from east to west in the dead of winter.

Frémont never imagined that the seventy miles to Sutter's Fort would take five weeks. Ten men on horseback forced a trail through the deep drifts until their animals fell from exhaustion. Others followed along afoot, leading the weaker beasts, repeatedly stumbling and falling headlong into the glistening snow. Struggling to regain their footing, they were as awkward as their animals. Some of the storms that descended upon them were so fierce that no one could see. The men were sometimes pushed along by the wind itself, feeling the bone-chilling effects of the thin air at such high altitudes. Others lost their footing, sliding hundreds of feet down the mountainsides.

When bogged down, sometimes for days in brush-strewn camps, they attempted to fashion makeshift snowshoes and sledges, also cooking up pots of watery pea soup and smelly mule stew. If it stopped snowing, they marched on, single-file, tramping down the snow with soggy moccasins. Those with axes cut a pathway through the icy drifts. They tried not to abandon one campsite until they found a new one within a day's travel.

On January 29, after dragging along the heavy howitzer for almost four thousand miles, Frémont finally decided to leave it behind in one of the canyons above the West Walker River east of the summit of the range. He only reluctantly, and he said temporarily, abandoned the fieldpiece, which he described as "invented by the French for the mountain part of their war in Algeria. . . . The distance it had come with us proved how well it was adapted to its purpose. We left it, to the great sorrow of the whole party."[28]

Protection of the animals against the harsh winter posed severe problems. When the party had left The Dalles in late November, there were still 104 horses and mules. The mountain crossing began with 67 animals remaining. But only 33 would reach Sutter's Fort in the Sacramento Valley. The creatures were so famished that one horse ate the tail of another. They also consumed tree bark, unguarded leather bridles, and parts of saddles. The men had to chop holes in the ice to make water available to the animals, which also continually pawed the snow in search of grass. The Sierra Nevada winter pack was so deep that year that they "sank into the snow up to their ears."[29] What looked like little pine trees were but the tips of larger ones buried beneath avalanches. Because the animals were too weak to shoulder all the baggage, Frémont ordered the fashioning of sleighs out of tree boughs, which his men pulled along the surface of the snow.

Finally the company was reduced to eating their little dog, Tlamath—as well as horses and mules as they died, boiling their heads for soup broth. Although Frémont ate the dog meat, it was difficult for him to give the order to kill his favorite young horse, named Proveau: "Mr. Preuss and myself could not yet overcome some remains of civilized prejudices, and preferred to starve a little longer—feeling as much saddened as if a crime had been committed."[30] When Preuss's mule, Jack, was also slaughtered, Preuss refused to eat the meat.

Days before, Preuss had ceased all sketching or painting, the intense cold having turned his brushes into icicles. With sheer survival at stake, he and several others tried to improvise some means of escape, evidently with Frémont's approval. But Preuss got lost for three days in doing so and was reduced to eating raw frogs taken from those streams not totally frozen over. After frogs were no longer available, he shoved his hand into an ant nest and licked the clinging ants off alive. Finally he stumbled into camp, rejoining the main party.

Others were even more deeply stressed. Baptiste Derosier and Charles Town, both dazed by what they were undergoing, actually became deranged. The latter could not be restrained from jumping into an icy stream "as if it were summer." Derosier eventually wandered off and was never seen again. When their last Indian guide also began to act strangely, singing his tribe's death chant, Frémont doled out to him his remaining hoarded ration of dried peas, tea, and sugar. But the guide considered their fate hopeless and deserted. Lost parties were at the mercy of Indian guides, who, when they felt totally unfamiliar with untracked territory, sought to escape personal disaster by fleeing.

Frémont next selected eight men to go with him in a more organized search of a route off the mountain crest. Quite unexpectedly, they topped a rise after a sharp bend westward in their trail, and before them lay a great plain—the Sacramento Valley. On February 20, 1844, they emerged from the western foothills of the Sierra. The men resembled a band of skeletons, but their miseries seemed temporarily over.

By insisting upon so rash a crossing of the Sierra Nevada, Frémont could have ended his second expedition in disaster. Only two years later, the unfortunate Donner party was to be decimated while also attempting to penetrate the great mountain range too late in the year. Frémont's own impulsiveness caused much of his own party's privation. It was as if he had unconsciously manipulated himself and his men toward self-destruction for a goal that was, at best, illusory. Was it really worth such excesses to skirt the fringes of Mexico's northernmost province? When he eventually reached Sutter's Fort, there were no Mexican troops there; the place was too far from the coast. Like Oscar Wilde's, Frémont's motto might well have been, "Nothing is good in moderation." Wilde also said, "You cannot know the good in anything till you have torn the heart out of it by excess." Frémont's flamboyance became a dangerous trait in the wilds of North America.

The legendary western hero Jedediah Smith in 1826, almost two decades earlier, had also crossed the Sierra Nevada, but from the California side. Because Smith, a fur trapper, did not map the mountains, Frémont and Preuss received credit for being the first whites to view Lake Tahoe. The leader named this body of water Lake Bonpland, after a French botanist whom he admired, though the name was later changed to an Indian one.

Not until March 8 did Frémont's party reach Sutter's Fort, or New Helvetia. Tattered and emaciated, most of the men limped. They smelled like the mules they had consumed and of their own excrement. The sight of Johann Augustus Sutter was a welcome relief. A Swiss, he had received a nine-thousand-acre land grant, spread between the junction of the Sacramento and American rivers, from the Mexican authorities, and in 1841 he had established a trading post there. Sutter's background was a checkered one. In the spring of 1834 this thirty-one-year-old bankrupt paper maker had deserted his wife and children in Switzerland. Although he had arrived in the West penniless and with no contacts, he had ended up the grantee of a vast rancho.

A generous but foolhardy man, Sutter welcomed all bedraggled overland parties, including Frémont's. Happy to sell them sorely needed supplies, he could not have imagined that in only a little over two years young Frémont would raise the American flag over his fort and take possession of it.

The party rested at Sutter's for several weeks, while their horses and mules were reshod. Frémont's men relished a "brown meal" prepared by the Indians; it was rich and spicy and stuck to the mouth like gingerbread. When they discovered that the substance consisted of pounded dried grasshoppers, they quickly lost their appetites for it.

On March 24, Frémont resumed the journey with 130 pack animals and thirty cattle, five of them milk cows. South of Sutter's Fort, clear streams were bordered with willows and sycamores. The party made its way through brilliant fields of wild poppies that stretched as far as the eye could see. Moving southward along the western foothills of the Sierra Nevada, they were no longer tormented by its snows. Members of the expedition resumed their collecting duties, crossing and recrossing California's San Joaquin, Stanislaus, and Merced rivers well out of range of the Mexican coastal settlements. The caravan traversed almost five hundred miles along the western base of the southern Sierra Nevada range before rounding its southern flank. Following the upper South Fork of the Kern, they next turned northeastward by way of Walker's Pass (named for Joseph Walker, who had served under Captain Bonneville) and then over the dry Tehachapi Mountains.

As they approached a remote northern segment of the Old Spanish Trail, both men and animals stretched out in a line a quarter of a mile long. Hardly more than a pathway, the trail bent in a northeasterly arc from Los Angeles in southern California toward southern Nevada and then into southwestern Colorado, dipping finally into Santa Fe. But Frémont used only the northern portions of this boulder-strewn route. Near today's Las Vegas (which Preuss marked "Vegas" on his map) Joseph Reddeford Walker, the seasoned discoverer of Walker Pass in California, joined Frémont's group, showing him a shortcut across the Colorado Plateau and toward the Rocky Mountains. This particular desert area was truly remote. Its tableland offered only searing heat and a harsh landscape.

Even for armed parties the southern trails were dangerous. Each afternoon the setting sun glared on the grey desolation of sand and rocks. One had to travel eighty parched miles from the Mojave River (which Jed Smith had called the "Inconstant" because it repeatedly disappeared and reappeared). Along the river notorious horse thieves lay in wait for unsuspecting overland parties. These *chaguanosos*, as they were called, were composed of renegade trappers and Indians. They regularly scavenged the carcasses of horses that dropped along the trail. Running off any unguarded stock, these ruffians did not hesitate to kill their owners.

Eventually Frémont came upon Andrés Fuentes and a boy, Pablo Hernández, the only survivors of a Paiute raid on their New Mexican party. Carson and Alexis Godey tracked the killers to Moqua, a remote Paiute village, where the Indians had skinned and butchered, and were about to roast, the haunches of stolen horses. Godey and Carson fired on the Indians' encampment, scattering the natives into the surrounding hills, then shot and scalped two Paiutes. After recapturing fifteen horses, they drove them back to Frémont's camp. Though his praise for these two favorite scouts would today be labeled racist, Frémont considered their act of revenge wholly meritorious.

Preuss did not agree with Frémont's and Carson's treatment of Indians. Offended, he charged that the latter and Godey had sneaked up on the Paiutes, killing and scalping at random. He also believed that Frémont himself "would exchange all observations for a scalp taken by his own hand" and that Carson "actually bought an Indian boy of about twelve to fourteen years for forty dollars. . . . In a few years he hopes to have trained him . . . so that he will at least be capable of stealing horses." On April 29, Frémont's retinue, accompanied by the survivors Fuentes and young Pablo, reached Resting Springs. There they found the mutilated bodies of Pablo's father and of the other dead New Mexicans. Only a little dog had escaped. Frémont took the shaken new orphan, Pablo, back east, eventually turning him over to the Benton women to rear.[31]

Before his return to Saint Louis, the explorer was to encounter furthern trouble with the local Paiutes. On May 9 they killed one of his most trusted guides, Baptiste Tabeau, and threw his body into a stream bed. This violence confirmed Frémont's belief that desert Indians could not be trusted; indeed, he called them "marauding savages," "wild men," and "horse thief Indians." Yet on one occasion he forced his Delaware scouts to back away from killing natives whose bows and arrows they had captured. He also saved the life of a starving elderly woman banished by her tribe. Carson and Walker were far more ruthless. Walker was accused of shooting Indians on sight for the pleasure of killing them, and was said to have shot and killed twenty-one natives.

One further loss had nothing to do with Indians. On May 23, François Badeau somehow shot himself in the head and died. It may have been an accident, but Frémont could not rule out the possibility of suicide caused by mental and physical exhaustion. Recalling Baptiste Derosier's mental breakdown, he wrote: "The times were severe when stout men lost their minds."[32]

The party reached Pueblo, in today's Colorado, on June 28, 1844. Several days later, with eyes red-rimmed from the blazing sun, they arrived at Bent's Fort in time to celebrate the fourth of July with a festive dinner. The route back to the then little town of Kansas on the Missouri River was easier than they had expected. When they reached it on July 31, 1844, the second expedition was virtually over. It had been a long, hard pull back to the Missouri outpost settlements. The trip had lasted a full fourteen months.

Upon his return to Saint Louis on the night of August 6, 1844, Frémont was in possession of the latest reliable data about the farthest West. For his efforts army chief General Winfield Scott promoted him to the rank of brevet captain. He and Jessie immediately began work on his *Report of the Exploring Expedition to the Rocky Mountains in the Year 1842 and to Oregon and North California in the Years 1843–44.*

Once again Frémont found it hard to work on his latest report. About its actual authorship, Jessie recalled, "the horseback life, the sleep in the open air, had unfitted him for the indoor work of writing." Seldom ill while out on the trail, John Charles developed more headaches and nosebleeds that for a time "convinced him he must give up trying to write his report." Jessie had to step in again as secretary and amanuensis. It took the remainder of 1844 to complete writing up the last expedition. Meanwhile, the Pathfinder experienced city life and Jessie's prim teas and parties as stifling.

Frémont's newest maps created a sensation. Jessie told him: "You are ranked with De Foe [Daniel Defoe]. They say that, as Robinson Crusoe is the most natural and interesting fiction of travel, so Frémont's report is the most romantically truthful."[33] Together they had fashioned best-sellers containing botanical, astronomical, and meteorological observations. Despite some mistakes in cartography, Frémont's report of his 1843 western hegira was a geographical triumph. Ten thousand copies were issued by an excited Congress, with subsequent printings.[34]

Historians have differed over whether his reports made Frémont truly "the West's greatest adventurer," "a man unafraid," or the "Pathmarker of the West." Was he merely a follower of other men's trails under government auspices? Most criticisms of him ignore the ways in which the Pathfinder was, indeed, "first" as an explorer. As unexplored wilderness sites shrank in number, the true discoverer became that leader who could get his experiences into print first, and for a big reading audience, too. Frémont's achievements cast new light upon the quite secondary matter of who actually went where first.[35]

The Pathfinder had, after all, covered the vast area from Kansas Landing to the Platte and Sweetwater rivers: over South Pass, skirting the northern Rockies and Wind River ranges; on to the Green River, the Snake, and the Columbia; to the British fur capital at Fort Vancouver; and finally to California. All of this changed the way in which future overland parties would view North America. Not only did Frémont provide a road map of the western trails, but his work also served as a model for future exploration.[36]

This expedition further established Frémont's reputation as both naturalist and cartographer. His and Preuss's trustworthy maps did more than fill in the blanks of western cartography, as some later critics would charge. He and his fellow topographical engineers were, in fact, creating a new professionalism. About his achievements, the best authority on early western mapping writes: "His grand reconnaissance produced the first scientifically accurate map of the American West ... and is of cardinal importance in the history of American exploration." Frémont collected his raw data entirely by himself, for he had no naturalist in his group. "Only Lewis and Clark as American explorers have exceeded Frémont in the diversity and plenitude of scientific observations made by a single explorer."[37]

Frémont's party had traveled 3,500 miles, naming many geographical sites, among them the Great Basin, which he described better than anyone had ever done before. In addition, he placed permanent names upon the land. For Carson and Walker he named separate rivers in today's Nevada, and for another of his men, Owens Lake in southern California. To the north of that lake, his was also the first systematic map of the Sierra Nevada mountains. Frémont's cartography showed the Columbia River to be the only waterway leading into the Pacific north of the Sacramento, thus erasing the mythical Buenaventura River from all subsequent maps. Jessie went so far as to claim that his maps even influenced the emperor of Germany in arbitrating the border of Canada as far west as the San Juan Islands.

A westering nation read Frémont's book almost as an adventure story, and many a boy was thrilled by accounts of the Pathfinder's councils with Indians as they sat in tepees on buffalo robes. The poet Joaquin Miller recalled reading Frémont's writings by candlelight on a Midwestern farm:

> I fancied I could see Frémont's men, hauling the cannon up the savage battlements of the Rocky Mountains, flags in the air, Frémont at the head, waving his sword, his horse neighing wildly in the mountain wind, with unknown and unnamed empires at every hand. . . . I was no longer a boy. . . . [N]ow I began to be inflamed with a love for action, adventure, glory, and great deeds away out yonder under the path of the setting sun.

Because Frémont drew upon firsthand knowledge about Indians, flora, fauna, and even pioneers encountered, his maps and reports were considered "trail bibles."[38]

Frémont had planned to prepare, conjointly with the botanist John Torrey, a full account of the fourteen hundred plant specimens he had gathered. Many had never before been collected. But more than half of them were ruined, mostly by rain and floods encountered early on the second expedition. Even those saved were badly damaged. He hoped to repair this situation by gathering new specimens on a third expedition.

Senator Benton, hinting at such a new venture, also wanted to make sure that President James K. Polk's new administration fully appreciated all this public adulation of his son-in-law. In the autumn of 1844, after Polk had won the election, Benton and Frémont met with the president-elect and with President Tyler's outgoing secretary of war, William Wilkins. Polk, in his inaugural address, was to assert that the American title to Oregon was "clear and unquestionable." He would also speak of the necessary "acquisition of California" from Mexico. Benton and Frémont thus had every expectation that the new president would be captivated by the latest details concerning the disputed cartography of the West. The president, a brittle and skeptical politician, listened to Frémont's glowing words. But he obviously considered the explorer's geographical claims inflated, muttering to his confidants that he distrusted the "impulsiveness of young men."[39] Frémont was then thirty-two years old, but Polk was only fifty.

Captain Frémont and Jessie tried to repair Polk's disparagements by attending his inauguration at the White House on March 4, 1845. They profusely congratulated him and his wife, who was only eighteen. Because Jessie was a close friend of Mrs. Polk, she regretted that the congenial young woman had not been in attendance when Frémont made his all-important report to the president.

The explorer quickly tired of the politicos in Washington, and he asked his superiors to return him to the West as soon as possible. His son, Frank, said that the "out-of-doors was life itself to him while the indoors was [merely] a place to be sheltered. . . . Stormy weather appealed to him as well as fair".[40] In his respect for nature's solitude, Frémont exhibited traits similar to those of other ascetic leaders who cherish a less complicated life away from urban complexities. T. E. Lawrence, of Arabia, for example, was happiest while on a "retreat into the desert, if not the desert, then into some wilderness."[41]

Although Frémont was not a complete ascetic, as was Lawrence, he did require repeated detachments from civilization's restraints. Like the mountain men he led, he cherished seclusion. He learned to hide his true feelings behind a private barrier, a gateway closed to others. Perhaps it is in the nature of some explorers to protect their self-sufficiency, nurtured by a willingness to leave women behind without guilt or regrets—as Jessie was learning.

As for his continuing risk-taking, one could argue that he found it necessary in order to validate himself while proving himself worthy of the Bentons. How else could he have made so instant a mark upon history except by taking chances? It was a heady experience to move in a few short years from being an unknown second lieutenant to a standing as one of the best known and admired of all American military figures. Such adulation could turn the head of almost any young man.

By the winter of 1845, George Bancroft, President Polk's secretary of the navy, prevailed upon the president to lay aside fifty thousand dollars for Frémont's

next venture. Benton's son-in-law was then asked to lead another exciting exploratory party. As yet, the young explorer seemed unable to do anything wrong. It
was as though he and Jessie knew exactly what the public wanted. Later, this
intuition would fail them, but for now a whole nation seemed ready to act upon
the unique strengths he imparted. ❖

The Third Expedition

The thirty-two-year-old Frémont spent the winter of 1844-45 in Washington planning a third expedition. He wrote the botanist John Torrey at the Princeton herbarium that the loss of important plant specimens during the second expedition had encouraged him to return to California. But that was a cover story that he and Senator Benton had concocted.

Frémont's superior, Colonel Abert, still had not authorized more than a limited scientific venture. He ordered Brevet Captain Frémont to survey "the geography of localities within reasonable distance of Bent's Fort." His instructions did not include striking out northwestward across the Rockies and onto the plains beyond those mountains. Although Abert's orders could have been a camouflage for the party to examine routes that might be used to invade Mexico, that seems unlikely. Abert may have sought to obscure the fact that the expedition planned to head west to California, but that, too, seems far-fetched. His new orders specified only that Frémont should lead a survey toward the Arkansas and Red Rivers. At the most, he was to map rivers that ran eastward out of the northern Rockies.[1] Frémont would disregard these official instructions. He planned quite another expedition to the farthest West. Senator Benton later stated that Frémont's exact intentions were not divulged even to persons high in Washington's officialdom.

No one could then have known how the rhythm of politics would make Frémont's next venture a momentous one. American expansion into the West had continued to resemble a grand design called "Manifest Destiny" by some. The United States had already extended the Louisiana Purchase by obtaining Florida in 1819. By the mid-1840s, public pressure mounted to annex Texas and to get American claims to Oregon Territory recognized by Great Britain. Catering to a national mood, President Polk's inaugural address asserted that the United States had a clear title to the farthest West. He and Senator Benton sanctioned doing anything to permit the republic to grow to its natural size, including seizure of California.

By 1845, as American infiltration steadily grew, Secretary of State James Buchanan sent an extraordinary instruction to Thomas Oliver Larkin, his confidential agent at Monterey. The mild and clerklike Larkin was quietly to persuade Mexican officials there that if they could somehow set the province free from

Mexico, the United States would welcome its annexation. He was also to win local good will as a means of converting the Californios to the idea of annexation, all the while staying in close touch with Americans trying to settle in the province.

Meanwhile, Frémont began to recruit men for his forthcoming expedition, determined to take along the best of those who had been on the last one. He again chose a passel of loyal French-Canadians, which included Alexis Godey, Basil Lajeunesse, Auguste Archambeau, and Raphael Proue. In addition to the usual Delaware scouts, he took along a young Indian boy named Chinook, whom he had found on the Columbia River during the second expedition. Having sent the lad to school in Philadelphia, Frémont thought it was now time to return him to his tribe.

There were new faces, too. Preuss, the controversial German mapmaker and artist on the first two ventures, stayed behind in Washington, and the long-legged Edward Kern took his place as a cartographer. This younger, more pliable draftsman still spoke of his leader as "the beau ideal of all that was chivalrous and noble."[2] He was lucky that Frémont chose him, for there had been forty-two applicants for Kern's position. He and a few specialists received $3.00 per day, while most others were paid $2.50, a spanking good wage in the mid-1840s. Based upon Kern's sketches, Preuss would in 1848 fashion a third important map of the territory west of the hundredth meridian.

At Saint Louis, hundreds of young bloods, anxious to volunteer, clamored around Frémont. They considered it a privilege to be personally selected by the Pathfinder. There were so many aspirants that he had to use a guarded house in which to make plans for the entire trip. One of the men he chose wrote his mother on June 15, 1845, that the excitement of organizing the party was such that it would "take us at least four or five days to reduce our chaos to anything resembling order." Although Frémont had treated him well, others were "afraid of the Captain." The writer, however, likened himself to their leader: "I am like Mr. Frémont in manner, mode of expression and even (heaven save the mark!) in face."[3]

At Boone's Fork, in Missouri, Frémont assembled the final party of sixty-two Caucasians and twelve Delawares. The actual jumping-off point for the Far West was Westport, today a suburb of Kansas City. Kern labeled it "a dirty place filled with Indians, Spaniards, Jews, & all sorts & sizes of folks." Its Indian women, he wrote his brother Richard in Philadelphia, "are up & down like a plained [*sic*] board, no grace, no poetry."[4]

Upon reaching the Arkansas River and Bent's Fort, Frémont divided his expedition into two parties. He sent Lieutenant James W. Abert, son of his superior, toward the Canadian River with one small contingent of men, while he moved west out of Bent's Fort with an instrument wagon, 150 horses, 200 pack animals, and a small herd of cattle. Kit Carson and Dick Owens had joined Frémont's larger party as scouts, and Joseph Reddeford Walker was to guide half of them to the eastern base of the Sierra Nevada. Beyond Pueblo, "Old Bill Williams," a scruffy, hard-bitten lone wolf, also joined Frémont's party. This 1845 expedition was the first officially to cross the complete width of the Colorado Plateau. Only in 1851 would a small party headed by Brevet Captain Lorenzo Sitgreaves again traverse virtually the same route.

Unable to find a feasible pass through the Rockies, Frémont headed northwestward. By mid-October the main party neared the southern shore of the Great Salt Lake. They crossed the desert below the lake with little trouble, moving next toward a lofty mountain that Frémont named Pilot Peak. Below it they came to some springs where the Bartleson party, the first overland group to make it to California, had camped four years earlier. Frémont gave the Humboldt River its final name. Then for a second time his group moved westward, one contingent over a well-established emigrant road and another, consisting of ten men under his leadership, through the deserts toward the south. En route he forced his Delawares to return some finely made arrows they had taken from a lone Indian hunter, telling his scouts that the Indian needed them in order to survive.

Yet in dealing with Indians, Frémont's main confidant, Kit Carson, continued to operate as a "hit man," killing with his chieftain's approval. Frémont did not overtly order Carson to slaughter Indians, although he clearly countenanced all reprisals against them. Carson, however, could be ruthless, though cool and steady, in his dealings with natives. More than two decades earlier he had set fire to Indian villages, burning them to the ground.[5] Frémont's memoirs portrayed Carson as a man of courage and devotion to duty; the ill-tempered cartographer Preuss remained jealous of the special relationship between the leader and the mountain man. In his diary Preuss castigated Carson's attitude toward Indians: "Unlike Kit, I don't see a murderer in every miserable human being." Other European travelers were also scandalized by frontiersmen's treatment of the Indians. Maximilian, Prince of Wied-Neuwied, a German contemporary of Preuss, once wrote that it was "amazing how much the [aboriginal] American race is hated by its foreign usurpers." While Frémont helped Carson to become a national hero, the latter's limitations were publicly unknown.[6]

Reaching Walker Lake near the Sierra Nevada, Frémont again split his party, and he and Carson again crossed the mountains, this time along the Truckee River and the pass later named for the Donner party, while another contingent under Walker used the Walker Pass route. This time the mountain passage was, mercifully, smooth. They reached Sutter's Fort on December 9, 1845, where "voluptuous but untidy" Indian girls—quite a contrast to the cootie-laden "plained boards" of the prairie—fed the party a feast. Frémont's men gorged themselves on ham, salmon, smoked tongue, and bear meat and washed down pumpkins, corn, and beans with a powerful local brandy called *aguardiente*.

After a stay of several days, it was difficult to leave all this indulgence behind and to press on toward Monterey, California's capital. Although Frémont's orders did not call for reentry into the province, his role as a topographical engineer was about to end. "I was given discretion to act," he later maintained, knowing full well that Senator Benton had continued to speak out about the need to fill the western power vacuum at a time when Mexico was politically soft.

Mexico's far-off province of California seemed almost to invite invasion. It had become virtually self-governing. Torn by personal and regional rivalries, it had suffered four local "revolutions" in the past twelve years. Outsiders were pouring in by way of the overland trails and by sea. Frémont's own published *Report of the Exploring Expedition to the Rocky Mountains* had described the place as a pastoral Eden. Benton's speeches in the Senate called for "thirty or forty thousand American rifles beyond the Rocky Mountains that will be our effective negotiators."[7] Frémont's men carried some of those menacing weapons.

In early March, the captain took along only eight men on his trip to Monterey, while the rest remained hidden in the San Joaquin valley. At the capital the Mexican flag flew over the customhouse, the sun having set upon Spain's former glory. Frémont was met there by Thomas Oliver Larkin, the New England merchant turned American consul, who had originally been appointed a confidential agent with orders to promote pro-American feelings among the Californians. Frémont wore a white felt hat and had a rifle slung across his saddle and a Bowie knife stuck in his belt. His party looked equally bizarre. When Frémont's men, with their untrimmed hair and beards, loomed up in the hills behind the capital, they seemed fiercely hostile. The natives were taken aback by the sight of so many "revolving pistols," rifles, and knives. Tethered under some sycamores outside the town, their horses churned up the dust throughout a makeshift camp, and the men quickly became a nuisance to the locals.

Consul Larkin took Frémont to see Monterey's two leading officials, Comandante General José Tiburcio Castro and Manuel Castro, the town's prefect. To them the consul stressed the peaceful intent of Frémont's exploring party. He also obtained permission for the captain to rest his men and animals and to buy eighteen hundred dollars' worth of supplies with money advanced by Larkin.

But once Frémont's main party reached the coast from California's central valley, trouble began. Several of his men went to the house of Don Angel Castro, uncle of General Castro, where they crudely "offered insult" to his daughters. The offended Castros consequently denied Frémont's request to winter in the province. They were in no mood to accommodate a young and obstreperous officer from a country in dispute with Mexico.

Frémont stayed at Larkin's home for several days. It was a lovely architectural combination of the two-story New England saltbox house and the California rancho. On its balconies Frémont felt the pleasing ocean breezes that wafted over Monterey's whitewashed adobe dwellings. After Larkin heard that General Castro remained suspicious of Frémont's intentions, he urged his fellow American to flee to Santa Barbara, where supplies had been delivered by sea. But then Frémont heard a rumor that as many as two hundred *Californio* volunteers might attack his encampment. This was followed by a threatening dispatch from Castro which he called "rude and abrupt" as well as "peremptory." As ever self-absorbed, he now refused "compliance to an order insulting to my government and to myself."[8]

Castro then ordered Frémont completely out of California. Instead of negotiating, Frémont equated his personal prestige with that of his government and appeared "ready to provoke war."[9] Irritated and obstinate, he seemed to forget that he headed an armed group within the borders of a foreign country, and he proceeded "immediately to build a rough but strong fort of solid logs and to raise the American flag amid the cheers of the men."[10] On a sapling flagpole he boldly unfurled the Stars and Stripes over a fort atop Gabilan (Hawk) Peak some twenty-five miles from Monterey, near today's Salinas. Any enemy would have to attack via a slippery cow path that led up the slope of a stone hillock. Frémont had backed into a standoff that would last for days. As with the rubber-boat crisis during the second expedition, he almost created tension. To stop distress entirely seemed to him to be a kind of empty disappointment.

At that time Frémont also oddly became embroiled in an altercation over ownership of a horse. One Sebastian Peralta came to the camp to complain that Frémont's men had stolen the animal. Acting as though he himself was the aggrieved party, Frémont disavowed the claim, stating that Peralta was lucky "to escape without [a] severe horsewhipping."[11]

While establishing his will in the midst of foreign territory, the intruder proceeded to ignore a series of sharp communications from General Castro delivered by Consul Larkin. As Frémont stood his ground atop his mountain, he was skirting the ragged edges of war. Yet he wrote to Consul Larkin in a heady mood: "I am making myself as strong as possible in the intention that if we are unjustly attacked we will fight to extremity and refuse quarter, trusting to our country to avenge our death. . . . [I]f we are hemmed in and assaulted here, we will die every man of us under the Flag of our country." Frémont also sent belligerent communications to California's Mexican authorities at a time when Larkin, following Polk's instructions, was seeking to conciliate them. The consul scarcely knew what to do about Frémont's ruffians, armed with "three to six guns, rifles, and pistols each."

While the Pathfinder anticipated a siege by General Castro's forces, some heavy winds toppled his willow flagpole. Frémont took this as a bad omen. Before a shooting match could erupt, he and his men descended the hill in the middle of the night of March 9. Yet, in a letter to Jessie of April 1, 1846, he explained his decision to leave the Monterey area in quite a different way. To her he grandly claimed that although he had received permission to winter in California, he had decided to retire "slowly and growlingly" before a force of three or four hundred men and three pieces of artillery.[12]

Having proudly hoisted the American flag only a few days before, Frémont decided to beat an ignominious retreat. Like a Gilbert and Sullivan operetta, the scenario reminds one of their sarcastic refrain: "He marched his sogers up the hill,/And he marched them down again." Joe Walker was disgusted when his chief announced that he would vacate Hawk's Peak. A tough Jacksonian nationalist, Walker promptly left the party in a huff, even though Frémont had always spoken highly of him and even named Walker Lake after the seasoned frontiersman. Walker said of Frémont that he was "morally and physically . . . the most complete coward I ever knew," adding, "I would say he was timid as a woman if it were not casting an unmerited reproach on that sex."[13]

The Pathfinder and his men next retreated northward toward today's Oregon border by way of Peter Lassen's Rancho Bosquejo, located on the upper Sacramento two hundred miles north of Sutter's Fort. During six days there, from March 30 to April 5, 1846, he bought some stolen Indian horses. Sutter, embarrassed and angered by this controversial act, had to explain it all to the touchy José Castro, from whom Frémont had craftily escaped.

While at Lassen's place, reports came in that as many as one thousand Indians were about to attack Americans who had settled in northern California. These fearful frontiersmen requested immediate help from Frémont. Once again the Indian menace had loomed up. Without checking the accuracy of such assertions, Frémont allowed Kit Carson and his men to use rifles and sabres to slash their way through several Indian villages. About this killing spree Carson later acknowledged: "The number killed I cannot say. It was perfect butchery."[14] He justified this bloody business by stating that the Indians would think twice before again contemplating attacks upon whites while Frémont protected them, an explanation that his superior readily accepted.

Absorbed by local events, Frémont had no way of knowing that in faraway Texas, General Zachary Taylor and a force of two thousand soldiers had been ordered by President Polk to move toward the Mexican border or that a military courier, Lieutenant Archibald H. Gillespie of the Marine Corps, was on his way to Frémont's camp from Washington, D.C. Traveling in civilian garb, disguised as a convalescing merchant, Gillespie came by way of Mexico and Hawaii. The lieutenant carried secret dispatches that he had committed to memory before destroying them. Once on a vessel bound for California from Honolulu, he again wrote out the instructions and in mid-April, 1846, delivered them first to Consul Larkin at Monterey before heading north to find Frémont's party.

Gillespie, later called a "messenger of destiny," overtook Frémont on May 9, 1846, on the south shore of Klamath Lake, just north of today's California border. Because the courier was exhausted by the trip, Frémont urged Gillespie to turn in early on his first night in camp. The explorer himself stayed up late, seeking to digest the messages that Gillespie had brought from Washington.

That evening Indians would again test Frémont's patience. When such natives were not trading, the horses in any white camp were fair game. Though the Klamaths had begun to barter their salmon with whites, Frémont's immediate party seemed past due for a raid. On the night of Gillespie's arrival, alas, Frémont failed (as he later admitted) to post a guard over the encampment. Fortunately, he had developed a keen sense of hearing. Kept awake by the excitement of Gillespie's dispatches, he heard the camp animals shuffling about in their make-shift corral. Drawing his revolver, he went out into the night to investigate. "A mule is a good sentinel," he firmly believed, "and when he quits eating and stands with his ears stuck straight out taking notice, it is best to see what is the matter."[15] After quieting the animals, he returned to the campfire and resumed reading. Then he grew drowsy and drifted off to sleep beneath some cedars that protected the campsite. When he awakened, it was to the shouts of Kit Carson's voice.

The thumping sound of hatchet blows on flesh aroused the camp. A wounded Delaware cried out in agony. During the fierce attack that followed, the trusted Basil Lajeunesse was tomahawked to death. A Delaware named Crane also had his head split open as he lay asleep. Yet another mixed-blood, Denny, died when a poisoned arrowhead made of iron pierced his side. Arrows, dispatched unseen during a night attack, were a terribly lethal weapon. But Frémont's men rallied. Soon the chief of the attackers—an English half-axe hanging from his wrist—lay on the ground dead. Carson seized the axe and beat the Indian's head to pieces with it; one of the Delawares then took the scalp. Frémont was "determined to square accounts" with the marauders. As an act of homage, he "left Denny's name on the creek where he died." Because his Delawares were aching for revenge, he ordered Carson to set fire to a nearby Klamath village. In his autobiography Carson recalled that there were fifty lodges in the village. Frémont recorded killing only a few Indians but admitted his wish for revenge:

"I had now kept the promise I had made to myself and had punished these people well for their treachery."[16]

Edward Kern wrote to his brother Richard: "We lost three of our men. They were murdered in bed. We revenged ourselves on the Indians by killing and burning whenever an opportunity offered. Lieut. Gillespie, the courier, had been followed for days by the Shasta Inds." Sea Captain William Dane Phelps, whose sloop would transport Frémont across San Francisco Bay in order to spike some Mexican cannon, recalled that the explorer punished Indian aggression by pursuing them "with his whole force and, falling upon a village belonging to the tribe of murderers, slaughtered the Indians."[17]

Because of fear of ambush, retribution was not only common but also expectable. The Castros, who had ordered Frémont out of California, may well have incited the natives to attack him and the other Americans. The Mexican authorities had also told Indians living near the "Buttes of the Sacramento" that American invaders would confiscate their lands.

Trouble with the Klamaths was not over. The explorer, riding his horse, Sacramento, suddenly came upon another native about to loose an arrow at Kit Carson. Frémont jumped the animal's hoofs directly upon the Indian and threw him to the ground, recalling: "His arrow went wild. . . . [I]t was a narrow chance for Carson. The poisoned arrow would have gone through his body." One of Frémont's Delawares, Sagundai, clubbed this Klamath to death and scalped him.[18]

Frémont did not blame the Californians for these ambushes, thinking that they were a result of the friendly relations of the Klamaths with the English, whose post on the Umpqua River in Oregon had supplied them with the iron arrowheads that had led to the loss of "one fourth of our number." A letter to Senator Benton reported that he had saved Gillespie's life, but Frémont worried about his party surviving: "We certainly commenced our voyage when some malicious and inauspicious star was in the ascendant, and we find enemies and difficulty everywhere."[19]

So many poisoned arrows had flown into their Klamath River campsite that Frémont and his men hung blankets on shrubs and low cedar trees as protection against these missiles. They spent each night thereafter with rifles cocked, anxious not only about Indians but about grizzly bears as well. On one occasion a one-thousand-pound bear charged the camp while they were having breakfast, sending the men shinnying up trees. Ultimately they killed eleven bears.

Frémont's advance guard of thirty-six men, on their way northward from Monterey toward the Klamath country, had not only slaughtered Indians with "lead volleys" but had also rushed in on the natives with sabres. "We made it a rule to spare none of the bucks," a participant wrote. One critic, Cardinal Goodwin, claimed that Frémont commended scalp-taking and treasured a picture of

Carson and Godey with such "glory trophies hanging from the ends of their guns." Earlier, Captain Phelps took a more forgiving view:

> I did not ask Capt. F. respecting this affair nor can I say he was justified in inflicting severe punishment. He has the name of being humane and forebearing. . . . I presume that his intimate knowledge of Indian character convinced him that the only and best way to protect his own party and secure . . . defenceless emigrants . . . from the depredations of the Indians was to punish this act of blood with a severity that should be remembered.[20]

Frémont did not discuss such matters with others. Captain Phelps said that his "intended movements are known only to himself . . . and are made with the utmost rapidity." Frémont dealt formally even with insiders, such as Gillespie. He had, after all, never before seen the marine lieutenant, who had brought the messages from President Polk, Secretary Buchanan, Senator Benton, and Jessie. Because of these messages, Frémont felt he had been relieved of responsibilities as a cartographer. But as the only visible American military figure yet in California, he refused to discuss his secret orders with anyone. Hence, we shall probably never know their full content.[21]

Did Lieutenant Gillespie carry a war warning to Frémont? The secret written orders could well have been a repetition of what Gillespie had told Larkin. President Polk sent Congress his announcement of war with Mexico on May 11, 1846. It seems impossible that Gillespie did not tell Frémont that Captain John B. Montgomery, commander of the U.S.S. *Portsmouth*, was then at anchor in Monterey Bay. Montgomery, furthermore, anticipated the occupation of California by Commodore John Drake Sloat, who took over that capital on July 7, 1846, in command of five warships.

Although Consul Larkin had personally watched and influenced all these operations, the Frémonts later refused to admit that he had played much of a role during the impending war with Mexico. They saw the real center of power back in Washington, where Secretary Buchanan regularly conferred with Senator Benton about the confusing scenario soon to unfold in California. Jessie would maintain that the "idea of a secret mission given Mr. Larkin has simply never been heard of by me before." In a letter to Secretary Buchanan of February 18, 1848, her father, the senator, had clearly suggested that Frémont's motivation be kept secret: "I do not think it necessary, nor desirable, to publish the instructions, nor in fact, any part of them." He wanted any public notice of both Frémont and Gillespie to remain "brief & . . . only to go to the general point of observing." To do otherwise would be to admit that his son-in-law had a wider mission. Benton continued to pry out of key Washington circles information unavailable to any other legislator, using it to achieve his military ambitions vicariously through

Frémont. Neither the army nor the navy could afford to risk offending the senator.[22]

Although the third expedition was technically a scientific venture, there was, in Frémont's words, a "new danger against which I was bound to defend myself; and it had been made known to me . . . on the authority of the Secretary of the Navy" that he had been instructed "to obtain possession of California." This, he later stated, "was the chief object of the President." A communication from Senator Benton "clearly indicated to me that I was required by the government to find out any foreign schemes in relation to California and, so far as might be in my power, to counteract them. . . . Act discreetly, but positively."[23]

After reading the dispatches Gillespie had brought, Frémont recalled:

> I saw the way opening clear before me. War with Mexico was inevitable; and a grand opportunity now presented itself to realize . . . the far-sighted views of Senator Benton, and make the Pacific Ocean the western boundary of the United States. I resolved to . . . return forthwith to the Sacramento Valley in order to bring to bear all the influences I could command."[24]

After California's conquest, Benton boasted that his son-in-law's activities there were carried on outside government knowledge and were "executed upon solicited orders, of which the design was unknown."[25] Benton's back-of-the-scenes conniving served to exalt Frémont before public. Whenever he was accused of intemperate actions, John Charles took the heat, yet he was frequently under the secret orders of his father-in-law as well as dependent upon the senator and Jessie to further his career in Washington circles. ❖

was but a pawn, and like a pawn, I had been pushed forward to the front at the opening of the game."[1] With these enigmatic words, Frémont described his role in the acquisition of California. He continued to put out a mixed story. On the one hand, he hinted at his secret power. On the other, he maintained that he became involuntarily involved with California's Mexican authorities.

Throughout 1846, tension with Mexico continued to rise. The winds of war were being fanned far off in Washington. Although Frémont became one of the chief actors in California's conquest, confusion later arose over the secret instruction warning him about the possible imminent outbreak of war with Mexico. Late in his life, George Bancroft, who had been acting secretary of war at the time, confirmed that such orders had, indeed, been sent to Frémont.

Although he was guided by Washington's army-oriented Benton faction, Commodore John Drake Sloat, commanding the Pacific Squadron, took his orders instead from Secretary of State Buchanan—as did Consul Larkin at Monterey.[2] There would follow a confusing division of authority among the navy, the army, and the Department of State during the subsequent American thrust into California.

Frémont would repeatedly assert that cartography alone had been his original goal, and he denied that he had gone to California under the pretext of heading up a scientific expedition. In a letter to Benton, he tried to explain how he had found himself in a thicket of political turmoil while attempting to leave California. When he turned back into the province from Oregon, that decision became, in his words, "the first step in the conquest of California," transforming him into a minor imperialist.[3]

Frémont, however, did not act quite as rashly as historians have claimed. His reminiscences are self-serving, but they boast that he knew where the real power lay: "Now it was officially made known to me that my country was at war . . . expressly to guide my conduct. I had learned with certainty from the Secretary of the Navy that the President's plan of war included the taking of California, and under his confidential instructions I had my warrant." A rather candid letter of Jessie's does undercut these assertions, stating that she had "no sympathy for the war nor has Mr. Frémont. Fighting is not his aim, and though he threw all his energy into the affair ... it was as if revenging a personal insult *for he knew nothing of the war*."[4]

Before the Mexican War actually broke out, President Polk had encouraged a subtle defiance of Mexico by Americans in California. If it was impossible to buy Upper California, he and Buchanan wanted a quiet revolt by native Californians, secretly encouraged by Consul Larkin. But there was little such support locally. American parties that reached Sutter's Fort on the American River found that they could barely count on that redoubtable Swiss to protect them. His loyalty to overland Americans who had crossed the Sierra Nevada and were regularly appearing at the gates of his walled fortress was ambivalent. Early in 1846, the master of New Helvetia predicted the arrival of more than a thousand such Americans. Sutter wrote to an acquaintance about California's military commandant and boasted that if "this Rascle of Castro" should undertake to interfere with his rescue activities on their behalf, "a very warm and hearty welcome is prepared for him." Sutter could not afford to be more explicit, lest his message be captured. In a letter to Jacob P. Leese, an American trader, the Swiss referred to the ten guns and two fieldpieces he kept in readiness to protect his fortress. He added significantly, if not grammatically: "I have also about 50 faithful Indians which shot their musquet very quick."

The waspish and mustachioed Sutter, at the very time he was assuring incoming Americans that he stood with them, secretly wrote to General José Castro, whom he obsequiously called "Your Worship," that Frémont was once more fomenting trouble. Sutter charged that the young commander "took twenty-one horses ... which his people bought from the Indian thieves."[5]

Larkin and other key local foreigners had meanwhile been marshaling support for American acquisition. Frémont's overt actions reversed this quiet approach as he swung back toward the Marysville Buttes along the Bear and Feather rivers. Sixty miles north of Sutter's Fort, Frémont met a band of dissident American settlers who were upset by rumors of impending conflict between Mexico and the United States. These were rough, leather-jacketed frontiersmen, part of a floating population of Americans considered uncouth by Larkin and Sutter. Although the Bear Flaggers were portrayed as smelly ruffians besotted by alcohol, there were decent folk among them. Most had gone west in search of land, hoping to improve their lot.

Such foreigners thought that California could end up under American rule, a wish expressed in a letter of March 9, 1846, from Charles Weber, a local German settler, to John Marsh, an American resident:

> Great News! War! War! Captain Frémont . . . with sixty or more riflemen has fortified himself on the heights between San Juan and Don Joaquín Golmero's rancho, the Stars and Stripes flying over their camps. José Castro and two or three hundred Californians with artillery are besieging their position. Captain Graham and sixty or more boys are moving to their rescue. Spaniards and foreigners are enlisting under their respective banners.[6]

On June 10 some of the Bears captured a band of horses being driven to the Santa Clara Valley by the Californios and took them to Frémont. On the fourteenth, these Americans raided Sonoma, the largest settlement in northern California. A day later they hoisted an improvised flag bearing the image of a California grizzly, creating what has come to be called the Bear Flag Republic. Some of the Bears eventually joined Frémont's forces as volunteers. During their short-lived episode the Bears feared a massacre at the hands of Joaquín de la Torre, Castro's military aide in the north. Indeed, Torre's men had tied Thomas Cowie and George Fowler, two Americans, to a tree, shot them, and hacked them to pieces, dumping their bodies in a ditch. Following this atrocity the Bears had no trouble recruiting several hundred vengeance-seeking adherents. Next, the capture of W. L. Todd led the Americans to fear that he would meet the same fate, but on June 23 a group under Henry L. Ford rescued Todd and attacked the Californios at Olompali, believing the Mexicans would cross the Carquinez Strait and slaughter the Bears at Sonoma. Among Ford's group was Kit Carson's brother, Moses. Kit, who spoke Spanish, now exerted influence upon Frémont to befriend the Bears.

In this violent atmosphere the Pathfinder reorganized his topographical engineers into the "California Battalion," placing Edward Kern in charge at Sutter's Fort. Prepared to do battle, Frémont protected scarce supplies behind its ten-foot walls. Kern manned the fort with some fifty resident Indians and a dozen Americans, all of whom Frémont promised to pay. Sutter was losing control of his personal bastion to Frémont, who began to sign himself "Military Commander of U.S. Forces in California," incidentally confiscating seventy-seven pounds of tobacco and a twenty-five-pound keg of flour from Sutter's stores, which would have to last until he was somehow resupplied. Frémont also issued an order for Kern to "iron and confine any person who shall disobey your orders—shoot any person who shall endanger the safety of the place."[7]

Sutter was actually humiliated by the capture at his home, Lachryma Montis outside Sonoma, of General Mariano Guadalupe Vallejo, a mild and friendly commander of Mexico's northernmost military region. Toward dawn on June 14, the Bear Flaggers burst in on the general and his wife while they were still in bed. They then took him to Sutter's Fort. Sutter, confused and embarrassed by this act, came to consider Frémont almost a tyrant. Sutter also feared that, at any moment, his military party might attract another ambush by Indians—this time stirred up by the Mexican authorities farther south. Edward Kern, temporarily in charge of Sutter's Fort, thought that General Castro had "bribed the Indians to burn the crops" of resident Americans. From Monterey, Castro, who now referred to all Yanquis as robbers, had indeed issued a proclamation ordering foreigners to leave the province "on pain of death."[8]

During all this confusion Frémont had given the volatile Bear Flaggers mixed signals. They believed that his return back into California from Oregon meant that he supported their uprising. He had, in fact, suggested California's "neutral conquest" to their leader, William B. Ide. This was somehow to be achieved by provoking Comandante General Castro "to strike the first blow" in a conflict with the United States. If the Bears encountered difficulty, Frémont suggested they should retreat back to the states. But the Bear Flaggers complained that this represented "falsehood and treachery dishonorably won," whereupon Frémont "became exasperated, and warned the Bears: 'I will not suffer such language in my Camp; it is disorganizing!' " Although he walked out on them, he later reversed himself, offering the Bears horses and supplies. He was to recruit some of them into his new California Battalion.[9]

It did not take long for Frémont's men to fraternize with the Bear Flaggers, their fellow Americans. On the fourth of July, Frémont helped them stage a fandango at Sonoma. A member of his party boasted that "Capt. Frémont is the only man who can command the California foreigners . . . needed to subdue the Spanish Californians."[10]

The Bears, who had come to count on Frémont's support, captured from 80 to 150 saddle horses and mares from Francisco Arce, Castro's adjutant. The general had ordered these animals herded northward in order to counter a perceived American threat. With General Vallejo locked up at Sutter's Fort, Castro had somehow to stop the *yanquis* from taking over the entire province. Communications between Castro and Governor Pío Pico were filled with alarm over the growing American threat to California, whereas the Bear Flaggers feared loss of their arms, livestock, and ripening wheat crop, if not outright extermination.

The Bears therefore hoped that Frémont might assume leadership of an uprising. Before the outbreak of the Mexican War became known in California they had already proclaimed at Sonoma a Bear Flag Republic that had lasted only twenty-five days. After Frémont arrived there from the north, he did nothing to impede their actions, yet he abstained from totally supporting the Bears. At one point, in fact, he nearly fired mistakenly upon some of them, thinking himself attacked by native Californians. "He came at a full gallop," the biographer of William B. Ide wrote, "right in the face and teeth of our two long 18's." Frémont's general tolerance toward the Bears thwarted the patient strategy of those Americans who had married into California's Hispanic families. Their less blatant approach coincided with the policy of Secretary Buchanan and Larkin, who hoped to gain California by peaceful means.[11]

In describing these events historians have not been kind to Frémont. Most have viewed his implied support of the Bears as "merely an early instance of his blunderings," portraying him as "a man quite without judgment, as his whole subsequent career indicates."[12] Although another Alamo disaster might have resulted from the Bear Flag Revolt, Frémont did not actually cause that incident, reaching Sonoma only on June 25 after the Bear outbreak was under way. His instructions from Washington actually implied that he should allow any such uprising to occur if local circumstances permitted. Even if no orders from Washington specifically authorized siding with the Bears, Frémont might well have been court-martialed if he refused to help beleaguered American settlers, especially if they were slaughtered—as General Castro had threatened. But back in Missouri, from which many Bears came, Frémont's abandonment of them could ultimately have led to violence against him. With scores of children among the Bear families, with some of their women pregnant, they could not have safely returned home. In a sense, he had to be their protector.

Frémont, however, did demonstrate insensitivity to local realities, taking over Sutter's Fort and approving the incarceration there by the Bears of General Vallejo. Some of them had previously gotten drunk on *aguardiente* at Vallejo's gracious table. This grand old man of Hispanic California supported its annexation by the United States. The courtly Vallejo had actually befriended Americans in the province, and his sister had married Jacob P. Leese, a prominent Yankee merchant. Of the 8 million acres held by eight hundred California families, Vallejo owned 175,000 acres—stretching from San Francisco Bay to the Napa Valley. Vallejo, charged with guarding the northern Mexican frontier against the Indians and the Russians at Fort Ross, had platted the town of Sonoma in an area the Indians called the Valley of the Moon. He had opposed the plans of Governor Pío Pico and of General Castro to move California toward rule by England or France, though he clearly favored a revolt against his own homeland:

My opinion is made up that we must persevere in throwing off the galling yoke of Mexico, and proclaim our independence of her forever. . . . We have indeed taken the first step by electing our own governor, but another remains to be taken, and this is annexation by the United States. In contemplating this consumation [sic] of our destiny, I feel nothing but pleasure. . . . Why should we go abroad for protection when this great nation is our adjoining neighbor?[13]

Despite Vallejo's good will toward Americans, Frémont allowed the general to languish as a prisoner for eight weeks.

Frémont's treatment of Sutter, another older man (born 1803), was no better. Short, fat, and with a broad head, the Swiss entrepreneur invited ridicule, and Frémont quickly grew impatient with his twisting and turning when asked for favors. Quick to forget that Sutter had been generous to his men following two crossings of the Sierra Nevada, Frémont now dealt with him with little compassion. Sutter, sputtering his indignation in German, became virtually a lackey in his own fort.

Far more serious than Frémont's ill treatment of Vallejo and Sutter was the charge, made later, that in these days before official hostilities began in California he countenanced a triple murder by Kit Carson and a small band of his men as retribution for the killing of the Americans Cowie and Fowler by the Californios. In this act of revenge Carson took out his anger upon Francisco and Ramón de Haro, twenty-year-old twins, as well as their uncle, José de los Reyes Berreyesa.[14] Years later, when A. H. Gillespie had become a political foe of Frémont, he placed responsibility for the counter-murders squarely upon Frémont rather than Carson. Gillespie recalled that when Frémont's party was at San Rafael, General Castro surreptitiously sent Berreyesa and the Haro brothers across San Francisco Bay to meet Joaquín de la Torre. Carson and his men did not bother to ascertain whether this was a peaceful mission. When they reported the killings to Frémont, he asked, "Where are your prisoners?" Carson answered, "Oh, we don't want any prisoners, they lie out yonder." Then Frémont allegedly exclaimed, "It is well!"[15] The dead bodies were left on the ground throughout the next night.

We have here another case of Frémont's apparently sanctioning murders committed by his subordinates. He had also covertly given orders not to take prisoners. For him a state of war already existed.[16]

Although he blamed his party's murders on his Delaware scouts, Frémont did state, "I want no prisoners, Mr. Carson, do your duty." Only after this order did Carson and his companions shoot the men. Thus, according to one viewpoint, "Frémont may be quoted against himself as a character witness for Carson. . . . The responsibility for the shooting of the prisoners rests upon Frémont."[17] This was not a simple trail killing by Frémont's men, but an act of retribution. Fowler and Cowie had been "lassoed, dragged alive, their tongues cut out, and other portions of their bodies mutilated while fastened to trees."[18] Punishment of the perpetrators seemed in order.

How were such acts viewed by those whom Frémont met in California?

William Hargrave observed that the Americans there did not at first feel friendly toward him, "but when we came to be in daily intercourse with him in trying situations, this feeling gradually wore off." Yet Frémont could not, said Hargrave, quickly "gain the deep affection of large numbers of his fellow men. . . . During those restless days which preceded the settlers' uprising he did not display any of the qualities of the conqueror. Even second-rate leadership must be denied him."[19]

This is too harsh an indictment. Frémont could be decisive. At Sutter's Fort, when one of his men, Risdon Moore, disputed an order, he placed Moore in an underground "dungeon" filled with what Edward Kern called "the most ungodly horde of the largest and hardest to catch, highest jumping, and hard-biting fleas that have ever worried man since the days of Adam." It took only one night of "solitary reflection" to convince the man, wrote Frémont, "that good reason was on my side and he rehabilitated himself and resumed his place." He had threatened to keep Moore and a companion, Richard Hughes, in irons. After some of his hunters accidentally killed a horse, "as a punishment Frémont gave the orders next morning that the whole twelve of us should walk 10 days, leading our horses."[20]

Despite this outburst of anger, Frémont still displayed his outwardly mild appearance. Though not tall, his height stood in contrast to his inner determination. Traveling artist Alfred S. Waugh expected to meet "a man of herculean frame," but found Frémont "small in stature and delicately formed— voice low and musical, and of manners bland and gentlemanly . . . quiet, well bred, and retiring." Although "his conversation was modest, instructive and unpretending, with a grace and suavity that irresistibly won all who approached him," here was a leader, wrote Waugh, "to be obeyed under all circumstances." Another member of the expedition disparaged Frémont's height as well as his marksmanship during one of his party's occasional shooting matches: "The magnanimous and justly celebrated Commander in Chief" was no taller than his horse pistol, and "just as the renowned Captain pulled the trigger and shut his eyes, an enormous dab of mud ploughed up by the ball in its downward course and proclaimed him victor."[21]

Frémont, however, really did not need to be much of a marksman, even during controversial actions. For example, in January 1846, six months before American military forces appeared at San Francisco, he took Carson and a small group across its bay to spike the shore artillery guns at Fort Point, located below the old Spanish Presidio; the fort had served as a decrepit Mexican outpost from 1822 onward. To reach it, Frémont requisitioned a launch off the brig *Moscow*, at anchor near Sausalito under command of Captain William Dane Phelps out of Worcester, Massachusetts. Phelps remembered Frémont as clad in a blue navy flannel shirt, blue cloth pantaloons, a deerskin jacket, moccasins, and a cotton bandanna around his head. As they stealthily rowed toward the Presidio of San Francisco, the water was so choppy that his landlubbers courted seasickness. About this sailing jaunt Kit Carson told Phelps: "Cap, I'd rather ride on the back of a grizzly than on this boat." Once they landed at Fort Point, finding no one on the site, it was easy for Frémont's band of fourteen men to scale its crumbling walls. After spiking three brass and seven rusty iron cannon with rat-tail files, they claimed the fort for the United States without a fight. Later Frémont would acquire a piece of land on the densely wooded promontory overlooking the Golden Gate, the name he gave to the entrance into San Francisco Bay.[22]

Not until July 7, 1846, did Commodore John Drake Sloat of the United States Pacific Squadron raise the stars and stripes at Monterey. In the event of war with Mexico, he was to occupy California's ports in order to establish American rule. Although he offered to fire a salute to the Mexican flag at Monterey, its port officials refused the honor because they lacked the powder to return it. The presidio (or armed fort) had only three cannon, each of a different caliber. California's entire navy consisted of only one ship without guns. Two days later Sloat hoisted his standard at Yerba Buena, today's San Francisco. Throughout the province the U.S. flag soon displaced both the crudely made Bear Flag and the Mexican flag.

After the American navy arrived in California, Frémont was no longer the only military commander there. In contrast to Frémont's previous encouragement of the Bear Flaggers, Captain John B. Montgomery, commander of the U.S.S. *Portsmouth*, starchily told their leader, William B. Ide, that he had "no right or authority to furnish munitions of war, or in any manner to take sides with any popular movement (whether foreign or native residents) of the country, and thus, sir, must decline the required aid."[23] But, knowing that Frémont was well connected politically, he could not bring himself to be equally harsh regarding the latter's previous support of the Bear Flaggers. Frémont kept up the pretence that he had no connection with them:

> The people and authorities of the country persist in connecting me with every movement of the foreigners & I am in hourly expectation of the approach of Genl. Castro. My position has consequently become a difficult one. The unexpected hostility that has been exercised towards us on the part of the military authorities of California has entirely deranged the plan of our Survey and frustrated my intention of examining the Colorado of the Gulf of California, which was one of the principal objects of this expedition.

Frémont had never before mentioned such a goal. He had told Captain Montgomery that he planned to head eastward to the Missouri frontier about the first of July, 1846. Now he complained: "In the meantime should anything be attempted against me, I cannot . . . permit a repetition of the recent insults we have received from Genl. Castro." He also explained that "between Indians on the one hand and a hostile people on the other, I trust that our Government will not severely censure any efforts to which we may be driven in defence of our lives and character."[24] Short of supplies, Frémont was grateful when Montgomery sent a launch with thirteen men from the *Portsmouth* up the Sacramento River bound for Frémont's camp to deliver carbines, pistols, gunpowder, balls, caps, and foodstuffs.

This gave the imprisoned Vallejo a chance to complain to Montgomery about his arrest and the proclamation of a Bear Flag Republic. The naval officer made "the most positive disavowal for myself and my Govt. . . . the same on the part of Capt. Frémont." Montgomery also assured General Castro that Frémont's mission remained a scientific one. This would be hard for anyone to believe. Castro had grumbled to Montgomery's superior, Commodore Sloat, that "a party of adventurers commanded by Mr. J. C. Frémont . . . took possession of the town of Sonoma . . . perpetrating assassinations and all kinds of injuries to the persons and property of the inhabitants."[25]

Once clearly informed that his country was at war, Frémont decided to report to the senior commander then in California, Commodore Sloat. When he boarded Sloat's flagship, the *Savannah*, he found its commander to be aged and sallow in appearance as well as nervous about the legality of the dramatic events exploding about him. An irritated Sloat took a much harder line than Montgomery, asking Frémont "by what authority" had he taken up arms against the Californians. "I informed him," Frémont replied, "that I had acted solely on my own responsibility, and without any expressed authority from the Government to justify hostilities. He appeared much disturbed by this information."[26]

Frémont averted another clash with an older man when Sloat suddenly relieved himself of command. Claiming ill health, Sloat headed eastward by way of Panama. Fortunately, Robert F. Stockton, his successor, was a political-minded naval officer. The new commodore cajoled Frémont—who described to him that he personally knew that all of Washington's most important leaders, "who at this time ruled its destinies and were the government, regarded the California coast as the boundary by nature to round off our national domain," and that he "had left Washington with full knowledge of their wishes."[27]

Duly impressed, Stockton authorized Frémont to form the "Naval Battalion of Mounted Volunteer Riflemen," later shortened to California Battalion. On July 5, 1846, Frémont activated this new force, and he was thereupon appointed by Stockton (with dubious authority) a lieutenant colonel—all courtesy of the Navy. Frémont returned to Sonoma and Sutter's Fort, where he enlisted 428 men, agreeing to pay each man twenty-five dollars per month, a handsome sum. With Gillespie now his second in command, they also recruited fifty Walla Walla Indians from Oregon Territory.

Next, Frémont moved south to capture, on July 17, 1846, the inland mission-pueblo of San Juan Bautista, where he found supplies hidden there by General Castro. Two days later, after also capturing San Jose, the battalion reentered Monterey, from which Frémont had originally retreated northward. Once again its residents were frightened by Frémont's ragtag forces, now even more sizable. He would later maintain that had he not reentered "the Old Pacific Capital," the British were poised offshore to pounce upon the town. Her majesty's warship *Collingwood* was, indeed, already in that harbor, but Frémont's boast of single-handedly protecting the province was surely overblown. He would, nevertheless, insist that "my taking possession of that coast in '46 is a matter of history. The English admiral was standing on and off for weeks, awaiting orders from home, and he afterwards declared to me that he would have landed and seized Monterey for the English that very day if I had not hurried in and raised the Stars and Stripes. That settled the status of the coast."

An English officer aboard the *Collingwood* recorded a fetching portrait of Frémont's hybrid party as they entered Monterey: "He was dressed in a blouse and leggings, and wore a felt hat. After him came five Delaware Indians, who were his bodyguard, and have been with him through his wanderings." The Englishman saw Frémont's men as "true trappers, the class that produced the heroes of Fenimore Cooper's best works. . . . The dress of these men was principally a long loose coat of deerskin, tied with thongs in front; trousers of the same, of their own manufacture." He also noted that Frémont allowed no liquor—only tea and sugar—and that he enjoyed "very strict discipline." Theodore Talbot, one of his own men, confirmed that his grizzled party again "frightened the Spanish ladies terribly," writing home that they were "such a half wild looking set."[28]

A thirteen-year-old midshipman on the *Collingwood* was, however, captivated by Frémont and his men. While ashore, this English boy stumbled past a sentry into a camp bristling with nine captured cannon and two hundred Mexican muskets. Bearded, wild-looking dragoons rested under oak trees, their long knives and "revolving pistols" glittering against their dusty buckskins, their camp sprawled over two acres:

> In the middle was a small tent occupied by Frémont himself . . . and he offered me a seat on skins. He is a middle sized man with an aquiline nose, very piercing eyes, and hair parted amidships. He had a beautiful rifle, and it was all inlaid with mother o' pearl, and he was guarded by the last of the Delaware Indians. I sat with him a whole half hour it must have been, and he was very kind.

Frémont was later invited aboard the young sailor's ship and "only nodded at me," the disappointed youth reported.[29]

In yet another first-hand view, naval lieutenant Louis McLane, who incongruously commanded two army fieldpieces in Frémont's unit, described him as an "ambitious Ass, and entirely wanting in Military Knowledge and feeling, though persevering and cunning."[30] Descriptions of the Pathfinder's role in the conquest of California vacillate between praise and contempt.

On July 26, 1846, Commodore Stockton dispatched Frémont's force of 150 men to San Diego on the sloop *Cyane*. They hoped to cut off General Castro's retreat into Mexico, where he might regroup for a new attack. By midday of July 29, Frémont was at San Diego. He and Commodore Stockton raised the flag at that old pueblo without firing a shot. Seeing no sign of Castro, they then marched northward.

Their united forces triumphantly entered Los Angeles on August 13, ran up Old Glory, and received pledges of allegiance from its citizens. Stockton then sailed on to Santa Barbara and to Monterey while Frémont marched his men back toward the northern Sacramento Valley. Both commanders were convinced that the struggle for California was over.

They did not know that Archibald Gillespie, the Marine officer they left in charge at Los Angeles, would soon experience a revolt there. He had treated the Angeleños as conquered underlings, issuing some resented curfew orders. Gillespie was besieged at Fort Hill; while at the nearby Domínguez Rancho, American sailors and marines on the way to rescue him encountered José Antonio Carrillo with a mounted force as well as a deadly cannon once used for firing salutes on festive occasions at the Los Angeles central plaza. After being dug up from its hiding place in a garden, it was lashed to the running gear of a wagon. The result of the revolt was American defeat and withdrawal to San Pedro. In fact, Los Angeles remained in rebel hands for three months. Gillespie held out for a week, then took refuge on a merchant vessel in San Pedro at the seashore. With only a token force there, Stockton, by then back in the north, could not possibly launch an attack until he could return both men and ships southward to aid Gillespie. Stockton thus asked Frémont to make plans for reoccupation of Los Angeles.

Frémont sailed again out of Yerba Buena on October 12 with one hundred men aboard the brig *Sterling*. They landed briefly at Monterey to pick up more horses, then moved south overland. On his way back toward Los Angeles, seeking to obtain the largest number of animals in the shortest possible time, Frémont seized livestock from ranchos all along the way, promising to pay later for cattle and horses. If the rancheros were friendly, he treated them courteously; if not, they "were mercilessly plundered," according to one source.[31] Thirteen "beeves" had to be slaughtered and replaced each day in order to feed his battalion. Sheep and horses were also requisitioned from rancheros, who suspected they would never be paid for their livestock. Because of Frémont's speed of travel and the roughness of the terrain, many horses gave out; others strayed and were not easily replaced. During the descent into coastal Santa Barbara by way of the San Marcos Pass, more than one hundred horses drowned in a torrential storm when Frémont marched his men off a mountain through deep gullies, slippery rocks, and torrents of water. Because he wanted to relieve Gillespie in the fastest time, the carcasses of countless animals littered the mountainside. Faced with an emergency, ends seemed to justify means, however reckless.[32]

After drying his drenched baggage and supplies, Frémont pressed on into Santa Barbara. An American who met him en route said that he planned to enter the town "with fire and sword, that with the exception of one or two houses he did not purpose [*sic*] to leave a single building standing. . . . I told him that I thought that would be rather brash and unjust."[33] Frémont replied that the Californios were all against him and merited such treatment. But, as he found Santa Barbara in a peaceful state, its troops having fled, he did not punish its inhabitants, though he did search their homes for concealed arms.

As Frémont converged on Los Angeles from the north, a new figure was about to enter the town from the south. Brigadier General Stephen Watts Kearny, U.S. regular army, had come west from Fort Leavenworth through Santa Fe, which he had on June 26, 1846, captured without firing a shot. Then he had suffered a punishing defeat. He had been told by Kit Carson (who had been sent east with dispatches for Washington officials) that California's conquest was over. As a result, the general had mistakenly returned part of his force to Santa Fe. In command of several hundred exhausted dragoons, he had been besieged at San Pasqual, near San Diego. His troops had to use sabres and mules to protect themselves against fine Californio horsemen, who attacked with sharpened willow lances.

When Kearny arrived at San Diego on December 12, 1846, he was out of sorts, sick, and painfully chagrined by his defeat at San Pasqual—the only sizable battle of the Mexican War in California. Frémont had met the general on his second expedition and knew him to be a strict disciplinarian. The younger officer was now to add to Kearny's insult by recovering some bronze mountain howitzers captured at San Pasqual from Kearny's command. Frémont, furthermore, would further discomfit the general by holding off the return of these weapons. In addition to Sutter, Vallejo, and Sloat, yet another older authority figure thus unexpectedly crossed his path—and that figure was a touchy army officer, too.

General Kearny had been humiliated at San Pasqual. Now he would encounter a rebellious young officer whose name had already become nationally known. A series of confusing episodes was about to unfold involving these two men. As a result of these events, California would become physically part of the American Union, and Frémont's military career would be placed in grave jeopardy.[34] ❖

On an overcast day early in January 1847 the two senior American commanders in California, Commodore Robert F. Stockton and Brigadier General Stephen Watts Kearny, marched northward together from San Diego toward Los Angeles. Hence, not one but three headstrong leaders converged on that rebellious pueblo: Frémont from the north and his erstwhile superiors from the south. As we have seen, Frémont had helped to occupy Los Angeles before the unexpected revolt there against the makeshift garrison that Gillespie had established on a hill. Stockton, who had commissioned and supplied Frémont's battalion, had ordered him to reoccupy Los Angeles.

Frémont, however, interpreted his orders as though he were the town's only true conqueror. On the outskirts of Los Angeles, at Cahuenga Pass, he signed, on January 13, 1847, a generous treaty with the commander of the native Californio troops. This was Andrés Pico, brother of the governor, who had ignominiously defeated General Kearny at San Pasqual. Frémont's unauthorized "Cahuenga Capitulation" ended hostilities in California. The document called for no punishment of the vanquished; conciliation was its pervading spirit. After its signing, Frémont's men entered the Calle Principal of Los Angeles, plastered with mud and drenched by a heavy rainfall, some without hats or shoes. But they were proud in spirit, as was their commander.

Frémont thus moved naively toward the center of a prickly fight for power between the two branches of the military. On one side stood Commodore Stockton; on the other, the crusty General Kearny. Relations between Stockton and Kearny—with Frémont in the middle—were to sputter along bickeringly. While we need not rehash the California conquest hill by hill, the clash of personalities it gave rise to is important to the Frémont story. In the midst of military hostilities, this squabble was reflected in a letter Stockton wrote to Kearny that was symptomatic of the tension between two commanders, one from the army, the other from the navy: "Now my dear General, if the object of your note is to advise me to do anything which would enable a large force of enemy to get into my Rear & cut off communication with San Diego. . . . I cannot follow such advice."[1]

The surrender of the Pueblo de Los Angeles to Frémont embarrassed both Stockton and Kearny, who had already occupied its southeastern portion.

Frémont, who had done relatively little fighting, had received the surrender of the main body of California's Mexican forces. Stockton, temporarily irate, called Frémont "a coward, traitor, and other harsh names." As neither Stockton nor Kearny could, however, take full credit for the surrender of Los Angeles, they momentarily patched up their own rivalry, turning their anger onto Frémont. General Kearny wrote Frémont on the day of the capitulation: "We are ignorant of your movements, and know nothing of you further than your armistice."[2] Frémont further irritated Kearny by writing letters that he signed with the outlandish title "Military Commander of the Territory of California."

Confusion reigned over who was actually in command. Within one week Vallejo received three letters, each signed "Governor and Commander-in-Chief of California." These messages were from Kearny, Stockton, and Frémont. When on January 16, 1847, Commodore Stockton decided to return to the east coast by sea, despite his pique with Frémont, he named him California's governor.

Commodore Stockton, in placing an irregular junior army officer in a key position over Kearny's head, did not realize that this act threatened the most important command the general had yet attained. With Frémont now free to act out his designated role, it became more difficult for General Kearny to claim his own supremacy. He now ordered Frémont to "cease all further proceedings relating to the formation of a civil government for this territory."[3] But Frémont refused to acknowledge Kearny's authority.

With the Mexican War at an end, Jessie eagerly awaited her husband's return to Washington. While he was in the field during the conquest, letters between Jessie and John Charles were few but revelatory of their concerted aims. She sent accounts of his valorous deeds to the *Washington Union* and other friendly eastern newspapers. One of these was Frémont's description of being besieged by a greasy General Castro on Gabilan Peak.

Jessie already knew about Polk's confirmation of Frémont's promotion ten days before the president announced it. She furthermore reassured her husband by a letter written on June 16 that his promotion had been achieved solely because of his own merit. This "advanced you in eight years from an unknown second lieutenant to the most talked about and admired lieutenant colonel in the army." She had "heard of no envy except from some of the lower order of

Whig papers who only see you as Colonel Benton's son-in-law," and she continued: "Dear, dear husband, you do not know how proud and grateful I am that you love me. We have found the fountain of perpetual youth for love, and I believe there are few others who can say so. I try very hard to be worthy of your love."

He, too, had written Jessie: "Many months of hardships, close trials, and anxieties have tried me severely, and my hair is turning gray before its time." To this she replied facetiously that he had never revealed how old he was, although they had been married for five years. "How old are you? You might tell now that I am a colonel's wife—won't you old papa? Poor papa, it made tears come to find that you had begun to turn gray." Little did either suspect the misery that lay ahead for both of them. In fact, she and her father were arranging for a new regimental command at Jefferson Barracks: "Father says you are to accept the appointment as it was given, with the understanding that you were to be kept on scientific duty under the direction of the Senate." Such a move would have taken Frémont beyond the control of the military establishment.[4]

Back in California, he was about to demonstrate his lack of capacity for self-regulation. Feeling slighted and obstructed, he continued the hostile struggle with General Kearny. Instead of showing deference to Kearny, Frémont set himself up as a *jefe político*. At Los Angeles he took over the Avila adobe near its plaza and began to entertain the newly conquered Angelenos. At first he showed no rancor, as if he wished to enter local society by inviting its leaders to galas and fandangos. According to Marius Duvall, a naval surgeon, he wore "the sombrero, and other things and makes himself ridiculous." But Frémont also sought, in the midst of all this turmoil, to hunt down Governor Pío Pico, who was still in hiding, thus frightening local residents:

> The women burst into tears, saying their husbands would never return, that Frémont would shoot them. . . . The people . . . are frightened at the very name of Frémont. He is represented . . . as being a Cannibal, a blood thirsty Barbarian [who] causes females to shudder, and crying children to be mute as death. . . . Those who [really] know the gentleman in question admire him for the childlike simplicity and unaffected kindness, justice and liberality which marks his every movement.[5]

Most of the Californios, though recently defeated, liked the picturesquely dressed young Galahad. He had shown some compassion by sparing the life of Jesús Pico, who was sentenced to death for breaking parole. Frémont thereby earned the lifelong friendship of the influential Pico family. He began to see himself not only as military governor but also as a prospective resident, soon to be purchasing property there.

But rumors of his personal corruption and immorality also arose. It was charged that Frémont "sought low associates in Los Angeles and patronized common prostitutes in public."[6] More substantial were charges that he borrowed so much money at Los Angeles that, as late as 1856 when he ran for the presidency, former California partisans refused to vote for him. It took years for the federal government to sort out and honor Frémont's expenditure vouchers, which were said to be padded.

After the conquest, Americans in southern California were especially critical of Frémont. The editor of the *Los Angeles Star* later made him the butt of ridicule, telling readers how during the war native leaders with only a handful of soldiers had outwitted their dubious conqueror. The paper accused Frémont of "timidity, duplicity, fraud, and peculation: "We have facts, names and dates—His harem, publicly established and maintained in this city, where sisters, mothers and daughters were indiscriminately collected, was the shame of the American people."[7]

One must remember that these later charges grew out of the 1856 presidential campaign. At Los Angeles, Frémont allegedly set up a menage around an elegant table at which all feasted sumptuously. This seems strange, for he was not a sybarite. He ate and drank sparsely, did not smoke, and retired early. With the celebration of victory in the air, however, the young commander may have deviated from rules established out on the trail.[8]

Frémont's old scout Alexis Godey labeled these "disgusting charges touching his moral character" as "unworthy of notice," calling "their grossness repulsive . . . proof of their falsity." He continued: "I knew Col. Frémont in this city to be, as at all times and periods of his life, the same high-minded, honorable man, possessing a private character far above his compeers—and the very last man in the world who would be likely to render himself to such vile scandal as appears in the *Star*." Godey maintained the Angelenos "all remember him as the man who afforded them more protection during the unsettled state of affairs consequent upon the invasion of the country than any other United States officer."[9]

Frémont knew how important Benton was to his future and should have curbed all this alleged scandalous behavior. The senator wanted him to be California's first governor. Although Jessie knew about the charges of immorality and corruption, she uttered not one word about them. She would instead choose to recall the power base her father established for her husband. In Washington the Bentons had unashamedly entertained all the major figures in California's conquest. Stockton, when commander of the *Princeton*, had dined at Senator Benton's home, as had General Kearny and even Lieutenant Archibald Gillespie before he boarded the sloop-of-war *Cyane* with his messages for Frémont. Paradoxically, Benton had written Kearny that he was to act as governor once the conquest was over. Although not an official order, this approval was significant because the senator was still chairman of the Senate's military affairs committee. Benton was also largely responsible for Kearny's appointment and the instructions given him officially. Yet Frémont foolishly refused to recognize Kearny's status because Frémont's battalion had been authorized by Stockton. All of this did not make sense to the rigid Kearny, who was so used to following all army orders.

During the ensuing standoff, the general believed he had every right to consider himself the major commander of American forces in California. He was furious over Frémont's lenient terms in signing the Cahuenga Capitulation. Although clearly outranked, Frémont continued to disregard Kearny's claims to the military governorship contained in explicit orders the general issued from January 16 to April 19, 1847. Kearny could not understand how so young a commander, under army authority, would continue to act as governor on the orders of Stockton, a navy officer who had left his post while California's military and civilian administration was still in chaos. Furthermore, Frémont remained unrepentant. He considered himself a military hero, and it was annoying enough to knuckle under to his father-in-law; to lick yet another man's boots was, for the moment, intolerable.

Although President Polk had increased Frémont's authority by confirming him as a lieutenant colonel, the newly promoted officer still retained the odd title of commander of "the Naval Battalion of Mounted Volunteer Riflemen." Polk also confusingly attached Frémont to a unit of cavalry then fighting in far-off Mexico to which he never reported for duty.

A surgeon with Kearny's dragoons, Dr. John S. Griffin, commenting upon Frémont's refusal to subordinate himself to the general, confided to his diary: "I only wish I could marry a senator's daughter; I might then set at defiance the orders of my superiors and do as I pleased. . . . General Kearny has been most outrageously used by Frémont and Stockton. They are both men of political influence, and of course they will go scot free, and in all probability throw the whole blame on Kearny." In a similarly resentful letter to his wife, Captain Henry S. Turner, an officer under Kearny's command, wrote: "Were I to behave as Frémont has done he would cause me to be put in irons. . . . Yet this man is permitted to escape without a murmur. He says he will prefer charges against Frémont. . . . I think he will do nothing to give displeasure to Col. Benton." Captain Turner, who would later testify against Frémont, complained that the general had been "effectually set aside by Stockton & Frémont, his rank & position treated with indignity & the orders & instructions of the President wholly disregarded." Kearny had "permitted Frémont to disobey his orders without arresting him. . . . The secret of the whole matter is he is afraid of giving offence to Benton."[10]

The Pathfinder had, in short, denied General Kearny the signing of a peace treaty, an honor that the general's rank deserved. When Frémont reentered the pueblo, furthermore, he had reported first to Commodore Stockton, only later

General Stephen Watts Kearny, who court-martialed Frémont following a bitter controversy over who was the military governor of California. The painter is unknown. Kearny died in 1848, soon after this portrait was made. (Used with permission of the Missouri Historical Society, Saint Louis; Accession 1933.1.1)

calling upon General Kearny. Frémont, who refused to stop executing orders from Stockton, was not only junior in rank, but also not a line officer. Few thirty-four-year-olds would have engaged in a jurisdictional controversy with a newly promoted general approaching sixty years of age.

Kearny angrily withdrew to Monterey, where he appropriated Consul Larkin's commodious house as headquarters. He proclaimed himself military commander of California, not bothering to inform Frémont of new army directives from Washington that officially appointed Kearny as military governor. Instead, he "strung out" Frémont, thereby producing grounds for a court-martial on charges of mutiny and insubordination. Frémont, totally alienated from General Kearny, repeatedly ignored the general's instructions on a variety of subjects, from the release of horses and men under his command to the payment of debts due local citizens. Kearny—angular, bony, and unyielding in temperament—determined to upstage the haughty Frémont. The general brusquely ordered him "to disband his forces and to cease the exercise of authority of any kind in the country."

A contemporary, William Tecumseh Sherman, later a great Civil War general but then a junior officer in California, left behind a description of the crusty General Kearny. Sherman described him as wearing an old dragoon's coat "and an army cap to which the general had added the broad visor, cut from a full-dress hat, to shade his face and eyes against the flaring sun." One of Sherman's fellow officers, upon seeing this sight, exclaimed: "Fellows, the problem is solved. There is the grand vizier (visor) by G——d!—He is Governor of California." Lieutenant Sherman had his doubts: "Feeling a natural curiosity to see Frémont, who was then quite famous by reason of his recent explorations . . . I found him in a conical tent with one Captain Owens, who was a mountaineer, trapper, etc. . . . I spent an hour or so with Frémont, took some tea with him, and left without being much impressed."[11]

Hard-bitten regular army officers in California clearly thought Frémont to be an irregular upstart. When Kearny and Sherman visited his Los Angeles headquarters, they were shocked to find him "dressed much as a Californian, with the peculiar high, broad-brimmed hat, with a fancy cord." Lieutenant Sherman and his fellow officers considered Frémont's command to be at loose ends, practically "in a state of mutiny. Some thought he would be tried and shot; others that he would be carried back east *in irons*. All agreed that "if anyone else than Frémont had put on such airs, and had acted as he had done, Kearny would have shown him no mercy, for he was regarded as the strictest sort of disciplinarian."[12]

The general continued to summon Frémont northward to Monterey. Finally, he dispatched a full colonel, Richard B. Mason, to Los Angeles to take command there, with orders that Frémont bring his archives northward to Monterey. Mason sent for Frémont several times per day to answer questions about his conduct, but the colonel received no reply. He also ordered Frémont to surrender 120 horses grazing outside the pueblo. Frémont was allegedly fattening these animal's with a view to joining General Zachary Taylor's forces in Mexico. Frémont considered the order to give up his horses especially insulting, for it would have immobilized his command.

Tension between Mason and Frémont mounted. Each took an immediate and intense dislike for the other. Mason, a full colonel in the regular army, threatened the lieutenant colonel forcefully: "None of your insolence, or I will put you in irons." Frémont finally surrendered his horses, which Mason sold for one to three dollars each. At this point Frémont sent two notes to Mason by Major Pierson B. Reading, an aide; one asked for a retraction of the colonel's abusive threat, and the other conveyed a challenge to a duel. When Mason sent no retraction, Frémont threatened to duel him with double-barreled shotguns. Both apparently chose such "unusual and unofficerlike" weapons because Mason liked to hunt with a shotgun. Frémont had never used such a weapon, although he was an experienced handler of most guns. On April 15, 1847, Mason replied that "it is necessary that I return to Monterey before I afford you the meeting you desire. We shall probably reach there within a few days of each other. I will then, as soon as circumstances permit, arrange the necessary preliminaries for the meeting."[13]

Frémont had finally agreed to go to Monterey, taking along Jesús Pico and his black servant, Jacob Dodson, with six loose mounts. They requisitioned a fresh mount every twenty-five miles or so and completed the 420-mile ride in less than four days. At the old Pacific capital, Kearny at last disclosed his Washington orders, which clearly placed the general in full command of all California. Thereupon Frémont offered to resign his commission and requested permission to take sixty men into Mexico. But Kearny, anxious to clip the wings of the young eagle, proceeded to strip Frémont of all his authority. Mason, too, was "to proceed no further" with the duel, and Kearny ordered the event "postponed to some future time and place."[14]

From aboard the U.S.S. *Columbus*, Commodore James Biddle, later in command of California's naval forces, likewise admonished Colonel Mason not to go forward with the duel: "You cannot but be sensible that, in the present condition of things in California, personal collisions between officers must be highly injurious to the public interest." Biddle pointed out that the effect upon the newly conquered Californians of two leading American officers locked in combat would be disastrous. He also wrote to Frémont, appealing to him "as your personal friend" and warning that "you cannot but know that it is the duty of all of us to suppress for the moment every angry feeling of a personal nature."[15]

The duel was never fought. Senator Benton later argued that the letters from Biddle, Kearny, and Mason were collusive, gotten up in order to extricate Colonel Mason from an embarrassing situation into which he had goaded Frémont. The duel became an issue after Kearny court-martialed Frémont. Under the Twenty-sixth Article of War, dueling had become an indictable offence, but although it was forbidden by army regulations, the practice was not uncommon. Mason went on to become military governor of California, and Frémont did not hear from him again until 1850, when, as a senator in Washington, he received a note from Mason offering to proceed with the duel. By then Frémont was no longer in a dueling mood. He paid no attention to the note.[16]

Kearny next ordered Frémont to follow him eastward. The younger officer was reduced to commanding only nineteen grumbling men who marched in the dust of the general's column. During this long march there was no longer any question of precedence. Frémont had become Kearny's prisoner. Sherman and his fellow army careerists saw Frémont's ouster from California as good riddance of a troublemaker: "With him departed all cause of confusion and disorder in the country."[17]

But when Frémont's own men learned that he would be court-martialed, some saw a conspiracy by the West Pointers. Theodore Talbot wrote, "As long as a man remains below a certain mediocrity all is well, he is promising, gallant, this, that and the other; but the moment he rises beyond that point, a host of enemies crowd round, their fawning turned to envious snarles [sic]."[18] Frémont's men began to wonder if their own future in the army would be influenced by the stigma being fastened upon their commander. It was his misfortune that he made either friends or enemies, leaving few persons feeling neutral. Frémont was naive when compared with Kearny—bolstered as the general was by the privileges of military rank.

When Jessie heard the news that General Kearny was marching her husband's party out of California, she and her black maid traveled westward to await his arrival. At Kansas Landing on the Missouri River, each day she went expectantly down to its wharf. She was still only twenty-four years old. He had been gone for five out of their six and one-half years of marriage. After a long wait in a stiflingly hot log cabin, he finally arrived on the steamer *Martha*. The villagers, carrying flags, greeted Frémont as a heroic figure. The couple next went together to Fort Leavenworth, where, on August 22, 1847, General Kearny formally presented his charges. Up to that time Frémont had been a nominal prisoner, not formally under arrest.

Ordered to the national capital to stand trial, Frémont traveled with Jessie to Saint Louis. Then it was on to Washington, where the couple escaped from Senator Benton for a few days of intimacy. Her recollections of the reunion were tender ones:

> For a week we lived alone together on a happy island surrounded by a sea of troubles. We arose late and had breakfast in our room before the fire. After the mail came, we went for a walk or a visit with friends. We even drove in the moonlight out to the school in Georgetown and looked up at the back window where the Colonel's first love letter had come up hidden in a basket of laundry.[19]

At the Washington Armory, where the court-martial trial convened on November 2, 1847, General Kearny widened his original accusations. He now formally charged Frémont with mutiny, disobeying the commands of superiors, and conduct prejudicial to military discipline. Kearny would have the support of the prestigious Major Stephen Long, the only explorer on the panel judging Frémont. Long still held fast to the idea that the Far West was a great desert, which Frémont's reports had seriously disputed. Long was taken off an assignment of building steamboats in order to serve at the court-martial, an event in which even the president became involved.

Fortunately for his biographer, President Polk kept a diary during the years 1845 to 1849, which covered the period of the Mexican War, the acquisition of Oregon, and the conquest of California and the Southwest. On April 30, 1847, he confided in its pages: "An unfortunate collision has occurred in California between General Kearny and Commodore Stockton, in regard to precedence in rank. I think General Kearny was right. It appears that Lieut. Col. Frémont refused to obey General Kearny and obeyed Commodore Stockton and in this he was wrong. . . . Indeed both . . . acted insubordinately and in a manner that is censurable."[20]

Frémont's insistence that the army do things his way got him nowhere. It was as though he wished General Kearny to have reversed that ancient commandment "Honor Thy Father" to become "Honor Thy Son." But the members of the court-martial jury, all regular army officers, could hardly be expected to understand. These jurors represented a military establishment that held a low opinion of his capacities. Indeed, these men had a deep-rooted contempt for the showman in him. Their forte was certainly not personal publicity. Nor had they any pity for a transgressor of army discipline.

By insisting upon an intellectual defense, Frémont hoped to vindicate his honor, if not to influence the final verdict. But General Kearny's chosen witnesses were nearer the working level of the jury's thoughts and therefore in closer touch with its members. In Frémont's eyes these men were anything but his peers. How could they possibly judge him? While he was in the witness box it was as though he remained in the dock, facing a sea of prejudice as the panel seemed to close in on their troublesome quarry. The accused was at one of those moments that try the human soul.

As the trial dawdled through many days and weeks, Frémont repeatedly claimed that the plans of the Navy and War departments were inconsistent with each other. Both services had indulged in poor planning in Washington. This had led each commander in California to believe himself to be the main authority there. Stockton had written to Secretary of the Navy George Bancroft: "When I leave the territory I will appoint Major Frémont to be governor." General Kearny, however, bore instructions from Secretary of War William L. Marcy that read: "Should you conquer and take possession of New Mexico and Upper California, or considerable places in either, you will establish temporary civil governments therein." This order, of June 18, 1846, was the principal evidence upon which Kearny's charges were based.[21]

The dispute was thus not solely a matter of Frémont's temperament. In Kearny's case, a seasoned army officer, although not a West Pointer, had been but newly breveted a brigadier general. Frémont's original commission, dating back to July 9, 1838, was with a partly civilian organization, the Corps of Topographical Engineers, described as a "bureau of the War Department." In his *Defense Before the Court Martial* he suggested that his selection for a regular lieutenant colonel's position over West Point rivals had led to their envy, and he noted that an embittered Captain Philip St. George Cooke, while in California with the First Dragoons, had sought the position in the new regiment that Frémont had received. Now Frémont posed as the underdog: "I was then brevet captain in the corps of topographical engineers, and had no rank in the army, nor did an officer or soldier of the United States army accompany me."[22]

In the midst of the trial the military tribunal learned how the Frémont-Benton axis maneuvered behind the scenes, lobbying even with the president on behalf of the Pathfinder. As early as June 7, 1847, while her husband was still in California, Jessie and Edward Fitzgerald Beale—who had helped rescue General Kearny after his defeat at San Pasqual—had stormed into the White House to see President Polk, giving him a letter from Frémont to her father portraying his side of the controversy. But the day after Jessie and Beale's visit, Polk's cabinet had agreed that both Frémont and Stockton had acted improperly.[23] Polk's cabinet had wished to let the storm pass over "as lightly as possible." The president was also visited, on Frémont's behalf, by Benton and William Carey Jones, the senator's other son-in-law, who would become the explorer's legal counsel.

Repeatedly the fiery senator himself had showed up in Polk's office, seeking punishment of Kearny from the president. But Polk considered Benton to be "a man of violent passions" who threatened a congressional investigation of the events in California, implicating the White House itself. "I know of no reason," Polk wrote in his diary, "why this case should produce more interest or excitement than the trial of any other officer. . . . [Y]et it is manifest that Senator Benton is resolved to make it so."[24] By his threat Benton actually widened the chances of conviction.

The senator was positive that Frémont's court-martial was because of his "not being regular army." He also believed Kearny to be an incorrigible martinet. The senator promised his son-in-law: "I shall be with you to the end, if it takes up the whole session of Congress." In October 1847, Benton wrote of Kearny: "We shall demolish him with all ease and overwhelm him with disgrace." In another letter he told Frémont:

I have full view of the case. You will be justified and exalted. Your persecutors will be covered with shame. The process through which you have gone is bitter; but it will have its sweet. . . . I shall know how to make advantage of all this . . . as your counsel. You may be at ease. The enemy is now in our hands, and may the Lord have mercy upon them; for I feel as if I could not.

In July 1848, Benton spoke for a total of thirteen days in the Senate, opposing the nomination of Kearny as a major general. His long speech, printed in the *Washington Daily Union*, revealed that Benton was a vengeful man for whom the trial had become a personal crusade.[25]

During the proceedings, as Frémont went rocketing toward his downfall, Benton charged that General Kearny had fixed his eyes upon his son-in-law as though he were a prisoner and had "looked insultingly and fiendishly at him." Others, too, reported that during the trial Kearny's face, reflecting hatred for Frémont, seemed almost to turn to stone. But Benton's remarks were labeled by one juror as "a violation of that respect which is due to the court." Yet Senator Benton could not be stopped: "I did today look at General Kearny . . . till his eyes fell upon the floor." The courtroom atmosphere had become so intense that Benton was willing to stop at nothing to punish Kearny. He even offered to produce the aged Henry Clay as a witness for the defense, although the latter knew nothing of the circumstances of Frémont's trial.[26]

The trial depressed Frémont's spirits. He had clearly aged. Upon his return from the West, after an absence of two and one-half years, his hair, still parted in the middle, was tinged with gray. After 1849 he wore a moustache and full beard. Jessie suddenly seemed to be married to an older man. For her,

> the great change was in the stern set look of endurance and self control which the past few months had forced upon him; and with it a silent repressed storm of feeling which entirely dominated his old lighthearted courtesy and thought for others. He . . . could not recover himself instantly from the long indignation of the return journey and the crowning insult . . . to be put under arrest.[27]

In the midst of the trial, Frémont's mother-in-law, Mrs. Benton, suffered a paralytic stroke. At the same time, his own mother, now Ann Hale, also became seriously ill in Aiken, South Carolina. Indeed, she died before he could reach her bedside. On September 20, 1847, he was allowed to take her body to Charleston for interment. Her third husband was not present for the burial, but only her son John Charles. Jessie went so far as to infer that the trial helped to kill off her husband's mother: "Her hopes centered on her only surviving son. The news of his returning home in arrest, and the vicious newspaper attacks, proved too much for an invalid. . . . When he arrived . . . her two years of patient waiting had been in vain. . . . [T]he open door was at once his welcome and farewell."[28]

Jessie tried to speed up the court-martial trial by continuing to appeal to President Polk, all the while apologizing for interfering "in a matter properly belonging to men." Polk wrote in his diary: "In truth I consider that Col. Frémont was greatly in the wrong when he refused to obey the orders issued to him by Gen'l. Kearny. . . . It was unnecessary, however, that I should say so to Col. Frémont's wife." Polk, the owner of plantation slaves, had also heard of the sympathy that the Frémonts openly expressed toward blacks. And he had already put up with Benton's repeated importunings and thus was in no mood to flatter the senator's pushy daughter.[29]

While the trial was still in progress, both Frémonts faced a mountain of daily correspondence. Accusations were being filed by the French ambassador alleging Frémont's poor treatment of consular officials in California, where he had seized $420 in French government gold. Frémont's response to such charges took the form of growing aloofness, which Jessie was powerless to prevent. Always elusive in personal relationships, he seemed steadily more remote and stoic.[30]

Another matter that came up at the court-martial concerned the pensions of men who had been on Frémont's expeditions as well as claims for supplies that he had requisitioned during the conquest of California. Repudiated by General Kearny, many of these "California claims" would be investigated for years to come. Congress's parsimony led to incessant pressure upon Frémont to do something privately about obtaining payment. Although Senator Benton introduced congressional relief bills on his behalf, most of them died. An act of 1847 did allow some claimants land or scrip payments.[31]

The legality of Frémont's having bought or requisitioned horses and property was also questioned at the court-martial. Writing to Secretary of War Marcy on May 19, 1848, Frémont defended these actions:

> My situation in California was difficult & arduous—3000 miles distant—without money—carrying on military operations— administering a civil government—getting supplies & small loans on the best terms possible—& actually getting supplies & loans from the conquered inhabitants, as an act of friendship to the United States.

He maintained that the navy would have paid all such claims had he been allowed to remain in California—just as Commodore Stockton had previously "paid other expenses of the conquest."[32]

The court-martial hearings ground on for eighty-nine days, from Indian summer of 1847 into January of the next year. The national press excitedly followed the proceedings day by day. When Frémont spoke of his trial as "a war," a group of admirers at Charleston offered the embattled soldier a specially designed sword and belt. With the court-martial still on, he declined a public recognition dinner to be held at Saint Louis, stronghold of the Bentons. Meanwhile, friends came to Washington offering to testify; among them was Ed Beale, a new and charismatic friend from a well-known family who had a knack for moving at ease in the company of prominent people.[33]

Still others favored neither side in the dispute. Historian Justin Smith rendered a Draconian verdict about each of the protagonists: "Frémont was a provoking unprincipaled [*sic*] and successful schemer, and Kearny showed himself grasping, jealous, domineering and harsh."[34]

President Polk, under pressure from Senator Benton, and partly because of the young officer's national prominence, confided to his diary: "I was not satisfied that the proof in this case constituted mutiny," but that "I ought to approve the sentence . . . remit the penalty and restore Lieut. Col. Frémont to duty.[35]

Frémont refused to stop his own cross-examination of Kearny. Spurred on by Benton, he persisted in counterattacking all of the general's charges and thus made the general into an underdog instead of the villain. Frémont went so far as to assert that the general had, through Secretary of War Marcy, planted newspaper articles for "the secret purpose of a future trial and arrest."[36] He bitterly portrayed himself as a victim caught in an elemental army-navy dispute. Thinking that he might enlist more support from California partisans, Frémont charged in a letter to one of them that "false and infamous charges made by Lieut. Emory and other agents of Genl. Kearny and published in newspapers from Havana to Washington had been industriously circulated to prejudice the public minds."[37]

When Commodore Stockton finally appeared in the courtroom, he so watered down his support that Frémont suspected a deal had been made with General Kearny. Stockton admitted that he had no orders or instructions, from either the secretary of the navy or the president, to commence government in California or to have appointed Frémont its governor: "I formed the government under the law of nations," he lamely testified.[38]

A disappointed Frémont issued this final statement:

> I consider these difficulties in California to be a comedy (very near being a tragedy). . . . I prevented civil war against Governor Stockton, by refusing to join General Kearny against him. I arrested civil war against myself by consenting to be deposed. . . . I am now ready to receive the sentence of the court.[39]

The trial produced 446 pages of testimony. A panel of thirteen officers deliberated for three more days, then handed down their verdict on January 31, 1848. Unimpressed by Frémont's defense, the jury sentenced him to be dismissed from the army. As a politician, President Polk approved this verdict, except for the charge of mutiny. Though he upheld the court's decision, Polk canceled Frémont's dismissal from the army. He thus endorsed the sentence, yet remitted it.

Frémont's supporters predictably maintained that a man of genius had been unfairly thwarted because of a wrangle between two superiors, who made him a cat's-paw of their rivalry. His all too brief six weeks as California's acting governor had been marred by army-navy conflict alone. The still intemperate Senator Benton arranged for publication of a seventy-eight-page pamphlet entitled *Defense of Lieut. Col. J. C. Frémont* (Washington, 1848), an *apologia pro vita sua* which is today a rarity. Benton and Jessie, enraged over what they considered shabby treatment by West Pointers, spoke darkly of "secret persecutors." Yet all except five of the presiding judges were not West Point graduates.

The final court-martial verdict had torn into shreds Benton's relations with the president and his cabinet. He resigned as chairman of the powerful Committee on Military Affairs in large part because of Secretary of War Marcy's antipathy. Polk's partial remanding of the trial verdict reflected the wish of his entire cabinet except for Marcy. Benton never again spoke to either Polk or Marcy.

Also rallying around Frémont in this moment of gloom was the young but already influential journalist James Gordon Bennett. His editorial in the *New York Herald* criticized the entire trial proceedings: "We saw from time to time evidences of hostility on the part of members of the court against Lieutenant Colonel Frémont, who held a higher commission and was a greater though a younger man than a majority of his triers; and what we then suspected has this afternoon been presented to us as actual truth." Frémont would not accept *any* verdict except one that found him innocent of *all* charges. After Secretary Buchanan urged him to resume an army command, he replied that he "would take pleasure in conforming my conduct to your opinion, if it were possible. But it is not possible. I *feel* the sentence of the court-martial against me to be unjust; and while that feeling remains I can never, by any act or word whatever, even by the remotest implication, admit, or seem to admit, its justice."[40]

Frémont would have none of Polk's feigned mercy either. Spurning all such conciliatory gestures, he resigned from the army on February 19, 1848. Almost immediately thereafter, Benton ran a letter in the *New York Herald* urging that the people of California organize their own civilian government. President Polk well knew that Frémont still had a political future among Californians. He believed that the purpose of Senator Benton's statement was "plain enough": to "make Col. Frémont the Governor of the independent government they shall form." The president saw this action as "arrogant in tone and calculated to do much mischief."[41] But one admirer wrote: "Col. Frémont is the most popular man that was ever in this country; in fact he is the only man that we have ever had here that has paid any attention to the interests of the people of California. He is popular with the Spaniards as well as with the Americans."[42]

The struggle with Kearny was erased only by death. When in 1848 the general lay dying, he requested Jessie to visit him. She refused. Convinced that she had lost her first son, Benton, because Frémont's trial had disturbed her pregnancy, she stated: "There was a little grave between us I could not cross."[43]

Cursing Kearny by ignoring him, Frémont placed this oracular statement in his memoirs: "I close the page because my path of life led out from among the grand and lovely features of nature, and its pure and wholesome air, into the poisoned atmosphere and jarring circumstances of conflict among men, made subtle and malignant by clashing interests."[44] He never again mentioned either his trial or Kearny. By stopping his memoirs at the very point where he was temporarily held up by life itself, he made it clear that more right and justice lay with him than with any general. Later Jessie bitterly called his conviction "a Dreyfus case to the end."

There were still forty-four years of life after his irksome court-martial trial. But Frémont, still only thirty-five, seemed at sea about his future as well as more dour and less likeable. He grew "more aloof . . . and sensitive about his honor and less sensitive about the welfare of the men who joined his expeditions." Yet, curiously, the court-martial added to Frémont's national reputation, fortifying the legend that "he had played a daring role in the acquisition of California."[45]

He certainly had not held its conquest together. Instead, he added numerous complications to that process. Exploration alone was his forte, not warfare. He persisted in portraying himself as a man who had not even been stunned, let alone wounded. Instead, he wanted to be seen as a leader who did not "look back, lose courage," or express regrets.

Although unable to avoid public scrutiny of his often bizarre behavior, he forever preferred, he said, "an unrestrained life in the open air," of being able to enjoy each day "as it came, without thought for the morrow."[46] What remained was a temperamental restlessness. Overwifed by "General Jessie," as some came to call her, he would again invite new blunders because of poor judgment.

Into 1848 the Frémonts deluded themselves into thinking that the Pathfinder could return to California to represent the president. Friends urged Polk to appoint Frémont to Consul Larkin's position at Monterey. They hinted darkly at "allegations" that would warrant Larkin's dismissal. But Polk was too wary to follow through.[47]

As one looks back upon the conquest of California and Frémont's subsequent court-martial, it is difficult to appraise the credit which should have gone to him. It is true that the acquisition of America's first Pacific state, together with the annexation of Texas, was the most important result of the Mexican War. But

California's conquest formed only one part of the war, not even its major portion. And Frémont was no more the conqueror of California than Commodore Stockton or General Kearny was. He deserves no greater credit than those leaders.

Those times had been turbulent, and problems with the Bear Flaggers, the Mexicans, and the high command were frustratingly confusing. Yet there need never have been a court-martial trial had it not been for the character flaws that Frémont so clearly demonstrated.[48] ❖

Following the court-martial trial, Frémont became embroiled in yet another fight. This time the acrimony erupted with Captain Charles Wilkes, U.S.N. Their rivalry dated back to Frémont's 1842 expedition, which some Washington officials had hoped would link up with a navy group headed by Wilkes. Frémont seriously underestimated Wilkes, who had proven that the frozen wastes of Antarctica were a separate continent. Wilkes's expedition of 1838–42 overlapped Frémont's but was much more extensive. It included civilian specialists as well as eighty-three officers and 342 seamen. In addition to his flagship, the *Vincennes*, Wilkes used five auxiliary vessels to explore sixteen hundred miles of Antarctica's coasts plus 280 Pacific islands as well as the western shores of north America.

Using the English mariner George Vancouver's 1788 charts, Wilkes probed considerably beyond the orbit covered by Frémont. He also first pointed out the strategic importance of Puget Sound if the United States were ever to drive the British out of the northern Pacific sea otter trade. Wilkes mapped the entire western coast beyond Fort Walla Walla, providing his superiors with secret plans for seizing the Hudson's Bay Company post ninety miles up the Columbia River. In California he roamed as far inland as Sutter's Fort. But some of his 180 maps and charts, unlike Frémont's, remained buried in archives, overlooked by cartographers. Although Wilkes had once also been backed by Joel Poinsett, the new Tyler administration ignored his achievements, for he had been appointed by members of President Van Buren's cabinet.[1]

The Frémont-Wilkes altercation first flared up when Washington's *National Intelligencer* for May 9, 1848, mentioned that the whaling ship *Hope*, out of Providence harbor, had foundered on rocky shoals off California. The newspaper blamed the shipwreck on Wilkes's faulty maritime charts. He had located Cape San Lucas from fifteen to forty miles too far eastward. Senator Benton was quick to charge in the *National Intelligencer* for May 15 that Frémont had corrected such a grievous error in his report on the geography of Oregon and Upper California "now in preparation." Benton, egged on by his son-in-law, asserted that Wilkes's sailing charts had placed the California coast too far eastward.

A few days later Wilkes replied in the same journal. Ignoring his own errors, he pointed out that Captain Frederick Beechey aboard H.B.M. *Blossom* during an 1826 visit to California, and confirmed by his fellow Englishman Captain Sir Edward Belcher (H.B.M. surveying ship *Sulphur*) during 1835, made observations reconfirmed in 1841 by Wilkes's United States Exploring Expedition.[2] Wilkes, furthermore, called Frémont, who claimed that his maps were far more accurate, "Young Bullion," in derision of the senator. Wilkes was saying that Benton and Frémont did not know what they were talking about whenever each vented pompous utterances about the geography of the West. Frémont's alleged "discoveries" were sometimes spurious, according to Wilkes.

As a result, once again Frémont decided to take on the establishment, this time represented by Captain Wilkes and the U.S. Navy. As he had not seen the English surveys (obviously withheld, he said, by Wilkes), Frémont asserted that his own astronomical observations on the Pacific Coast were uniquely correct. Furthermore, Wilkes could not "claim any share" in his vital data. Frémont charged the captain with having left the true geography of the coast more unsettled than before. Labeling Wilkes's maps as replete with errors, he continued: "Our seamen need something more accurate than they have available" from Wilkes's navigational charts.[3]

Wilkes took exception to what he called Frémont's criticism of minor points "as though they were major ones." A few days later Frémont again rebutted Wilkes's "imputing unfairness in my references to his observations." Frémont affirmed that he had tested the latitudes in question and stood by his findings. According to him, Wilkes was simply guilty of "propagation of error." Wilkes expressed resentment of such "sweeping charges." Their correspondence ended when Frémont claimed that "the truth is Capt. Wilkes led me into error," never once "apprising me of his mistake." He continued: "If then, there was any error . . . it is attributable entirely to Capt. Wilkes." He closed by accusing Wilkes of provoking the entire controversy.[4]

Both protagonists in this quarrel over the merits of their cartography thought that the other claimed too much credit. Actually, their ventures had been quite different in scope. Wilkes's observations, being mostly by sea, and quite secretive, too, were thus not really comparable to Frémont's. But once again, in Frémont's eyes a nasty, older authoritarian, Wilkes (born 1798), had wronged him and "left me in ignorance." Meanwhile, two of the nation's leading explorers at such loggerheads undermined public confidence in either navy surveyors or the army's Topographical Corps.[5]

When Wilkes's *Narrative of the U.S. Exploring Expedition* (1844) appeared in five volumes plus an atlas, it was much more elaborate than Frémont's reports. Wilkes's only biographer tells us that "one of the most important results of the elaborate Wilkes expedition was to establish . . . the essential unity of all parts of the Pacific Coast—Puget Sound was an inherent part of Oregon, and the Columbia Basin was essential to the development of American commerce in the Pacific."[6]

The Pathfinder believed his own achievements were greater than those of Wilkes or of any other explorer. Once again, he wanted but a single story to emerge, and one favorable to him alone. His detailed map of the Oregon Road (1846) was, indeed, of inestimable value to settlers; in addition to offering new topographic data, it included descriptions of meteorology, ethnology, natural resources, and safe camping sites along the overland trail. Frémont's map of Oregon and Upper California published in 1848 in seven segments, furthermore, represented the first detailed charting of both northern California and the Great Basin, forming the most practical guide to Oregon and California—a far more accurate one than Lansford W. Hastings's irresponsible *Emigrants Guide . . .* (1845).

After the quarrel with Captain Wilkes fizzled out, Frémont next turned to a tedious but less contentious task—the preparation of his report of the third expedition's achievements before the conquest of California had interrupted that work. So meticulous was he in caring for the details involved that, for example, he complained to John Torrey, the botanist then authenticating his one thousand plant specimens at the Princeton herbarium, that the species *Frémontia vermicularis* had been renamed *Sarcobatus vermiculatus*. (Incidentally, Frémont named the gnarled Torrey Pine, which grew along California's shoreline, after the botanist.)

Having reassumed the role of geographer, Frémont also had to check out many mapping coordinates with one of the country's leading astronomers, Joseph Stillman Hubbard. He and Jessie ultimately managed to prepare a fifty-page *Geographical Memoir upon Upper California*, published in twenty thousand copies as a U.S. Senate document in 1848. To print this report, which he called "the cursed manuscript," the government allowed only about eight dollars for each day's work on the document.[7]

The *Geographical Memoir* downplayed the dangers of going west—the Indian menace, the risks of encountering half-ton grizzlies, or the bleakness of the deserts. Instead, Frémont was the first writer to call California "the Italy of America." Here was a potentially verdant orchard of vegetables, figs, peaches, and grapes. Easterners, chilled by the ice of winter or sweltering in summer's humidity, would read this refreshing report with alacrity. Inexpensive reprints became highly popular, especially after the gold rush to California began—in the very year the memoir was first printed.

Because of Frémont's engaging reports, it did not really matter whether he had won or lost his battles with General Kearny and Captain Wilkes. His name would be the more enduring one when the history of the American West was finally written. ❖

A t last the court-martial trial was over. Though painful, that event had
made Frémont nationally known. Jessie boasted that her husband was
offered a salary of five thousand dollars per year to be president of
the railroad that ran from Charleston to Cincinnati, the roadbed of which he had
once surveyed. Amazingly, Frémont had also been tendered a position on the
faculty of the College of Charleston, where his past transgressions had been
forgiven. Jessie recalled: "I saw only the proud lonely man making a new start
in life." In that process, she added, his temper was "as sweet as his will was
strong."

In mid-1848 the Frémonts made plans to leave Washington for California,
where Larkin had purchased the Rancho las Mariposas for them. It was a seventy-
square-mile tract located in the interior south of Yosemite Valley. The rancho lay
undeveloped. Benton and fellow senator John Dix loaned Frémont money with
which he ordered a corral, barn, and house built there. He also sent farm
implements and shipped an entire sawmill to San Francisco on the Aspinwall
steamer *Fredonia*.

Instead of going immediately to his Mariposas property, however, Frémont
was lured into the wilderness by a disastrous fourth expedition that should never
have taken place. With the backing of Benton and three Saint Louis merchants,
he hoped to survey a railroad route along the thirty-eighth parallel to find
whether passes in the southern Rockies were usable in midwinter. He sought
government backing for so costly a venture. Although the Senate appropriated
thirty thousand dollars for the enterprise, the House of Representatives rejected
that appropriation by a decisive vote of 128 to 29. Feeling still ran high against
both Frémont and Benton in Washington.

Frémont mistakenly hoped for good morale after informing the party that
they would end their midwinter journey in sunny California. Because his men
were to serve without pay until he could somehow reimburse them, he had to
make certain concessions. One of these was to allow the writing of journals. For
that reason we know the grueling details of an expedition that would start out
well enough but that ended in terror. By receiving no remuneration, Frémont's
men actually helped finance the undertaking. One was convinced that "when the
work was finished [the] Govt. would pay us."[1]

Frémont's retinue was a varied one. He took along the three merchants who had subsidized the trip. Grouchy old Preuss was again the topographer. All three of the Kern brothers, acting as artists and official physician, came too. Richard and Dr. Benjamin Kern were the greenhorns. The former saw this expedition as "an opportunity to improve myself [in] landscaping painting." Also on board was the mustachioed Captain Andrew Cathcart, an Ayrshire Scot observer from the Eleventh Prince Albert Hussars who had sold his commission in that British regiment. He expected a sporting holiday in America's Great West, planning to travel on to Canton in China. Cathcart, a soldier for eleven years, had seen service in India. He delighted in shooting bison; as he wrote a friend, "I peppered anything, whether cow, calf, or bull." Frémont attracted yet another new face, Frederick Creutzfeldt, who came along as botanist. Fifteen other men had traveled with previous Frémont ventures. All offered their services for nothing and furnished most of their own supplies. Edward Kern estimated that Frémont himself dispensed only eight thousand to ten thousand dollars of his own money.[2]

The party left Saint Louis on October 3, heading up the Missouri on the *Martha*. Jessie accompanied her husband part of the way westward. She was again pregnant and brought along their first boy, Benton, named for Jessie's father. The baby suffered from a weak heart. On October 5, 1848, two days up the Missouri from Saint Louis, he died aboard the *Martha*. At first Jessie refused to admit that the child was dead, acting as though he had merely fallen asleep. Finally, her husband had to take the baby away from her. "I understand," she said hazily, "but I have had him such a little while." The next day the infant was quietly buried ashore. As her husband's men lowered the tiny casket into the earth, Jessie bitterly blamed her loss on the ordeal of the court-martial trial.[3]

A grieving Jessie continued on up the Missouri with her shaken husband. For a while she stayed on in a flapping tent while he provisioned the expedition. On October 20, Frémont left his wife behind at Westport, then on the frontier. Jessie would go back to the East Coast to board a vessel for California. So long a journey once again would separate Jessie from her wandering husband.

Frémont was able to track as many as twenty-five to thirty miles per day along the Kansas River toward today's Topeka and Salina, Kansas. The men grew nervous when a band of Kiowas temporarily accompanied them for some miles. By November 4, snow began to fall. Four days later, the group reached the banks of the familiar Arkansas River, from which they proceeded down the Santa Fe Trail southwestward. Now visible was the front range of the Rockies, with snow already on the high peaks, which the Indians called the Breasts of the World.

It would be a long winter. The signs were everywhere. Overnight frosts stayed on the ground until late in the day. The beavers were working fiercely, and livestock were growing heavy coats of fur. The party reached Bent's Fort on November 16. Accommodations there were much like those at other camps and stations of the West. The inhabitants endured frigid weather and meals of boiled maize from rat-infested cribs. Frémont nevertheless wrote Senator Benton that, although the snow was deeper than in other years, he was not alarmed. At the fort John Charles also wrote Benton:

> Both Indians and whites report the snow to be deeper in the mountains than has for a long time been known so early in the season. They predict a severe winter. . . . Still I am in no wise discouraged by the prospect and I believe we shall succeed in forcing our way across. Should we have reasonable success, we shall be in California early in January, where I shall expect to hear from all by steamer.[4]

These remarks concealed a terrible miscalculation; but by now Jessie was getting used to her husband's unrealities. She half wished that he were less resolute in the face of danger.[5] At Bent's Fort, Frémont refused the advice of two seasoned mountain men, "Uncle Dick" Wooton and Tom Biggs. They thought it folly to move along the thirty-eighth parallel in a straight line across the southern Rockies in midwinter. But, Frémont reasoned, how else would he find out whether an all-year railroad route was feasible?

Jessie's father desperately wanted a Pacific railroad that would be firmly anchored in Saint Louis. Benton and the merchant community there dreamt of a bustling trade with the Orient. But first Frémont must establish a viable overland link from the East Coast to the western shore. Manufacturers would then send goods by train over the Rockies toward the riches of Cathay. Traders at Hong Kong and Shanghai, too, could ship Asian luxuries—silk, ginseng, and ivory—to Boston and New York through Saint Louis. Frémont planned a railroad route down the Old Santa Fe Trail and across the mountains north of Taos. There, above the headwaters of the Rio Grande, key passes could be surveyed to the Pacific.

Frémont allowed only three days' rest at Bent's Fort, after which the party again headed west. When one of their campsites was caught in a prairie fire, Captain Cathcart wrote that they started backfires to prevent being engulfed by the flames. "These lines of miles of flames are a magnificent sight," he reported. But at night, especially, the fires kept the group "in perpetual anxiety." Cathcart recorded other details of daily life on the trail: "We breakfast by star light, travel all day, and eat again in the evening. Heavens, how I enjoy the tea." They also dined on buffalo, racoons, and fat badgers so heavy that they had to be dragged into camp, boiled overnight, and eaten cold the next day. Cathcart soon realized that he had joined no cozy Sunday afternoon shooting party.[6]

Frémont had lingered too long in Washington, awaiting his expected assignment to Larkin's California post. He now had to rush the expedition forward in order to minimize the snows of winter. On some days they traveled as much as fifty miles, heading for today's Pueblo, Colorado, then called Fontaine qui Buit, or "Fountain that Boils." The place was a sleazy compound of crumbling adobes with peeling whitewashed walls. By the time Frémont reached there, several of the original thirty-five men who had left Westport had already quit.

The Pathfinder now engaged a new mountaineer as guide. William Sherley ("Old Bill") Williams was reputed to know the southern Rockies as well as any guide. He had lived in those mountains and among the Indians for years on end. Williams had been wintering at Pueblo because one of his arms had been shattered by an Indian bullet the previous July. Still waiting for it to mend, Williams hesitated before signing on with Frémont. Temperamentally, Williams was not the man Frémont should have chosen as his principal guide. Some members of the party grumbled that the leader had to agree to Williams's every wish in order to obtain his services. The creole Alexis Godey, younger, more prudent, and loyal to the Pathfinder, had guided the party into Pueblo. Williams was sixty-two years old, a heavy drinker, touchy, opinionated, and hard to handle. At his side Frémont would naively march into the San Juan Range.

The last tiny settlement they reached before heading into the mountains was called Hardscrabble; it was a miserable assemblage of huts belonging to trappers and their female Indian companions. The party feasted there on chickens and baked pumpkins, and Frémont managed to purchase 130 bushels of corn from the locals. The corn proved to be a burden. Because of the extra load on their horses and mules, the men were forced to enter the mountains on foot. By December 6, Richard Kern recorded the first results of the freezing temperature: "We all looked like old Time or Winter—icicles an inch long were pendant from our moustache & beard."[7]

Frémont insisted that they travel as far up the Rio Grande, yet as near the thirty-eighth parallel, as possible until they reached the massive San Juan Range. Located in today's southern Colorado and northern New Mexico, these mountains are the youngest in the Rockies, the least eroded and most jagged. Their fourteen-thousand-foot peaks created a towering backdrop to the silhouettes formed by Frémont's party. With the group cupped securely within impenetrable heights, Williams, deceived by the heavy snows that lay on the mountaintops, turned off the river some fifteen miles too soon. This miscalculation, which he was too stubborn to admit, led the party onto the side of the rugged La Garita Mountains, a forty-mile-long spur that included Boot (elevation 12,422 feet) and Mesa (12,944 feet) peaks.[8]

Godey later maintained that after reaching Carneros (Cochetopa) Pass, Frémont doubted that Williams was pursuing the right route. The diaries of the Kern brothers suggest that Frémont himself made the fatal cartographic errors. But Williams apparently told both Godey and Frémont that "he knew every inch of the country better than the Colonel knew his own garden." With the assurance that Williams had crossed and recrossed the San Juans over a period of thirty years, the party plunged onward. "I advised the Colonel," wrote Godey, "that I was perfectly willing to follow him and was confident that everything would result favorably." He added: "For the subsequent misfortunes that befell us, Col. Frémont is not reprehensible [*sic*]; he trusted to his guides, in whose representations he was bound to place confidence, and that they were deceived was no fault of his."[9]

Yet Frémont had been repeatedly warned that this crossing, especially during such an early winter, was dangerous. Yet he persisted. As with his second expedition, Frémont's gamble clearly meant sacrificing his men. Anticipating privation, he had even bought amputating instruments in Philadelphia. As the group slogged through heavy snow flurries, Richard Kern's diary entries grew especially alarming. That for December 10 reads: "The deep snow of today should have warned Col. Frémont of his approaching destruction, but with the willfully blind eyes of rashness and self-conceit and confidence, he pushed on."[10]

Like other risk-takers, the colonel flirted with disaster, walked a tightrope, yet would expect forgiveness if transgressions were ever charged. Once more, he was poor at realistically discerning the level of chaos into which he was about to plunge.

Rudderless in a mountainous sea, Frémont rashly slogged on. Overtaken by blizzards, his men had to march onward like numbed ghosts or die. On December 16, as the mountain weather unleashed its fury on the expedition, Richard Kern recorded the following about their most recent stop: "Had we remained there a half hour longer the whole party might have been lost." Their remaining corn had been eaten, and the animals were munching on saddles and leather straps as well as nipping at one another's tails and manes. Two days later, Benjamin Kern wrote: "I waked up and found 8 inches of snow on my bed, peeped out and told Dick that the expedition was destroyed and if we all got to some settlement with our lives we would be doing well."[11]

The fourth expedition was now hopelessly bogged down in ice. Daily snowstorms wrapped them in paralyzing folds, with the wind-chill factor estimated at minus seventy-five degrees. A lucky survivor, Thomas Salathiel Martin, recalled: "The depth of the snow must have been fully 150 feet, as the tops of tall trees were in some places barely peeping through it." The men cut these tree tops for firewood. Their feeble pathway "was sunk down in the snow in places eighteen feet deep, quite wide at the top but gradually narrowing until at the bottom it was only a foot wide." To keep from freezing, the men slept together on rubber blankets. When they awoke each morning they found "from 3 to 6 feet of snow on top of us."[12]

The party had traveled west across almost three-fourths of Colorado's length before bogging down south of the Gunnison River. By Christmas day, faced with split loyalties, Frémont divided the remaining members of his exhausted party as he had done on the 1844 midwinter crossing of the Sierra Nevada. He sent a relief group under Williams down the mountains—it was composed of the moderately strong men, including Thomas Breckenridge, Frederick Creutzfeldt, and Henry King.

Some 120 mules had perished, and Frémont had wasted precious time and dissipated his men's strength by insisting that all the baggage (including saddles and pack gear) be hauled down to La Garita Creek. The worn relief party was supposed to walk more than a hundred miles to obtain supplies and animals for the stranded expedition, hoping to make it back in eleven days. But after waiting for sixteen, Frémont, with several other men, decided to go in search of the vanished party. After dividing the last provisions, he instructed the rest of the group to wait three days before doubling back southward down Embargo Creek to the Rio Grande. These wretches were to encounter blizzard winds strong enough to blow mules off a mountain and snow so deep that it took them sixteen days to reach the river."[13]

Frémont would be accused of abandoning twenty-four marooned men weaker than himself. Among them were the Kern brothers, who had stayed on with Lorenzo Vincenthaler (sometimes Visonhaler) at what they named Camp Dismal during "days of horror, desolation and despair." Vincenthaler had been a sergeant in Frémont's California Battalion, the members of whom the Pathfinder always favored, but he would prove to be an unusually poor choice as leader. Nevertheless, Frémont ordered him to pack up the expedition's baggage and to move down the Rabbit River, "where we would meet relief." Frémont's orders were not only confusing but also self-serving. According to the reminiscences of Micajah McGehee, another survivor, Frémont had urged the remaining men to "hurry as he was going on to California." Meanwhile, Vincenthaler hoarded scarce supplies. Richard Kern called Vincenthaler "totally unfit," a coward who "left the rest of us to perish" and who "cared for self alone."[14]

Frémont's men were now dispersed in several directions. He did finally locate the relief party, one of whom was dead and the other three of whom were half-starved. They had looked in vain for pinecones with edible nuts, a food staple of the New Mexico pueblos. Remnants of the main group that had stayed behind were reduced to eating frozen rosebuds, water bugs, and even the soles of their moccasins. Buried beneath twenty feet of snow lay the carcasses of their horses and mules, but the weather was so numbing that no man could be induced to dig out these animals in the freezing blasts of winter.

The members of this fourth Frémont expedition not only had to endure deathly privation but would also be charged with a serious crime: cannibalism. When survival is paramount, the now dated notion that sexuality is the first of human drives falls by the wayside. Ten of the expedition's thirty-three members ultimately lost their lives, as did 130 of their frozen pack animals. Although Henry King was originally one of the strongest men, Charles Taplin reported that more than half of his frozen body was eaten by his trailmates. Frémont and Senator Benton would repeat these grave accusations. Preuss, too, confirmed such charges in his diary, as did Martin, who wrote: "I know positively that the men we left behind lived on those of their companions who gave out." Martin's actions were especially reprehensible. One night he and Vincenthaler waited until the weakest men were asleep. Then they "crept out of Camp."[15]

Vincenthaler luckily hunted down a stray deer, by which he and Martin kept themselves alive at the expense of their abandoned compatriots. Martin's narrative confirms Richard Kern's accusation that the stronger men deserted the weaker ones. When a rescue team failed to return, Captain Cathcart, the Kern brothers, and several Indian boys started down the mountain. They dragged along a two-hundred-pound load of medicines, medical instruments, sketches, and a collection of flora and fauna. As they moved along the trail that the relief party had used, the going got so tough that they left behind most of the baggage at a cave they named for Raphael Proue, who had already perished.

Frémont had, meanwhile, shuffled toward Taos with Godey. On January 21, 1849, they appeared at Carl Beaubien's store. The expedition was in shambles. Seldom did Frémont lose mastery over his environment. This time his leadership was clearly irresolute. He was now off keel, like a sailor hard-a-weather and without true bearings for reckoning a vessel's whereabouts, or like a wooden chip lost in a turbulent sea of mountains. As he staggered onward, even his speech was disoriented.

The Sangre de Cristos, like the court-martial, had taken their toll. Frémont was hollow-eyed, limping with a badly frozen foot, ragged and drawn. But always the risk-taker, he knew that he personally would survive. He hated quitters who did not possess similar determination. Weakness was not only a danger but also a disgrace.

Meanwhile, the small Kern splinter group groped its way toward the Rio Grande. As they were about to give up hope, a vision appeared before them. It was Godey. Snow-blinded, they mistook him for Frémont, who in fact was far away:

On the 28th of January about 12 in the morning during a snow storm as we all sat silently around our little willow fire, Taplin suddenly exclaimed by God there is a halloo. Tis but a wolf again we said—rising to his feet he said Christ there's a man on horseback over the river, we gave a shout you may be sure, almost in an instant Godey was with us. . . . Oh he has bread we cried and some of us trembled with joy at the sight of it.[16]

Godey had reentered the mountains from Taos with a relief party of four Mexican muleteers, thirty animals, food, and blankets. He now guided the remnants of the expedition back to that pueblo. After the Pathfinder was reunited with them, he wrote Jessie not so much about the loss of his men but of how he had left Bent's Fort with "upwards of a hundred good mules." He also deplored inadvertently leaving behind in the mountains a sack containing twelve hundred dollars in gold doubloons. It belonged to Thomas Breckenridge, and he had agreed to keep it safely among his scientific instruments. Although Frémont promised to "see that the loss is made up to you," Breckenridge, who acknowledged that "human life at that time was of more value than Spanish coin," later grumbled, "I have never had the loss made up to me by the government as promised."[17]

"The courage of the men failed fast," Frémont wrote Jessie. "In fact," he continued, "I have never seen men so soon discouraged by misfortune as we were on this occasion."[18] He still acted as if his men should also follow his self-imposed struggles. Meanwhile, emaciated and downcast, the survivors hardly had the strength to give thanks for being spared from death. Captain Cathcart had become a hollow-eyed skeleton who no longer resembled the polished Scotch officer of resplendent glory.

Richard Kern's diary entry of February 9 tells us that, upon Frémont's arrival at Taos, "Major Beall, commander of that post, ordered the commissary to issue to the colonel thirty days' full rations for the twenty-five men still in the mountains and expected in. These rations were never turned over to the men, and were probably taken to California by Frémont!"[19] All of this was vehemently denied by the faithful Godey. Whereas he stood up for his leader, most of the men condemned Frémont for failing to accompany him back into the mountains to search for marooned survivors.

At Taos, a dusty outpost of grubby adobes, Kit Carson's wife, Josefa, following local custom, served him chocolate in bed each morning. Frémont and Carson still felt comfortable with one another. Neither could utter a harsh word about the other. When Carson later dictated his memoirs, he paid tribute to his old commander, who he had heard was a rich man: "All that he has or may ever receive, he deserves. I can never forget his treatment of me while in his employ and how cheerfully he suffered with his men when undergoing the severest of hardships."[20]

The Kerns told a different story about the fourth expedition. They called Frémont "the accuser of others to shield himself."[21] Richard charged that "the greatest dread" Frémont had felt was "that a *true and correct* account of the proceedings ... may be made public."[22] Even Edward Kern (who had thought more highly of Frémont than had his brothers) did not choose to follow him on toward California. He and Richard joined Lieutenant James Hervey Simpson's expedition, which happened to be heading west to make the first survey of the Navaho country. Simpson was grateful to employ skilled artists; their meeting was a lucky happenstance for the Kerns, too.

Simpson's journal entries contain a severe indictment of Frémont's fourth expedition, but he expunged these strictures from his printed report to the Topographical Engineers. Simpson obviously feared reprisals from the Benton-Frémont camp, because his original notes blamed Frémont for the entire catastrophe. Simpson claimed that after Frémont had secured help at Taos, he apportioned food and supplies unfairly—even that he sought to leave Taos without paying the quartermaster there for food.[23]

Frémont was tight-lipped with anger at members of the expedition who, he claimed, had let him down. Unable to express any compassion toward them, he sought to paint his disaster as a success. Even the dead had seemed to betray him. Infuriated that one of his men, Raphael Proue, had fallen into a deep slumber from which he never awakened, the Pathfinder saw duty as a cruel but necessary master. Death by freezing thus seemed an act of cowardice. To surrender oneself to the elements was unmanly. Indeed, all emotional weakness represented forms of defeat correctable by stiffening one's backbone.

Frémont also concocted the story that Old Bill Williams had deliberately misled the expedition, encouraging the rumor that Bill went back along Embargo Creek with Dr. Benjamin Kern not to locate the expedition's abandoned records and supplies, but because he planned to gather up and resell the belongings of the men who had died. Whatever Bill's motives for returning into the mountains, in March, 1849, he and Kern were ambushed and killed there by either Utes or Jicarilla Apaches.[24]

These events made for great drama worthy of national attention by the press. Frémont's letters back to his wife and to Senator Benton were excerpted in the *National Intelligencer*. They were then reprinted in other newspapers and by his earliest biographers, John Bigelow and Charles Upham. His dispatches still portrayed the Pathfinder as a flawless leader whose associates had failed him. All critics had to be made to appear wrongheaded. After all, most seasoned scouts had called his guide, the best in the country, "a man whose name was a synonym for mountain knowledge and trapper's lore." How could one possibly have known that Old Bill Williams was capable of "fanciful superstitions and odd performances that evinced a want of balance?" How could Frémont have done anything else but trust Williams? Jessie joined her husband in attacking the dead Williams, a man of "low morals" that resembled the "naturally predatory instincts" of Indians. Also labeling him an unemployed "itinerant preacher," she quoted Kit Carson: "In starving times no man who knew him ever walked in front of Bill Williams." Such depreciation was nothing new. We have seen how the Frémonts treated Larkin's role in the California conquest. Senator Benton now joined his daughter and son-in-law in labeling Frémont's late guide as "a passport to disaster."[25]

The fourth expedition produced such a record of disintegration that the Frémont clan needed Bill Williams as scapegoat. In death he could not answer their charges. Undeniably an eccentric, Williams had a foggy reputation. Despite his oddities, he undoubtedly had not wished to risk his life any more than his companions had. Some evidence persisted that he had not wanted to follow the route Frémont prescribed. In the words of Antoine Leroux, "Williams had himself traveled it several times in company with me. His knowledge of that part of the country was perfect. The course which was taken by Col. Frémont was an impracticable one in winter and no sensible mountaineer would ever for a moment have entertained the idea of taking it."[26]

The remaining Kern brothers, after Benjamin was murdered alongside Williams, experienced a heightened aversion to Frémont. Edward claimed that the leader "loves to be told of his greatness." A letter to the Kerns' sister, Mary, explained why the brothers had not gone on with Frémont to California:

> Hardly one time has he treated us with the respect due . . . and jealous of anyone who may know as much or more of any subject than himself, for he delights to associate among those who *should* be his inferiors, which may . . . account for the reputation he has gained of being, for a man of his talents, so excessively modest. A thing by the by which many adopt to hide their want of depth.

Edward also maintained that Frémont had "begat a dislike for Doc" (his brother Benjamin) and that he "took no small pleasure of showing it to others." Thus, "twas best to part before coming to a rupture with him." For "he has broken faith with all of us. Dick and I were to have accompanied him as his Artists and Doc as Medico and Naturalist," Edward continued. Instead, Frémont had left them "without even his good wishes or a thought of our future—and owing *me money*."[27]

A fourth Kern brother, John, wrote Richard and Edward that Frémont refused to talk to anyone from their native Philadelphia if he suspected "they were acquainted with the Kerns." John also accused Frémont of having stolen letters sent to his brothers "Care of Col. Frémont." John had received a note from Henry King's mother complaining that she had been unable to retrieve from

Frémont a journal that her dead son had written during the fourth expedition and that unaccountably disappeared once he borrowed it.[28]

After only two years passed, despite some scathing criticisms Richard Kern had released to several newspapers, Frémont met Richard in San Francisco and they, quite surprisingly, became reconciled. In the mid-1850s, Edward, too, stopped criticizing the Pathfinder after he ran for the presidency. Edward even offered to hand over notes and drawings for Frémont's future writings. Although Edward could not go so far as to back Frémont for the presidency in 1856, when the Civil War broke out he enlisted as a captain of topographical engineers in Frémont's Army of the West. A letter from Simpson to Richard Kern reveals that Frémont ultimately patched matters up with the Kerns: "I am glad you and Frémont have become reconciled to each other. There can be no doubt that he has done great injustice to individuals in his public career, but the first step toward improvement is to confess error, and as he seems to have done this in your case, there is hope that this experience will not be lost upon him."[29]

The Pathfinder had some loyal partisans among survivors of the calamitous fourth expedition. Even before that event, Captain Cathcart had called him "a very nice fellow, very gentlemanlike and quiet." Cathcart later sent Frémont from Britain a specially made steel-mounted sword, on the blade of which was etched the motto of the American Union. Solomon Carvalho, too, remained captured by Frémont's magnetism: "A half hour previously, if anyone had suggested to me the probability of my undertaking an overland journey to California . . . I should have replied there were no inducements sufficiently powerful to have tempted me. . . . I know of no other man to whom I would have trusted my life."[30]

Yet another Frémont favorite, Alexis Godey, was, next to Kit Carson, the explorer's most stalwart adherent. He, too, could say little wrong about the leader: "Frémont, more than any man I ever knew, possessed the respect and affection of his men. . . . In his private character he is a model. . . . I never recollect . . . anything like blasphemy issue from his lips . . . and the truth of these things can be attested by all of the old companions of Frémont."[31]

As he looked back upon his catastrophic fourth expedition, Frémont stuck to the role of misunderstood hero. His sense of blamelessness was reflected in another letter to Jessie: "I wish for a time to shut out these things from my mind, to leave this country . . . so signally disastrous as absolutely to astonish me with a persistence of misfortune which no precaution has been adequate on my part to avert."[32]

Although his fourth expedition would be seen as "harebrained," indeed as an "insane illusion,"[33] one of its few tangible remains was the collection of unique specimens. After the third expedition, Frémont had already sent eastward by sea from San Francisco some soldered tin cases, wrapped in stretched green California cowhides, to Professor Torrey's herbarium. Now came, through the Brooklyn

Navy Yard, hitherto unknown plants collected along the Gila River and as far south as Sonora. Frémont also sent thousands of plant and geological specimens to Asa Gray, professor of natural history at Harvard, and to James D. Dana, professor of natural history at Columbia.[34]

The explorer had mounted his last two expeditions to fulfill Senator Benton's dream of proving the workability of an overland railroad route along the thirty-eighth parallel. Both men reasoned that if this line of march was moved further south, their scheme would have been compromised. Yet no railroad was ever to be built through the mountains where Frémont had risked the lives of his men.

It is difficult to believe that a leader would sacrifice his expedition by following so dangerous a course unless he was a driven man. The searing experience of the court-martial had impelled him once more to take death-defying risks in the wilderness. From his point of view, he had conquered the Sierra Nevada in midwinter five years earlier, so why not next the San Juans? Lack of judgment became compulsive, an imprudence that he could not alter. He botched both the fourth and fifth expeditions in large part because his and Benton's single-mindedness ran roughshod over geographical facts. Erratic leaders dare death by confronting it on mountaintops or in deserts. Some seem to favor destruction over rationality.[35] ❖

Frémont left Taos only two days after his men straggled out of the San Juan Mountains. He and Jessie had arranged to meet at San Francisco during April of 1849. In anticipation of their reunion, Frémont quickly left behind whatever remorse he had felt. He borrowed one thousand dollars at Taos from a French-Canadian from Saint Louis, Francis Xavier Aubry. But he had to wait until the circulation in his leg improved before leaving.[1] An explanatory letter of January 27, 1849, to Jessie reached her only the following May while she was delayed in Panama.

Because she had never been to sea, Jessie's father made precautionary arrangements with Colonel William Aspinwall, whose steamers carried the mails to San Francisco. Jessie would be accompanied only by her brother-in-law, Richard Jacob, who had gone with John Charles on other expeditions. They were to be met at ports along the way. After Jacob became violently ill from sunstroke in Panama, Jessie was alone except for her six-year-old daughter, Elizabeth, and their maid. From New York she took a packet steamer down the Atlantic Coast to Chagres, which she called "the worst hellhole in Christendom." Because of the dangers of the trip, travelers insured their lives before setting out across the Isthmus of Panama, but a clause in each policy declared that remaining in Chagres even overnight would forfeit their claims. After she reached Chagres, Jessie almost turned back. She found no housing, few supplies, and malaria as well as yellow fever and dysentery.

She next had to take native dugout canoes, or *bungoes*, to cross the first eleven miles of swamp and river through alligator-infested waters. Indian porters poled her craft through dense jungles alive with alligators, boa constrictors, and swarms of mosquitoes. Her arms, legs, and face were soon covered with nasty bites and welts. Jessie's ankle-length woolen skirts were hardly suited for steamy weather. Thick stretches of swamp forced members of her party to step into the ooze outside their dugout, risking leeches and tropical disease, in order to pull it forward. Exhausted at the end of each day, a homesick Jessie and her fellow passengers slept on the ground in native huts, "told at every turn" to go back, for they could never survive the tropics.

At Cruces, which marked the end of the Chagres River, her party hired mules for seventeen more miles of dangerous mountain trail to the Pacific. In the nine-month rainy season, the pack mules floundered up to their bellies in the muddy mire. Following another two-day mule trek to Panama City, which she called "a nightmare," Jessie and her daughter stayed there with a family rather than in one of its pestilential hotels. Its American military hospital and cemetery could well have marked the end of the trail for Jessie, as they did for many who tried to cross Panama.

While she was awaiting her steamer, its crew deserted. It took seven long weeks for the next vessel to arrive, during which she contracted "brain fever" after receiving news that her husband was frostbitten and might even lose a leg. But whether his fortunes were up or down, Jessie's praise was unfailing: "From the ashes of his campfires have sprung cities," she would proudly write in her reminiscences.

When another ship finally arrived at Panama City, she became one of four hundred passengers on a vessel designed to carry eighty persons. Space was so tight that "sleeping berths" on deck were marked off in chalk lines. The shipboard trip also had its dangers. In 1853, Captain Ulysses S. Grant would come through Panama on a ship that experienced eighty deaths by cholera. Grant recalled the abominable condition of his fellow passengers as a memory worse than that of any battle. En route to San Francisco, Jessie could scarcely imagine that gold, which would make the Frémonts instant millionaires, was about to be discovered on the Rancho las Mariposas. This wealth would also move her husband into national politics as one of California's first two senators. Before that could happen, however, he, too, had to get to California, leaving behind the wreckage of his fourth expedition.

Upon reaching San Diego from Panama, Jessie received important news aboard her Aspinwall steamer: "The colonel's safe; riding up to San Francisco to meet you there; he didn't lose a leg—was only badly frostbitten."[2] She could not wait to press on to the Golden Gate, which he had named. That was her husband's final destination.

When Jessie's ship landed there, San Francisco's docking facilities were still primitive. Her rowboat tossed precariously on the incoming waves. Finally she had to be carried through the surf by a sailor. San Francisco was a wild tent city. Telegraph Hill was still conical; its eastern slopes had not yet been quarried for

In 1849, at age thirty-six, Frémont sat for this daguerreotype, probably in San Francisco. The strains of his court-martial trial and the disastrous fourth expedition are beginning to show. (Reproduced by permission of the Huntington Library, San Marino, California; Album 188)

rock to provide ballast for outbound ships. As she gazed at the half-formed town, it presented a dismal picture to a poised, upper-class woman. She hardly expected to find anyone of her social and intellectual background in such a ramshackle environment, although the town's sixteen American ladies all turned out to welcome her. Once her husband arrived, they would somehow have to make the best of their new life at the Golden Gate.

But he was still out in the wilds. Twenty-five adherents followed him toward California. Traveling with some sixty horses, the group had dipped below today's Mexican border to avoid the cold weather that brought seasonal snows as far south as the Gila River in Tucson. On the way westward, Frémont had encountered twelve hundred Sonorans on their way to Alta California. They were the first to inform him that gold had been discovered near Sutter's Fort, with which he was well acquainted. The fort was north of his new property. When Frémont finally reached California, he enticed twenty-eight of these Mexicans to join his group, promising them employment on his own land.

They traveled by way of "the Angels," as Los Angeles was then called, to San Francisco, where Jessie and John Charles were reunited at its makeshift Parker House. Like other such "hotels," it was little more than a series of loose boxes nailed together and with rooms divided by thin cloth partitions. But the place teemed with Gold Rush addicts whose enthusiasm Frémont caught; he was propelled toward mining. Bayard Taylor, a travel writer, gives us this detailed description of him at that time:

> In the morning we went with Lieutenant Beale to call upon Colonel Frémont, whom we found ... wearing a sombrero and California jacket, and showing no trace of the terrible hardships he had lately undergone. It may be interesting to the thousands who have followed him ... on his remarkable journeys and explorations for the past eight years, to know that he is a man of about thirty-five years of age; of medium height, and lightly, but most compactly knit. ... I have seen in no other man the ... lightness, activity, strength, and physical endurance in so perfect an equilibrium. His face is rather thin and embrowned by exposure; his nose a bold aquiline and his eyes deep-set and keen as a hawk's. The rough camp-life of many years has lessened in no degree his native refinement of character and polish of manners. A stranger would never suppose him to be the Columbus of our central wilderness.[3]

The California of 1849 offered Frémont unique opportunities for profit. Each bark that landed at San Francisco discharged a stream of passengers from ports throughout the world. Rampant inflation, fueled by the Gold Rush, drove prices skyward. Articles of every sort suddenly became valuable. Horses brought up to two hundred dollars per head and mules as much as three hundred dollars. It even became worthwhile to capture wild beasts of burden.

When he had broken up his expedition at Isaac Williams's Rancho del Chino, Frémont had awarded each member a pony and a pack animal. He had nothing further to give. Before pressing on to San Francisco after a hurried visit to Los Angeles, he had arranged for purchases, on credit, of cattle to be shipped to the mines on his property. The Sonorans who had traveled west with him ended up working at the Mariposa lode. He would employ some of them also at a steam sawmill that he set up near San Jose. Like cattle, lumber was scarce during the Gold Rush. It fetched five hundred dollars per thousand board feet.

An invading foreign culture was beginning to deprive California's Latinos of the soil on which they had so long been settled. As one of the new dominant *yanqui* leaders, Frémont was in a privileged position to benefit from expropriation by a greedy invading society. The Hispanic owners of property, unaccustomed to the intricacies of U.S. law, were slowly forced to surrender their heritage piecemeal.

Land prices rose rapidly. Within a year, San Francisco lots that had sold for two hundred dollars went for ten times that. Because of the government's refusal to reimburse Frémont, he temporarily remained the owner of Alcatraz Island. Later, in 1860, he also bought twelve acres at Black Point, overlooking San Francisco Bay, and he owned land adjacent to Mission San Francisco d'Asis. Jessie borrowed the money for some of these purchases from her family and friends; all had to wait a long time for repayment.

Frémont's little family was temporarily sheltered in a two-room prefabricated dwelling located in the makeshift Happy Valley district near the future Palace Hotel. The little house had been brought from China and put together with pegs. Other Chinese in San Francisco had reassembled it like a puzzle without using so much as a nail. Its inner wall was a cotton cloth partition. Chinese also acted as servants, doing the cooking outside. Toilet facilities were al fresco on the windswept sand dunes nearby. This modest house cost ninety thousand dollars, reflecting the exorbitant prices charged during California's Gold Rush. It was, however, to go up in flames during one of the fires that swept the tent and wooden metropolis, which was not yet built in stone and brick.

Two years earlier, after the California conquest, Frémont led a parade of former military officers who, seeing the opportunity for vast profits, bought land there. By 1850 one of his lots, at the corner of Sansom and C streets, produced a rent of $1,655 per month. Frémont formed a little syndicate that also owned the orchard of former Mission Dolores. But squatters descended like locusts on that property, and he sold his share. Backed by Palmer, Cook & Company, San Francisco's most affluent bankers, he speculated on other properties and ultimately conveyed his claim to Alcatraz Island to that organization.[4]

The strain of the fourth expedition was still upon Frémont, who suffered from headaches and unexplainable nosebleeds and other irritations. During a camping trip through the Tulare Lake region, he complained that "the mosquitoes torment me here so much that I absolutely cannot write." Edward Beale and Frémont now camped together throughout California. Indeed, Beale stretched a leave of absence into resignation from the navy, then turned to disposing of mining claims located on Frémont's land that belonged to Commodore Stockton.

The Pathfinder meant to lose no opportunity for investing in California. He asked B. D. Wilson to reserve both cattle lots ("much cheaper in the south than in the north") and town lots for him at Los Angeles. In 1851 he also unsuccessfully offered Abel Stearns $300,000 for Rancho los Alamitos.[5] Frémont did, however, purchase, with Palmer, Cook & Company, the Pescadero grant on the San Joaquin River north of today's Tracy, California, but its eleven square leagues never yielded a cent of revenue. Invading squatters ran thousands of head of cattle on it as though it were their land. He also asked that Pierson Reading buy for him the Rancho las Pulgas, located in San Mateo County on the western shore of San Francisco Bay, after his land agent, former Consul Larkin, had failed to do so.[6]

Instead, Larkin in February 1847 had bought a much more important property: ten square leagues on the western slope of California's Sierra Nevada ridge. It was called Las Mariposas, "the Butterflies." Larkin charged a commission of 7.5 percent for obtaining this piece of land. It ran for fourteen miles along both sides of the Merced River, but its 44,386 acres (nearly 70 square miles) seemed so barren and rocky that Frémont considered trying to get back the three thousand dollars that Larkin had paid for it. That would have been a serious mistake. Bear Valley, where the ranch was located, was in the heart of the rich Mother Lode region.

Before they could take full possession of the Mariposas property, the Frémonts temporarily moved from San Francisco to Monterey. There they lodged at the former governor's adobe, owned by José Castro, Frémont's former bête noire, now in Mexican exile.

Jessie's baggage had arrived packed with rugs, brooms, willow baskets, and scarce eastern household items. These made her instantly popular at Monterey, where she shared disposable treasures with the wives of future Generals Bennet Riley and E. R. S. Canby. Unfortunately, she stored some of her most precious furnishings in a San Francisco warehouse while awaiting completion of the Bear Valley home, and in one of the fires that swept the city she lost precious family possessions.

Although Jessie did not say so openly, she now experienced the first of many periods out west during which she felt out of sorts. But this was no time to tell John Charles, who was now with her each day instead of in the wilds. She had so resented their separations. As she once put it: "Being away from you is a kind of death. Only with you am I fully alive and well." Despite Jessie's private ailments, these were among the happiest times of her marriage.

The Frémonts were now also surrounded by unending excitement. On January 24, 1848, James Wilson Marshall, once a member of Frémont's battalion, had discovered the first California gold in the millrace of the sawmill he was building for Sutter on the middle fork of the American River. This find set off a worldwide gold rush. Frémont's Sonoran laborers also suddenly struck high-grade ore on his Mariposas tract. They shipped it to him on the coast in one-hundred-pound leather sacks. An elated Jessie claimed that each of these bags was worth $25,000 and that "the bags of gold, in lumps, in dust, in rich bits of rock," began to fill all the drawers and cupboards of their Monterey house.[7]

After news of Frémont's gold discovery reached eastern newspapers, on November 13, 1849, a correspondent for the *New Jersey Daily True American* announced:

> By far the most magnificent discovery is that recently made upon the ranch of Colonel Frémont on the Mariposa river. It is nothing less than a vein of gold in the solid rock. . . . The stone is a reddish quartz, filled with rich veins of gold. . . . Some

stones picked up on top of the quartz strata, without particular selection, yielded two ounces of gold to every twenty-five pounds. Colonel Frémont informed me that the vein had been traced for more than a mile. . . . The discovery has made a great sensation throughout the country.[8]

Las Mariposas was two hundred miles inland from San Francisco. Nearly the size of the District of Columbia, it was shaped like a frying pan. Well timbered by oak and pine trees, the property, raw and undeveloped, was not like a typical rancho. The earliest placer discoveries, free-floating gold "miggets" and flakes in its streams, were quickly exhausted. Freeing the remaining gold from the rock would take large quantities of money to develop veins of auriferous quartz streaked with the blue and green carbonate of copper deposits.

Without clear proof of title, Frémont would find it difficult to obtain a final legal confirmation of this Mexican land grant, which in 1844 had been given by former Governor Micheltorena to Governor Alvarado and which had then been conveyed to Frémont on February 10, 1847. The grant's boundaries were chaotically imprecise and defense of the property's title was costly and time-consuming. On January 21, 1852, Frémont had to file a fresh claim to satisfy U.S. law. He kept secret his personal resurvey of the property's boundaries, because it included mining sites claimed by others. The Merced Mining Company maintained that it had spent $800,000 developing these resources and that Frémont possessed only grazing and agricultural rights, not subsurface ones.

In 1853 the attorney general of the United States, Caleb Cushing, sought to reverse the decision of a federal land commission that had confirmed the grant. Cushing won his case before the Supreme Court of the United States. Frémont then had to engage his lawyer brother-in-law, William Carey Jones, to appeal that decision. Not until 1854 would Jones obtain the Court's confirmation. To quash lingering doubts regarding validity of title, Frémont's personal attorney, Montgomery Blair, also hired former senator and U.S. Attorney General John J. Crittenden. In an impassioned appeal before the Supreme Court, Crittenden recounted Frémont's brilliant services to his country and deplored his constant legal expenses to defend Las Mariposas. Even the grave members of the bench applauded this dramatic performance. Technically, they stopped further appeals against Frémont's claim. Finally, on February 19, 1856, Frémont was invited to the White House, where President Franklin Pierce personally conveyed a signed copy of the confirmed grant to Las Mariposas.

There would be continuing legal hassles about precise mineral rights and boundaries. Frémont had leased questionable mining claims to Biddle Boggs, his first Bear Valley caretaker, for seven years at one thousand dollars per month. Boggs had to defend title at the Mariposa courthouse, the land for which Frémont had given in order to satisfy tax liens. By 1855, Frémont's position was that as long as his properties were in dispute, he refused to pay the eight thousand

Early photograph of the Princeton Mine, one of the richest gold and silver producers on Frémont's Mariposas property. (Reproduced by permission of the Huntington Library, San Marino, California; John F. Duling Collection, box 3)

dollars in taxes due on them. He helped win the Boggs trial on July 2, 1857, but the next year Boggs lost a further appeal to the California Supreme Court, with only Justice Stephen J. Field dissenting. In November 1859, however, the state supreme court reconfirmed the original decision in favor of Frémont. This trial helped affirm Chief Justice Field's advocacy of the rights of large property owners, a doctrine he would later perfect when he joined the U.S. Supreme Court.

It would take Frémont's various lawyers years to collect their legal fees from him. Senator Crittenden was especially bitter that as late as 1861 he had still not been paid. After the senator's death, his son, Robert, threatened Frémont with a duel after the latter refused to admit that he owed the money. On August 11, 1863, Montgomery Blair also complained that he had not been paid for ten years of representing Frémont and offered to settle his claim for only three thousand dollars. Both Gwinn Harris Heap and Frémont's erstwhile friend Beale also ultimately filed suits against him.[9]

Frémont did not hesitate to ruin even old friendships over financial matters.

He never escaped the need for lawyers, especially after he and his partners, Palmer, Cook & Company, extended his claims onto unsurveyed government lands being worked by others. Despite the huge sums Frémont spent for mining operations and legal fees, his creditors might have received their money if he had lived less extravagantly.

Whether at Las Mariposas or San Francisco, John Charles liked to pamper and show off the still young and attractive Jessie. Men outnumbered women by fifty to one in California, and they were expected to please their women. He thus ordered a new lightweight surrey, especially built for her in faraway New Jersey. Accompanied by Ed Beale before they had their falling out, the Frémont family traveled through fields of wild oats flecked with green oak trees in this six-seated carriage, drawn by two sturdy, mismatched bays, trailing a cloud of dust.

Elizabeth Frémont recalled, "We lived a nomadic life at first, driving back and forth between San Jose, Monterey, and San Francisco, very rarely sleeping even for one night under a roof. My mother had the cushions drawn together in the surrey so as to form a mattress, while I slept in the boot. . . . My father and the other men slept in the open on their blankets, or in hammocks."[10] How reminiscent this was of Frémont's boyhood travels in his parents' carriage.

Always a fine horseman, Frémont sometimes went ahead astride one of his two favorite mounts, Sorrel or Abogado. Jessie wrote of their pursuing "bridle paths among the trees," because there were so few definable roads. Wherever they camped, two Indian servants, Juan and Gregorio, knew how to broil quail deliciously or roast eggs for their party in the hot sand. Whenever they reached outlying ranchos and farms, John Charles was greeted as "Don Flemon." Like carefree gypsies, his party presented the Californios with what Jessie called a picture of "youth and health and happiness."[11]

During trips to the coast, Frémont visited his sawmill at San Jose. With lumber at a premium, he used proceeds from the mill to buy vital supplies and equipment for his Mariposa operations. At San Jose he also received the news that President Polk's successor, Zachary Taylor, had offered him an appointment to the international boundary commission. While Jessie expressed pride at such new "government employment with dignity," an appointment "for which his past life had fitted him," she did not want John Charles to go off on another journey, "even though the President had told Frémont that the appointment was compensation for the harsh finding of the military court." Her husband agreed and decided not to give up his newly found independence. As Jessie put it: "That long white envelope, with its official stamp in the corner, which brings such terror into officers' families, and sounds the note of separation to so many, was not again to come to us; henceforth we would direct our own movements."[12] Little did she know how short-lived their bliss would be.

Temporarily, John Charles was having some luck in attracting capital for mining operations. Friends and relatives alike invested in the Mariposas grant. The Aspinwall shipping family sent Frémont money, too. Beale and Frémont's brother-in-law, William Carey Jones, joined former Commodore Robert F. Stockton in leasing quartz diggings on the property, importing in 1850 the first ore-crushing machinery to reach the California mines. Palmer, Cook & Company also invested in a stamp mill there powered by two steam engines. Eventually they would own half of Las Mariposas, leasing parts of it to the Agua Fria Mining Company.

Though visitors described mountainous Bear Valley as resembling in beauty the grandeur of Chamonix in France—even Grindelwald in Switzerland— the Frémonts could not stay put for long. Theirs was a lifetime spent moving from place to place. ❖

Politics would take Frémont away from Las Mariposas. By 1849 a state constitutional convention had framed an antislavery document to his liking, and its delegates had petitioned Congress for admission to the union as a free state. At San Jose, partly as a result of his antislavery views, a convention chose Frémont to be one of California's first senators. Jessie boasted that he could have had the governorship had he wished it. Proudly, he rode through the rain from San Jose back to Monterey—140 miles in thirty-six hours—to bring her news of his selection as senator.

On New Year's Eve of 1850, the Frémonts heard the gun salute of the sidewheeler *Oregon*, which would carry them from Monterey to the East Coast. Jessie recalled that "the rain was pouring in torrents, and every street crossing was a living brook. Mr. Frémont carried me down, warmly wrapped up, to the wharf, where we got into a little boat and rowed out." They were now reconciled to leaving California: "I have found that it changes the climate and removes illness to have the ship's head turned the way you wish to go." The Frémonts left the Mariposas property in the hands of overseers and, almost in a spirit of vindication, headed back to Washington, the scene of the humiliating court-martial.

Once arrived in the East, they found, for a change, even a little comic relief in the air. In 1850 the circus showman Phineas Taylor, alias P. T. Barnum—alert to sensational money-making possibilities—announced that Frémont had captured a "wooly horse" out west. Barnum placed a story in New York newspapers that described this creature as a mixture of an elephant, a deer, a horse, a buffalo, a camel, and a sheep. Its fine, curled camel's-wool hair was nature's last blessing—and could be seen for twenty-five cents, with children at half-price admission. Frémont did not protest this hoax, which was advertised by placing his picture on a large New York billboard. In his autobiography Barnum described the gullibility of the public: "Like a good genius, I threw them not a bone but a regular tit-bit, a bon-bon, and they swallowed it at a single gulp."[1]

On April 23, 1850, San Francisco's *Alta California* reported that the Frémonts had finally reached the nation's capital. There they found that admission of California to statehood would be delayed for months. Senator Frémont and his newly appointed cohort, William M. Gwin, were unable to take their Senate seats until September 11, 1850, the day after California was formally admitted to the Union. In the interim, Frémont did not hesitate to carry on personal mining business, lobbying potential investors in Washington and New York. He and Gwin, in long speeches, had pleaded for the admission of California.

Inquiries about California "came in bushels" from prospective settlers throughout the country. The new senator was not skillful in handling constituents, who formed lines outside his office hoping to meet him. Gold Rush millionaires came to Washington expecting Senator Frémont to present them to President Zachary Taylor. They also wanted quick and decisive action of all sorts.

Instead, Frémont introduced some inflammatory antislavery legislation. The debate that led to the Compromise of 1850 was then raging in Congress. He now infuriated his native South, choosing not to identify himself as a Southerner. As an outsider, he sympathized with downtrodden blacks, for he had experienced the destruction of his own family in the South. Within the substituted Benton family, and especially from its women, he received sympathetic understanding of his antislavery views. In Washington the Bentons introduced him to moderate Southerners who believed in quietly freeing the slaves—as opposed to northern abolitionists who, with less to lose, clamored noisily for their freedom.

In the Senate, Frémont joined a club of gentlemen in stiff collars, with beards and whiskers askew, who argued every procedural point that divided South from North. The southern legislators were his obvious enemies. Frémont's short tenure on Capitol Hill occurred during an age in which senators loaded partisan speeches with truculence. Insults replaced moderation in a Congress racked by sectional discord.

At the beginning of his mere twenty-one working days in the Senate, Frémont ran into a rival of Benton's—the feisty Senator Henry Stuart Foote of Mississippi. On the floor of the Senate, Foote had already drawn a pistol upon Jessie's father, knowing "that Senator Benton was unarmed." Foote, who carried a weapon while he bullied other senators, had even exchanged blows with his fellow Southerner, Jefferson Davis, later president of the Confederacy. Small of stature and with a large bald head, Foote had also engaged in four formal duels and "numerous lesser encounters." During a tense evening session, Foote, obviously upset and transferring his anger from Senator Benton onto his son-in-law, burst into the Senate chamber. Purposely avoiding the slavery issue, Foote instead accused the Pathfinder of sponsoring legislation concerning mining that favored his own California interests. Disoriented, excited, and intoxicated, Foote actually mistook a naval appropriations bill for one concerning California lands. He called that particular legislation disgraceful, stating "that the republic would be dishonored if it passed." Elizabeth Blair Lee wrote to her husband that Senator Foote's disguised violence toward John Charles deeply upset Jessie. While visiting the Blair estate, Silver Springs, "she looked pale enough to make me suspect she was not comfortable in her sensations." Though "self-possessed, she ate very little and would not talk about either her husband or the senate."[2]

Senator Foote's fellow Southern legislators, one of whom called the Path-finder "a thoroughly bad man," charged that in the anteroom of the Senate Frémont "struck Foote and brought blood," ceasing the attack only when separated by other senators. An angered Frémont did indeed tell Foote that he took exception to language "which a gentleman in his position could not use, and which was unworthy of a senator" and insisted upon a retraction "to be signed in the presence of witnesses." When this demand was refused, Frémont threatened a duel. Foote then grazed Frémont's face with his fist before they could be separated. According to the *Albany* (New York) *Atlas*, a day or two later Foote stated that, although he had declared "corrupt private motives" to be behind Frémont's legislation, he had meant no personal denunciation but was merely criticizing a bad piece of legislation. Foote next leaked a message signed "X" to the *Baltimore Sun*, stating that he refused to retract any of his previous statements and censuring Frémont for attempting to prevent free discussion in the Senate. Frémont replied in the *Sun*, on September 30, 1850, that "to avow no retraction is to reaffirm the original insult." He called the notion that he "should attempt to gag senators" absurd. Foote, a hothead, had also insulted Henry Clay, John C. Calhoun, William Seward, Jefferson Davis, and Senator Hale of Vermont, in addition to Benton. Frémont, seeking to avenge these insults, had again proposed a duel, once more courting physical danger. He closed the episode by stating: "Mr Foote went out of his way . . . to deliver a deliberately considered insult and defiance to me."[3]

As in Frémont's earlier encounters with General Kearny, Colonel Mason, and Captain Wilkes, an older man (Foote was born in 1804) had again wronged him. On the one hand, he seemed lodged in these unresolved struggles with authority figures. On the other, seniority was central to the attainment of power. Frémont's opponents—commanding officers, senators, congressmen, and secretaries of state and war—were older than he. Because most young aspirants to power know better than to seek control over their superiors, one is tempted to conclude that Frémont's head-on battles with men like Senator Foote were once again derived from his feelings about his father.

Violence had become a pervasive aspect of national life. Senators were subject to expulsion for carrying concealed weapons; at that time members of

Congress secreted stilettos and revolvers on their persons. The sergeant-at-arms manned a rack in the capitol rotunda where lawmakers were supposed to check their derringers. In 1856, Representative Preston Brooks of South Carolina caned Charles Sumner of Massachusetts on the floor of the Senate, inflicting severe damage to Sumner's spinal cord. Duels were still common. Shootings of all sorts occurred. Family feuds, even retaliatory murders, were unregulated, with guns instantly procurable.

In this chaotic atmosphere Senator Frémont's abolitionist views did not stand him in good stead. Nor did his and Benton's desire to speed confirmation of land titles in California in order to outwit squatters. Although that state had been admitted to the Union in 1850, Kansas remained a battleground between North and South. Behind the scenes, Senator Benton sought to avoid lengthy investigations of existing land grants by federal attorneys. Both of his sons-in-law had acquired extensive acreage throughout California. Their real estate purchases were partly bankrolled by Benton's backers and Frémont's Mariposa gold. Some California grants, furthermore, had not met the legal conditions of either Mexican or American law. Frémont had to prove their validity. Although his brother-in-law Jones issued a report (commissioned by Benton in the Congress) which called the California grant titles nearly perfect, another lawyer and future enemy, Henry Wager Halleck, saw in them convincing evidence of fraud.[4]

With North-South tensions mounting, the proslavery forces in California, a faction loyal to Frémont's colleague, Senator Gwin, wished to unseat the testy young legislator who spoke so openly against owning slaves. Yet Frémont wanted "to be a candidate for re-election," as he wrote a friend. He hastened back to California with Jessie in the fall of 1850, absenting himself from the second session of the thirty-first Congress. In order to receive his pay and per-diem reimbursement, he had to certify falsely that this absence was a result of illness.

In order to get to California, he and Jessie once more had to endure the miseries of Panama. She had once vowed never again to recross the dreaded isthmus. But the alternative would have been long weeks of travel across the plains. Yet Jessie knew all too well that Central America's exotic beauty obscured the dangers of cholera and crocodiles. On the trip her husband's mysterious "Chagres fever" waxed and waned, as did the aching in his left leg, which he had almost lost on the fourth expedition.

When they finally made it back to San Francisco, Frémont found that his brief senatorial career was virtually over. The wayward senator met a barrage of criticism within the state. Its political leaders had instructed him to introduce a law calling for construction of a transcontinental railroad. Instead, he had made the slavery issue his main interest, all the while representing a seriously divided state. "He was not clever in politics," his harshest critic claims.[5]

Senator Gwin tried to excuse Frémont's failure to sponsor railroad legislation by stating that he had simply forgotten to do so. Gwin, however, more than hinted that he himself had written the eighteen bills that Frémont introduced in the course of one day alone.[6] This disparaging revelation severely reduced Frémont's chance to be renominated. Because senators were elected by the legislature, Frémont did make some attempts to lobby its members, asking Abel Stearns, who had power in southern California, to sponsor him at its next meeting. But at the end of 1852, Frémont lost his bid for the Senate on the 144th ballot.[7]

Agreeing with Jessie that politics was "too costly an amusement," he next turned to obtaining more California land. Frémont and his brother-in-law continued to push for speedy confirmation of its 813 pre-American claims, amounting to fourteen million acres. So recently a senator, he was still theoretically in a position to influence legislation that would speed up confirmation of land titles for himself and his associates. His remained the richest mining claim in California.

Little wonder that settlers in the central valley accused Frémont of being uninterested in their claims to public lands. Jones had quietly purchased the twelve-league San Luis Rey and Pala Mission Rancho and also laid claim to thousands of acres near San Mateo and in the Potrero of San Francisco. The latter had been the property of the Haro family, whose two brothers had been murdered by Frémont's men.[8]

Frémont and Jones also used muscle to achieve their acquisitions. John Forster, who had taken possession of lands once part of San Luis Rey Mission, complained that Frémont had galloped into the mission courtyard "with the determination of capturing and executing me, under the idea that I was working against the interests of the United States." In addition to scaring Forster out of his wits, Frémont and his brother-in-law filed for title to the former mission's valuable properties.[9]

Frémont eventually had to give up these time-consuming escapades across the new state by horseback. He returned to remote Las Mariposas, where his presence was truly needed. There Jessie tried anew to put together their former life in the rancho's one-story frame house. The locals were calling it "the Little White House," as if the Frémonts might one day enter the portals of more than this replica of the nation's first mansion. Jessie tried to make up for its starkness by laying down some crimson Brussels carpets and installing costly draperies to cover the bare window frames. She also imported some handsome furniture, including a rosewood piano. All these possessions would be lost when the place burned down in 1866.

Prospective investors and even employees were put up at the Mariposas White House until they could find housing. When Jessie published her *Far West Sketches* (1890), she expressed pride that "the Colonel would not employ men who drank." But he did feed them well on the ranch, importing a German baker to create superb pastries.[10] Frémont kept busy in nearby Mariposa as well as on the ranch. He owned the whole town and established an assay office in its two-story Oso House. He was not only lord of the manor, but also head of a fiefdom. Founded in 1850, his town of Mariposa was the county seat, and its streets—Jessie, Charles, Bullion, and Jones—he named for members of the family. That year the place numbered twenty stores and a hotel. Some fifteen hundred people lived in town and another three thousand around its perimeter.

Unable to placate resolute miners who had settled like locusts on his lands, Frémont faced seemingly endless litigation over the title to Las Mariposas. Both Indians and squatters raided the rancho's stock of cattle and horses. Driven from their lands by miners in search of gold, the Indians had been reduced to starvation. The federal government sent peace commissioners to investigate their plight. To soften their transition to reservation life, treaties were signed that promised them food in return for good behavior. Frémont was to figure in their relief program. Though he was an invaded landowner, he and Beale supplied the natives with beef.[11]

Before Beale was appointed California's superintendent of Indian affairs, he contracted with Frémont to supply $183,825 in beef for the Indians of northern California. Together they drove close to two thousand head of cattle up from Los Angeles; for them Frémont charged $90 per head, less 25 percent to Beale for loaning money to purchase the animals. His old scout Alexis Godey was to sell this meat, intended for the Indians, to miners, while Frémont maintained that the animals were strays and not part of the herd bought for the government. He did not escape charges of irregularities concerning these cattle purchases. Back in 1847, he had procured twenty-eight horses and mules as well as sixty-six cattle, presumably for his troops, but these animals had ended up at Las Mariposas. The army refused to approve payment for them.

As for the livestock Frémont had acquired to feed the local natives, Indian Commissioner George W. Barbour had promised reimbursement by means of a treaty he had negotiated with the Mariposa Indians. Frémont had paid for the cattle with treasury drafts at the rate of twenty cents per pound. When he needed cash, he sold these promissory drafts at a discount. The notes were repeatedly resold. Purchasers hoped that Senator Benton could persuade Congress to rescue Frémont's obligations by a special appropriation. But, suspicious of fraud, it refused to pass such a bill and, furthermore, failed to ratify Barbour's treaty. The Indians therefore never received their promised beef. Both Frémont and Beale had to answer charges of corruption. Beale threatened to sue his partner for payment of overdue bills resulting from their cattle speculations—a total of $150,000, then a huge sum.

In 1854, partly as a result of his dealings with Frémont, Beale was removed as superintendent of Indian affairs following charges of financial irregularities.

Frémont in one of his pensive moods: he had a studious side to him and, like other explorers, consulted the best books available about the regions he planned to traverse. (From the C. C. Pierce Collection, Huntington Library, San Marino, California.)

Both men lied about their cattle contracts. Frémont and Beale claimed hundreds of thousands of dollars, including interest, for the overpriced beef they had supplied to the government. Their fraudulent bills of lading were repeatedly repudiated by the War Department and the secretary of the interior.[12]

All the turbulence surrounding Las Mariposas was hardly making it the retreat Frémont had hoped for. Jessie was becoming openly critical of life there: "Indians, bears, & miners have made it lose its good qualities as a country place & it is very out of the way," she complained to the Blairs. "California has no attraction for me and I trust a stay of a few months may be all it requires of Mr. Frémont. We should only be in his way for any visit that was not to last for a year or two," she maintained. As the Mariposas was so infernally hot in the summer and cold in the winter, she was delighted when Frémont sought again to buy Stearns's Rancho los Alamitos, located in a more temperate climate near Los Angeles. But Stearns at age forty-four had taken a bride of fourteen, Arcadia Bandini, who wished to stay on the land. His offer of $300,000 refused, Frémont alternatively tried to develop the southern part of Las Mariposas for cattle raising and agriculture.[13]

Always looking beyond Las Mariposas, which was not ideal for cattle raising, he next bought a third of Rancho el Pescadero in San Joaquin County for five thousand dollars, but squatters soon descended upon the property. Confirmation of Frémont's grant to the Rancho Laguna de los Gentiles (Casamayome) and other Mexican grants remained long delayed. Located on geyser and quicksilver lands in northern Sonoma County, that rancho's title was clearly fraudulent. On one occasion the *Alta California* called its owner "the great national scapegoat for all great land-grabbers."[14] In 1851 he purchased a half-interest in the Rancho San Emigdio from Pablo de la Guerra for two thousand dollars, and he hired Alexis Godey to run cattle on its 18,000 acres. Ed Beale would in 1869 buy out Frémont's portion in order to help him raise sorely needed funds. The ranch later became the nucleus of the giant Kern County Land Company. Frémont also tried but failed to buy the rich Almaden quicksilver mine (with William A. Leidesdorff) for thirty thousand dollars, and he attempted unsuccessfully to acquire the Santa Anna del Chino rancho, consisting of over 100,000 acres. Finally, in 1854 he and a group of speculators sought to use the land grant of José Santillan, a priest, in order to claim title to San Francisco's Mission Dolores, but this effort, tied up for years, ended in failure.

Frémont's Washington, D.C., and California setbacks encouraged him to look elsewhere for the adulation he sought. Jessie, too, was more than ready to join him in that search, even if it meant going abroad for a time. While he was fiddling with so many land deals, Europeans had begun to discover the magic of his earlier explorations, and they were ready to honor him in ways that no longer seemed available in California or at his nation's capital. ❖

Worldwide, naturalists and scholars whom Frémont called "men of science" began to appreciate anew his past contributions to exploration. He was comfortable in the social and intellectual circles in which naturalists moved, compared to the society of self-serving politicos and unbending military commanders against whom he had struggled. At a time when science was being professionalized and amateurism was disappearing, he called the naturalists "the world's true cosmopolitans."

Among these scientists was the naturalist-explorer Alexander von Humboldt, who praised Frémont in his book *Aspects of Nature* (1849). Years earlier the Pathfinder had named the Humboldt River for the eminent scientist. Baron von Humboldt, the most renowned of his generation of scientists, had traveled to Mexico, South America, and parts of the United States. His brother William was Prussia's minister of education. Together they smoothed the way for Frémont to receive a high international honor. Humboldt, writing from Sans Souci, former home of Frederick the Great, sent Frémont a great golden medal, "for Progress in the Sciences," bestowed by the king of Prussia. Humboldt also transmitted to Frémont membership in the Berlin Geographical Society. After the death of the English writer Thomas Babington Macaulay, in 1859 Frémont would also receive the Prussian "Cross of the Order of Merit," replacing Macaulay on its roster of notables.[1]

Frémont's new-found popularity coincided with an explosive period of discovery. At midcentury it seemed as though the entire world had become an outdoor museum of natural history. Frémont himself, as a student of nature, had collected more than a thousand specimens. His fellow naturalists greeted each exotic new animal or plant with wonder. From unexplored areas of the world collectors brought back the moon moths of Java as well as California's 275-foot-high redwoods, which the English called Wellingtonias rather than Sequoias. Frémont's expeditions had brought back mule trains laden with specimens far more unusual than the potted ferns and palms to be seen at most municipal "conservatories."

The Pathfinder's cartographers had also supplied unique maps and charts to geographical society libraries throughout Europe at about the same time that the Indian paintings of George Catlin stirred interest in distant America. Frémont's artists were not as well known as Catlin, but their sketches of the American West helped to flesh out its features dramatically.[2] In the landscapes of American naturalist painters the human being seemed but a small part of the wilderness, engulfed by the immensity of strange and exotic creatures and plants.

As the study of natural history was systematized, the fauna, flora, and geology of the Far West were displayed in Old World museums. In both Europe and America spectators crowded into circuses, Wild West shows, and zoos to see the West's buffalo, beaver, and land otter. In an age about to be captured by the evolutionary theories of Charles Darwin and Thomas Huxley, the archaeological digs of Heinrich Schliemann at ancient Troy and Frémont's western exploits attracted big audiences that craved visual contact with the unknown. As early as 1845, Catlin had opened Wild West shows in Paris and London that featured *tableaux vivants* of costumed Indians. Frémont, too, would bring his own "moving diorama" of the American West to London.[3]

Frémont's new fame led Professor James Rhoads to proclaim that "the three greatest events in the world" were connected with the rise to power of the United States. He saw Frémont at the very center of this process: "Columbus marked a pathway to the new-found world. Washington guided and sustained the patriots who consecrated that world . . . and Frémont lifted the veil which, since time first began, had hidden from view the real El Dorado."[4]

In 1836, Ralph Waldo Emerson had introduced similar thoughts in his essay entitled *Nature*. His European audiences yearned for knowledge of the Golden West that lay beyond the boundaries of "civilization." Emerson, attracted by the Pathfinder's *Report of the Exploring Expedition to the Rocky Mountains*, called him, quite erroneously, a "buffalo-hunter." In 1850, Emerson's journal entries gave Frémont and other explorers credit for having "outlived their robuster comrades by more intellect." Though he had some doubts about Frémont's behavior, he envisioned a mythical "American College" with academic chairs filled by "Allston, Greenough, Nuttall, Audubon, Frémont, and Irving."[5]

The poet Walt Whitman also extolled Frémont's explorations. Whitman shared his abolitionist stand as well as a continuing faith in the credo of America's Manifest Destiny. Yet another writer, Henry Wadsworth Longfellow, in his *Evangeline* (1847) used Basil Lajeunesse, one of Frémont's hardiest voyageurs, as a central character. Longfellow acknowledged that Frémont had deeply "touched my imagination."[6]

With all this emerging adulation as background, Frémont did not need much coaxing to decide upon a trip abroad in order to receive his European decorations. Furthermore, David Hoffman, a New Yorker whom he had sent to London as an agent, seemed to be causing nothing but trouble. Though purportedly there to sell or lease Mariposas land, Hoffman wrote letters back to the States saying that he was most disturbed by Frémont's "petulance," "irresolution," and "unsuitable economy." He also thought the explorer possessed "a little of the leven of humbug."[7] All the while, Hoffman sought to impress his employer back in California by sending Frémont his glowing dispatches to the *Times* of London, which he had beautifully bound in red Morocco leather. The agent, who was himself quirky and eccentric, was unable to handle Frémont's contrary moods.

Frémont may have had it in mind to fire Hoffman even before he left for England on the sidewheeler *Cunarder Africa*, taking along Jessie, who had been ailing and needed a change of climate. They were accompanied by their infant son, John Charles, Jr., who had been born at their Stockton Street house in San Francisco on April 19, 1851, and Frémont's niece Frances Cornelia (known as Nina). The family landed at Liverpool on March 22, 1852, tired from so long a voyage.

Hoffman made elaborate arrangements to meet his superior. He had worked for Frémont in London for more than two years, but the Pathfinder now proceeded to ignore him. Meanwhile, confusion resulted when two Americans, Thomas Denny Sargent and J. Eugene Flandin, called the land that Hoffman had leased fraudulent. As a result, Frémont was sued in an English court. Hoffman, meanwhile, was in the middle, confused and irritated. Although Frémont refused to see him, he kept ordering him by letter to produce records of land sales. Months passed without Frémont's acknowledging Hoffman's communications concerning English leases.

Frémont also undercut Hoffman by entering into negotiations directly with foreign prospects. At one point even Senator Benton, in trying to sell the property himself, thought he had disposed of the whole of Las Mariposas to Sargent for one million dollars in a negotiation later repudiated by Frémont, completely outside Hoffman's knowledge or power. The legal complications, foreign and domestic, were becoming massively wearing on both men as distrust of Frémont's land claims made English investors wary of risking their capital. Never a good businessman, Frémont failed to furnish his agents accurate data about the mining sites he wished to lease. As a result, Hoffman had difficulty borrowing capital. Hoffman's correspondence is filled with secret complaints concerning "the colonel's most impenetrable and most impossible indifference" as well as Frémont's "disreputable laziness."[8] Mostly that indifference was another example of Frémont's old habit of keeping people at arm's length, or distancing.

Hoffman did not realize the pressures that Frémont was experiencing. On June 6, 1850, the *San Francisco Chronicle* had reported that representatives of the Pathfinder were making leases to all sorts of speculators, among them Charles Savage Homer, father of the American artist Winslow Homer. Homer followed Frémont to London, begging him to lease a particular Mariposas mining site said to be of "incredible richness."[9]

In these years creditors who thought the Frémonts truly rich dunned them incessantly. Mexican War claims dogged him all the way to London. One night, the international celebrity, who had recently been honored with the gold medal of Britain's Royal Geographical Society, escorted Jessie to London's Clarendon House to attend a grand dinner. Suddenly, in front of that building four tweedy constables arrested him, then took him to Sloman's Lock-Up on Chancery Lane. They alleged that he had to pay notes for $19,500 that he had drawn in Los Angeles when acting as California's governor. Those drafts had been sold to English holders. Secretary of State James Buchanan had not honored the drafts because Congress had made no appropriation to cover them. The Englishmen who had bought this "paper" had denounced Frémont as a swindler. After he was released from prison, Frémont immediately wrote Benton from the Clarendon. He implored the senator to use his influence in order to obtain congressional appropriations to cover past debits accrued on behalf of the government:

> I have been arrested for $50,000. . . . I spent one night in a "Sponging House" (ante room to the jail), being arrested at night, and was bailed out the next day, by George Peabody, the eminent American merchant here. . . . If I was a great patriot as you, I would go to jail and stay there until Congress paid these demands, now over a million, but my patriotism has been oozing out for the last five years. As my detention here promises to be long, you will greatly contribute to our comfort by getting me appointed chargé to some neighboring power, to protect me from further arrests and help to pay expenses.[10]

Once again Frémont sought to enlist his father-in-law's power. His letter, however, dripped with sarcasm about the senator's interference in the sale of his properties. Although Benton sent the communication on to Daniel Webster, the new secretary of state, tension again mounted between Frémont and Benton, especially after Frémont nullified his father-in-law's sale of Las Mariposas. About the rift between them, Jessie wrote a friend: "This is only the expression of years of distrust of Mr. Frémont's judgment. Since the revoked sale of the Mariposas . . . father has put great constraint on his temper and now he has what he considers a fair occasion for an opposition."[11]

In London, Jessie, who was panicked by the jailing of her husband, had burst in on Hoffman during the night of the arrest to ask him for bail money. He responded that Frémont had not granted him even half an hour to deal with matters "that consumed more than two years of the most precious part of my life." Hoffman had found that both Frémonts displayed a tendency to disconnect, showing no regard for his own financial distress. They were his debtors, not creditors. She would not hear any of these excuses. Hoffman thereupon refused to give her any money, having already organized a total of twenty-one separate "companies" for Frémont and having not received a farthing for his loyal efforts. Instead, Jessie labeled him "a great rascal."[12]

Frémont next filed suit against Hoffman in Chancery Court. Incensed, Hoffman scribbled the words: "Wonder of wonders! Inconsistency of inconsistencies! Impudence of impudences!!" He wrote to the Frémonts that their best advocate abroad was being treated by them as a villain. While receiving no salary, he had dutifully paid all the bills in Frémont's London office and had also financed both English and European land sales out of pocket.[13]

In London, Frémont hired a solicitor, John Duncan, to draw up *An Answer to the Pamphlet of Mr. David H. Hoffman* (1852). Frémont labeled Hoffman's allegations "a jumbled and confused mass of assertions, slanders, untruths, and very few facts" and "stupid effusions." Senator Benton also condemned Hoffman's leases as fraudulent in the *London Globe*. Hoffman wrote a final letter that accused Frémont of personal cruelty: "You have taken the whole matter out of the hands of honesty, devotion, faith, to entrust it all to villainy."[14]

Finally, Frémont fired his bewildered London agent, though the legal proceedings would prove prohibitive. As for Hoffman, he suffered a breakdown. Frémont, having virtually ignored his agent's very presence until litigation between them began, seems to have "disturbed his emotional equilibrium."[15]

In addition to Hoffman, Frémont had deputized other agents to act on his behalf abroad. Among them was George Washington Wright, a partner in Palmer, Cook & Company, who had accompanied Frémont to England. Another agent, Charles F. Mayer, endured relations that were no more happy than Hoffman's. Mayer described Frémont as a "spoiled child of fortune and of too sudden and too superlative fame. He is the most provokingly dilatory and fussy man. . . . Even in passing through Baltimore he did not give me the chance of an hour's conference with him . . . as he is on the wing." Repeatedly, Frémont made excuses regarding why he could not meet with his own agents, about which Mayer wrote: "His immediate remissness is unpardonable. He called Frémont's "indifference the most impenetrable and most impossible and laziness the most disreputable."[16]

For both Frémont and his wife, London provided too many exciting distractions. Their days were crammed with teas, dinners, and receptions. Jessie chose to attend a London school of court etiquette before being presented to Queen Victoria. For that occasion, to emphasize her good figure she wore a pink silk gown with moire train, and she was accompanied by a little girl, suitably hired for the event. One might be dying of social fatigue, Jessie averred, "but no sign of it must be made" when curtsying before the queen and her adored prince consort, Albert, in the throne room of Buckingham Palace. In turn, the Frémonts invited members of the court to view displays of ore samples from the Mariposa mines at the Crystal Palace's 1851 Great International Exhibition.

John Charles, now an honored explorer, also met Britain's greatest living hero, the Duke of Wellington, and he was subsequently invited to Woolwich, where he visited vessels being readied to search the polar regions for the missing explorer Sir John Franklin, who had been lost in the Canadian wilds since 1846.[17]

Never publicity-shy, Frémont used a new means of advertising his California properties. He hired a lecturer to speak twice daily at London's Egyptian Hall. Audiences of up to 600 persons showed up to hear a mixture of the Pathfinder's exploits and fulsome descriptions of his realty holdings. During a period of six months, 300,000 persons attended these sessions. A colored "moving panorama," subsidized by Senator Benton, with an accompanying pamphlet advertised the gold locked within the slopes of the Sierra Nevada. Frémont presented his oil-painted diorama first in Boston during 1849, then later in London. Put together by John Skirving, an enterprising Englishman, it was 25,000 feet in length and took two hours to unreel. The pamphlet that accompanied the show boasted that Frémont had "discovered a vein of solid gold stretching for two miles."[18]

Both George Catlin's and Buffalo Bill's more famous Wild West shows had also opened in London before Queen Victoria—replete with a panoply of Indians and cowboys—long after Frémont's diorama promoted his California properties. Eventually he took this moving tableau to Paris's Théâtre de Variétés. There Frémont enticed Prince Louis Lucien Bonaparte to act as president of the Nouveau Monde Compagnie, which planned mining operations on the Mariposas tract.[19]

On the continent the Frémonts frequented the company of the Bonapartes. They took special pride in meeting Eugénie de Montijo, about to become empress of France, and in attending her wedding to Napoleon III at Notre Dame Cathedral. His was called a "carnival empire," gaudy, glittering, and in stark contrast to Frémont's American West. Jessie described their Parisian life ecstatically:

> After many years of sleeping on the ground, and a wet saddle for a pillow, it was delightful for Mr. Frémont to have the silk hangings, the down pillows of his warm room, where a Sevres bowl of roses near his head replaced the weapons so long needed. Yet he had a boyish satisfaction at times in taking a long walk in the teeth of sleety wind and rain.[20]

The Frémonts would on a later trip meet Hans Christian Andersen, the renowned Danish writer of children's fairy tales. Although Jessie called him "a supreme egotist," he latched onto her and John Charles as hardy representatives of a frontier America that enthralled this sentimental storyteller. All his life Andersen, like Frémont, craved acceptance. Born ugly, and barely legitimized, he had failed as an actor, singer, and playwright, but his fairy tales had gained him the company of celebrities, including the Frémonts, who were equally flattered.

Jessie, who relished the glitter of European society, compared her limited perquisites at home with those of Parisian women of similar status but much greater power than she possessed: "In France she might have ruled openly in the councils of the nation; in America she merely gave suggestions and advice to those who controlled the people's destiny."[21] Their Paris apartment was staffed by a retinue of French servants from whom she selected two maids to take back to the States. There they would serve her family for twenty years.

Despite heavy indebtedness, the Frémonts at different times maintained residences in New York and San Francisco and on the Champs-Elysées. Now there were French governesses for the children, sleek carriages, and silk gowns for Jessie. A profligate world of fine china and glassware, deep-piled carpets, and rare French wines transformed luxury into excess. Each grand tour of Europe would see Jessie bringing home more fine Meissen, Sèvres, and Wedgewood services. The oil paintings, silver trays, and furniture with inlays of brass, Delft porcelain, and mother-of pearl imitated the world of Queen Victoria.

Abroad or at home, only credit supported the family's high living. Palmer, Cook & Company, formerly squatters on Las Mariposas, became Frémont's biggest creditors. By 1851, that banking firm owned an undivided half of that neglected property. While debts piled up, the family stayed on in Paris for fourteen months, partly because Jessie was pregnant again. After a hard delivery, Anne Beverly, named for John Charles's mother, was born there on February 1, 1853. Jessie had to stay long abed thereafter.

When she, in late spring of that year, returned with the children to America, she again took along Nina Frémont, her husband's troublesome niece. Unpredictable and impulsive, the girl caused incessant problems. Halfway across the Atlantic, a discouraged Jessie wrote the Blairs: "I have had the blues desperately." These close friends were lately alarmed by her not-so-hidden sense of desolation. The crossing was a long one, with the water rough and the sea grey. John Charles again was not with her but was to follow on another ship. (Later, it was more than gossip that he traveled across the Atlantic with another woman.)

On July 11, Jessie reached Francis Blair's Silver Springs estate outside Washington. There, little Anne died of a "digestive ailment," probably intestinal influenza. John Charles, who eventually showed up, reacted to this loss by praising Jessie: "It was she who remained dry eyed to comfort me, for I was unmanned over the cruelty of this bereavement. Her calm stoicism, so superior to mere resignation, soon shamed me into control."[22]

As for her husband, he would seek other outlets to quiet his sorrow. Another chancy adventure would, as usual, win out over practicality. In his memoirs one finds the possible boyhood origin of this conflict within him: "A single book sometimes enters fruitfully into character or pursuit. I had two such. One was a chronicle of men who had made themselves famous by brave and noble deeds, or infamous by cruel and base acts. With a schoolboy enthusiasm I read these stories over and over again." A second book that he admired "was a work on practical astronomy," which appealed to Frémont's second side—the observer of nature.[23]

The Pathfinder needed once more to combine the excitements of the trail with the life of explorer and scientist. Whether in Europe or America, Frémont again felt the emotional tug of the American West as if it were a magnet. Unable to bear the crowded cities of either continent, he could have said, as did Sir Richard Burton, that "discovery is mostly my mania."[24] Both men were adventurers who had to rove, just as their parents had been inveterate wanderers.

In 1853 a fifth expedition would offer another escape back across the western mountains and deserts. Each such venture provided a sort of self-renewal. Frémont's long involvement with the West's many landscapes had not yet ended. ❖

The Fifth Expedition

By the early 1850s the American Congress, responding to widespread public interest, finally stood ready to consider a series of transcontinental railroad surveys. Frémont believed himself to be the ideal leader to head up such plans. No one had worked harder than he and Senator Benton to keep the idea of a Pacific railroad system alive. But the politicians who fashioned this legislation had not forgotten his court-martial trial, undistinguished senatorial career, or the disastrous fourth expedition. Meanwhile he yearned, almost pathologically, to be on the move again, to be at the head of a new exploratory party, one that was firmly his own.

Writing for London's *Sunday Morning Chronicle* of January 4, 1851, Frémont tried to minimize the ill effects of his last expedition. If he was to implement a transcontinental railroad system, he must overcome public doubts about the treacherous mountain passes through whose snows his men had already slogged so disastrously.

Late in 1852, Congress authorized $150,000 to survey five midcontinental all-weather routes. Jefferson Davis, then secretary of war, designated these routes to run from the thirty-second to the forty-seventh parallels. Staffed with natural scientists, artists, and collectors, several exploring parties would travel a range of trails from a northern Saint Paul-to-Seattle line to a southern route through Texas and the Gadsden Purchase. The principal mountain passes along each route were critical to selection of a final trackway.

The key role in determining choice of a final route would be played by Jefferson Davis. This future president of the Southern Confederacy, a gaunt and juiceless man, became Franklin Pierce's secretary of war in 1853. He, too, had fought in the Mexican War, but unlike Frémont, he was a West Pointer who had distinguished himself at the Battle of Buena Vista. Davis had also been a senator from Mississippi during Frémont's brief period in Congress. He well remembered Frémont's quarrel with his colleague, Senator Foote. And he continued to look down upon a sniveling former Southerner turned abolitionist. Davis and Foote had opposed California's admission to the Union and detested Frémont's racial views.

As the federal government would choose only one ultimate route, Davis favored a thirty-fifth parallel line that ran through his native south. He went along with surveying various routes, however, as a gesture of political good faith toward the northern states. Sidelined, Frémont and Benton still believed that the avenue to the Pacific lay along the thirty-eighth parallel.

Several antagonists vied for the right to explore one of the routes to the Pacific. High in the pantheon of the topographical engineers was William Emory, the West Pointer who had served on Kearny's California staff and a fierce enemy of Frémont during the court-martial. Emory from 1848 to 1853 was chief commissioner and astronomer in determining the boundary with Mexico under the Gadsden Treaty. He and other officers had not frittered away their careers by thwarting key government figures.

An ailing Senator Benton again entered the fray, wanting Frémont finally to prove that the thirty-eighth parallel route was not too far north for winter use. Benton was no longer a senator after his defeat in 1851, but was serving as a congressman, his political clout vanished. Though still angry with Frémont, for Jessie's sake he insisted that his son-in-law was still the ideal person to carry on the best transcontinental survey. Benton also wanted Edward Fitzgerald Beale as co-commander of the expedition. Beale had conducted a reconnaissance of a wagon route to California, where he had been appointed superintendent of Indian affairs. Beale and his cousin, Gwinn Harris Heap, agreed with Benton and Frémont that a central route to the Pacific was indispensable, and they, too, wrote effective letters to newspapers on its behalf.[1]

Congress allotted forty thousand dollars for exploration of the central route. Here was a chance for Frémont to wipe away the record of the disastrous fourth expedition. Instead, Davis appointed Captain John Williams Gunnison, another West Pointer, to the new command. Gunnison, forty-six years old, was already known for his reconnaissance of the Great Basin, with Captain Howard Stansbury, which had resulted in a report entitled *The Mormons ... Their Rise and Progress, Peculiar Doctrines, Present Condition, and Prospects* (1852). He now set about to explore a route through the Cochetopa Pass instead of the controversial Bill Williams Pass that Frémont still stubbornly favored.

When it became apparent that Benton would be defeated in his struggle to gain government backing for the thirty-eighth parallel route, he once more raised private funds for a new expedition. In September 1853, Frémont recruited twenty-

During the 1850s the office of the secretary of war produced the thirteen-volume *Reports of Explorations and Surveys to Ascertain the Most Practicable and Economical Route for a Railroad from the Mississippi River to the Pacific Ocean* (Washington, D.C., 1855–60). Although Frémont was left out of that effort, this prairie scene by G. Sohon Del on a lithographic plate illustrates the artistic possibilities available during Frémont's fifth and last expedition.

two trail companions, first at Saint Louis and later at Westport Landing. These men included ten of his favorite Delawares and four Wyandot Indians who were to hunt game for wages of two dollars per day. The natives would furnish their own horses, and Frémont would provide saddles and ammunition. Each pack animal had a large letter *F* branded into its hide. Other stores included India-rubber blankets and preserved cream, milk, and eggs to be tested for the supplier. Although Frémont carried along bank drafts, he never fully paid his Indian scouts.[2]

Quite appropriately for an abolitionist, Frémont took along, as on his second expedition, a freed black man, the mulatto Albert Lea, who had worked for the Bentons. But the Pathfinder also broke his practice of past expeditions by appointing a second in command, William H. Palmer, whose family owned Palmer, Cook & Company in San Francisco, Frémont's bank. The banking family provided some funds, but for the most part Benton and various Saint Louis merchants subsidized Frémont's latest attempt to recross the southern Rockies in winter.

Now there entered a new firsthand witness to Frémont's activities at age forty. Solomon Nuñes Carvalho, painter, photographer, and Sephardic Jew, like Frémont was born at Charleston. Frémont took him along after reading Humboldt's *Cosmos*, which suggested use of a daguerreotypist on scientific expeditions. Carvalho's account would become a major source concerning the explorer's last expedition. Because Richard Kern had joined the Gunnison party, Frémont needed other specialists as well.[3]

To operate the scientific equipment he had bought in Paris, he signed on Frederick Eggloffstein, a twenty-nine-year-old Bavarian topographer and landscape artist who would become the "father" of the half-tone photographic process. More highly educated than Carl Preuss, he was every bit as exacting in his cartographic work, and less cantankerous. But, like Carvalho, Egloffstein had never gone to the farthest West. Max Strobel, who had been with an expedition to survey the forty-ninth parallel, also joined Frémont's expedition at his own expense. These technicians were to plot railroad construction sites by sketches and by the use of calotypes or "talbotypes," brownish-tinted prints made by a process that was an improvement over daguerreotypes.[4]

Frémont had hoped to complete the fifth expedition in only two months. But his illness, either from rheumatic fever or sciatica of the leg, delayed departure for almost sixty days. Even then he could leave only by taking along a German physician, Dr. A. Ebers, from Saint Louis. He had previously ordered his small party to move out of Westport toward Shawnee Mission, and when the explorer finally caught up with his men, they were pleased to hear the jingle of his spurs. Camped in Kansas for weeks on end, they feared that the expedition would never really get started. As Carvalho recalled: "No father who had been absent from his children could have been received with more enthusiasm and real joy."[5] Carvalho, when asked why he would risk his life with such an adventurer, replied: "My estimation of character is seldom wrong. . . . If I felt safe enough to impulsively decide to accompany him, without personally knowing him, how much safer do I now feel from the short time I have known him."[6]

Practically before the fifth expedition got underway, the party was trapped by a great prairie fire, probably caused by the carelessness of the group itself. When a fireball jumped the Saline Fork of the Kansas River, Frémont and his men escaped only by making a fifteen-mile dash on horseback through the blazing grass that threatened to trap them on all sides.

By November 18, 1853, the group reached William Bent's old fort on the Arkansas River, which they found virtually destroyed. Repeated Comanche raids had caused its abandonment after Charles Bent had been killed in an 1847 insurrection. As the old location had also fallen prey to cholera transmitted by overland parties, Charles's brother, William, had blown up the site in 1849. He then moved downstream to the Big Timbers region to start another fort. During previous expeditions Frémont had spent days on end with the Bents. This time he could spare only one week for rest and provisioning. He obtained several buffalo-skin lodges from Bent that were large enough to house not only himself but the men as well. He also needed fresh horses and bought heavy stockings, gloves, moccasins, and other necessities in addition to dried meat, coffee, and tobacco.[7]

At the new fort Frémont cashiered one of his men, James F. Milligan, a roisterous ne'er-do-well whom the leader accused of leaking his diary entries to newspapers. On both the fourth and fifth expeditions Frémont could not afford to pay all of his men, but Milligan was actually on his payroll and therefore had none of the rights of those group members who had grubstaked themselves. Furthermore, the Pathfinder could hardly be blamed for not wanting acts of cannibalism described, should they occur again.

Milligan recorded his own sacking: "Col. Frémont gave me a lecture about 'contention in camp' and exercised his power by suspending me from duty until I became better tempered." Meanwhile, the offender resented the way in which Frémont and his "nigger" servant remained "snug in his little tent," hoarding "cannisters of soup" while other members of the expedition had to make do with lesser rations. In fairness to Frémont, it is impossible to substantiate these charges of self-indulgence.

Rather than leave Milligan stranded at the edge of the wilderness, Frémont put him in charge of some lame horses and mules left behind at the fort. The Pathfinder hoped to obtain fresh mounts for the return trip from Beale in California. But he never returned to pick up Milligan at Bent's Fort, for which the aggrieved man severely criticized him: "Selfishness, the predominant feature with which he appears to be endowed, has been fully illustrated." Milligan also accused him of using his men as "tools for a greater one's designs." Rationalizing his dismissal by Frémont, he told members of the expedition that he did not want to stay in the service of such "an ungrateful man." He expressed pity for those who continued on with such a selfish and ambitious leader, "totally devoid of gratitude."[8]

Frémont left Bent's Fort on November 25, 1853, with twenty-one men and fifty-four animals. Although the arduous terrain he had faced in 1848 lay ahead, he hoped to avoid wintering in the high country. By traveling lightly, he would achieve greater speed through the dangerous mountain passes. But his estimate of making it to California in sixty days was unrealistic. Indians met along the way were predicting a long, heavy winter, based upon the evening "fire light," or aurora borealis. In addition, the buffalo had migrated much farther south than usual. But because there was less snow on the ground than during the fourth expedition, passage over the mountains was somewhat easier this time. Frémont followed the wagon ruts left by Captain Gunnison over the 10,160 foot Cochetopa Pass, or Buffalo Gate, which they reached on December 14, 1853. Trees felled by Gunnison's expedition cleared a path even through snowed-in country. Gunnison and six of his men, including Richard Kern, would be slain by Paiute Indians in Utah. Trying to avoid previous mistakes, Frémont pressed on beyond the valley of the Rio Grande over the Sawatch Mountains.

As his party lumbered onward in a northwestward direction, they found the Indians in a state of high excitation. The Utes, Cheyennes, Pawnees, and Arapahos at turns were at war with one another. The resultant confusion created fear among the men. At one point some Utes threatened to attack the camp of the "Great Captain" because of controversy over a horse that his men had slaughtered. But he refused to give these natives gunpowder as compensation and did not venture outside his lodge to deal personally with them. Carvalho was impressed by his firmness: "He at once expressed his determination not to submit to such imposition, and at the same time laughed at their threats. I could not comprehend his calmness. I deemed our position most alarming, surrounded as we were by armed savages."[9]

Carvalho also described Frémont's need for privacy while on the trail in an account that varies greatly from Milligan's sarcasm. His "lodge was sacred from all and everything that was immodest, light, or trivial; each and all of us entertained the highest regard for him. The greatest etiquette and deference were always paid to him, although he never ostensibly required it," wrote Carvalho. Respecting his sense of reserve, Carvalho also reported an "unexceptionable deportment demanded from us, the same respect with which we were always treated and which we ever took pleasure in reciprocating."[10] As he wrote these gushing comments in support of Frémont's candidacy for the presidency in 1856, Carvalho hoped for a government post. His nephew, in fact, criticized the way in which he toadied up to the Pathfinder, having earlier criticized him: "It would astonish you to hear him talk *now* in favor of Frémont, after having heard his conversation on his return from California," the nephew wrote in a cynical letter, "Alas! Money! Money!!"[11]

Carvalho also reminds us of Frémont's severity when the occasion required: "One of the officers on guard [Frederick Eggloffstein] left the animals and came into camp to warm himself. Col. Frémont saw him at the fire and asked if he had been relieved. He said 'no'. Col. F. told him that he expected him to travel on foot during the next day's journey." Although the punishment struck Carvalho as quite heavy, the party had already lost five horses and mules to thieves who had done their stealing only after Eggloffstein left his midnight post. Fortunately, they were apprehended and the animals recaptured. "Had we lost our animals, we must have perished," Carvalho lamented, "exposed as we were on those vast prairies to bands of Pawnee, Comanche, and other hostile Indians."[12]

As the expedition traversed remote spots that no one would again visit for decades, both Carvalho and Eggloffstein encountered difficulty using their scientific equipment. Each day they had to be sure that the packers carefully handled the delicate apparatus. Though the thermometer at times stood at from twenty to thirty degrees below zero, in addition to calotypes they produced surprisingly good daguerreotypes. Eggloffstein sometimes stood up to his waist in snow, buffing, coating, and mercurializing photographic plates in the open air. Following a tremendous snowstorm, they finally had to abandon the equipment, saving only the daguerreotypes.

After the party moved higher into the mountains, its members shivered at night and covered themselves with flea-infested buffalo robes. Bone-tired, their collars pushed up around their ears against the numbing cold, they moved across uncharted mountains well beyond the headwaters of the Rio Grande del Norte and the Colorado River. In the sage-covered valleys, instead of antelope and beaver the party shot an occasional raven, hawk, or porcupine. When the supply of these gave out, they resorted, as on previous expeditions, to eating their horses. Each mule or horse lasted for only about six meals. Furthermore, every beast killed "placed one man on foot." Carvalho himself one night stole a piece of raw and frozen horse liver, pronouncing it "the most delicious morsel I ever tasted."[13] Every time a thin, starving horse died, the cooks saved the blood in their camp kettle, boiling the entrails and roasting the bones. Even the hide of a horse or mule, fried in tallow from melted candles, was preferable to eating porcupines with their quills singed off. For fifty days, when there was no meat available, the men lived on broiled cacti, wild rosebuds, and water bugs.

Ordinarily Frémont ate with his officers, but now he "requested that they excuse him," recalling the cannibalism during his last expedition. According to Carvalho, Frémont "begged us to swear that in no extremity of hunger would any of his men lift his hand to prey upon a comrade; sooner let him die with them than live upon them." He continued: "If we are to die, let us die together like men." He then threatened "to shoot the first man that made or hinted at such a proposition."[14] All twenty-one of his men solemnly took this oath against cannibalism as they stood in the snowy *poudrerie*, with heads bowed, while Frémont admonished them to stick together, but not as barbarians.

Deep snows again clogged the high mountain valleys of southern Colorado. Beyond Pueblo the lower elevations were clear of snow but barren of game. The hunters covered wide swaths of territory on horseback, but the rest of the group slogged along on foot. Frémont's party dissolved into a broken line of cold, half-starved stragglers. The scrawny fifth expedition stumbled through sleet, mud, rattlesnakes, dysentery, and scurvy over Roubideau (sometimes Robidoux) Pass.

Frémont's men had to surmount the Wasatch mountains of southern Utah near the rim of the Great Basin. On a steep slope of today's Gunnison River the party's lead mule slipped on the ice and plunged into a deep chasm, pulling fifty other animals to the bottom, hundreds of feet below. Miraculously, only one of them died. After the last of his horses had given out, Frémont, though his pack mules were weakened, unloaded them, cached their loads, and mounted his party on the remaining animals. Until the mules began to give out, this afforded the party temporary relief.[15]

Hardly ever did Frémont's own stamina fail him. In fact, he recovered from exhaustion even before his men realized their commander had temporarily lost his customary strength. Carvalho tells us that Frémont was proud that he could still tramp a "pathway for his men to follow." Toward the end of their march, however, most were "entirely barefoot." Some, who had not eaten the soles of their moccasins, had only "a piece of raw hide on their feet, which, however, becoming hard and still by the frost, made them more uncomfortable than walking without any."[16]

Beyond Green River, Oliver Fuller, assistant to Eggloffstein, gave up after fighting "a wild waste of snow." Frémont tried to save him by remaining "at this dreary place near three days," then pulling him along on one of the few mules left. The half-frozen Fuller did not respond even to scarce rations of food. With great sadness, they "wrapped him in his India rubber blanket" and laid him to rest.[17]

In the southern Great Basin, some friendly Utes appeared. Their leader was the brother of the celebrated Wakara, with whom Frémont had exchanged blankets back in 1844. These Indians helped guide the beleaguered party toward the Mormon outpost of Parowan. Frémont's ragged file of men finally stumbled into that tiny settlement on February 8, 1854. Luckily, he still had some credit among traders who had read his exploration reports while coming over the western trails in 1846. Two of Frémont's letters to Senator Benton tell us most of what we know about the bedraggled arrival in Parowan. "The Delawares all came in sound," he wrote, "but the whites of my party were all exhausted and broken up and more or less frostbitten." Although he acknowledged losing one man, his brief comments clearly understated their suffering.[18]

When rumors spread that some of Frémont's men had deserted the expedition, Benton was quick to deny this to the newspapers: "No man ever deserted him. His men die with him, as for him, but never desert."[19] Behind the scenes, however, Benton knew that the fifth expedition had realized no great achievements. Thereafter he would show even more distrust of his son-in-law's judgment.

After fresh provisioning, the party moved westward toward California's Tejon Pass, entering the state by way of today's town of Big Pine, the Owens River, and the San Joaquin Valley. When at last Frémont stumbled into San

Francisco on April 16, 1854, he was tendered two testimonial dinners, but he characteristically managed to wriggle out of both events. Had Jessie been along, she would surely have forced him to attend, for his letters tell us how much she vicariously cherished such honors.[20]

Frémont pronounced his pathetic little expedition a success, although professing that "this winter has happened to be one of extreme and unusual cold." About the route followed, he congratulated his father-in-law on "verification of your judgement." Both men still doggedly believed in vain that a railroad could be built along a "central line" and that this latest expedition had been designed merely to "daguerreotype the country over which we passed." These facsimiles, later developed by the photographer Matthew Brady, were salvaged but ultimately destroyed in a fire. As a result, Eggloffstein's rendition of the Black Canyon of the Gunnison River is the only remaining pictorial record of the fifth expedition. Having almost lost his life with Frémont, at Parowan he and Carvalho left the party, heading for Salt Lake City.[21]

Frémont intended to write an account of the fifth expedition, but the report was never completed. Once again he did history a disservice by not keeping his own diary, leaving behind but a fragmentary account in a letter of June 14, 1854, to the *National Intelligencer*. That letter was subsequently published by newspapers throughout the country and as a government document, but Solomon Carvalho's memoir, which Frémont allowed him to print after abandoning plans to publish his own account, became the main source concerning the expedition.[22]

On his earlier explorations Frémont was able to protect publication plans by prohibiting his men from keeping journals. This stricture stood in sharp contrast to the practice of Lewis and Clark, who had ordered their "serjeants" to write personal journals. But Frémont remained wary of any further unflattering publicity. In 1854 his *National Intelligencer* dispatch, and a printed version of letters he wrote to the Pacific Railroad Convention, were designed to keep alive the viability of the central route. "The West's rich valleys only await cultivation," he continued to argue, if the nation would only construct "this one completing link to our National prosperity. ... Build this railroad and things will have revolved about: America will lie between Asia and Europe—the golden vein which runs through the history of the world will follow the iron track to San Francisco."[23] Frémont again saw reality as larger than life, reflecting the grandiosity that he and Jessie so often fashioned—as if what he said would really come true. As we have seen, she was not above doctoring his reports.

At San Francisco he released yet another statement for its local newspapers. Steel rails, he again predicted, would replace the worn-out, dusty paths of the Far West. Should a war break out between North and South, furthermore, the advantages of a nonsouthern rail link to northern unionists would be decisive.[24]

This rare daguerreotype shows Frémont about April 1854, following his fifth and last expedition. He was haggard and worn out by ordeals suffered on the trail. It is presumed that the daguerreotypist was Solomon Nuñes Carvalho, but there is no absolute proof that he took this photograph. (From Collection of the Oakland Museum, Oakland, California; used by permission; Accession 68.93.2)

But no one ever used the midcontinental passes that Frémont favored. The Union Pacific and Central Pacific lines instead selected a route better suited to service between Chicago and the Pacific Northwest than to the few Saint Louis merchants who had backed him. The Mormon leader Brigham Young, personally fond of Frémont, was bitterly disappointed when the Union Pacific bypassed Salt Lake City. And on May 10, 1869, when the first transcontinental line was finally celebrated at Promontory Point in Utah, Frémont was not invited to attend that dedication.

The Pathfinder's days of exploration were coming to a close with still more accusations that he had become the follower of other men's trails. The fifth expedition had indeed traveled over old ground for the first seven hundred miles and in the wagon ruts of the Gunnison party for more than several hundred of the sixteen hundred miles Frémont traversed. Accusations continued to be heard that his last expeditions were mounted not for the pursuit of new discoveries but for publicity; self-interest and vanity had begun to supplant the image of conscientious explorer.[25]

Yet there is no other case in which an American explorer mounted two successive expeditions without a trace of government aid. Most nineteenth-century explorers were content to lead one or two expeditions. It was his misfortune that his fourth and fifth ventures ended in suffering and death. This tragic result discouraged him from publishing the journals of either expedition. The fifth one finally terminated his career as an explorer.

Although Frémont's last expedition was a pale facsimile of his earlier exploits, his mapmaking, along with that of Wilkes, Gunnison, and Emory, represented an important rung on the ladder of exploration established earlier by Lewis and Clark, Pike, and Long. Each explorer brought back specimens and some of the earliest ethnological records of remote tribes and preserved a detailed account of ecosystems that would not survive the human tide that overran the American West. Others had preceded Frémont in all this activity, but none became America's most charismatic pathfinder of empire.

Frémont stayed on in San Francisco only briefly. Then, borrowing money from Palmer, Cook & Company for the journey, he returned eastward with his Delaware Indian scouts on the Nicaraguan steamer *Cortes*.[26] He now permanently turned his back on those western campfires in whose embers his personal glory was once reflected so brightly. ❖

Frémont returned to Washington at a time when the beaver, Indian, and buffalo were being overwhelmed on the western plains and mountains. With the men who had accompanied the Pathfinder on his five expeditions also passing from the scene, there were some compensations in not being out on the trail. One of them was that he no longer had to remember Jessie by looking at the ivory miniature of her in the waterproof compartment she had stitched into his clothing. After this last expedition, he seemed more ready to join her in the big, comfortable white bed awaiting him in Washington.

This reunion, however, was soon followed by sad family losses. In September 1854, Jessie's mother died. The following February, her father's Washington home went up in smoke. Senator Benton's treasures of a lifetime, including a fine library, manuscripts, and memorabilia, were all lost. Destroyed also were records relating to Frémont's explorations, the loss of which would obscure vital parts of his life from future generations of historians.

The Frémonts moved their main residence to New York in 1855, partly because of Washington's political atmosphere. During his short senatorial tenure, a sharpened North-South antagonism had divided the nation. But even outside the capital, Frémont, who still held strong abolitionist views, could not escape politics. The newly founded Republican party, and even some members of the Democratic party, began to speak of him as a presidential candidate—a situation similar to that of Dwight D. Eisenhower, another military hero courted by both parties a century later. The American people have frequently confused romantic heroes with political ones.

Frémont seemed a safe-enough candidate for either party's nomination. The initial approach on behalf of the Democrats came from a family member, John B. Floyd, late governor of Virginia, who would one day become Buchanan's secretary of war. Floyd had married Sally Preston of Virginia, one of Jessie's in-laws. A states-rights Democrat, he hoped that Frémont could run on a combined Democratic–Know Nothing ticket. At the Saint Nicholas hotel in New York, members of the party argued with Frémont for several days, hoping that he would accept their offer. The South-dominated Democratic Party virtually controlled the federal government. But the Democratic bid was conditional upon the candidate's acceptance of measures sought by the South as protective of slavery.

To his credit, Frémont issued several public letters on slavery in which he refused to reconcile his compassion over Negro rights with the racism of the Know Nothings. Had he become the Democratic nominee, he probably would have been assured the White House if he had agreed to drop his opposition to the extension of slavery. But then he would have needed to support the return of runaway slaves, endorsing a horrific Fugitive Slave Law that allowed slaveowners to track down blacks like animals. Ultimately, the Democrats decided that James Buchanan would make a safer candidate.

The new Republican party firmly opposed the extension of slavery. Furthermore, the Republicans refused to back repeal of the Missouri Compromise and were against the Kansas-Nebraska Bill of May 25, 1854, which countenanced slavery throughout the West. Although originally from the South, Frémont, like Poinsett and Benton, was never a sectionalist. His expeditions had, after all, been federally funded. His appeal was national, although he was strongly identified with the West.

Before Frémont was nominated by the new Republican party, a whole year went by—from the summer of 1855, when the Southern-inspired offer was made to him, until that of 1856. The process was complex, and it featured such powerful political figures as Edwin D. Morgan, Gideon Welles, Thurlow Weed, and members of the influential Blair family. Also involved were Horace Greeley's *New York Tribune* as well as William Cullen Bryant and John Bigelow's *New York Evening Post*. These backers had the good fortune to rely upon Palmer, Cook & Company, Frémont's California bankers, for campaign financing.

Other prospective candidates for the Republican nomination included Senator William Henry Seward of New York, who had originally enjoyed the backing of political king maker Thurlow Weed. Weed, however, persuaded the influential *National Intelligencer* to champion Frémont. Seward resented the amateur, but because the senator was an even more uncompromising foe of slavery than was Frémont, Seward was feared by Southerners, who thought that if Frémont were elected president, Seward might become the real power behind the throne, stopping at nothing to destroy slavery. Another possibility was the ambitious Salmon Chase, former Free Soil senator from Ohio, currently its governor. He would become secretary of the treasury under Lincoln and later chief justice.

In the end, Frémont's lack of political partisanship furnished good reason for making him the candidate of a new party of fusion. Its founders, who met for the first time in Pittsburgh during February 1856, included men who deserted the Whigs, Free Soilers, and Democrats because of inaction over the slavery issue. They would submerge their differences in favor of Frémont. No other prospect could match the popularity of a candidate who already had seventeen towns and counties named for him.

On June 19, 1856, in Philadelphia, Frémont accepted the Republican nomination for the presidency. His choice was partly a gamble that his dashing reputation would attract independent-minded Democrats. Unfortunately he refused to fight for his first choice as a vice-presidential runningmate, Simon Cameron. Instead, he had to accept the colorless William L. Dayton. The candidate was actually more interested in his once favorite project—construction of a transcontinental railroad as well as river and harbor improvements—than in the more pressing issue of whether national union would be disrupted by continuing national discord.

Publishers rushed campaign biographies of Frémont into print. Both he and Jessie furnished materials to John Bigelow, who published a chapter per week about the explorer's life in the *New York Post*. These chapters were bound into a book that the *New York Independent* said would silence an "immense brood of malignant slanders."[1]

In an age when politicians routinely employed scurrilous invective against their enemies, Frémont could not believe the reckless charges leveled against him by such unfriendly newspapers as the *Washington Union*. Unlike Abraham Lincoln, who made over ninety speeches on his behalf, the candidate seemed unable to roll with the punches. He winced at every criticism. To counter charges of political ineptitude, Lincoln spoke of the Pathfinder as "our young, gallant, and world commander" and "the man for the day." Neither man could abide the scourge of slavery, but Frémont had the misfortune to encounter that dangerous issue prematurely. Even in 1860, when Lincoln became the first Republican president, the issue almost cost him the White House. That year his wife, Mary, had to assure her family, the Todds of Kentucky, that her husband, unlike Frémont, was not a true abolitionist but a former Whig who merely wanted to replace that stale old party with a new leadership that would merely oppose the *extension* of slavery. This was something that Jessie in 1856, as the first Republican candidate's wife, had been unable to tell her kinfolks.

Lincoln and his fellow Republicans could hardly have guessed what a thin political reed Frémont would prove to be. Yet the Pathfinder, however listless he seemed, did prepare the way for Lincoln to run successfully four years later.

Some conservatives who wanted to support Frémont in 1856 considered him to be too young, at forty-three, as well as untried, too impersonal, and awkward. Something was missing. He had almost no sense of humor and was rarely known to laugh or to engage in small talk. And, alas, more serious personal charges, most of them false, would not go away. They were effectively used by his opponents. Among the most damaging of them was the inference that Frémont had become a drunkard—and a Catholic one, too.

Religious bigotry played a big part in the 1856 campaign, as did widespread fear that the South would secede from the Union if an antislavery Republican ever made it to the White House. In the face of both issues, Frémont tamely asserted that under the Constitution no religious belief should disqualify a candidate for office. He supposedly had made the sign of the cross in public and had then erected a crucifix on Independence Rock. He also allegedly had been seen crossing himself in Washington's Catholic cathedral. His marriage by a Catholic priest fueled the rumor that he was secretly a Catholic and had confessed belief in the doctrine of transubstantiation. To counter these assertions, friendly Protestant clergymen provided evidence that he had worshiped at Grace Episcopal Church, that Jessie had become an Episcopalian after being reared a Presbyterian, and that their children had been baptized as Episcopalians.

Members of the Know Nothing party, who favored former president Millard Fillmore, openly contested his alleged Protestant past. The anti-Catholic sentiment fostered by the Know Nothings was fierce. Although, like them, Frémont stood for immigrant restriction, he could not quiet the uneasiness of persons who believed that a Roman Pope might run the country if a Catholic were ever elected president.

Pamphlets continued to pop up everywhere filled with confusing defamations of his character. Among these slurs was one that promised

> Proof of His Romanism
> Proof of His Pro-Slavery Acts
> Proof of His Conviction of Mutiny
> Proof That He is a Duelist
> Proof That He is a Bully
> Proof of His Swindling the Government
> Proof of His Complicity With the Swindling Operations of Palmer, Cook & Co.

Another publication, entitled "Frémont's Romanism Established," charged: "We have linked together the names of Bishop Hughes, Wm. H. Seward, and John C. Frémont and charge upon this trio the most foul combination."[2]

Frémont steadfastly refused to declare that he was not a Catholic. About his stand Jessie said: "He was a Protestant, and had never been anything else, but took the position that the main issue of the canvass was freedom." Hence he declined even to state his religion. Yet had he done so, the candidate might have defused the religious controversy that surrounded him. Thurlow Weed called a conference at New York's Astor House to get him to declare he was not a Catholic. Although it was difficult to deny that Frémont's French-Canadian forebears had been Catholics, some dissident Know Nothings would have urged Millard Fillmore to withdraw as their candidate had Frémont been willing to head up a fusion Democratic–Know Nothing ticket. But he, quite courageously, would not cooperate in any such denial.[3]

As if the Catholic issue were not trouble enough, the candidate's career as conqueror of California became another campaign issue. He was depicted as a phony conqueror who had fought no major battles there. Edward Fitzgerald Beale, who had testified on his behalf during the court-martial trial, now spoke out against him. Their legal squabbles had ruined a fine relationship.

The editor of the *Los Angeles Star* warned readers not to vote for a man who had on his hands the blood of a cruel murder of three Californians "because he had no room for prisoners." This was a reference to the murder of the Berreyesa brothers during the conquest era. The *Star* maintained that there was no room for a tyrant, no room for a robber, no room for Frémont as president. Although former governor Pío Pico absolved him from these charges, the previous accusations of immorality surfaced again. So did reproaches about Frémont as "master monopolist" of the Mariposas claim, as absentee landlord and "land-shark," and as the tool of the powerful banking house of Palmer, Cook & Company. The Democrats alleged that Frémont planned to appoint Joseph Palmer secretary of the treasury; another of that company's officials, George Wright, was allegedly to become assistant secretary. According to the *Star*, Frémont was the candidate of a dishonest clique that was determined to pry open the U.S. Treasury, and his inexperience with politics, limited success as a senator, and military escapades unfitted him for the presidency.[4]

To counter all this negative California publicity, Thomas Oliver Larkin, the former consul at Monterey, provided a testimonial regarding Frémont's role in the conquest of California. A strong abolitionist, Larkin espoused the newly formed Republican party. Although in 1848 Frémont had sought to block Larkin's government appointment as a naval agent, Larkin betrayed neither hostility nor resentment over past bickering. He and the explorer-turned-politician were, however, temperamentally poles apart. In California, Larkin had been the cautious, orderly merchant facing a power-backed young chameleon as war approached. He recalled Frémont as "of reserved and distant manners, active & industrious in his official duties, anxious to finish the business on hand & before him & to be on the march to accomplish more, generally remaining in tent if

not house. Rather adverse to company & to extending the circle of his acquain-
tances, but polite, kind, and courteous to every one." While Larkin found his old
associate to be "not communicative unless drawn into conversation by others,"
he described him as "without any coarseness or profanity." Larkin ended his
testimonial with the statement: "I consider Mr. Frémont a just, correct, and moral
man, abstemious, bold, and persevering. While he was in my house we had
several balls and parties in Monterey. He attended one or two but did not appear
to participate in the pleasures of the company, although occasionally he joined
in the dance." This statement was intended to offset charges that Frémont had
comported himself lasciviously during the conquest era. Larkin reassured critics
that "the Native Californians saw much of Frémont & in general speak favorably
of him to this day."[5]

Much harder to discount were recurring charges of Frémont's past relationships with a variety of women. To prove his dissoluteness, his opponents dredged
up what they called "an *affaire d'amour* in which young Frémont played an
unfortunate part" while he wintered among the Cherokee Indians back in 1837.
Another critic asserted that he kept a Hispanic mistress at Los Angeles when
acting as governor of California.

More seriously, the Republican National Committee seems to have bought
off a "French mistress" who threatened to expose her relationship with Frémont
before the election of 1856. At about that same time, according to John Bigelow,
Frémont got "a servant girl," perhaps the same woman, pregnant. This caused
Bigelow, the campaign biographer, to break off relations with the candidate.
Gideon Welles, who would become Lincoln's secretary of the navy, also had
reservations about Frémont. His correspondence reflected this distrust: "It has
been vaguely whispered privately in my ear that he has been guilty of abortive
or disreputable conduct . . . which, if true, would make it desirable that we say
as little as possible. The subject is so delicate." Preston King, also high in the new
Republican party, reflected upon the 1856 campaign, confiding to Welles: "There
were reasons personal to himself which would prevent his being a candidate.
Mr. Bigelow of the Post . . . specified a reason which I deemed sufficient to
abandon any such expectation." King urged Welles to burn his letters regarding
this subject, all the while specifying what Frémont had allegedly done: "The
specific charge I heard was that he had debauched, while living on 9th Street,
New York in 1856, a chambermaid or servant girl whom you may have seen
come to the door to answer the bell." A note, undated, to Governor Rodman
Price of New Jersey stated that Frémont was coming through Trenton and wanted
hospitality for himself and "a lady whom I shall have in charge." Who was she?
Later one finds still more evidence of Frémont's philandering.[6]

The Republicans feared that the slander about him, like a shadow in outline,
would be taken as true if it became common knowledge. Though in the midst

of a political campaign, Frémont had seemed to follow that French proverb: "In love and war don't seek counsel." But the charges of his womanizing, alas, had more validity than the religious nonsense written about the candidate, or whether he parted his hair down the middle (an affectation distrusted out West). Jessie was right to call the campaign "a trial by mud."

Frémont's stand on slavery also kept resurfacing, including an obviously planted rumor that he secretly owned seventy-five slaves. The abolitionist issue stirred up opponents, who carried placards down San Francisco's streets that read, "Frémont: Free Niggers and Copper Cents," as well as "Frémont: Free Niggers and Frijoles," the latter referring to his supposed pro-Hispanic views. At the University of North Carolina, chemistry professor Benjamin S. Hedrick would actually be dismissed from its faculty for supporting Frémont's antislavery candidacy.

The Democrats were equally determined to undermine Frémont's record as an explorer. They rehashed his western disasters, exhuming the charges of cannibalism. Critics also accused him of pretending to be the discoverer of South Pass, an achievement he had never claimed. The *New York Daily News* for June 30, 1856, stated that real mountain men and trappers considered Frémont a "fancy amateur tourist," an "over-grown schoolboy playing mountaineer." Saint Louis's *Daily Missouri Republican* on July 8, 1856, quoted Henry Minayell, "a trapper from Bent's Fort," as saying:

> The general opinion of the boys is that he is a very young beaver—that he is as vain and self-conceited as a young squaw looking at herself in a spring. And as for that last trip of his . . . we all feel that no one but a fool would have attempted it at that time of the year, and that none but a cold-hearted, selfish devil would have lost his men and animals in the way he did.

Further injurious testimony about Frémont as a leader of men came from Edward Kern and his brothers, who were urged by the Democrats to reveal all that they knew about the disastrous fourth expedition: "The man who could be guilty of the acts that he has been guilty of is certainly not the man to be the successor of Washington."[7] Though Richard Kern was dead, Frémont's foes dug up a pejorative version of his original journal, published in May 1849 at Quincy, Illinois. This diatribe reappeared in the *Washington Daily Union* on July 31, 1856.

As the campaign venom grew more scurrilous, Frémont withdrew inwardly. His daughter Lily said that her father was "used to life in the open and wanted a square fight." She observed that he was urged not even "to look at his mail during the campaign, nor [to] read the newspapers until they had been blue pencilled by my mother." Jessie's role, as later during the Civil War, grew especially complex. While she again acted as his protector, in that age she could scarcely dominate the powerful men who surrounded him. She tried to do so tangentially in the only way open to her, by charming them.

In censoring her husband's mail she tried to reduce the daily strains upon him. But this cut him off from some of the realities of the campaign. She also urged his handlers to "keep up his splendid condition by fencing every morning early and by tremendous walks after dark." Jessie personally reassured him that he was the most handsome of all three candidates, being slender and with a still well knit frame.

She also had a family to care for. In the summer of 1856 she took the children to Siasconset on Nantucket Island. The reluctant candidate remained behind to fend off admirers and critics alike amid the rude political hustings of New York. His son attested to the fact that "Public speaking he disliked. He was anything but what is called nowadays a mixer."[8]

Not only was it difficult to coax the candidate to show himself in public, but he also kept a distance even from key local politicians. On one occasion an impatient crowd set up a clamor for his appearance. Finally he emerged onto the front porch of his house at 56 West Ninth Street, accompanied by campaign aides. Wearing a suit of black broadcloth, he was as handsome as their campaign literature pictured him. Although his grey blue eyes seemed tired, a well-trimmed beard imparted an air of composure to a crowd anxious to see the great Pathfinder in the flesh. Press stories about mountain trails and western gold mines accompanied rediscovery of a hero, though he personally was fuzzy about political specifics.

For a candidate, he was also touchy. Frémont reacted with great anger to a speech made at Richmond by Virginia Governor Henry A. Wise, who launched an attack upon the candidate's illegitimate birth. Wise, whose roots reached far back into the history of his native Old Dominion, spared no mercy:

> Tell, me, if the hoisting of the Black Republican Flag in the hands of an adventurer, born illegitimately in a neighboring State, if not ill-begotten in this very city—tell me, if the hoisting of the black flag over you by a Frenchman's bastard, while the arms of civil war are already clashing, is not deemed an overt act and declaration of war? His mother was a strumpet of a Richmond brothel. Old Colonel Pryor married her. Frémont's father . . . ran off with her to Norfolk, afterwards to Charlestown. Fry him up to cracklings!

Should Frémont secure the election, Wise even threatened "a prompt declaration of martial law followed by the calling up of 150,000 militiamen"—in short, secession itself.[9]

Tormented by such accusations, Frémont was desperate somehow to legitimize his origins. According to John Bigelow, he implored Canadian archivists to search for his parents' fugitive marriage certificate. But he was never able to prove his legitimate birth. Another campaign pamphlet, entitled *Black Republican Imposture Exposed*, was subtitled *Fraud Upon the People: Frémont and His Speculations*. It purported to show his "astounding disregard of the public interest, only to be accounted for by extravagance, recklessness, or an utter want of judgment!"[10]

There were still other skeletons in Frémont's political closet. Charles A. Dana, editor of Horace Greeley's *New York Tribune*, implored Bigelow not to mention the candidate's various challenges to duels in his campaign biography, lest he lose the Quaker vote:

> I asked General Frémont if John Bigelow's allusions to his duels in the Campaign Life of '56 repelled the Quakers from him, and he answered, "Not greatly, I am sure. Quakers are sensible people, and when I gathered that fine army of sixty thousand around me in Missouri, several of the foremost young Quakers of Pennsylvania joined me and put on the uniform and took up the sword at the risk of expulsion from their church. I believe a few actually were expelled. I'll tell you what repelled the Quakers, and everybody else . . . the horrible woodcuts that they made to represent me and the pictures on banners and transparencies. I am not handsome, by a good deal, but I don't feel that I have ever done anything to deserve those caricatures. To my certain knowledge the villainous woodcut of me printed by the Tribune the day after my nomination lost me twenty-five votes in one township."[11]

Frémont used Bigelow's biography to answer accusations stemming from the 1848 court-martial. Jessie personally wrote part of that book, refuting the most blatant allegations made against her husband. Though little more than a campaign tract, the volume reached sales of forty thousand copies. She boasted that it replaced the family album on half the living room tables in the United States. The Pathfinder's western exploits were paraded before a wider audience than he had ever before enjoyed. For some voters this background provided an undeniable appeal. One of them saw "intelligence breathed in every utterance; resolution was portrayed upon every feature; modesty, ability, integrity were written as plainly as the alphabet upon the whole."[12]

To help an inept political Galahad defend himself against attacks, Greeley commissioned a hack writer, W. H. Bartlett, to write a thirty-two-page pamphlet that the *Tribune* distributed for twenty-one cents a copy. The pamphlet (also translated to gain German voters in the Midwest) claimed an amazing similarity between the explorer and George Washington. Both men, its author maintained, reflected a "calm steadfastness" and a "strength of will." At a meeting in Camden, New Jersey, a spokesman for the God-fearing, antislavery Greeley even compared Frémont to Jesus Christ.[13]

His campaign handlers commissioned yet another hyperbolic tract, Charles W. Upham's *Life, Exploration and Public Service of John C. Frémont*, published at Boston. The volume sold thirty thousand copies at one dollar per copy. It, too, featured the candidate's heroics, including an effective quote from the Delaware chieftain Sagundai: "Frémont brave man. Brave man Colonel Frémont." One other campaign biography, Samuel W. Smucker's *The Life of Col. John Charles Frémont*, claimed a similarity between Frémont and Andrew Jackson. Both were America's frontier heroes.[14]

The Republicans encouraged rural towns to rename themselves "Frémont," and the parents of newborn girls were to call them Jessie or Jessie Ann or Jess. This campaign featured the wholly new participation of women, partly inspired by Jessie's role in it. Campaign songs spoke of "Sweet Jessie, our liveliest and best, our Liberty Queen." Jessie relished the torchlight parades in her honor that highlighted the image of a plucky woman who would make a great first lady. These honors were accompanied by a book of songs entitled "Frémont and Jessie" and by publication as well of twenty-seven poems titled *Signal Fires on the Trail of the Pathfinder*. The Republicans distributed these keepsakes along with cloth banners that read, "Free Speech, Free Soil, and Frémont."

Frémont had some powerful political writers in his corner. They included the Quaker poet John Greenleaf Whittier, whose Philadelphia newspaper offices had been sacked and burned back in 1838 because he had publicly expressed antislavery sentiments. Whittier wrote Frémont's campaign poem, "The Pass of the Sierras"; other adherents included newspaperman Horace Greeley and Massachusetts politico Anson Burlingame. Another powerful figure, Nathaniel P. Banks, speaker of the House of Representatives, stumped New England on Frémont's behalf. Banks even turned down the Know Nothing nomination for himself after Frémont was nominated in June 1856.

The candidate's backers, however, grew ever more fearful. Greeley called him the "merest baby in politics" and confided to members of the Republican electoral committee, "He don't know the ABC's." Though Greeley was tired of apologizing for the candidate's weaknesses out on the stump, when the Democrats criticized Frémont's beard, the old newsmaker concocted a cock-and-bull story that the noble Pathfinder would never cut it off. After all, the beard had guarded his face, and even his teeth, against frostbite in the wilderness. But Greeley privately complained: "We shall all be sorry if we get him elected."[15] He saw that Frémont's own aimlessness aided the Democrats in discrediting him, for the candidate did not really understand politics. Not only did the Democrats marshal money from slave states to defeat him, but Northern business interests, too, feared that a Frémont victory would mean loss of Southern markets and economic disunion.

Hoping against hope that Frémont's abolitionist views would not harm him unduly was Bronson Alcott, most transcendental of the transcendentalists. Alcott wrote in his journal for September 11, 1856, that with Henry David Thoreau he had discussed "politics, Frémont, Garrison, Emerson and the rest all morning in my study." Alcott's New England circle of literati were taken by their candidate's association with nature and his antislavery obstinacy, though he was hardly that model of an intellectual that they would have preferred. Yet he continued to retain the support of Henry Ward Beecher's famed Plymouth Church.[16]

Another scion of the Boston literati, Josiah Quincy, also endorsed Frémont. "Personally, I know him not; but I have read the history of his life, and believe him to be a man as much marked out by Providence for the present exigency of our nation as Washington was for that of our American Revolution. . . . Nursed in difficulties, practiced in surmounting them; wise in counsel; full of resource; self-possessed in danger; fearless and foremost in every useful enterprise; unexceptional in morals, with an intellect elevated by nature . . . he is destined to save the Union from dissolution.[17]

By far the most effective charge against Frémont concerned his antislavery sentiments, which dated back to his days as senator. The *Richmond Enquirer* suggested a parodied slogan for his campaign: "Free niggers, free women, free land, and Frémont."[18] The Republicans, anxious to counter charges that he was a renegade Southerner who had become an abolitionist turncoat, sought moderate newspaper support wherever they could find it. The *Agitator* of Wellsborough, Pennsylvania, described Frémont as "a truly national man whose whole career has been spent in the service of the whole country." He had done more of it, the paper continued, "than any living American."

As the campaign progressed, large crowds turned out, particularly in the Midwest, to honor the Pathfinder. In Alton, Illinois, 35,000 showed up; at Kalamazoo, Michigan, the throng numbered 30,000. At Indianapolis a parade took five hours to pass a Republican reviewing stand: fifty bands were in the line of march, the daytime festivities were followed by a torchlight procession.[19]

From the Southwest came an unexpected endorsement from the influential Sam Houston of Texas. In the Senate he voiced confidence that Frémont was not actually dangerous: "There will be neither bustling, bayonets, nor secession, if Colonel Frémont shall be elected by a majority of the people." In the House of Representatives, Thaddeus Stevens, Pennsylvania's antislave political titan, also spoke in favor of Frémont. But he deeply regretted continuing charges that the Republican nominee was a Catholic, about which he said: "The cry of Frémont's Catholicism has lost us the nation."[20]

The candidate never ventured south of the national capital. Savannah, the city of his birth, remained a hotbed of antislavery. The city fathers had once offered ten thousand dollars for the capture of a prominent abolitionist, Amos Phelps. Other Southern communities proposed to pay even more for these "ignorant and infatuated barbarians," as Congressman J. H. Hammond of South Carolina had called abolitionists back in 1836.

The Republicans prayed that Frémont would control his own abolitionist vitriol in Washington, a Southern city where he spent a good deal of the time. In its suburbs lay Silver Springs, the beautiful estate of the powerful Blair family. Though they owned slaves, they were relatively sympathetic to his views. But his candidacy posed severe problems of loyalty among Jessie's old friends and members of her family.

Senator Benton had spent weeks trying to dissuade Frémont from running; he argued that his family should not support an untried sectional party that would divide the union, believing that the idea of a new antislavery party, the Republicans, would prove too provocative to the South. During the election the senator and the Frémonts were sharply divided. Benton and his wife's family had owned slaves, yet he was antislave. But he was also a loyal Democrat who thought Southerners had a right to protect slavery in the South. Benton wished to keep that institution from disrupting the entire union, whereas his son-in-law's backers thought they should obey a higher law made by God, even helping slaves escape to freedom.

Jessie confessed her disappointment over what she considered her father's betrayal, labeling his defection from Frémont's candidacy a "Brutus stab." Eliza, Senator Benton's eldest daughter, and her husband, William Carey Jones, also both Democrats, sided politically with the old nationalist, which further divided Eliza from Jessie. The Frémont grandchildren, who loved their Grandpa, found it confusing to hear the Blairs speak of Benton as "Ole Bull." So Jessie and John Charles encouraged them to blame the family rift on Aunt Eliza and her jealous husband. Jessie complained that, within her family, her husband "was dropped by every relative." She herself continued to be attacked publicly. "Have we a Presidentess among us?" one critic rudely asked.[21]

Frémont saw his father-in-law's repudiation as personal, although Benton rationalized it in a rambling, emotional speech that turned out to be his last:

> Mr. Frémont, standing near to me, in a relation dear as it could be to me not to be my own child. He has had an eventful life—great difficulties, great dangers, great trials to undergo. I stood by him in every one of them as a father would stand by a child. [Long continued applause.] . . . I spared nothing which I could raise and deliver him, in order to carry him through . . . knowing from the first that Mr. Frémont was to be the candidate of a sectional party, I told him from the beginning that it was impossible that I could support any such nomination. [Cheers.] No matter what came, he must be national, he must have a vision that could look over the Union. He must not be on a dividing line . . . or I cannot [*sic*] only not support him but I must take ground against him.

Estranged old friends like the Blairs, would say of him: "Tom Benton's stubborn stand cost us many a vote outside Missouri."[22] The patriarch and his defensive son-in-law both suffered almost simultaneous political defeats in the same year. After losing his seat in Congress, Benton in 1856 had run unsuccessfully for the governorship of Missouri—his last campaign—before dying of cancer on April 10, 1858. After the polar tension between the two men was finally over, Jessie would write a glowing vignette about her father that John Charles allowed her to place at the very head of his own memoirs. The old tyrant never quite left their beings.

The 1856 presidential results had been mixed. Although Fillmore's Know Nothings diluted the final vote, the new Republican party did not do too badly, winning in eleven states. Frémont polled 1,341,264 votes to Buchanan's 1,838,169 and would have prevailed if he had carried Pennsylvania and either Illinois or Indiana. Only two states, really, blocked his way to the presidency. But with the breakup of the American Union increasingly threatened, Frémont came closer to uniting North and West against the militant South than had any previous presidential candidate. He carried every state north of the Mason and Dixon Line except Indiana, Illinois, Pennsylvania, New Jersey, and California, to win 114 electoral votes. He received 33.1 percent of the popular vote (45 percent in the North) as compared to 45.3 percent for Buchanan and only 21.6 percent for Fillmore. If Pennsylvania's 27 electoral votes had gone to Frémont, the election could have been decided by the House of Representatives, where he might have won. Serious charges of voting fraud and bribery, and rebuttals to those charges, came out of Pennsylvania.

Frémont also lost California's four electoral votes. That state's Bear Clubs, his supporters, ran into conservative Whigs who were alarmed that his election would stir further sectional conflict. Frémont made a poorer showing in California than nationally, gaining only twenty thousand votes. Not only had that state become strongly Democratic, but his reputation had also tarnished since he had been its first senator. His connections with Palmer, Cook & Company proved especially harmful. That firm, as part owners of Las Mariposas, had recently defaulted on $100,000 worth of San Francisco bonds. Some California precincts registered no votes for him at all. He drew but 18 percent of the state vote and only 6 percent in the three mining counties of Mariposa, Tulare, and Stanislaus.

What really destroyed Frémont's chance for the presidency was his stand against slavery, but there were still other reasons for his defeat. Frémont was conveniently vague on some other issues, but some believed that he would be dominated by the Blairs, Greeley, Thurlow Weed, and other political professionals. Weed, by means of the *National Intelligencer*, had indeed supported Frémont's expansionist ideals. Instead of crediting Frémont for his explorations (as von Humboldt and admirers abroad had done), fault-finders said that mountain climbing did not prepare a leader to understand the constitution or world affairs.

Frémont's foreign origins, his Catholic father, and his marriage by a Catholic priest continued to be held against him.

Buchanan, an aging but crafty Democrat, became a minority president at a time when the country was on the verge of tearing itself apart. A sixty-four-year-old bachelor, he had spent most of his adult life in public office. Referring to himself as "the Old Public Functionary," Buchanan projected an image of stability that Frémont could not match. Also known as "Old Buck," his pseudonyms highlighted the reliability of a seasoned war horse, which Frémont was not.[23]

Frémont emerged from the campaign with a reputation as a political goose who had refused to accept advice. John Bigelow's reminiscences reveal his disgust with Frémont's ineptness: "As a candidate . . . he did everything pretty much that he could do to bring his party into contempt." Bigelow added: "He lived long enough . . . to satisfy everyone that he might have proved a disastrous failure as President. A wedge may be useful in splitting a log, but useless in converting either of its parts into a chest of drawers."[24]

The metaphor of Frémont as a wedge is apt. Although some followers saw him as a dynamic candidate, his campaign had been divisive, stiff, even wooden. "He possessed all the qualities of genius except ability," Josiah Royce later said. Yet another criticism described him as "a spoiled child of fortune" whose "activities were so near the line between great deeds and charlatanism that it was difficult to distinguish the pose from the performance." Ulysses S. Grant, later commanding general of the Union armies, said that he did not vote for Buchanan in the election but, rather, against Frémont—the ultimate humiliating comment.[25]

Unlike Grant, Frémont never reached the presidency. The defeated candidate stoically repressed his loss better than did Jessie and their daughter. "To a girl of fourteen," Lily wrote, "the result of the election was more than the loss of one great party pitted against another. My life in Washington, as a member of Senator Benton's household, had implanted in my young heart a love of political honors, and the White house [had] loomed up as a delightful place to spend four years or more."[26]

With the presidential election finally over, Jessie looked for new ways to keep her husband's mind off his loss. She urged him to get on with assembling his long-delayed report of the fifth expedition. Solomon Carvalho had worked on the plates for such a book—also writing his own unofficial *Incidents of Travel and Adventure in the Far West* (1857). But it remained difficult to reproduce daguerreotypes for printed books. Jessie complained that she had to turn her New York drawing room into a retreat for Carvalho's artist and photographer friends. The house was permeated with the stench of hot mercury vapors. Throughout the winter of 1856, the renowned photographer Matthew Brady worked there on Carvalho's daguerreotypes. By May 1857, artists began to render these into oil canvases and wood engravings that Brady prepared for wet-plating, the latest method of producing photographs.

Jessie described the family's role with the book as the creation of "our baby and pet." Since the "election looks ages back," she added, her house was in turmoil. In Lizzie's bedroom lay "a grand collection of oily rags and bad smelling bottles and paints, but the results are beautiful." While supervising production of the book, Frémont, homebound, was once more getting reacquainted with his children, as Jessie also recorded: "Frank and Mr. Frémont grow young together over imaginary buffalo hunts located in certain valleys which look out upon them like nature from a canvas."[27] The whole family worked hard on their father's book. But it would all come to a sudden end in 1859 when his publisher, George Childs of Philadelphia, asked for the return of money advanced Frémont five years before and then canceled the contract.

Once the presidential campaign ended, Jessie suggested that they all go back to California. Now that sleek eastern carriages had replaced the jingling spurs of the rancho era, San Francisco had become a place that Jessie would come to prefer over Washington and New York, if not Paris.[28] Also, the Bear Valley property needed serious attention, and Frémont likewise had to provide for the care of the thirteen acres of land surrounding Black Point, their San Francisco property. So, it was back to the Golden Gate once more, if only temporarily.

Not only did their California properties need attention. Family morale, too—especially the relationship between Jessie and John Charles—required serious bolstering. Their personal lives had been scarred by too many losses. As a result of frequent changes of residence, including fires, relatively few of their personal letters survived. But from these we can reconstruct Jessie's feelings as she expressed her continuing love for John Charles.

Jessie's passion for him remained unquestioning, romantic, and as complete as ever. She brushed aside all charges by others of his selfishness or egotism. After the family returned to California, she wrote to him during his travels. On Sunday evening of July 25, 1857, Jessie took pen in hand and wrote of their relationship with other people. By living so much of their life in public, this was bound to alter how they felt about each other. She yearned for greater closeness: "I don't think you have given your liking to any who really did see your highest qualities—the Blairs I except. But I get indignant when I see you wasted on people to whom you are simply a rich man or a society man. You laugh at my 'infatuation' but you must see how many share it, although you say truly only I know you well."

Capable of passionate emotion, verging at times upon the obsessional, she had a right to have her needs satisfied by a devoted husband. His sexuality, however, was of a different order, wandering and less intense. Furthermore, throughout her life Jessie had to keep propping up John Charles. She continued to write that she hated people who are "stone-blind to your best side" or who "cannot comprehend you." And she added: "You must always let me feel you trust me and keep nothing from me that touches you." Four days later, on July 29, 1857, she wrote her husband again, as though she had been deprived of his love by more than their current separation. More intimacies followed: "Love me in memory of the old times when I was dear to you. I love you now much more than I did then." She told John Charles that she wanted "for a little kind word from you—seriously dear Master," and she stated that she had grown disgusted with French novels that depicted love fading after marriage.[29]

In the Victorian age, marriage was both a moral and a public institution, its proprieties to be maintained at all cost, however they might be privately worn and damaged. One finds not a word in Jessie's correspondence about the transgressions of which he was accused. Although she knew more than an occasional detail, Jessie used both repression and denial as personal defenses. For John Charles, the closing off of sentiment hardly allowed him to express intimate emotions. No single set of factors caused this shutting-down, which led Jessie to yearn for his continual reassurance. When Jessie had to return eastward in 1857 before her father's death, she missed John Charles even more. Another letter to her husband expressed her feelings:

> My darling, I want to see you more than you can think. I am well, but I am such a great fool I want to be still beside you, with nothing to think or do but sit and wait for a kind word from you—Sirius by the dear master. I am trying to make the sun go from west to east, that is, trying to look young and pretty. *Je deviens coquette dans mon vieux temps pour te plaire. . . .* One affectionate look from you will give me more life than all the rules. You see, I have nothing to tell, sweetheart, much to wish and hope and, my darling, so much to thank you for . . . the only real happiness we know. Most of all, darling, I love you and want you.
>
> Your JESSIE[30]

One further letter spoke of "trying to make the sun go from west to east— that is trying to look young and pretty." She pathetically sought "to follow all the rules," exercising and dieting for her absent lover. To please such a bird of rare plumage, Jessie was at turns adoring, admiring, and entertaining. All these measures helped to cover anger over so many separations. Though both a loyalist and his watchdog, she sometimes had relatively little influence over her solo performer. Frequently he was simply not around, and in any case he did not join well with her friends, remaining mostly *hors concours*.[31] ❖

The Mariposas property continued to exert severe strains upon Frémont and his family. Although mining operations promised tremendous wealth, their complexities were enormous. His excavations were located at remote, widely separated sites, among them the Princeton, Josephine, Mount Ophir, and Pine Tree mines. He collected fifteen hundred dollars per month from prospectors who individually paid four dollars to ten dollars for the right to mine more than thirty auriferous quartz and granitic locations. His overseer sold the miners supplies as well.

Frémont also leased lots in the town of Mariposa on which stood a row of hardscrabble wooden houses and tents. The main dirt road was lined with a double row of saloons. Bear Valley's only hotel, the Oso, had walls made of cotton bed sheets tacked to wooden partitions. Because meat from domestic animals and fresh vegetables were scarce, its guests were served odd meals whenever supplies of rice, beans, and salt pork ran out. Flapjacks for supper, washed down with mugs of heavily watered coffee, were not an unusual menu at the Oso.

The Mariposas grant produced, Frémont maintained, from sixty thousand to one hundred thousand dollars per month, half of which was supposed to be profit. His overblown advertising brochures claimed that one iron mortar alone had pounded up three barrelfuls of select ore worth thirty thousand dollars. Frémont's agents, from San Francisco to London, gave out similarly inflated assertions to attract gullible investors—supporting the charges of Hoffman, his London agent, that Frémont had "a bit of humbug in him." Indeed, Josiah Royce later asserted that Frémont was an outright liar. The hazy history of California's overlapping land grants, as well as its vague mining laws, helped the Frémonts make up charming myths about their holdings.

Las Mariposas' original grantee, Governor Alvarado, had neither occupied nor improved the property, as required by Mexican law. Although Frémont knew this, he continued to assert that the grant was not only a developed one, but legally valid as well. He also expanded its original boundaries, claiming land that was never in the initial grant. His land surveys, conducted in secret, led to serious discrepancies regarding its mineral deposits. Only in 1863 would Clarence King, who later became nationally known for his geological work, begin to survey the eastern Sierra Nevada, including the Mariposas tract. King was invited there by Frederick Law Olmsted, who came to the estate in the fall of 1863 as its new overseer. After two years there, New York City offered him a commission to design that city's Central Park, and he returned east. He had been unable to clear up the confusion, some of it deliberately planted by Frémont, regarding the true size of Las Mariposas.[1]

After 1851, one of Frémont's largest sources of income came from the Merced Mining Company, which paid him twelve thousand dollars per year in lease fees. That firm built tunnels and roads and installed expensive machinery, but its owners were chagrined when Frémont could not deliver a clear title to his land. Furthermore, he proceeded to release some of the company's mining sites to Biddle Boggs, a yellow-haired, mustachioed Pennsylvania speculator. Boggs was to pay a fee equal to that of the Merced Mining Company for seven years. The company's subsequent lawsuit against Boggs further clouded the legality of Frémont's mining operations at a time when squatters swarmed all over his property.[2]

"Squatter judges" and "squatter juries" repeatedly favored the rights of individual miners in disputes over California's Mexican claims. During one prolonged squatter case, Frémont faced Judge David Terry, a vinegary Kentuckian who carried a Bowie knife for protection. Terry saw the litigant as an incorrigible Free Soiler. An ardent pro-slave Southerner, the judge had little sympathy for the abolitionist Frémont's murky land and mining deals. His opposition led Jessie to complain that if theirs "were the property of a southern democrat, it would have every legal protection" from Judge Terry, whereas he gave her husband nothing but trouble.

Frémont retreated, at the end of days filled with legal controversy, to the comfort of Jessie's "little white house," which one reached by taking a dusty lane that wound through Bear Valley. There, with the wind whistling through the tall timber, she tried to create a cozy and secure inner world for him and the children. As she wrote eastern friends, they all loved to curl up in front of the stone fireplace. Also, each family member was, fortunately, an inveterate reader:

"We have books and lots of papers and light reading & it is such a rest to Mr. Frémont to cut off business and put this high wall between himself and the money making."[3]

Jessie had also, as she said, "magnetized" her husband into accepting more family responsibilities. She was proud to tell Elizabeth Blair Lee:

> He takes part in & likes all the details of our household—the children's plays & witticisms and lessons—he looks after our comforts & is in fact head of the house. No "wild turkey" left. . . . I feel now as if we were a complete and compact family, and really Mr. Frémont used to be only a guest—dearly loved and honored but not counted on for worse as well as better. To him the palms. To us the shade. Now we share & share and he is far the happier for it.[4]

The thirty-four-year-old Jessie ran a lively household. A visitor to Bear Valley in these times described her as still a powerful personality, with her wavy brown hair, expressive eyebrows, sparkling eyes, and body fullness already underway. Jessie's male guest likewise found her "incessantly interesting, well-read, witty, genial, with a grasp of affairs, feminine intuitions . . . and a gift of irony" as well as overflowing with maternal feelings.[5]

Jessie was also pleased that the bond between her husband and their son was strengthening:

> Frank imitates him as nigh he can. He is a most beautiful boy and has developed the right paternal foolish fondness in Mr. Frémont at last, and the door once opened, the rest have gone in also. . . . By six they are scoured & nightgowned and have said their last jokes to Mr. Frémont & each in his own room is singing himself to sleep. For them this long stay here has been all good."[6]

Jessie wrote her publisher that Frank was "petted & magnified by us until, in his loving confidence, he feels quite our equal. He often advises his Father & we amuse ourselves by meeting his notions with all gravity." She and her husband lavished praise on their son: "No one treats Frank with levity, he is such a miniature of his Father. . . . At the same time he believes in fairies & is quite sure about the chimney fairy at Christmas."[7]

A charming letter to his son Frank discussed fairies, or "cabletosos": "I think that . . . everybody has a Cabletoso. . . . When a fairy whispers to you, you always hear it whether you seem to or not. . . . You must remember this, and always, when your Cabletoso whispers you to do something good, be sure you do it at once." Frémont pointed out that his cabletoso (or good fairy) had just saved him from a railroad accident. Another letter to "Franky" stated that he was happy that his son was putting sails on a toy sloop that worked with a magnet. This communication ended with the phrase, "You know I always am pleased when you do well."[8]

Frémont was never cruel to his children, and these communications suggest that he could actually be quite affectionate with them. Like Jessie, they complained that he too often was absent from the family. But at Las Mariposas, away from other women, she admitted feeling "more than justified in being here when I see how much I do to keep Mr. Frémont where his interests require." With her father dead, she came to look upon her husband as the real head of the household. He had finally taken the place of Senator Benton.[9]

John Charles also took a new interest in Lily, their rather homely daughter. She remembered, half regretfully, how his tenderness toward all the children was almost odd: "My father rarely talked of himself or what had happened to him out on the plains." Lily also noted his reserve and "aversion to personal display." Despite this, "on my father's birthday" she recalled, "we always made it a practice to decorate the house with flowers," his favorites being white roses and heliotropes.[10]

These and other amenities helped to shore up life at Bear Valley, which had been named for the grizzlies who made it their home and who now feasted upon the remains of hogs raised on Frémont's property. Conditions there remained quite crude. Both men and women used separate outside privies, located over a flowing stream. In the little wooden frame house, however, wax candles and oil lamps lit up its pretty French wallpaper, which Jessie pasted over flimsy wooden walls. She enlarged the bare, one-story white cottage and covered its floors with a crimson Brussels carpet. Jessie also got Frémont's men to lug a heavy piano made of cherry wood overland from San Francisco. Many years after the Frémonts had departed Bear Valley, antique hunters found her abandoned piano and dining room set.

At their ranch the Frémonts were surrounded by Indian helpers from 1849 onward. Their French cook complained that too many meals had to come out of their storeroom, which he called *le grocerie*, for it was hard to keep a vegetable garden in winter's quasi-Alpine weather when the land frosted over.

Out behind the ranch house lay Mount Bullion, a landmark given Senator Benton's nickname. This mining site, rich with ore veins, would attract a good many squatters. Jessie, who feared the dangers they posed, would entitle a chapter of her *Far West Sketches* (1890) "Besieged." Her husband did not venture forth each day without a derringer in a small holster strapped to his belt. On one occasion John Charles personally and courageously served a writ of eviction upon a group of French squatters who had occupied his Guadaloupe Mine. Such claimants could legally "jump" a mine once it was left empty, which was how he lost the valuable Black Drift Mine. A guard, left there to police its entryway, was bribed away long enough for squatters (who called themselves the Hornitas League) to take possession of the mine.[11]

When, on July 9, 1858, seventy-five raiders from the Merced Mining Company "jumped" Frémont's Pine Tree vein, he threatened that "they'll find they have jumped the wrong man." He positioned workers in the brush below the tunnel's platform and threw up barricades of rock, mining equipment, and powder kegs, which were themselves quite dangerous. Tension between the two opposing forces mounted, but Frémont refused to budge. The standoff lasted several days. Had the invaders descended into the mine, by way of an abandoned shaft called the Black Hole, Frémont planned to use dynamite against them.[12]

Next, the claim jumpers sought to isolate five men inside the Pine Tree Mine in order to starve them out. Frémont resourcefully got food to his trapped men by using a Mrs. Ketton, who ran the local boarding house, as a courier. Her husband was one of those besieged inside the mine, and twice each day she talked herself past its squatter guards. Had she been a man, they might have shot her. Under Frémont's direction, she also managed to carry in a layer of gunpowder and bullets secreted in the bottom of a picnic basket. Finally, Frémont, with eleven rifles leveled at his head, made a dramatic appeal to the squatters to lift their barricade at the mine entrance.

But next the squatters threatened to burn down the Frémonts' house. One night the family withstood the invaders with thirty-two rounds of ammunition, as Jessie explained in a letter to Francis Blair: "Five nights we kept guard with Lee and Isaac—our trusty colored men . . . both good shots—a fierce dog named Randy & Mr. Frémont made up the home force. With pistols and double barrelled guns we had 32 shots."[13] Bombs made of gunpowder in tin cans continued to explode near their home for weeks thereafter. Both Frémonts stayed on despite this intimidation.

Finally, the five-day siege of the Pine Tree Mine ended upon command of California's governor, to whom Frémont had appealed for help. As a result, a force of five hundred state troopers restored order. Jessie was convinced that members of the Hornitas League were "criminal outcasts exulting in their escape from Botany Bay and Sydney in Australia." After the governor ordered these invaders to disperse, they repaired to the Oso Tavern, where one of Frémont's men killed one of them and wounded three others.[14]

The *Sacramento Union* for December 7, 1858, crowed over Frémont's victory, suggesting that he "has been the subject of more bitter personal enmity and abuse than any man we have heard of. So far as we know there is no reason for it, and for the benefit of all concerned, it should stop until it fully appears that he *is* the autocratical swindler, scoundrel, and rascal that it seems the heart's desire of some men to make out."

All this friction with his lessees and with squatters weakened Frémont financially. The scramble for capital with which to develop the ores that lay below a forest of pines and red clover was unceasing. His machinery began to rust as he intermittently stopped mining operations because of lack of money for repairs, payrolls, and fuel. County taxes were also due on each load of ore. In the little settlement of cabins and tents that lined Bear Valley's main road, his men grumbled. The scarred mountainside hid its wealth from them whenever the stamp mills lay silent. The only answer to Frémont's continuing lack of funds was to attract outside investors.

To find that capital, he and Jessie therefore invited a procession of visitors. Among them was T. A. Rickard, who would become the foremost mining engineer of his time and who, like his fellow Cornishmen, was lured to California by its mineral wealth. Another celebrity whom the Frémonts entertained during the summer of 1859 was Richard Henry Dana, author of *Two Years Before the Mast*. A third well-known visitor, whose chin-whiskers were the talk of Bear Valley— the eccentric journalist Horace Greeley—became a one-man publicity bureau for Frémont's mining properties. Since the presidential campaign three years before, Greeley had viewed Frémont as unfairly maligned. In a daily newspaper column, the writer portrayed Frémont to his readers as an entrepreneur who arose each morning "with the lark" to mine a vein of ore eight to sixty feet wide. The ebullient and naive Greeley pointed out to a national audience that the Pathfinder paid taxes of "no less than sixteen thousand dollars per annum" on land "wasted" by squatters, who dug his soil "into utterly worthless chasms and heaps in quest of gold" and who cut down timber and fed off his grasslands "at their own discretion, leaving to the fortunate owner only the privilege of paying the taxes." Frémont had become a "manager, chief engineer, cashier, accountant, and is at the head of every other department but that of law." Greeley reported that two of Frémont's stamping mills, "which he hoped to increase to one hundred," were producing gold "at the rate of at least two hundred and fifty thousand dollars per annum, at an absolute cost, I am confident, of not more than one hundred and fifty thousand dollars."[15]

The squatters who invaded the Mariposas diggings were not all the evil figures that Greeley portrayed to the outside world. Strapped for capital, once the Sierra Nevada's surface placers gave out, they left them behind to technically better organized groups who worked the Mariposas hydraulically or with dynamite, scarring the mountainside with flumes and ditches, as did Frémont.

A Vermonter who worked for Frémont at Bear Valley admired his courage in handling these squatters but expressed misgivings about his character:

> I considered him a brave, enterprising, honest man, but he always had the idea that he was a great man and much smarter than most of the people. He was daring, dashing, and brave . . . just the man to take hold of a desperate job. He laid out and planned more . . . than any other man I ever saw. [But] in money matters he had no more judgment than a ten year old boy.

In the battle against the squatters, however, Frémont registered higher marks as he proved to be

> no coward, nor were his men. The "jumpers" were armed with guns and pistols but we had about thirty Springfield rifles and plenty of revolvers. Some of our men had two or three "blunderbusses" made of brass, small at the breach but gradually flaring at the top ... loaded with powder, shots, bullets, and slugs. ... Frémont came to us on his horse, often day and night. Whenever he appeared, the boys who were awake would cheer him long and loud. ... Our brave front made the "jumpers" lose heart and courage.[16]

Jessie and her husband both regularly read absorbing tales of battles won by heroic leaders, and she saw him as one of those courageous knights. An agent for Frémont's bankers, Edward Bosqui, described the way in which their ranch house reflected her courtly ideals: "Mrs. Frémont was a highly accomplished woman of fine intellect, with a towering ambition and courage equal to her husband's. The acquisition of power and the love of display and leadership were her ruling passions and caused much of her husband's troubles and disappointments." Jessie pinned onto one wall of the house "an illustration from Shakespeare's 'Henry V,' where the King is made to say 'By the sword I gained my titles, and by the sword I will maintain them.'" About this she wrote: "The horse is as essential as the man in the knight complete— man, sword and horse made the war trinity."[17]

All this interest in the trappings of chivalry occurred at a time when European genealogists were busily validating coats of armor for wealthy American clients. This authentication "provided an upper class under stress with valuable emblems of unity and exclusiveness."[18] Jessie seemed to seek such identification for her husband, perhaps as mutual reassurance of his superiority to other mortals who dared to challenge him on his own domain. He was the knight; the squatters were mere peasants.

Jessie meddled in a variety of other activities, too. Even the ranch's outlying Indians fell within her purview. She pitied these miserable creatures, who, starved for food, were reduced to making sandwiches of bread, warm suet, and potato peelings and whose labor was routinely exploited in the mines. To his credit her husband would not use black slaves for such work. Slavery, furthermore, was legally forbidden in California.

John Charles also tried to help the natives acculturate to the waves of invading white settlers. In fact, he would get into still deeper financial trouble seeking to secure government funds with which to feed the local Indians. To help settle his forty-thousand-dollar government claim over food for them, Frémont employed Montgomery Blair, then a judge at the Washington Court of Appeals.

Their relationship would become a long and complicated one. Blair was only one of a succession of attorneys constantly in Frémont's employ.

In protecting his property, Frémont, unlike harassed property owners of Hispanic background, knew what his rights were under American law. But legal fees were high. By 1858 he had five different cases pending before the courts. Always suspicious, he wrote Blair that these legal actions formed "part of a general attack upon me." By this he meant that the hated Merced mining group was out to destroy his hold over Las Mariposas.[19]

The Pathfinder now presided over no small operation. Some sixteen thousand workers either mined or were otherwise employed within the borders of his properties. One assayer estimated forty dollars' value per ton of gold mined. Although some of the gold in the quartz veins was high, it was expensive to extract. By importing more modern machinery to reduce labor, and by constructing canals and centralizing his mining and logging operations, Frémont hoped to make the property more efficient.[20]

Because of his economic miscalculations, Frémont became, as we have seen, the object of bitter criticism by his London agent, David Hoffman. Back home, too, Frémont was called an autocrat, swindler, scoundrel, rascal, even thief. Henry A. Wise (author of the book *Los Gringos*) described him in a private letter as "a very unscrupulous character." Yet Wise admired his scientific explorations and "the indomitable energy, perseverance, and skill with which he accomplished them."[21]

Finally, on March 10, 1855, the U.S. Supreme Court reversed earlier California decisions that had held up confirmation of the Mariposas claims.[22] A celebration was clearly in order. The family, anxious to take a vacation away from the ranch, went by carriage to Stockton, where they boarded a paddle-wheel steamer to San Francisco.

When she was at Black Point, overlooking San Francisco Bay near today's Fort Mason, Jessie found greater satisfaction. She would come to love that seaside home, its fogs punctuated by the tolling of a warning buoy that floated offshore alongside the seals of the bay. But the couple's troubles, financial and legal, were hardly over. Tight money made it necessary for Frémont to sell off or to lease yet more mining claims. Among them were "the Belgian Mines," advertised as traversed by a thick vein of silver. His mining sites were so spread out (seventeen miles in length and five to twelve miles wide) that Frémont had to spend $150,000 on new roads to link up each location.[23]

The mines allegedly provided an income of almost $40,000 per month, but the monthly payroll alone amounted to $10,000. Frémont required even more capital for tunnels, shafts, and machinery. Furthermore, a technological revolution had taken place since he first began to work the lode. The eastern United States soon reverberated to the whir of factory wheels, the clangor of foundries, and the scream of locomotives, one of which he imported from Pittsburgh to run over a four-mile track connecting the mines with the Merced River. The train was supposed to save $200 per day in transport charges by making a descent and ascent of fourteen hundred feet in a short distance. But its rolling stock alone cost over $120,000.[24]

Lobbyists, mining engineers, and lawyers proved costly, too. Among the specialists Frémont hired was the great geologist Professor J. D. Whitney, after whom Mount Whitney, California's highest mountain, is named. In addition, Charles Douglas Fox, an English mining engineer, and Justus Adelberg, a renowned metallurgist, traveled together to San Francisco and then on to Bear Valley to advise Frémont. In 1857 the Pathfinder offered Charles Ellet, another civil engineer, the job of constructing a canal seventy-five miles long to bring water from the Merced River to the Mariposas mining sites. Frémont also constructed the Benton quartz stamp mill six miles north of his town.[25]

In the summer of 1859 the Frémonts built a camp eighteen hundred feet above Bear Valley on the east side of Mount Bullion. There they erected a large tent with a wooden floor. Nearby was a cold-water spring that formed a miniature lake. The family, while camping there, could escape the heat that wafted up into Las Mariposas from the San Joaquin Valley. They and their visitors especially enjoyed a good view of the snow-covered Sierra Nevada.

The running of complicated mining and milling operations left little time for such vacations. Because Las Mariposas required constant new capital, early in 1858 Frémont traveled eastward to raise more money. Each such voyage attracted the attention of the press. Because he had little luck in getting money from New York bankers, he sailed back rather hastily for California on the bark *Moses Taylor*. After crossing the isthmus of Panama by land, Frémont boarded another vessel, the *Golden Age*, on the Pacific side. Worn out by the long sea voyage, he arrived at San Francisco on April 12, 1858.

There, Frémont was hounded by creditors, who met his ship at the Embarcadero. Perennially late paying off loans, Frémont had repeatedly come close to losing Las Mariposas, and after this trip he brought back only a small infusion of capital but installed more machinery and hired better trained men to work his claims. Repeated lawsuits had depleted not only his resources but also those of Palmer, Cook & Company. Partly because of Frémont's heavy money requirements, that firm failed later in 1858. "It takes a mine to make a mine" was an old Spanish saying.

Frémont now also engaged Frederick Billings (later a leading developer of the Northern Pacific Railroad, after whom Billings, Montana, is named) as his principal attorney. During the gold rush of 1849, Billings had the good judgment to open a law office in San Francisco instead of digging for ore. That office became the city's leading legal firm, Halleck, Peachy, and Billings. Commanding in appearance and possessing superb social graces, Billings, who was ten years younger than Frémont, became one representative whom the mine owner could trust. Although Billings and Frémont often used a code system to convey telegraphic business messages to each other, Billings wisely did not mistake this for closeness, for Frémont treated the lawyer as an employee throughout their long relationship.

Both men left for Europe during 1861 in another search for foreign loans, stopping off at New York's Astor House to meet President Lincoln amid hostile tension between North and South. The former presidential candidate was pleased to be recognized by almost as many people as was Lincoln himself. But Frémont's mind was on matters more intimate. Rumors were unceasing that he continued to consort with various women.

Jessie had stayed on in San Francisco, suffering from repeated fainting spells related to injuries sustained after her runaway carriage careened wildly down San Francisco's Russian Hill. This freed her husband to travel to Europe with a Margaret Corbett. We know little about that woman except that she had a child and that, before embarking, she and Frémont spent time together in Philadelphia. He made elaborate travel plans to disguise his dalliance with her, even suggesting that Billings should sail on another vessel in order to confuse gossips. But news of the affair leaked out, even though she occupied a separate stateroom on board, for which Frémont paid—a deceit that Billings considered "disgusting." Frémont's other aide, the rapacious Trenor Park, also knew of the Corbett affair, and Jessie probably did as well. Billings wrote to Park that Frémont was "ashamed to take his woman on the same ship that I go on. For he takes to Europe the same woman and child he brought from San Francisco."[26] Billings liked Jessie but distrusted her husband, calling him an employer who used a sawmill to destroy the California redwoods though he was a self-advertised lover of nature.

Also traveling aboard the vessel with Frémont and his paramour was George W. Wright, a founder of the Mariposa Mining Company. Wright would try to cover up for the couple, but after they reached London, Frémont unexplainably took Mrs. Corbett for a visit to the U.S. Legation. Its secretary, Benjamin Moran, wrote in his official consular log for Tuesday, March 12, 1861, that the Pathfinder was "enroute to Paris with a Mrs. Corbett."[27]

Once the news became known, Francis Preston Blair, a consistent backer of Frémont in Washington, importuned Wright immediately to issue a letter of defense to a select group of Jessie's friends: "A slanderous report . . . is that Col. Frémont left California in company with a woman of bad reputation—that he had been living with her in New York and that finally he had taken her to Europe." Wright sought to assure Montgomery Blair that this female was a friend of Jessie's and had been placed in Frémont's care while traveling, a highly unlikely story.

Wright named a suspect, probably Horace White, a journalist, of making the affair public: "The slander was first put in circulation on board the boat by a low born wretch by the name of White who is seeking a certain position under the Federal Government. . . . This man White obtained by fraud and falsehood a letter from Mrs. Frémont to your Father." The Frémonts' marriage was clearly in trouble, but Jessie managed not to give out any indication of her unhappiness to anyone. Only one letter of hers hints at any sort of revenge. Both John Charles and a long-suffering Jessie conformed to Victorian secrecy about marital matters. As for Mrs. Corbett, she dropped out of sight in London after she, Frémont, and Billings enjoyed a public reading by the celebrated novelist Charles Dickens. We do not know if she completed the trip to France with Frémont, as did Billings.[28]

Billings found that Frémont's English agents had done little to attract new investors since his last visit—partly a result of the mine owner's failure to delegate responsibilities regarding the announcement of which mines were for sale or lease. Therefore, Billings took along only an "imperial-size" folio of Mariposas photographs by Carleton E. Watkins to accompany a handsome prospectus entitled *The Mariposas Estate*, published in England, which reproduced Professor Whitney's glowing report on the Bear Valley mines.

When Frémont and Billings reached Paris in search of funds, they sought out a Baron Jarnoc of the banking house of Rothschild, along with William L. Dayton, Frémont's vice-presidential running mate in 1856, who was now minister to France. Frémont and Billings invited potential investors to Las Mariposas to inspect its mining prospects. These included the Counts de Blandville and Wass as well as a Major Uznay; they offered to loan $1,250,000 rather than become outright investors.[29]

The continuing Mariposas financial mess made Frémont look like an economic idiot, constantly dependent upon a coterie of consultants. During 1862, Billings tried to sell the entire property to an English syndicate, which he might have done had the Civil War not broken out. Foreigners became wary of investing large sums in a country at war with itself. Next, Billings appointed his former law partner, Park, as overall manager of Las Mariposas, also striking an unfortunate bargain with a group consisting of George Opdyke, mayor of New York City; Morris Ketchum, Frémont's New York banker; and one James Hoey. The details of their joint involvement emerge from the transcript of a libel suit in which Frémont was a correspondent and witness, which makes him look like a lamb shorn of wool by shysters.[30]

At the end of 1862, Frémont ceased to receive royalties from the property, although "experts" still said he could count on a gross monthly income of $200,000 in gold and an overall annual revenue of $1,920,000. But interest charges on outstanding liens of $3,250,000 reached $13,000 per month. His telegraph bills alone cost as much as $150 "day after day," as Frémont testified in the Opdyke trial. The syndicate fleeced him of $2,600,000.[31]

After the American Civil War exploded, Frémont stayed on in Europe for a time, preoccupied with military purchases. Neither he nor Jessie returned to the Mariposas estate until after the war, having conveyed to Billings and Park one-eighth of the property each for legal and management fees. Defense of the title had recently cost over two hundred thousand dollars. Ultimately Frémont gave Billings an added one-sixteenth of the estate, while Charles Dudley Field, another attorney, received a one-fiftieth share. As a result, its seventy square miles had slipped from Frémont's control. After some of his creditors founded the Mariposa Mining Company, throwing its stock onto the market, he complained to friends that when he first went to California, he was worth nothing but, that after all the furor caused by defending Las Mariposas, he owed two million dollars! ❖

A General versus Lincoln

There had been talk in 1860 of Frémont again running for the presidency. But, now he no longer had the backing of the Blair family, nor of Gideon Welles and other Republican stalwarts. They still harbored misgivings about him as a leader. Nevertheless, for a time he was mentioned as a prospective minister to France. William H. Seward, President Lincoln's secretary of state, also confidentially proposed him as secretary of war. But Lincoln did not act on this suggestion. The president did, however, query Seward regarding an appointment to Paris, to which Seward replied: "The prestige is good. But I think that is all. If, as I have heard, he is to be engaged in raising money there for his estates, it would be a serious complication."[1]

When the Civil War broke out in April 1861, Frémont was still in Europe with Frederick Billings seeking new Mariposas investors. By then, eight southern states had seceded from the Union. The Confederates had also seized ten federal arsenals and forts. With no official authority, Frémont dropped private business plans and began to contact European weapons merchants in order to purchase arms and ammunition for the U.S. government. He wrote Francis Preston Blair from London's Athenaeum Club: "I have succeeded in procuring the control of funds sufficient to purchase three or four batteries of guns . . . and perhaps 10,000 rifles." After visiting English and French foundries and arsenals, he confided to Blair: "I trust that you have already offered my services to the President. . . . My great desire is to serve my country in the most direct and effective way that I possibly can."[2]

Frémont lamented the activities of Confederate agents in England who were busy obtaining everything from ammunition to "war steamers." Pledging his own frail personal credit as payment, he and Frederick Billings contracted for seventy-five thousand dollars' worth of cannons and artillery shells from England and France. For these purchases he had, unfortunately, only the begrudging support of the distrustful Charles Francis Adams, American minister to the Court of St. James.

In the spring of 1861, after receiving rumors that President Lincoln planned to appoint him to a high government position, John wrote to Jessie in California asking that she take the family to meet him in New York. She found it difficult to tear herself away from Black Point. After the two grueling years at Las Mariposas, she reveled in Black Point's twelve acres of scenery, "a combination of every beauty in nature." It had been wonderful to relax in "the prettiest little house you ever saw, furnished like a picture." He had also built adjoining stables for the family horses and carriages while she spent twenty thousand dollars of her own money in enlarging the parlor and bedrooms and in adding a three-sided glass veranda and a summer cottage. At her teas there she invited the popular orator-minister Thomas Starr King, the writer Francis Bret Harte, as well as Ed Beale, who had become California's surveyor general. Nearby lived Leonidas Haskell, a wool and hide dealer whose daughter Nellie, brighter than Jessie's Lil, became a member of her circle. As Jessie packed up the family's belongings, she did not know that never again would they all experience the glow of Black Point's fireplace.[3]

Frémont found the political and military atmosphere back in the states to be chaotic. As the summer of 1861 approached, Lincoln faced a severe shortage of general officers. The army's senior commander, Lieutenant General Winfield Scott, was then seventy-four years old, and the president sought younger leaders. Frémont, therefore, became one of the first four major generals appointed following the outbreak of war. The army had two departments, that of the East and that of the West, the latter headquartered in Saint Louis. Frémont accepted command of the Department of the West, arriving there with Jessie on July 25, 1861.[4]

Lincoln ignored the fact that Frémont had never commanded more than a few hundred men. Furthermore, the Pathfinder was to head up a far-flung area in which fighting raged—Tennessee, Missouri, and Kentucky were implacably divided—and he had to maintain long lines of communication. Frémont found himself in command of thirty thousand raw troops in all the states between the Mississippi and the Rockies, one-third of the nation's entire territory.

Saint Louis was as much a part of the South as of the North. Confederate influence there was so strong that Union officers were unwilling to appear alone in uniform on its streets. Secessionists flew the Stars and Bars from a Confederate recruiting center downtown. Furthermore, the federal government had no local credit. Merchants did not trust its ability to repay them for goods furnished to Frémont's army. The general himself considered Saint Louis to be a rebel city.

Indeed, some of its most influential and wealthy citizens remained friendly toward secession. On August 4, 1861, the general declared martial law, suppressing the *Saint Louis Republican* and imprisoning its editor. He believed that secessionists might well take over the city should Confederate troops appear on its outskirts.

With Senator Benton long since gone, Frémont had to face local dissidence alone. The "Rebs" wandered at will throughout the divided state, and "irregular warfare" flourished. In order to contain attacks on his green troops, Frémont blundered into a completely illegal and sub-rosa agreement with Confederate General Sterling Price that each would not encourage bushwhacking bands of renegades. As long as these irregulars pillaged the countryside, Frémont somehow had to stop the hemorrhaging of his scattered forces.

The federal garrison in Saint Louis never numbered more than eight thousand men, of which only three thousand were well armed. Frémont repeatedly marched them through the city's streets to give the enemy the impression that he had over ten thousand in reserve. His critics asserted that he remained tactically immobile for a period of five weeks and never went farther from his front door than onto the sidewalk to review newly arrived troops.

Frémont installed his staff in a large house that he rented for six thousand dollars per year from one of Jessie's relatives. Upstairs in this command post he sought to bring order into a chaotic military situation. Hunched over long tables covered by war plans, papers, and reports, the Pathfinder fended off innumerable callers. These were said to bother the life out of him. He was surrounded by carping and resentful West Pointers. Yet, early in the war, it was Frémont who appointed Ulysses S. Grant, a West Pointer, to his first significant command—control of the Cairo, Illinois, military district. Grant, who had been a low-ranked quartermaster during the Mexican War, had faltered as a peacetime army officer, farmer, and merchant. But eventually he would emerge as a major commander, whereas Frémont's role became that of an untrusted visionary.

Frémont's headquarters was also filled with visiting dignitaries. They included a Prince Napoleon as well as Dorothea Dix, who was busy creating a nursing corps for the Union Army. Frémont asked her to open hospitals for the wounded. Jessie confided to Miss Dix that it was "such a relief" that "my dear Chief" was doing his duty for God and country despite neglect from Washington. It was, Jessie continued, "simply a shame and a crime to hamper him so." Although she sympathized with her husband's plight as head of the impoverished western command, her own role was also a difficult one at Saint Louis. Married to so prominent a northern general and political figure, she simply had to side with him against old Southern friends. Her war experiences, she later claimed, turned her hair almost overnight from chestnut brown to yellowed white, and she was only thirty-six. But, infuriated that Washington continued to treat Frémont's

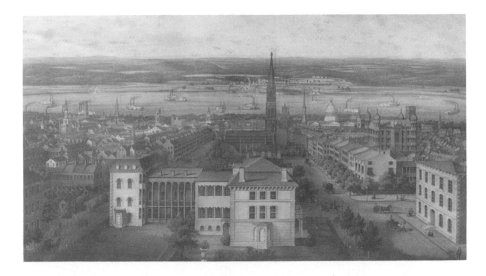

View of Saint Louis from Lucas Place about 1865. Major General Frémont had established his headquarters in that city once dominated politically by his father-in-law, Senator Thomas Hart Benton. For the Frémont family, Saint Louis was a second home. (Used by permission of the Missouri Historical Society, Saint Louis)

command like a weak stepchild, she began to act, some said, like a female general.[5]

Frémont's command was to last only one hundred days. With severely limited funds, he had to raise an army of trusted volunteers, to transform river ferries into gunboats armed with mortars for the reinforcement of undermanned outposts, and somehow to win a few battles. His forces included seven ironclads that patrolled the Mississippi; one of them he named the *Benton* in memory of Jessie's father. He launched all of these vessels at Saint Louis.

Most of Frémont's forces were located west of Saint Louis. Two Confederate armies were gathering for an invasion of Missouri along the state's southern border, not to speak of the guerrilla infestations. Four days after Frémont assumed command, six thousand Southerners crossed the Mississippi from Tennessee and occupied New Madrid, where they threatened Union soldiers at the river junction of Cairo, Illinois.

For a time Frémont gave serious thought, as did other commanders, to mounting an expedition down the Mississippi to capture New Orleans. He believed that his troops might thereby actually win the war by splitting the Confederacy in two, after driving through its southeastern region, and then

LINCOLN: *"Well, Master Frémont, that's rather a long reach, ain't it?
You might fetch it with your sword, in the proper time, but it is n't
ripe yet."*

This admonishing cartoon from *Leslie's Weekly* refers to the last attempt in 1864
by Frémont's backers to run him again for the presidency. (From W. A. Crofutt,
An American Procession [New York, 1914], p. 271)

sweeping up the East Coast to his native Charleston and then on to Richmond. Professional military leaders saw this as the pipe dream of an amateur short on troops. Only parts of Frémont's original strategy were coincidentally followed independently of him by the high command, and certainly without attribution.

As he fussed over one strategic plan after another, Frémont *thought* he had powerful allies back in Washington. Across the street from Lincoln's White House lived the Blair household, distantly related to the Bentons. An alliance between the two families had endured for years. Francis Preston Blair, patriarch of his clan, had been a Jacksonian colleague and the editor of the Democratic party's Washington newspaper, *The Globe*. Without his influence, Frémont would not have received the Missouri command.

The Blairs were, however, "a composite of conflicting characteristics . . . able, aggressive, patriotic, and vindictive." Francis's two sons were strategically placed—Montgomery in Lincoln's cabinet and Frank as chairman of the House Military Affairs Committee. In return for past favors, they expected Frémont to endorse nomination of Francis's son Frank as a general. When this was not forthcoming, and for other reasons, too, the Blairs turned against Frémont. They not only sought to run the war in Missouri by proxy, but also wanted a measure of control over an inexperienced president as well as his field commander in Saint Louis. From there, a gullible Jessie implored Montgomery Blair to "send . . . both arms and money by the most rapid conveyance." As she also complained to Ward Hill Lamon, "her general" was thwarted on every side by Lincoln's confused cabinet, which had no right "to send Genl. Frémont out with the fullest security for his plans not being sustained."[6]

Frémont was so strapped for funds that he had to persuade his troops at Cairo to stay beyond their three-month enlistment period. Soldiers who had served without pay were ever on the verge of mutiny. The general called both his draftees and volunteers an "unmanageable mob"; they were constantly threatening to go home to their farms and villages. Without the help of seasoned veterans, he sought to whip raw recruits into shape by interminable drills. Faced with their defection, he personally guaranteed their wages. In order to obtain sorely needed supplies for them, he had to pay greatly inflated prices for contracted goods. The Saint Louis branch of the U.S. Treasury had refused him one hundred thousand of some three hundred thousand dollars originally appropriated to him. Desperate for these funds, on one occasion he raided the district treasury office to seize money with which to meet his payroll.[7] As Jessie again wrote the Blairs: "He is doing the best he can without money, without arms, without moral aid"; she complained that equipment destined for her husband's forces was "moving to the East."

Jessie reminded all her correspondents that her husband, through Frederick Billings, was dutifully continuing to buy weapons abroad on his own. To one she wrote that, indeed, "his battery rifles and pistols might save the state." In a bold hand he scrawled across one of her pleading letters the words, "Money and Arms without delay and by the quickest Conveyance." Billings continued to ship arms from Brussels, Frankfurt, and Paris as well as London. One of Billings's shipments consisted of 204 cases of artillery shells, 450 revolvers, fifteen hundred rifles, 102,000 cartouches, and several million percussion caps plus six-pound cannons, carbines, and sabres.[8]

Trying to shore up so poorly equipped a command seemed a hopeless cause. Frémont was to testify before the Committee on the Conduct of the War that he never was "furnished with any particular plan of campaign. . . . Not a line of written instructions was given me."[9] Washington had made practically no preparations to conduct a war in the West. Of course, despite the western general's objections, the higher priority of supplies for the eastern commanders was justified. The Union Army simply could not have afforded to lose the war in the East. Furthermore, most of the Confederacy's most potent commanders, including Robert E. Lee, operated in the eastern theater of operations.

Because Frémont commanded so many inexperienced recruits, he created the Benton Cadets, a school for conscripted infantry officers. He also formed the regiments of Benton Hussars and Frémont Hussars.[10] These irregular units drew the criticism of West Pointers, who, moreover, hated to serve under a political appointee. Two brigadier generals—John Pope, a rival from Topographical Corps days, and Samuel D. Sturgis, who had also served in the Mexican War—were unsparingly critical of their commander. Pope never relented in coveting Frémont's command, and Sturgis, a drunk, was defeated at Brice's Crossroads in 1861. Both charged that Frémont consistently favored dubiously talented Hungarian and German hussars. Whole regiments, such as the Twelfth Missouri, were in fact German-speaking. Other units included a peculiar mixture of adventurers, among them old California friends.

But the foreign soldiers who flocked to Frémont's command were relatively undemanding, and they sometimes brought along ancient European muskets and old sabres. Others even furnished their own absurdly gaudy uniforms. Colonel Anselm Albert, a veteran of the Austrian army, was only one of the general's eighteen personal aides, some of whom were called "decayed aristocrats." Hovering like peacocks round Frémont's headquarters, they deferred to a newfound master who favored their cosmopolitan background.

Major Charles Zagonyi organized an entire cavalry battalion, which acted as the general's personal guard. Jessie heroicized them in her *Story of the Guard* (1863). The renowned "Zagonyis" consisted of only three companies of some fifty men each. Though scoffed at as "show soldiers," they were model cavalrymen. At Springfield they lost one-third of their men while charging a body of several thousand Confederate infantry and mounted scouts, shouting "Frémont and the

Union." After routing the enemy, Zagonyi said in his quaint English: "We did use sabers only. Pistols is a trooble—and not so sure!" Their daring raid drove the enemy out of Springfield.[11]

Frémont's chief of staff was another foreigner, Brigadier General Alexander Asboth, a participant in Kossuth's Hungarian revolt, and his topographical engineer was Colonel John T. Fiala. German General Franz Sigel, a swashbuckler from Baden still in his thirties, commanded one of Frémont's best regiments. Frémont appointed as a civilian aide Gustave Koerner, with a Heidelberg doctorate, who had been lieutenant governor of Illinois. Major William Dorsheimer, a German-American lawyer, became postal chief, and a Captain Waldaner was Frémont's musical director. Others who bore foreign names and who spoke with accents joined Frémont's military rolls: Saccippi, Occidone, Cattanco. John Schofield, an officer then in Missouri, charged that these foreign adventurers possessed greater access to scarce weapons than did regular army personnel like himself.

Furthermore, Frémont made strenuous efforts to obtain even more foreign recruits. In a letter to Francis Lieber from Saint Louis he wrote: "Are there any experienced artillery officers or men . . . Germans, Prussians, or French, in New York who can be enlisted immediately and sent to me here without any loss of time? I am distressed for want of men to man my guns and the enemy is at our door."[12]

Frémont again stirred the usual loyalties in some of his men, though he was never a soldier's soldier, at ease with troops or living with them, eating the same food, sleeping on the ground, or setting an example of camaraderie. While in Missouri he showed the hauteur of the staff officer instead of the line commander. Old trail hands were surprised that he had aged so much; he now wore a full beard, and his long, curling hair was heavily streaked with gray. Though haggard and overworked, he was pleased to see even former enemies such as Ned Kern, who, along with Pope, had once declared Frémont incompetent. He now directed Kern to work with a French engineer and a former officer of the Russian army who had fought in the Crimean War. Theirs was a delicate assignment: to go behind Confederate lines and to reconnoiter and sketch the earthworks south of Saint Louis.[13]

Frémont was clever in his use of spies, though he had no experience with espionage. He was in dire need of more detailed information regarding enemy operations as well as roads, forts, and bridges in western Tennessee and Kentucky. Some of his telegrams went to his agents in Hungarian and other languages. A few messages were routed through General Grant, who was grateful for the invaluable Confederate information about Forts Henry and Donelson unearthed by Frémont's foreign-born personnel. Grant, writing to Captain Charles de Arnaud, acknowledged that he was able to take Paducah, Kentucky, "solely on information given by yourself." Frémont paid de Arnaud three hundred dollars for "secret service" forays into "the rebel parts of Tennessee and Kentucky" at great personal risk. Later confined to an insane asylum, de Arnaud claimed that his hallucinations were a result of the extraordinary service that Frémont had demanded. With Lincoln's endorsement, de Arnaud later received most of an additional claim for thirty-six hundred dollars.[14]

Useful for espionage was the tiny fleet that Frémont created. These boats also did splendid service for Grant at Forts Donelson and Henry on the Mississippi. President Lincoln took a special interest in the creation of this "western flotilla." But Frémont could not resist giving lucrative contracts to his friends, including James B. Eads, for the conversion of riverboats and rafts into ironclads. The taint of corruption in his command lingered on as the general relapsed into the role of a loner who isolated himself by using three sets of sentries to bar the door to his command post.[15]

While his praetorian guard cut him off from the realities of command, Frémont's military reputation, like that of other "radical generals" such as Butler, Hooker, McDowell, and Burnside, darlings of the abolitionists whom President Lincoln had to appease, did not improve. Not all irregular officers were political hacks, however. Among the exceptions were Generals Cyrus Bussey, William Campbell, and John Sanborn. None of the latter, however, tried to integrate foreign officers, regulars, and volunteers under one command as did Frémont.

Although Francis Lieber wrote to Senator Charles Sumner that "Frémont is worshipped by his command," closer observers complained that his "illegal appointment of Dutch officers," or Germans, was producing "ruinous destruction" within the Western Department. "Frémont's love of pomp makes him surround himself with a bodyguard of about 50 or 100," a critic charged. These "parasites," he continued, "are instructed to drive back and beat away with the flats of their sabres any of the injured citizens who might in their desperation seek to see the great Mogul." The writer described presenting an important letter to "the grand Monarque, who chucked it behind him without even opening it . . . conversing in a royally condescending style of pleasantry with the officer who led me up, taking no more notice of me than if I had not been in existence, save in a single supercilious glance." After Union supplies ended up in the hands of Confederate General Sterling Price, the same correspondent wrote to Horace Greeley describing the outlandish behavior of troops headed by a Frémont favorite, General Sigel: "Nothing you can possibly hear from any quarter of the mismanagement, pillage, and utter ruin in this Department can at all approach the reality."[16]

Recording all this confusion was the future author Francis Grierson, who acted as a young page at Frémont's headquarters. Grierson recalled that the local response to the appointment of so many foreigners in order to give the command "some idea of military tone and style" was one of indignation: "They could not understand such a whim on the part of a democratic leader at a time when action and courage meant everything, personal appearance nothing." One of Grierson's duties was to help keep visitors away from Frémont. When the later renowned William Tecumseh Sherman, then a mere brigadier general on his way to Kentucky, attempted to gain access, a fellow guard admonished him: "What do you want with General Frémont? You don't suppose he will see such as you?" Frémont was portrayed to Sherman as "a great potentate, surrounded by sentries and guards," and also as possessing "a more showy court than any great king; [he] kept senators, governors and others waiting for days before granting an interview." Sherman would not forget such nonsense. Even members of Frémont's past western expeditions, "who expected to be admitted to his presence without any trouble . . . waited a long time, returning day after day." Some never did gain admittance.[17]

In addition to not imposing discipline on his bloated staff, Frémont acted as though Washington's bureaucracy was as much the enemy as the Confederacy. This intemperance aroused the anger of Frank Blair, a tall and handsome authoritarian with drooping mustache. The Frémonts had named a son after Blair, who not only remained chairman of the congressional Military Affairs Committee, but also became the spearhead of conservative Unionism in Missouri and an opponent of Frémont's Free Soil notions. Salmon Chase, President Lincoln's treasury secretary, wrote the general privately that he considered Blair dangerously selfish. But Chase was more interested in obtaining the presidency than in helping Frémont against Blair. Chase, working underground to unhorse Lincoln in 1864, used the politically naive Frémont against the Blair family, whose members wished to make Frank a future president.

The Blairs, as former slaveholders, knew that the war probably meant the end of slavery. But these would-be rulers of Missouri were not genuine abolitionists, as was Frémont. The Blairs favored gradual emancipation at best. Postmaster General Montgomery Blair, Frank's brother, also excoriated Frémont's tendency to become a cult figure: "Our people are not man worshippers, and if they were, there is nothing in Frémont's recent conduct to attract any enthusiasm. . . . He will subside into insignificance and . . . wise acres will say behold how foolish and capricious are the people. . . . I confess to great mortification at the failure of Frémont. I had taken up the general opinion that he was a great man."[18]

The Blairs also grew to resent Frémont's continuing popularity among Missouri's Germans. As long as he was in command there, he could back his power with raw force on the scene. Their quarrel went beyond matters of military strategy, or whether he was a do-nothing general. Wartime Missouri was split by two political factions. A group known as the "Claybanks" believed in gradual emancipation of all slaves, while the "Charcoals" advocated Frémont's view that slaves should receive immediate freedom.

As a result of the falling out between the Blairs and the Frémonts, their children no longer moved in and out of each others' houses, as they had in former times. Almost overnight Jessie experienced a sort of selective amnesia concerning the help the Blairs had extended as far back as the election of 1856. Both Frémonts also chose to forget a number of other matters about Montgomery Blair. A West Point graduate, he had been Frémont's personal attorney and had also become district attorney and mayor of Saint Louis. Blair knew many personal details about Frémont's mining controversies and his cattle and Indian claim problems, yet Blair had been unable to collect for his legal services to Frémont.

As President Lincoln's postmaster general, Blair had tried to get the western command for an old family friend, Nathaniel Lyon. When that proved impossible, the Blairs had backed Frémont for the job. Montgomery's father, the family patriarch Francis P. Blair, was a close friend of General Lyon. Both of these older men felt themselves to be more than the equal of Frémont, who, after all, had once been tarnished by a court-martial trial. Therefore, when Frémont failed to reinforce Lyon, a West Pointer who refused to retreat from Springfield in southwestern Missouri, Blair blamed the western commander for Lyon's death.

Lyon had faced terrible odds. In order to reinforce Cairo, Frémont had to withhold reinforcements from Lyon's six thousand men. Lyon, quite alone, had confronted the combined armies of Generals Sterling Price and Ben McCulloch. This Confederate force was twice the size of Lyon's. On August 10, 1861, instead of retreating, Lyon, accompanied by General Franz Sigel, made an impetuous attack on a Rebel encampment at Wilson's Creek, ten miles from Springfield. Although the Southerners initially fell back, they regrouped and routed Sigel, who managed to escape. Lyon was outnumbered three to one and ran out of ammunition. He lost not only many men but also his own life—and with severe implications for Frémont. Lyon was the first Union general to be killed on the field of battle during the Civil War.

General John Schofield, who was on Lyon's staff and a witness to the events at Wilson's Creek, did not believe that Frémont sacrificed Lyon. Schofield had personally urged Lyon to retreat. Because Lyon disobeyed that advice, Schofield concluded that "the fruitless sacrifice at Wilson's Creek was wholly unjustifiable" and that "Lyon ... threw away his own life in desperation. Frémont maintained the defence of General Lyon at Springfield would have taken a week's march." He continued: "And before I could have reached it, Cairo would have been taken." Schofield recorded on August 28, 1861: "Today we had quite an excitement. The body of Gen. Lyon, who fell so nobly at Springfield was brought to the [Brant] house in a metallic case ... draped with U.S. flags."[19]

The Blair family never forgave the failure to "rescue" General Lyon, maintaining that Frémont had over fifty-five thousand troops in the field available to aid Lyon. But the latter's defeat, and the capture of General J. A. Mulligan's forces at Lexington as well, occurred before Frémont could counterattack. The lost Battle of Wilson's Creek was not Frémont's folly. He maintained long lines of communication from the East along a thousand-mile border, whereas Confederates could move into his command from nearby supply bases.

Opinion remained divided over Frémont's role. A close student of this episode concluded that the general "must bear the charge that he lost himself in details and moved too late to save a brave but disobedient general." A contemporary believed Frémont possessed "a certain . . . heaviness and circumspection that made him over cautious and slow to act."[20] As a result, Frémont adopted that spirit of procrastination with which generals are frequently charged. He could hardly be said to have followed Napoleon's dictum that incidents ought not to govern policy, but policy should dictate incidents.

Sensitive to this unwillingness to act except on his own terms was Frank Blair, who, after the defeat at Wilson's Creek, wrote to his brother Montgomery about Frémont: "He talks of the vigor he is going to use, but I can see none of it, and I fear it will turn out to be some rash and inconsiderate move—adopted in haste to make head against a formidable force which could not have accumulated except through gross and inexcusable negligence. . . . My decided opinion is that he should be relieved. . . . The sooner the better."[21]

The Confederate victory at Wilson's Creek opened up southern and western Missouri to a full-scale invasion. General Price next attacked thirty-five hundred Union troops at Lexington, Missouri, near the Kansas boundary, and they surrendered on September 20. Frémont had lost much of Missouri within only two months. The scarcity of both men and supplies throughout the Union Army crippled each of his attempts to launch any semblance of a unified attack from Missouri. After the Union defeat at the first Battle of Bull Run, the War Department ordered quantities of arms diverted eastward to the Army of the Potomac, leaving Frémont's remote Western Department desperately short of rifles and ammunition. Frémont was so anxious for parity with other field commanders that he exaggerated to Lincoln the achievements of his junior officers. Among them was Grant, who prevented Confederate General Leonidas Polk from seizing Paducah and Cairo where the Ohio and Mississippi rivers converge.[22]

But the Blairs continued to charge Frémont with spending weeks uselessly waiting for supplies instead of attacking Sterling Price's troops, which regularly raided western Missouri. The Blairs steadily pressured Lincoln for Frémont's removal. Fortunately, on September 30, 1861, Frémont did occupy rebellious Jefferson City, Missouri, naming his camp headquarters there "Camp Lily," after his daughter.[23]

By the Western Department commander's insistence upon his own military fiefdom and commissioning of too many officers, his command became a subject of continual derision. General Lewis Wallace, later the author of the novel *Ben Hur*, who served under Frémont in the Western Department, claimed that creation of "a special command territorially so vast as to be itself a temptation to a weak man" isolated Frémont, who "surrendered himself to politics." As a result, "everybody looked his way suspiciously, if not in dread." Wallace even likened Frémont's activities to Aaron Burr's earlier sinister western conspiracy.[24]

When Wallace first reached Frémont's command post, he, as had Sherman, tried in vain to report the arrival of his regiment, one of those units of recruits organized by cities across the country. Although the place was "well-equipped with saddle furniture, nobody received me or so much as noticed my presence." Wallace was chagrined that Frémont would not even interrupt his lunch to receive one of his own commanders. Instead, Frémont's foreign officers preened themselves before Wallace. One, a haughty Bulgarian dandy, was dressed in a flaming scarlet uniform yet could not speak a word of English. Wallace boasted that his men were fully ready to fight, and he saw a real contrast between them and the stand-pat attitude prevalent at Frémont's headquarters. Wallace rode away convinced that he had seen a nest of Frémont apologists instead of a military post. He asked to be reassigned to General Charles F. Smith at Paducah, Kentucky, who operated under Grant's command. Frémont did not interfere with Wallace's redeployment, and they did not meet. Each would suffer serious adversities in battle—Wallace by Jubal Early at the Battle of Monocacy and Frémont by Stonewall Jackson in the Shenandoah Valley. Both would also become governors of western territories long after the war ended.[25]

Smarting from the mounting criticism against her husband, Jessie persuaded John Charles that she should go to Washington, see President Lincoln, and present their side of so many complicated accusations personally. On September 8, 1861, she left by train with her personal maid. Her trip proved to be rushed and exhausting, and it produced mixed results. When she reached the White House on the night of September 10, 1861, the president's reaction was not favorable: "She sought an audience with me at midnight, and tasked me so violently with so many things, that I had to exercise all the tact I have to avoid quarreling with her."[26]

Jessie's own recollections of her confrontation with Lincoln were entirely different from those recorded by his two young secretaries, John G. Nicolay and John Hay. Her hasty trip to Washington had left her dead tired after sitting up for two days and nights in a steamy and overcrowded train. She had not even been able "to undress or lie down since leaving Saint Louis." Nor had she yet bathed before being "commanded," she said, to visit Lincoln late at night at the White House. There is, however, not much question that she spoke to the president in a testy mood. And, according to her, he never offered her a seat. She chose to recall that it was he who became angry: "Strange, isn't it, that when a man expresses a conviction fearlessly, he is reported as having made a trenchant and forceful statement, but when a woman speaks thus earnestly, she is reported as a lady who lost her temper."[27] Conversely, most historians (admittedly males) agree that Lincoln received her with courtesy and dignity. Jessie, however, claimed to detect in the president's voice that he had already made up his mind about her husband's future. From Washington she sent John Charles coded telegrams about "enemies" who lurked there. Chief of these was Lincoln himself, who, she said, especially resented his having placed the slavery issue up front in the midst of a war. She assured her husband that he had an indisputable right to free any slaves who had come across his front lines.

There was actually a great sense of fairness displayed in a letter that Lincoln addressed to "Mrs. Genl. Frémont" two days after he had met with her. Concealing his feelings of injury, Lincoln wrote her that "no impression has been made on my mind against the honor or integrity of Gen. Frémont; and I now enter my protest against being understood as acting in any hostility towards him." Lincoln went on to maintain that he had not impugned her husband's "honor or integrity."[28]

Schuyler Colfax, who would become speaker of the House of Representatives, made an unexpected speech in defense of Frémont that the press called "a magnificent burst of eloquence." Colfax personally liked both Frémont and the Blairs, but privately Colfax did not underestimate Frémont's dilemma: "Confidentially, and the details not to be published, I do not wonder that he feels chagrined. He's denounced you know by some as a humbug, inefficient, etc." As for Jessie's unfortunate visit to the president, Colfax wrote: "Mr. Lincoln expressed himself personally in the warmest language towards Frémont," even though she insisted on denying it.[29]

Lincoln, hoping for reelection in 1864, had to take account of Frémont's popularity with the midwestern Germans and his following among diehards who refused to see him as a blunderer at the center of a web of inefficiency and corruption.

Frémont's field letters to Jessie back in Washington continued to complain about Washington officials' sabotaging him with the high command. On October 10, 1861, he wrote: "I want the Secretary of War to put an end to the kind of action which is impeding me by producing want of confidence." He spoke of General Lorenzo Thomas, adjutant general of the Union Army and a West Point mediocrity who was visiting the western command at the time, as "not friendly to me, and therefore I have a right to demand that he be at once removed from my department. I think that he has been purposely sent with the object that being unfriendly, he would embarass me. I ought not to have impediments." Frémont wrote again on October 11, 1861, to complain that Adjutant General Thomas, "contrary to usage and regulation, ordered [Justus] McKinstry and others from my department without doing it through me. It is a discourtesy and military offence." The words "discourtesy," "disobedience," and "neglect" repeatedly appear in Frémont's wartime correspondence to his wife. Numerous foes litter the pages of his letters: "General Thomas is my enemy. He is one of those who opposed my appointment, and I am told indulged in some of the abusive and false language which a certain class about Washington has habitually permitted to themselves in reference to me." Frémont wrote as if he expected Jessie, then in Washington, to put an end to his many grievances.[30]

In a letter of October 18, 1861, from "Camp on the Banks of the Osage," he addressed her in a braver frame of mind concerning a cattle contract about to be annulled by higher-ups. That order, though "intended to cripple me," could not succeed. He added: "When left to my own resources I have no fears." Such contracts would, however, lead him into further difficulty because he was drawn unsuspectingly into speculations such as that foisted upon the army by the then young John Pierpont Morgan. That fledgling financier was about to enrich himself by buying defective weapons directly from government arsenals at $3.50 apiece and reselling them, unrepaired, to Frémont's command for $22.00 each. When front-line soldiers tried to fire these arms—advertised as "new carbines in perfect condition"—they shot off their own thumbs. President Lincoln stated that those profiteering in such defective weapons "ought to have their devilish heads shot off."[31]

Frémont continued to deny that he did business with dishonest firms. He complained of "all manner of disobedience and neglect on the part of . . . paymasters, quartermasters, and all feel that my orders may be disregarded with impunity." He complained to Montgomery Blair: "In time of war the orders of the General commanding a Dept. ought to be obeyed. If he issues an order or calls for aid which circumstances do not justify, he may be held responsible for the consequences but he should be obeyed by every subordinate to whom he issues an order." The government's disapproval of his orders to buy Canadian horses at a higher price than scarce American mounts led him to lament that "such a course is intolerable not because it seriously impairs my efficiency by lessening the respect in which my conduct is to be held by officers of my command, but also by the discouragement it inflicts on myself." He asked Blair to implore Lincoln to "put his foot down" on junior officers sent west to negate his orders. He was also upset by Charles Francis Adams ("that mean and selfish man"), who, as American minister to Great Britain, constantly blocked Billings's purchases of arms abroad.[32]

Frémont seemed incapable of understanding that President Lincoln had to delegate responsibility both to cabinet officers and to military staffs. Yet Lincoln was not without fault in his command practices, repeatedly dispatching hostile politicians and military figures to check up on a military commander. This bypassing of the martial hierarchy undermined confidence within the Missouri command. For his part, Frémont, again taking every suggestion personally, acted as if the president should deal individually him. This was an impossible wish, given the large number of generals under Lincoln's command. As time passed, Frémont's complexities had become too much of a constant. Seldom a team player, he reminds one of the modern General Douglas MacArthur, who when his failures could not be hidden, attributed them "to a conspiracy in Washington."[33] Unlike Grant—phlegmatic but stolid, with less nervous energy to quell— Frémont could not seem to mediate between competing pressures upon him from both below and above. All the while he exasperated the Washington high command.

Jessie, also a grumbler, and forever blind to his shortcomings, wrote, in a letter to James T. Fields, her publisher: "I'm savagely tired of injustice to my chief." She also resented the "aged and spiteful old army officers" who impeded her husband's contribution to the war effort and the "negligence and niggardliness and ignorance of the war managers."[34]

Quite suddenly another bad judgment would stain her man's record. It was as if the wild horses of fate were about to run away with his light chariot of fortune. And what the end would be, no one could forecast. On the afternoon of August 31, 1861, Frémont boldly scrawled his signature across his own emancipation proclamation. He was not only acting in defiance of President Lincoln, but also thereby setting aside the power of Missouri's civilian governor. Frémont would henceforth rule the state under full-scale martial law, silencing all political opponents and even ordering persons possessing illegal weapons to be shot. All slaves who entered his command were to be freed in Missouri, which was, as we have seen, a touchy, divided state then only partly loyal to the Union cause. Frémont's ill-timed general order not only freed slaves, but also confiscated the property of "rebels." He regarded his proclamation primarily as a military measure, having no idea of its political and legal implications. The president had laid aside his own deep personal antipathy toward slavery in an effort to retain the support of loyal slaveholders in the border states. Lincoln had carefully refrained from interfering with slavery in delicate border-state situations.

The president, dumbfounded by the continuing turmoil within General Frémont's command, simply had to take action to control this knight errant who had become a law unto himself. He had to be admonished, if not relieved of command. Part of Frémont's unauthorized proclamation provided for shooting prisoners of war. For this reason Lincoln sharply warned him: "Should you shoot a man, according to the proclamation, the Confederates could very certainly shoot our best men in their hands in retaliation; and so, man for man, indefinitely. It is, therefore, my order that you will allow no man to be shot . . . without first having my approbation or consent. In fact, on the very day that Lincoln sent the above communication to his most quixotic general, Missouri's Confederate commander announced that for every Southern soldier put to death, he would "hang, draw, and quarter a minion of Abraham Lincoln."[35]

Paradoxically, because of Frémont's order, Lincoln, symbolically at least, almost joined the Confederates in opposition to Frémont. The president had also objected to a second part of Frémont's proclamation. As he wrote the general: "In relation to the confiscation of property and the liberating of slaves. . . . Allow me, therefore, to ask that you will, of your own motion, modify that paragraph so as to conform to . . . the act of Congress. . . . This letter is written in a spirit of caution, and not of censure."[36]

Frémont, one of those leaders who hated ever being wrong, now wrote his commander in chief that he had issued his proclamation because he was caught between Confederates and "home traitors," though he did add: "If upon reflection, your better judgment still decides that I am wrong in the article respecting the liberation of slaves, I have to ask that you will openly direct me to make the correction. The implied censure will be received as a soldier always should the reprimand of his chief." Despite these words, Frémont, ignoring Lincoln's wishes, had two hundred copies of the original uncut proclamation printed and distributed. Lincoln finally issued the following order to him: "Your answer, just received, expresses the preference on your part that I should make an open order for the modification, which I very cheerfully do. It is therefore ordered that the said clause of said proclamation be so modified.[37]

Frémont's emancipation proclamation had been intended to quell guerrilla warfare and to penalize disloyal slaveowners in the North, but its wider significance was to drive a deeper wedge between radical and conservative Northerners. If not countermanded, it would have sought to convert a war fought to preserve the Union into an effort to free slaves. Frémont's threat to confiscate the lands as well as slaves of anyone who aided the Confederates endangered Missouri's and Kentucky's shaky loyalty to the Union. Lincoln's worries over the larger political situation stood in contrast to Frémont's defiant act, which led to the further accusation that the general wanted to arm freed slaves to fight against the South. The president, alarmed by the prospect of alienation from the Union of politically divided border states, was forced to rescind Frémont's order.[38]

The abolitionists, among them Harriet Beecher Stowe, however, exulted over Frémont's plan to free Missouri's slaves. When Lincoln annulled that order, her husband Calvin wrote a letter to Salmon Chase, still a member of Lincoln's cabinet, which accused the administration of rewarding treachery and imbecility as well as punishing just acts. Although the Beechers were to suffer abuse for their support of Frémont, they arranged a New York dinner for their reprimanded hero at a time when the general's enemies charged that Henry Ward Beecher's sermons were preached from a pulpit in the church of "Saint John C. Frémont." Frémont's controversial order had importance for the abolitionists. To them, he had instilled a realization among slaveholders that emancipation of their human property was now in jeopardy. Lincoln somehow had to clip the wings of a Pathfinder, who had lost his way. Frémont's immediate response to the president's admonition was to sulk. Despite the cabinet's repeated doubts about his activities, he resented Lincoln's decision to void his proclamation. Lincoln remained certain in the "conviction that it was a measure right and necessary, and I think so still."[39]

Ignoring Lincoln's presidential powers, Frémont had presented the president with an impossible fait accompli. Like the Beechers, some newspapers, among them Horace Greeley's *New York Tribune*, the *Missouri Democrat*, and the *National Intelligencer*, continued to endorse Frémont's rash acts, but most journals called his moves abominable.[40] Congressional reaction was mixed. Senator William Fessenden of Maine saw Frémont's personal emancipation proclamation as a masterstroke. Benjamin Wade of Ohio also praised it, as did Zachariah Chandler of Michigan and Orville Browning, one of the organizers of the Republican party in Illinois. These men later became anti-Lincoln radicals. As for President Lincoln, he could not have imagined that the general would be so imprudent as to usurp presidential prerogatives. Though no one doubted Frémont's patriotism, within the cabinet anti-Frémont sentiment festered anew. Attorney General Edward Bates joined in demanding his immediate discharge.

Lincoln, who proved to be more tough-minded than either Frémont's friends or enemies, did not rashly dismiss the miscreant general. Instead, he called on the army to investigate the Saint Louis command, specifying that, in addition to Adjutant General Thomas, Quartermaster General M. C. Meigs and Postmaster General Montgomery Blair go to Missouri to gather evidence.[41] Resentful of these intruders, Frémont ordered his sycophant foreign guards to deny access to all Washington emissaries. The visitors sent by Lincoln found Frémont arrogant and supercilious, presiding over a headquarters that resembled a showy court.

The president next transferred a junior commander, General David Hunter, commanding near Rolla, Missouri, to Frémont's staff as assistant commander, hoping that Hunter could stave off further rash decisions. Lincoln's instructive letter of September 9, 1861, to Hunter hinted at his distrust of Frémont, yet also suggested accommodation: "Gen. Frémont needs assistance which it is difficult to give him. He is losing the confidence of men near him, whose support any man in his position must have to be successful. His cardinal mistake is that he isolates himself, and allows nobody to see him; and by which he does not know what is going on in the very matter he is dealing with. He needs to have by his side a man of large experience. Will you not, for me, take that place?"[42] Hunter ultimately would obtain the western command. Frémont, meanwhile, feeling more and more harassed, resorted increasingly to that psychological defense mechanism known as isolation, which only further confused both his local commanders and Washington superiors.[43]

Among the enemies who remained unrelenting in their determination to oust Frémont was the vitriolic Congressman Frank Blair. Soon Blair's interference within the army's Western Department precipitated yet another injudicious act by the general. On September 18, 1861, Frémont arrested Blair himself for "insidious and dishonorable efforts to bring my authority into contempt with the government, and to undermine my influence as an officer."[44]

Blair's arrest created still more rancor in Washington against Frémont. Secretary of the Treasury Chase, formerly well disposed toward the general, now wrote to Secretary of War Simon Cameron: "For Heaven's sake bear in mind that we must have vigor, capacity, and honesty. If Frémont has these qualities sustain him. If not, let nothing prevent you from taking the bull by the horns. We have had enough of dilly dallying, temporizing and disgrace. Let us have decision, action."[45] Cameron's personal investigation turned up what were described as "robbery, fraud, extravagance, and peculation." The secretary of war reported that a scene of disarray and confusion existed at Frémont's new field headquarters in Tipton, Missouri. Although Cameron possessed Lincoln's authorization to remove Frémont from command, he withheld any decision about dismissing the controversial general until his return to Washington. He considered Frémont a political hot potato and wanted Lincoln to make the final decision about getting rid of him. Cameron secretly wished that Frémont might resign on his own, for Frémont's well-known defiance could prove embarrassing to Secretary Cameron, who would himself be sacked subsequently by Lincoln on charges of fraud and mismanagement.

Meanwhile, Jessie had the audacity to demand copies of Frank Blair's complaints to Lincoln, although these personal letters to the president were filled with secret information. After Montgomery Blair managed to obtain his brother Frank's release from Frémont's stockade, Frank, in a hot letter to Missouri's former governor, wrote: "If the President does not remove Frémont, I intend to prefer charges against him and force him to a trial, and make him defend himself before the Bar of the Nation." Blair did bring such charges. This time, however, the Pathfinder would fortunately escape another court-martial, although a congressional investigative committee examined claims that Frémont had paid far more for arms, supplies, and fortifications than necessary. There followed the arrest of Brigadier General Justus McKinstry of his command on charges of issuing fraudulent contracts, after which the committee began to investigate Frémont himself. Jessie, too, was charged with receiving three hundred dollars from contractors toward the purchase of a handsome horse and carriage, and other members of the Frémont entourage were faulted for profiteering if not outright embezzlement.[46]

The select investigating committee focused upon Frémont's disobedience of orders as well as his "despotic and tyrannical conduct." Frank Blair denounced Frémont's testimony before this "Committee on the Conduct of the War" as "an apology for disaster and defeat." The congressman wrote Montgomery Blair that Frémont had published his own "silly and frivolous charges," as well as his wife's correspondence with Lincoln, in various Missouri newspapers in order to drum up popular support. He added: "If the Administration will submit meekly to such castigation at the hands of such a nincompoop, it deserves to be treated with contempt."[47] Following weeks of sworn testimony, the committee finally exonerated Frémont. Although he was cleared of impropriety, his management policies were termed "unwise." This relatively mild rebuke also reflected corruption and waste in the inefficient War Department. In short, McKinstry, Frémont's quartermaster general and purveyor of goods and services, took the rap for whatever transgressions had occurred.

Frémont's response to all this trauma was ambivalent. Those who thought they knew him well had noticed a gradual change in his personality. Elizabeth Blair Lee flatly charged that his "seclusion and torpor" could be explained "by the fact of his being an opium eater."[48] We cannot be sure of how destabilizing was his possible use of drugs, or if indeed Frémont used opium. If the charge was true, he may have been able to control the habit, as did the English author Samuel Taylor Coleridge. Frémont may have originally taken the substance to alleviate pain in his leg following the fourth expedition. Then called laudanum, it was used widely as a sedative and sleeping potion and dispensed by drugstores. It was imbibed orally by use of a glass dropper.

Whatever the cause of his erratic behavior, which Lizzie Blair and others saw as enhancing his personal shyness, Frémont also seemed in public to employ increasingly a kind of false modesty to disguise his mounting arrogance. Lizzie Blair thought the results were devastating for her friend Jessie: "I cannot tell you how sorrowfully I think of Jessie. No wonder she has run after her unhappy husband, struggling to protect him against himself & yet [he] has such a stormy temper that she is as unfit to control him as herself. I do pity them & the poor children more than all else." During this same period, Lizzie's brother, Montgomery, wrote to President Lincoln about a disquieting meeting with Frémont: "He seems stupefied and almost unconscious and is doing absolutely nothing." While "the Rebels were daily growing in strength," he continued, "Frémont was not really defending Missouri." His mind, instead, was "busy with petty aspirations & of course he is prey to . . . petty jealousies. . . . I have telegraphed you to say that I think General Meigs should be immediately put in command here."[49]

When Frank Blair reminded Jessie of all that the Blairs had done to promote her husband's career and to protect his property by legal means, "she bridled up at this & put on a very *high look*. I told her . . . she was to play the part of Empress Catherine. Not 'Catherine but Josephine,' she said. I said You are too imperious for her & too ungrateful for me." Jessie had always called the old man "Father Blair," and in a letter to him she attacked his son, Frank, stating that Frémont would hold Frank personally responsible for the damage he had done to her husband. "But the old man told her very gently that the Blairs did not shrink from responsibility," Lizzie wrote. Frank bluntly wrote his father about Frémont: "I believe firmly that he is such an ass that he is determined to refuse obedience to the order of the President. . . . You may think this absurd but I have good reason to know that his flatterers have persuaded him that he can do this successfully."[50]

Both the national and local press, resenting Frémont's clamp-down on unfriendly newspapers, played a part in his downfall. When on September 23, 1861, the *Saint Louis Evening News* rebuked him for allowing Lexington to fall to the rebels, he arrested the editor and closed it down. Lincoln, finally succumbing to heavy pressure, on November 2, 1861, dismissed the general. The power of the Blairs, of dissatisfied cabinet members, of Adjutant General Thomas, and of General Hunter, who coveted the Missouri command, not to speak of insubordinate Generals John Pope and Samuel Sturgis—all this proved overwhelming. Jessie maintained that it was the president himself who had stymied her husband.[51]

But Lincoln had little choice. Within the army Frémont was considered a weak commander. Unlike Grant, he had not gotten the most out of his own officers; he played favorites and thereby created rivalries. Grant handled subordinate generals shrewdly and did not take sides in their feuding. Frémont remained unable to comprehend standard army politicking and could be nobody's old boy.

In addition to all these negatives, General George C. McClellan, Lincoln's major commander, continued to weaken other Union armies of scarce reserves of men and materials. Furthermore, Frémont, thus frozen out of the military hierarchy and deprived of its support, tried to hang on to several exposed salients against superior forces. Outgunned and outmanned, his troops probably did well to hold Cairo, Jefferson City, and Saint Louis itself.

Other questionable decisions irked the high command. In the face of so many disabilities, Frémont refused to give up or reorganize several showy but largely ineffectual elite units, the latest of which he named the "Jessie Scouts" for his wife. He had also renamed the Missouri Home Guard "Frémont's Rangers." As for the three-hundred-man "Zagonyi Hungarian Guard," he and his ten-year-old son, Charley, had watched them finally gain a limited local victory near

Springfield paradoxically on the very day Lincoln signed his order removing Frémont from command of the western armies.[52]

The harassed general had followed a piecemeal strategy, coordinating his operations neither among subordinate units nor with adjoining theater commanders. Although this happened elsewhere during the Civil War, one knowledgeable military man called Frémont "certainly the most stupendous failure of the war." Lincoln, who as commander in chief had observed many generals, said, after he had shelved Frémont: "I thought well of Frémont," but "he has absolutely no military capacity."[53] John Hay, whom Lincoln had sent to observe his headquarters, called him "quiet, earnest, industrious, but imperious." Much later an English military analyst, Major General Sir Frederick Maurice, came to the conclusion that Frémont was "an incompetent soldier."[54]

When an array of supporters, including Karl Marx in faraway Vienna, heard of Frémont's dismissal, they came to his defense. Marx, writing in *Die Press* on November 26, 1861, called him "a man of pathos, somewhat bombastic and haughty" but "an idol of the northwestern states, which . . . regard his dismissal as a personal insult." Marx believed that "this striking figure" had become a "dangerous rival of Seward" and had offended all defenders of slavery.[55] Frémont's good friend the poet Whittier again publicly praised him for issuing, albeit prematurely, his emancipation proclamation:

> Thy error, Frémont, simply was to act
> A brave man's part, without the statesman's tact. . . .
> It had been safer, doubtless, for a time,
> To flatter treason, and avoid offence. . . .
> Still take thou courage! God has spoken through thee.
> Irrevocable the mighty words, Be Free!

Despite Whittier's "Roland blast heard from the van of freedom's hope forlorn," the Pathfinder was once again without command.[56]

It did him precious little good also to be lauded at New York's Cooper Union Hall by so powerful a senator as Charles Sumner or to hear the plaudits of Thaddeus Stevens, fiercest of all abolitionists in the House of Representatives. Though even *Harper's Weekly* praised his furtive proclamation order, he now joined other sidelined political commanders awaiting assignment at a time when there were fifty-two major generals in the Union Army. Although the abolitionists and radical Republicans were unable to save his command, Frémont did remain the pet general of both groups. Along with Ben Butler, he was also the best known antislave general.[57]

After President Lincoln sacked him, Frémont's Missouri adherents strewed flowers on the streets of Saint Louis where he passed. Torches flared and sabres glittered as his magnificently uniformed Zagonyi Guards escorted their hero regally from place to place. His recall produced outright threats of mutiny within the ranks of midwestern Germans, who, though sometimes puzzled by Frémont's behavior, remained fiercely loyal. Senator Sumner told Francis Lieber that the German troops in Missouri looked upon Frémont's dismissal "with unusual dissatisfaction."[58] To midwestern Germans, he was like the great Alexander von Humboldt, who had honored him, or the Duke of Wellington, a giant restrained by political pygmies.

For all the controversy he engendered, Frémont also never lacked some loyal adherents among his own troops. One of them whom he would never meet was Austin Crabbs, who had dutifully enlisted as a private in Indiana at age twenty-one, emerging as a captain four years later. Writing from Camp Slack at Indianapolis on December 31, 1861, Crabbs vented his feelings at Frémont's mistreatment:

> If it be true that the public service required the removal of Gen'l Frémont. . . . [H]e had not only put his army in motion but had driven the rebels flushed with the victory of Lexington out of seven-eights of Missouri. He had performed a longer march than has been made by any National Gen'l during the war. Whatever may have been his previous errors, it is undeniable that his career since he took the field had been a complete military success, and his removal when he had almost overtaken his flying forces and when in the leaving of his guns was, in my opinion, not only a blunder but an act of injustice and one which will recoil with crushing force on those who advised it.[59]

The fiancée of another Union volunteer, a cavalryman who had been a sharecropper, wrote: "I *do* think Frémont is a noble patriotic man. . . . Certain it is that he deserves much praise. His conduct in the *past* has been that of a hero, and I believe the future will reveal to his friends and foes alike that he has a patriotism not to be chilled by all the envious devises of those who would cripple his power."[60]

Another member of the Senate, James Grimes of Iowa, wrote to his fellow senator, William Fessenden of Maine, on September 19, 1861:

> When it was reported that Frémont was suspended, cold chills began to run up and down people's backs; they bit their lips, said nothing, *but refused to enlist*. I know nothing of the merits of the controversy, but it is evident as the noonday sun that the *people* are all with Frémont. . . . My wife says . . . that the only real noble and true thing done during this war has been his proclamation. Everybody of every sect, party, sex, and color approves it in the Northwest, and it will not do for the Administration to causelessly tamper with the man who had the sublime moral courage to issue it."[61]

About Frémont's dismissal Grimes also announced: "I learn from . . . a member of the cabinet that before the Administration would bestow the appointment of major general upon him a promise was exacted from him that he would not be a candidate for the presidency." When Frémont issued his proclamation, however, "the embryo Presidents in the cabinet at once took the alarm, and required him to modify it. This he refused to do. . . . Then . . . a conspiracy was entered into to destroy his influence . . . and finally to depose him." A White House cabal, according to Senator Grimes, had honed in on Frémont: "Yet with all their sifting of testimony, taking it from the mouths of disappointed rival contractors . . . and with no opportunity to rebut it . . . they have been unable to bring home the perpetration . . . of a single one of the alleged frauds to General Frémont." Grimes had originally doubted Frémont's fitness for command. "I would never have made him a general of the regular army" he wrote in vain: "but being one, I intend to insist most strenuously and persistently that he shall have complete justice done him."[62]

Looking back upon Frémont's Missouri record, John F. Hume, later the author of *The Abolitionists*, believed that "no man in this country was made the victim of greater injustice." Although Hume considered Frémont to be a relatively "weak man in some respects," the general had laid down the strategy that led to the capture of Fort Donelson and Henry in Tennessee, "for which Halleck got the credit."[63]

But it was General Grant who captured Fort Donelson, and only after Frémont was dismissed from command. Because this was almost the first significant Union victory of the war, it helped to transform Grant from a local commander to a rival of Generals Halleck and McClellan, both clearly more prominent than Frémont. Yet there are those who today still feel that Frémont's superiors bear part of the blame for what happened to him in Missouri. A modern military specialist points out that while in command there, Frémont not only faced Herculean odds but also operated under "a cloud of viciousness . . . that made rational thought and behavior difficult."[64] His poor sense of timing and impetuous nature, however, had overcome both judgment and tact.

When the general and Jessie boarded a train from Saint Louis for the East Coast, yet one more difficult period in their lives had ended under a cloud of controversy. He would be lucky to receive another command. ❖

When John Charles and Jessie returned to Washington, they found other adherents ready to cheer them. One night the general and his popular wife attended a lecture by their friend Horace Greeley at the Smithsonian Institution. Their appearance created, according to an observer, "such a furor" that two prominent politicians, Schuyler Colfax and George W. Julian, "induced them to go upon the platform. Their reception by Mr. Greeley was the signal for another prolonged outburst. This meant a criticism of the President. ... The Smithsonian audience was vociferously on the side of Frémont."[1]

At a reception that the Frémonts gave in a Washington hotel, the general "spoke modestly and quietly" of his differences with the president, "saying confidently that the people could be of but one opinion when the whole truth was out. Mrs. Frémont, witty, graceful, and brilliant, was less reticent and forbearing." An admirer recalled "her standing in the centre of a group leading an animated conversation concerning the indignities to which she thought her husband subjected. She spoke warmly and even defiantly, with the sharp emphasis of outraged honesty . . . and her eyes flashed as she exclaimed 'Justice! Justice! Justice!'" She still portrayed her husband as the victim of a conspiracy headed by the Blair family.[2]

Back in Chicago, a mass meeting of the Society of German-Americans unanimously adopted a resolution urging that Frémont, General Franz Sigel, and General Benjamin O. Butler replace the entire army high command, including General Henry Wager Halleck, who on November 19, 1861, had taken over a newly created Department of Missouri, including western Kentucky, and who would go on to become Lincoln's "General in Chief."

The plump and self-satisfied Halleck was another of those West Pointers who had loathed Frémont during the Mexican War. Halleck's credentials were, however, superb. Sporting old-fashioned ginger-colored mutton-chop whiskers, he cut a striking figure. After a period as a San Francisco lawyer, he had reentered the army in 1861. Known as "Old Brains," his lectures on strategy, published in book form, Lincoln himself read. Halleck believed that Frémont had been more interested in freeing slaves and enlarging his reputation than in running a military command. Discipline was ingrained in Halleck, who, on July 11, 1862, went on to become general-in-chief of the army.

Deeply suspicious of nonacademy "political generals," including Frémont, Butler, and Sigel, Halleck asked Secretary of War Edward M. Stanton to oust them from any command whatsoever. Although General Sigel, like Frémont, recruited thousands of Germans for the Union cause, he seemed to be basically an inept commander. Little better was Butler, who hung on to his command virtually to the end of the war, repeatedly claiming he was number one on the army's seniority list. As for Frémont, General McClellan warned Halleck that he would find, upon assuming the Missouri post, "a system of reckless expenditure and fraud perhaps unheard of in the history of the world."[3] Halleck had, indeed, unearthed much extravagance. Though pressure upon Lincoln to give Frémont a new post mounted, Halleck thought he had himself squelched any possible "application of Genl. Frémont for further command."[4]

Allied with General Halleck were all the members of the Blair family, who continued their attacks on Frémont. This time their goal was to prevent him from gaining another command. On March 2, 1862, Frank Blair, in a speech on the floor of the House of Representatives, denounced Frémont as not only an inept commander but also one who had regularly signed fraudulent purchase orders for favorites whom he had appointed to their posts. In reply, Frémont claimed that it was his refusal to approve a contract recommended by the Blairs themselves that had started the feud with them, to which charge Blair shouted in the Congress: "A man to be great must be able to do great things with small means. And when we hear of a fellow going around the country trying to give the reasons for his being whipped . . . nobody will ever select him as a fit person to fight battles and to carry on war."[5]

Frémont's immediate future depended not upon Halleck or Frank Blair. It was Lincoln who would make the decision about whether an upstart general merited any further command. Both Frémonts for their part distrusted the entire presidential administration. Thurlow Weed attested to the fact that "Frémont and his wife are bitter towards Mr. Lincoln and blind with ambition. I heard this directly from them."[6]

Yet the president continued to seek out some sort of post for the Pathfinder. The *New York Tribune* for June 1, 1863, carried a Washington dispatch that stated, according to Senator Charles Sumner, that President Lincoln had asserted "he would gladly receive into the service not 10,000 but ten times 10,000 colored troops" and that "he would with all his heart" offer such a command to General Frémont. Lincoln changed his mind, however, for nothing came of this idea.[7]

Lincoln well knew that Frémont's ultimate goals were political. But while ambition and drive are traits found among commanders, Frémont never bothered to conceal both attributes from his civilian superiors. This sort of hubris led Ulysses S. Grant, in the middle of the Civil War, to comment upon personal guile in any commander: "So long as I hold a commission in the army I have no views of my own to carry out. Whatever may be the orders of my superiors and the law I will execute. No man can be efficient as a commander who sets his own notions above law and those he is sworn to obey." Such were not the thoughts of Frémont's partisans, ever ready to produce favorable testimonials on his behalf at any time. One of their tracts compared his career with that of General McClellan: "While a portion of the people of the country appear to regard Frémont as a military failure, and McClellan as possessing wonderful military abilities, others are enthusiastic in their admiration of Frémont's entire career as a soldier and fail to see the evidences that McClellan is entitled to the favor which the Administration has shown him." The pamphlet went on to point out that Frémont was never educated at government expense, as all West Point generals had been, and that his expeditions and commands had all been underfunded. The writer suggested that Frémont be considered for the post of commanding general of all the armies. From November 1861 until the following March, McClellan remained general-in-chief. Neither he nor Frémont then knew that each would become a presidential candidate in 1864.[8]

As the Frémont stalwarts kept up pressure on the administration for one more command, another friendly publication labeled the Blair brothers as "political rats who sought to wound a great general." As for the West Point generals Halleck and Thomas, who had hamstrung Frémont on the eve of victories in Missouri, "Shame on such men!" the writer scolded.[9] His critics had every right to wonder whether such publications, which sprang up every time Frémont got into trouble, were not heavily solicited. Yet these encomiums seemed necessary to overcome so much opposition. Almost every member of the cabinet was opposed to Frémont's reinstatement in any command.

Trying to overcome such determined opposition, Benjamin F. Wade, abolitionist radical and chairman of the powerful congressional Committee on the Conduct of the War, was among those who leaned heavily on the president, urging another assignment for Frémont. On February 5, 1862, Lincoln, responding to such pressure, invited both the Frémonts to a White House reception. For the occasion Jessie extracted from her traveling trunk "a white and violet dress of thulle & blonde & fragile beauty & fearful cost." But they stayed only one hour, as she told Frederick Billings two days later: "Stopped by the President in person in the hall and made to take off my cloak & be introduced to Genl. McClellan, I behaved myself perfectly well but I didn't like it. I had my compensation in seeing the eyes that followed us across the hall & East Room, the President & Mr. Frémont, Mr. Sumner & myself while the introductions were gone through."[10] Lincoln not only treated the Frémonts with decency on that occasion but also soon thereafter, quite surprisingly, announced the general's reassignment to command the Mountain Department of western Virginia, including parts of Kentucky and Tennessee.

When Private Austin Crabbs heard this news, he wrote to his fiancée from Tiptonville, Tennessee: "Yes, 'the restoration of Gen'l Frémont' is highly gratifying to me for I still retain my high opinion of him. . . . Had he the same advantages that McClellan has had he would have been the hero of this fearful struggle; and I also believe that had he remained in command of the Western Department, the Mississippi Valley would have been ours." Not everyone was that happy about Lincoln's decision, as journalist Horace White reported to his *New York Tribune* superiors: "Washburn went up to see the President last night about the reinstatement of Frémont & told him flatly that he was not going to chase down any more robbers if they were to be promoted to high places of responsibility as soon as convicted of crime. Lincoln replied that the act was done in response to 'everlasting popular clamor!' " White repeated Chase's assertion that although cabinet members protested against Lincoln's restoring Frémont to command as "a disgraceful self-stultification, it was to no avail."[11] Lincoln had obviously assuaged the radicals.

His fiery secretary of war, Stanton, who had once argued against Frémont's land claims before the Supreme Court, immediately tried to stop him from setting up a new headquarters with "just such a gang" as the Pathfinder had in Saint Louis. Stanton was piqued because the general had requested staff appointments by name, about which he stated: "I will not allow Generals to carry on the war . . . holding court in New York, taking proposals for appointments on their staffs." Although a tough administrator, Stanton could hardly control Frémont, who later complained to Senator Sumner that Stanton "has been an insidious enemy of mine since his advent to office."[12] Once more, a towering authority figure seemed to thwart Frémont's wishes.

Secretary Stanton not only menaced his political rear; Frémont was also about to encounter new military complexities in West Virginia. He assumed command of a topographical cauldron within which broken mountain ranges and valleys favored the Confederate defenders. As in Missouri, he lacked innovative officers who knew how to fight in such terrain. Furthermore, he had no power to raise troops locally or to requisition supplies from the citizenry. The situation was so chaotic that his officers bought cavalry mounts from one another. For most troops, "a pair of blankets and a bit in the saddlebags had to suffice."[13]

Confederate armies in northern Virginia used the Shenandoah Valley to threaten Washington, thereby drawing Union pressure off their own capital of Richmond. To counter rebel forces, Frémont set out to assemble twenty-five thousand bluecoats for a drive 250 miles southward to capture Knoxville, for President Lincoln wanted desperately to liberate east Tennessee.

On March 29, 1862, at Wheeling in West Virginia, where he took along his wife and two children, Frémont relieved General William Starke Rosecrans. From this base he first had to secure the Shenandoah, a two-hundred-mile corridor that extended from Harper's Ferry on the north to Roanoke, the valley's southwestern gateway.

Stonewall Jackson had some special advantages over Frémont. Before the Southerner began any campaign, local spies helped him to scout out the terrain in a way not available to northern commanders. Jackson's seventeen thousand Confederates, by swift and deceptive thrusts, continually harassed all Union forces. His guerrillas and bushwhackers moved up and down the Shenandoah Valley almost at will, humiliating the Union armies by quick, piercing, uncontrollable raids. Frémont devised a retaliatory makeshift strategy that changed from day to day. He also set up a field headquarters named Camp Jessie, from which he jabbed out sporadically against "Seceshdom," as the Confederate lines were called. Amazingly, Jessie joined her husband in the midst of the war in West Virginia, writing to Frederick Billings from Wheeling that she had gone to his camp "deep in the mountains."

Accompanying Frémont into the Shenandoah Valley as aide-de camp was Colonel Albert Tracy. Tracy's journal reveals that despite all the fuss in Missouri over his foreign-born officers, President Lincoln's newest general in the valley still relied heavily upon these volunteers while in pursuit of Stonewall Jackson. Welcomed to his new command was Brigadier General Carl Schurz, who, on June 10, 1862, was assigned a division and who later became a major general. Throughout the war Schurz corresponded directly with President Lincoln, an anomalous, perhaps unwise, procedure. He was also shifted about, at his own request, from command to command. Another German reassigned to Frémont was Major General Franz Sigel, who, like Brigadier General Louis Blenker, headed up a ten-thousand-man brigade, mostly German. Colonel Anselm Albert, a Hungarian, became Frémont's chief of staff. A Bohemian, Colonel John Pilsen, was his chief of artillery. Colonel Charles Zagonyi, the Hungarian who had headed Frémont's elite Missouri cavalry guard, also joined the general along the Shenandoah. That guard unit had been mustered out of service without pay for alleged disloyalty following a Confederate raid on Springfield, Missouri. In great haste, during the midst of the war, Jessie had written her *Story of the Guard* (1863) for their relief.

Frémont's units were all badly equipped; indeed, some of the men were shoeless. When thrown against Jackson, a tactician of the first rank, they were at a great disadvantage. Despite the disabilities of the troops, the secretary of war ordered Frémont to "break" the Virginia and Tennessee Railroad, which connected Bristol, Tennessee, and Lynchburg, Virginia. The commander was also to march toward Harrisonburg to join the forces of General Irvin McDowell. But heavy rains bogged down the arrival of supplies. To move in any direction was an impossibility. "Our people were next to starving," Colonel Tracy wrote, "and this was the country of the enemy." With fences leveled, fields laid waste, and buildings torn apart by cannon fire, Frémont's men had to loot cellars, pantries, and barns in order to survive. Drenched by heavy downpours of rain, his troops were frequently immobilized.[14]

Loyal to his commander, Tracy tells us that "the General" well knew that if he did not corner the elusive Stonewall Jackson, his future would be bleak. Tracy pictures Frémont as eager to fight, although the general's foreign scouts kept reporting to him that the enemy was in too large a force to engage frontally. For a time, at least, Frémont seemed a different commander than he had been in Missouri. "Well up towards the head of all, rides, with his staff, the General, earnest and determined, impatient only of delay in any form," his aide, Tracy, wrote in his diary as Frémont pursued Jackson up the north fork of the Shenandoah, hoping to cut off a Confederate retreat.[15] Jackson also had to defend against the Union forces of Generals James F. Shields and N. P. Banks, so the Confederate leader ordered all bridges across the river destroyed. This action cut off any communication between Union forces on opposite sides of the Shenandoah. Although Frémont was now prevented from crossing the river, he did lead eleven thousand men in pursuit of Jackson's superior numbers. He was, however, slowed down by hauling along river-crossing equipment that had been rendered useless, and for which he had personally paid. This episode resembled somewhat Frémont's stubbornness when he refused to give up a cumbersome howitzer during his second government expedition.

On May 29, 1862, Jackson began a masterful retreat, escaping through a narrow corridor between Banks's and Frémont's armies. Speed and secrecy were the keys to Jackson's success. At one stage of the retreat, he had to cover forty-four miles while his enemies needed to traverse only eleven. Jackson won that race, fighting off savage thrusts at the battles of Cross Keys and Port Republic. He not only held off Frémont but in addition drove him and Shields back to the upper Shenandoah Valley. All the while, Jackson fled southward, but only temporarily.[16]

Frémont, in addition to facing bridges burned by Jackson, now became involved in another unfortunate dispute with a West Pointer, General McDowell.

It concerned who possessed battlefield seniority after a running fight that went on day after day through abandoned farms and burned-out villages. Frémont blamed McDowell for Jackson's escape. McDowell had refused to carry out Frémont's order to burn a vital bridge across the Shenandoah before Jackson crossed it. As in the past, once Frémont took a position, it was as if his decision was set in concrete. McDowell believed that all the forces facing Jackson should be under a single command, a condition that Lincoln would not countenance. About all this, however, Stonewall Jackson said that "if McDowell had done his part in the Luray Valley as well as Frémont did his in the Shenandoah, there wouldn't have been many of us got away to Richmond." Jackson escaped in time to help another hero, Robert E. Lee, defeat McClellan at Mechanicsville on June 26.[17]

At Cross Keys, Jackson had succeeded in fully checking Frémont's pursuit as Confederate fire cut tattered Union brigades to pieces. After each fusillade Jackson retreated, only to reappear menacingly. All the while, Frémont's artillery lobbed shells across the river into Confederate ambulances gathering up the wounded, sometimes hitting federal prisoners. At Cross Keys, Frémont lost 114 killed and 443 wounded, with 25 men missing. Jackson probably lost 800 troops, giving rise to the claim that Frémont had somehow won the battle of June 8–9, 1862. It was really a standoff. At no time were Union forces able to corner Jackson, who was said to encourage the belief that he would shoot deserters who surrendered. Lincoln finally ordered Frémont to halt at Harrisonburg and to pursue Jackson no further.[18]

The men were pleased to have several days of respite, with time to rub down their horses and to dry grimy shirts on bushes. Soon they were again on the march, however. Lincoln next ordered Frémont to move twenty thousand of his troops from Franklin to Harrisonburg. The general wired a reply: "On the march. Will be there tomorrow noon—John Charles." A critic wrote in dismay: "Frémont has been and done it!" By this he meant that the War Department

> was thunderstruck to learn that Frémont was at *Moorfield* with his whole army, almost due north of Franklin instead of at Harrisonburg southeast! Of course, Stonewall Jackson escaped. Lincoln is a good deal groveled by this unaccountable disobedience & cowardice, but I fear he is too irresolute and too much of a coward himself to inflict the proper punishment. If Frémont had obeyed orders, the whole rebel force under Jackson and Ewell would have been bagged.[19]

This is an oversimplification of the problems Frémont faced in a fruitless effort to trap Jackson. Lincoln had divided Virginia into too many competing commands, with little coordination between his commanders.

Yet a displeased President Lincoln now ordered, as he had done in Missouri, another personal emissary to give him an appraisal of Frémont's command. This was General Carl Schurz. Charming, lanky, and German-born, Schurz was, like Frémont, popular among his midwestern countrymen. Though still only thirty-two years old, Schurz was a revolutionary hero in his native land. He would also become a distinguished statesman and soldier in his adopted one, having already served as Lincoln's minister to Spain from June 1861 to January 1862. Schurz reached Frémont at Harrisonburg in June 1862, the day after the Battle of Cross Keys. He reported to Lincoln that Frémont's troops were shockingly ill-equipped, "largely destitute of clothing, tents, and even shoes, many marching barefoot. Their pioneer companies in this mountain country had no axes, picks, or saws; their hordes were barely able to drag the artillery." Schurz, whom Frémont promised command of two brigades, noted that the general once again felt sorely impeded by orders from Washington. He tended to excuse Frémont's excesses: "It has been said that there was much of the charlatan in him, but his appearance at that time certainly betrayed nothing of the kind. There was an air of refinement in his bearing. His manners seemed perfectly natural, easy, and unaffected, without any attempt at posing. His conversation, carried on in a low, gentle tone of voice, had a suggestion of reticence and reserve in it, but not enough to cause a suspicion of insincerity."[20]

Inspectors from Washington did not enhance the military realities that Frémont faced. Hampered by serious storms, his bedraggled forces had proved no match for those of that brilliant general called "the wizard of Southern Cavalry." Nevertheless, Frémont actually thought he might defeat Jackson, voicing grandiose aspirations to Jessie: "We march eastward tomorrow, but already there is an indication that Jackson is retreating. Maybe we can catch him. Our Army is in good condition and if we have anything to do it will be done well."[21] How could Frémont possibly describe his forces as in good shape? And why?

National factors influenced battlefield decisions by President Lincoln, who had become engaged in bitter political in-fighting that threatened his prospects for reelection in 1864. Military conscription was deeply unpopular. Rioting, procurement scandals, and national battle fatigue were endangering his war efforts. If Union triumph was to be accomplished, Lincoln needed to defeat the elusive Confederates somewhere, anywhere, in a decisive military showdown.

"Get your force in order," Lincoln commanded Frémont: "Now do not misunderstand me. I do not say you have not done all you could . . . and I beg you to believe that as surely as you have done your best, so have I. I have not the power now to fill up your corps to 35,000. I am only asking of you to stand cautiously on them."[22] Had Frémont and McDowell met at Strasburg, the pincer movement planned by Lincoln might have prevented Jackson's hasty retreat, but even their collaboration would not have caused a Confederate defeat. As a drenching rain never stopped, turning all local roads into a quagmire, Schurz wrote Lincoln that field conditions made it impossible for Frémont to execute the president's recent order and that his forces had meanwhile been forced toward Moorfield in order to meet desperately needed supply trains. Had Frémont encountered Jackson head-on, Frémont's emaciated troops would surely have been ground up.

General Schurz, from Frémont's headquarters in Wheeling's McLure Hotel, wrote to Lincoln: "This morning I found General Frémont in a somewhat irritated frame of mind, and I must confess I understand it. The government has plenty of provisions and our soldiers die of hunger, plenty of shoes and they go barefooted, plenty of horses and we are barely able to move." Schurz was surprised that Frémont had held up under the strain. A member of his staff said that he retained "an eye like a falcon for keenness and earnestness," though Frémont's fine features were now furrowed by lines of worry and fatigue, his eyes bloodshot.[23]

Lincoln continued to telegraph orders for Frémont to cross the mountains into eastern Tennessee. The president and Secretary Stanton still wanted the general to sever the Virginia and Tennessee Railroad, to relieve Union forces further west, and to capture Knoxville. But Confederate forces, though in retreat from Port Republic, struck again and again at both Frémont and McDowell along a fiery trail down the Shenandoah.

For a brief time Jackson seemed to be trapped in the middle of a triangle with Banks at its peak while Frémont and Shields guarded the two base angles. The only way out was to prevent Frémont and Shields from linking up their forces. Jackson's subordinate commanders were frustrated in trying to decipher his maneuver plans—from whence arose the silly suggestion of his personal lunacy. General Ewell once said that "he never saw one of Jackson's couriers approach without expecting an order to assault the North Pole." It was, however, such audacity that led to the delay of Frémont's advance.

Even while they were withdrawing, Jackson's Confederate commanders continued to capture thousands of muskets and other equipment. As a jubilant General Richard Taylor reported to Jackson: "I thought the men would go mad with cheering." On June 12, President Lincoln, mistakenly believing that Frémont had bloodied Jackson's Confederates, sent him a congratulatory cable: "Many thanks to yourself, officers, and men for the gallant battle of last Sunday."[24] But the great valley of Virginia was Stonewall's Shenandoah, certainly not Frémont's.

The president, despite his recent message of congratulations, doubted Frémont's boast that he could capture the rail hub at Staunton in Virginia if only he had a force of thirty-five thousand men. Though critics in Lincoln's White House told him that Frémont should once more be dismissed outright, he instead decided to create one overall command under Major General John Pope.

Frémont's relationship with Pope was a touchy one. Another West Pointer,

Pope was a native of slaveholding Kentucky, junior in years to the Pathfinder. In 1849 an army board had accused Pope of plagiarizing one of Nicollet's maps while conducting a Minnesota expedition. As a captain, in 1854 Pope had headed one of the Pacific railroad surveys through Texas along the thirty-second parallel, something that Frémont had been denied. Still later, when serving as a division commander under Frémont in Missouri, Pope had been repeatedly insubordinate. Although Pope was a garrulous loudmouth, he had one advantage over other generals. He knew Lincoln personally.

The president's telegram of June 26 to Frémont was unequivocal. It relieved him of command of the Mountain Department forthwith. He and his troops were to be reconstituted into the First Corps of the Army of Virginia, while Nathaniel P. Banks's Department of the Shenandoah became the Second Corps and Irvin McDowell's Department of the Rappahanock was restructured as the Third Corps. These commanders were all ordered immediately to report for duty under General Pope. Not only did tension continue between Frémont and Pope, but Pope was no better commander. He was soon to suffer an ignominious defeat at the second Battle of Manassas, or Bull Run. Frémont, once again humiliated by Lincoln, asked that the president release him from subordination to Pope. On June 27, Lincoln granted his request. The president had shifted Pope into the unified Shenandoah command in part because of Frémont's continuing lack of cooperation with regular army sector commanders, who complained incessantly to Secretary of War Stanton.

After Grant and Sherman emerged from the confining chrysalis of service within the army's western theatre of operations, they abandoned the previous no-win strategy in which generals like Frémont had been engaged. That strategy had been to march large armies onto Southern soil, principally in Virginia, and to engage the Confederates in hopes of annihilating them. For three years in a row each such thrust along the South's borders had failed. Repeatedly, bloodied commanders, including Frémont, would retreat to lick their wounds and regroup for another try. But for Frémont there would be no further such chance to defeat the enemy. Grant and Sherman would bring to bear forces large enough to press the Confederates relentlessly, no matter what the cost.

Following his second relief from command, Frémont, though still outranked on the army's seniority list only by General McClellan, had virtually no credibility left in army circles. Yet he felt entitled to a leave of absence in order to go to Washington to fight this humiliation. But Secretary Stanton gruffly refused to grant even this request. Neither Stanton nor Lincoln wanted a former presidential candidate lobbying behind their backs in wartime Washington. Furthermore, hard-line regulars now saw to it that Frémont's showy Zagonyi Guard was promptly mustered out of the service without pay, quarters, or even forage for their horses. The War Department also promptly annulled all of Frémont's outstanding contracts for supplies and animals, gathering evidence against malfeasance in his command.[25]

As after the failure of Frémont's Missouri command, adherents sought to reargue his military capabilities. Among these friends was the ever faithful John F. Hume, who now purported to claim that Frémont had actually "defeated Stonewall Jackson in Virginia—at Cross Keys—which was more than any of the other Union generals then in that department could do. . . . It was the misfortune of Frémont that his independence caused him to clash with selfish interests, and he was sacrificed."[26]

From among his troops came forth the usual apologists for Frémont. A Captain Pike, who had built a bridge for him across the Ohio River at Paducah, Kentucky, avowed that he "wouldn't have missed what that man has said to me for all the rest of my years." When in Frémont's headquarters tent, Pike "was never so happy," and he added: "I'd go to hell for him." Another officer, however, who had not fully obeyed one of Frémont's orders, reported being promptly dressed down by the general: "When I send you on any special service . . . always my orders must take precedence." Frémont had also known how to show pleasure when his orders were followed, as an admirer attested: "There was a light on his face that helped to account for the devotion of his followers . . . and perhaps the more that he said so little."[27]

Colonel Tracy, Frémont's aide, hated to see the general take leave of his troops: "A sense of bitterness of the injustice done pervaded us all; and with the reading of the final dispatch, announcing the General relieved from all present command, a silence fell upon our little group such as no one then in attendance can soon forget." Accompanied by Colonels Albert, Pilsen, and Zagonyi and a small retinue of other foreign officers, Frémont waved farewell and, "striking spurs, was soon, with those about him, past the corner of a little wood and upon the road to Winchester," en route to New York, where Secretary Stanton ordered him to await further orders.[28] The orders never came.

After staying for a time at New York's Astor House, Frémont and his family moved on to Washington, where he was unwanted. Taking a house on Fourth Street, with the aid of friends in Congress Frémont prepared a defense of his Missouri activities not unlike that produced during the court-martial trial so many years before. But the White House and War Department let him sit idly by without further command.

Secretary of War Stanton did momentarily revive the impractical idea that Frémont might yet command some colored troops. This notion was floated as an attempt to allay radical Republican displeasure over his second loss of command. Actually, Stanton, who had repeatedly brought the general up short for loose command practices, as in Missouri, saw to it that Frémont would have no real chance for an unprecedented third Civil War command.[29]

As the war raged on, Frémont remained in the shadows while other generals received national plaudits—Sherman for the fall of Atlanta and Grant for his victories at Vicksburg and in defense of the capital. Grant, silent, unkempt, and once reduced to selling firewood on street corners, had been far better suited than Frémont to leading the volunteer armies of a populist society. Though unassuming in demeanor, he possessed strategic brilliance and ended up commanding an army of more than a million men. The nation rewarded Grant with the rank of full general; he was the first officer to hold that title since George Washington. On May 10, 1863, Frémont's archenemy, Stonewall Jackson, fatally wounded by the fire of his own men, became a Southern legend. General Halleck too, who had replaced Frémont in Missouri, far outstripped him in military credentials. Lincoln was at pains to explain that although he was general in chief, Halleck had "nothing to do" with the removal of either Frémont, Butler, or Sigel:

> Sigel, like Frémont, was relieved at his own request, pressed upon me almost constantly for six months, and upon complaints. . . . In the early spring Gen. Frémont sought active service again. . . . He holds the highest rank in the army, except McClellan, so that I could not well offer him a subordinate command. Was I to displace Hooker, or Hunter, or Rosecrans, or Grant, or Banks?[30]

The out-to-pasture generals had been reduced to watching military events from the sidelines. Yet Lincoln, thinking ahead to reelection in 1864, had to keep them in uniform.

For Frémont the war was over. Although he had seemed to be an ineffective leader and appeared to exert little effect on the war's outcome, one cannot simply dismiss his role as totally ineffectual. Although he had lost two successive commands, both of them had been laden with baffling logistical problems. Each theater of operations was especially poorly supplied, partly because Frémont did not receive the backing he thought he deserved. Whether or not this lack of support was primarily a result of his abrasive nature, there were, furthermore, generals even more incompetent than he, but perhaps none with quite his pretenses.

On March 18, 1863, a disgruntled Frémont, still drawing the pay of a major general, took his small staff back to New York City. On August 12 he resigned his last military commission, said goodbye to his entourage, and received from the head of the Secret Service a check for $2,924.22 from confidential funds.[31] He was once more out of the army—this time forever. All that remained was to be photographed in uniform, along with other generals, at the studio of Matthew

Brady, who, after helping with the preparation of the western daguerreotypes, had become a prominent figure in his own right. Brady included Frémont in a compendium of military notables. But because all the major military figures were being photographed, that was no great honor. Back in 1850, Brady had placed Frémont in his "Gallery of Twenty-four of the Most Eminent Citizens of the American Republic Since the Death of Washington." Among Brady's other nominees had been Calhoun, Webster, Clay, and Audubon.[32] How the mighty had fallen.

In New York a powerless Frémont, while witnessing the death throes of the Confederacy from afar, came to know what it meant to live in a divided union. There were thousands of arrests for sedition against the Union. He personally experienced an attempt to burn the first city of the North. During New York's July 1863 draft riots, a secessionist mob planned to burn down his home on west Nineteenth Street. Young Frank Frémont recalled that "our house was one of those marked in chalk, to be destroyed"; someone had scrawled "queer designs" on the residence. The city of New York, according to Frank, had a Democratic administration that refused to defend the Frémont family—this at a time when blacks toward whom the general had shown such compassion were threatened with hanging from lamp posts. Frémont therefore sent his family to safety in the countryside. Members of his household secured the windows and doors of his residence until the riots passed. Once more nothing had gone his way.[33] ❖

To be relieved of command during a war would have crushed most leaders, but Frémont retained some political clout along with a loyal coterie of followers. Without such power, Lincoln would never have restored him to the mountain theater of operations after the first dismissal. Even before Frémont went to West Virginia, there was talk of renominating him for the presidency. "The western people, especially the Germans, begin to be blatant about Frémont," Francis Lieber wrote to General Halleck early in 1864. "Frémont cannot, I take it, be elected, but it may defeat another election and help Great McClellan."[1]

Lincoln had fired George B. McClellan, increasingly called a do-nothing general who had refused to fully commit his troops to battle. But McClellan also possessed a political following. If "Little Mac," as he was called, won the Democratic nomination, people said he would welcome the South back into the Union with slavery intact. Others feared a soft reconstruction policy under Lincoln. Radical Republicans and uncompromising abolitionists, hence, again swung toward Frémont. There was even talk of his receiving the Democratic nomination should he be able to arrange peace with the Confederacy, a nonsensical proposal.

Had Frémont not ignominiously sat out the last years of the war, he might not have listened to talk of renomination, which was incessant. Early in 1864, the *New York Weekly World* ran an editorial, entitled "Mr. Lincoln as a Presidential Candidate," that noted that "a large section of the radicals hate and despise Lincoln, and if he is nominated they mean to put Frémont into the field as an independent candidate." The article continued: "The danger as things now stand is not that he will fail of the nomination, but that Frémont will defeat his election by drawing off the radicals. We shall not be surprised, therefore, if the crafty politicians in the Lincoln interest proffer an alliance with the friends of Frémont."[2]

The midwestern Germans held the balance of power in Missouri, Wisconsin, and Illinois. Gustav Koerner, a German once on Frémont's staff and a close friend of Lincoln's, found the president "extremely uneasy, not to say alarmed" that Frémont might recapture the nomination of the Republican party as he had done in 1856.[3] McClellan, too, could win the presidency if Lincoln and Frémont split the Republican vote. There were continuing whispers that certain backers were willing to buy Frémont the nomination. A proposal that both he and Lincoln should withdraw in favor of a compromise candidate did not please the president, who refused to consider it.

The great newspapers of the country were of a mixed mind about all the candidates. Horace Greeley's editorials in the *New York Tribune* favored Chase and Butler as well as Frémont. Regional papers, especially in the Midwest, were strictly for the Pathfinder. The *Illinois Staats Anzeiger* (which Lincoln once owned) and the *Westlich Post* were for him as was the *Cincinnati Enquirer*. The *New York World* came out for Frémont as a "victim of jealousy and injustice." As early as August 20, 1863, the *New York Herald* reported:

> The friends of General Frémont, from Massachusetts to Minnesota, are beginning . . . an active campaign . . . to take the wind out of the sails of Chase. . . . Frémont will be brought out as an anti-cabinet Republican candidate, taking bold ground against arbitrary arrests, military blunders, and conscription measures of Chase, Stanton, and the radicals and a clear and definitive position as an emancipation candidate.[4]

The *New York Weekly World* for January 28, 1864, asserted: "In general character Frémont contrasts favorably with Lincoln in two respects: Fearless promptitude of decision against Lincoln's timid vacillation, and intellectual and social cultivation against Lincoln's uncouthness." But the *Chicago Tribune*'s June 4 edition claimed that Frémont was committing "political suicide by the course he has taken. . . . And he will not harm a hair on the head of Lincoln." James Gordon Bennett's *New York Herald* called Frémont's fellow recalcitrant, General Benjamin Butler, "a bag of wind" and considered Frémont himself "of no earthly account."[5]

Despite such misgivings, in 1856 and again in 1864 Frémont inherited the banner of the radical abolitionists, who had "courageously sought to curtail human bondage," to use the oft-repeated language of the times. He did, however, hesitate to be renominated, realizing that his chances for election to the presidency were relatively slim. The president of the Central Bank of New York said that he had not met one man yet who was determined to vote for Frémont.[6] As for the South, had that region been back in the union, he would certainly have received few votes there. During the war, in a Southern melodrama entitled *The*

Guerrillas by John D. McCabe, Jr., Frémont was cast as a villainous traitor; the play featured wanton Union destruction of property in western Virginia, not far from where his mother was born.

Ignoring these southern disabilities, on May 31, 1864, 350 radical Republican dissidents held a rump convention in Cleveland's Cosmopolitan Hall, once again putting forth Frémont's name for the presidency. Opposed to renomination of the moderate Lincoln, the delegates included Wendell Phillips, Schuyler Colfax, black leader Frederick Douglass, feminist Elizabeth Cady Stanton, and that faithful old friend, the journalist Horace Greeley.[7] This splinter group could hardly be viewed as a small group of cranks, as their opponents suggested. "If I turn to General Frémont," said Phillips,

> I see a man whose first act was to use the freedom of the negro as his weapon; I see one whose thorough loyalty to democratic institutions, without regard to race, whose earnest and decisive character, whose clear-sighted statesmanship and rare military ability, justify my confidence that in his hands all will be done to save the State, that foresight, decision, and statesmanship can do.[8]

Joining in this renewed praise was the *New York Tribune* for June 14, 1864, which stated that Frémont "embodied the Republican character and ideas as no other man on the continent represents it." On June 4, 1864, at Cleveland, Ohio, the fifty-one-year-old candidate whom Lincoln had called a bespattered hero allowed himself to be nominated for the presidency a second time.

This time around, Senator Sumner could not support Frémont for the presidency as he had eight years earlier. Sumner was one of those sometime friends who had tried to get Frémont an independent command after the general had been relieved during the war. But the senator's mood changed when he learned of Frémont's renewed political interests. Whereas Sumner had once considered Lincoln a dictator for annulling Frémont's emancipation proclamation, by the end of the war the senator was a constant visitor to the White House and a favorite of Mrs. Lincoln. In 1864 Sumner viewed Frémont's reemergence into politics as divisive for the Republican party.[9]

"I see that the Ragtail convention has nominated Frémont," a grumpy General Halleck wrote Francis Lieber on June 2, also in disapproval of Frémont's candidacy. "I don't believe there are bladders enough in this country, if every one should be inflated to its utmost capacity, to float such a mass of corruption and humbugs," he further asserted. General Halleck went on to state that the whole purpose of "that rump convention was to arrange to be bought off by a major party." Halleck maintained that when, in 1864, Frémont had started a journal named *The New Nation*, its first two issues had slandered him. There is no further mention of such a publication, but Halleck swore that he "had nothing whatever to do with either of Frémont's removals, and . . . every officer to whom he was assigned sent him off as a charlatan and a nuisance."[10]

As for Lieber, although he professed to be for Frémont, he had refused to head up a "Frémont Campaign Club" on the grounds that the general's nomination was about to divide the Republican party. Lieber had come to believe that "most people in New York City think that the whole Frémont concern will sell out to Grant, should he be nominated, bitter hatred against Lincoln being the chief motive."[11] In Congress, Thaddeus Stevens urged Carl Schurz to push for a reconciliation with mainline Republicans. Stevens, though forever a radical who had championed the earlier Frémont candidacy, stood aside from yet another endorsement of him.

Frémont's challenge both to McClellan, who became the Democratic candidate, and to Lincoln was to be short-lived. But before the main Republican convention met at Baltimore in June 1864, Lincoln had forebodings of defeat. Rather quickly, however, people began to view Frémont's recent nomination as "ridiculous," according to an observer who predicted that he "will not carry [even] one state" and who labeled his prospective political ticket as "the weakest of all combinations."[12]

There was talk, however, of a possible deal between McClellan and Frémont regarding Democratic opposition to Lincoln. Historians James G. Randall and Richard Current believe that Frémont was willing to make an accommodation with the Democrats. His former Missouri aide, General Justus McKinstry, actually offered Frémont's support to the Democratic nominee in exchange for the Pathfinder's restoration to his original command at Saint Louis, although one cannot be sure that Frémont authorized McKinstry's overtures. Colonel R. E. Marcy, McClellan's father-in-law, wired the Democratic candidate in code that he had met with McKinstry about Frémont's withdrawing in favor of McClellan and the Democrats.[13]

Although Frémont possessed little potential for victory, he retained latent bargaining power. Back in 1844 a tiny vote for the obscure James G. Birney, head of the Liberty party, had cost Henry Clay the presidency. In closely divided states no one yet knew what Frémont's influence might be on either of the two major political parties. Both Lincoln and McClellan feared a close election. There was still talk of Grant becoming a candidate, but the heavy casualties that Grant's forces were sustaining along the Potomac in the summer of 1864, with the Confederates at one point menacing Washington itself, had worked against his candidacy.

Spokesmen for Frémont continued to seek accommodations with both major parties. In the opposition was S. L. M. Barlow, corporation lawyer and backstage impresario of General McClellan's campaign. Barlow's personal papers contain the following strange letter to a friend: "McKinstry of St. Louis, Frémont's agent, left yesterday for Chicago, where I believe he is a delegate. He takes with him a written pledge from Frémont to declare for an immediate armistice and a convention, and with this he proposes to secure the Democratic nomination."[14] McClellan, who did receive that honor, repudiating Frémont's "peace stand," left behind a fragmentary record of Frémont's challenge to him: "The Frémont interview was a strange one, & confirms many little hints that had reached my ears. We will talk over it more fully when we can . . . be prudent as a letter in these days when the mails are so."[15] McClellan's letter then trails off incomprehensibly, its message mysteriously torn away, with no indication of what Frémont's agents had offered the Democrats.

Another incredible rumor regarding a trade-off was to the effect that McClellan would promise Frémont the position of secretary of war should McClellan become president. Yet another scenario would see McClellan in the position of general in chief of all the armies should Frémont, instead, win the presidency. McClellan reacted negatively to all these suggestions: "If these miserable intriguers think they can use me for their purposes, I will soon show them that they have mistaken their man—I am sick of the whole thing." McClellan, however, did believe that Lincoln promised Frémont "a position in the cabinet and dismissal of the two Blairs, Frémont's great foes" if he would withdraw and advocate reelection of the president, to which Frémont "replied that it was an insult."[16]

In fact, Lincoln would never have wanted Frémont in a future cabinet, and Frémont had nowhere else to turn except back into the Republican fold. Frémont had accepted the nomination of the Cleveland convention only with hesitation, yet he had resigned his army commission in order to speak out against what he called Lincoln's military dictatorship and usurpation of power.

By September 1864, Frémont was ready to withdraw from the race. He did achieve one verifiable goal out of his pseudocandidacy that year: the dismissal from Lincoln's cabinet of Montgomery Blair, who had so damaged his reputation. Henry Winter Davis, a congressional radical who also wanted Blair deposed, engineered Frémont's vacating the presidential race in exchange for Lincoln's dropping of Blair. After a meeting at New York's Astor House, the general withdrew from the campaign. In return, Lincoln, on September 23, the day after, sacrificed Blair to the Frémont radicals, announcing his resignation from the cabinet.

This sacking, the motives of which would be long denied, greatly pleased Frémont, who had not personally demanded it. By the end of the war the Blairs had collected too many enemies. Davis, Benjamin Wade, and Zachariah Chandler all continually put pressure upon Lincoln for the dismissal of both the Blair brothers as either advisers or officials. Frémont played no central part in this procedure, standing apart from the fray. Schuyler Colfax, as well as Secretary of War Stanton, Secretary of the Treasury Chase, and Thaddeus Stevens in the House of Representatives were also Blair enemies. Chase, furthermore, had an ulterior motive, seeking the Republican presidential nomination. Lincoln soon also dropped him from the cabinet. Almost four decades after these events, Chandler, in 1864 senator from Michigan, stated that Frémont had asked no price for withdrawing from the race. Blair's resignation, however, was clearly a precondition arranged by Washington enemies who hated him even more than did the Pathfinder.[17] It allowed Lincoln to go on and win the election of 1864.

In truth, the president had not quite known what to do about Frémont's spurious yet real candidacy. About it all, John Hay, one of Lincoln's young secretaries, had written in his confidential diary: "Frémont would be dangerous if he had more ability and energy. 'Yes,' says the American [Lincoln], 'he is like Jim Jetts' brother. Jim used to say that his brother was the d——dest scoundrel that ever lived, but in the infinite mercy of Providence he was also the d——dest fool."[18]

Despite his distrust of Lincoln, on this occasion Frémont was not a spoiler. With the war still raging, he did not want to play into the hands of McClellan and the Democrats. His poet friend Whittier summed up his decision to withdraw from the election of 1864 in these words: "There is a time to *do* and a time to stand aside."[19] ❖

After the war finally ended, Frémont and his family stayed on in New York, where he and Jessie proceeded to create a special world of luxury and privilege. In Manhattan they bought a residence similar to that of the wealthy folk who traveled in their circle, a handsome brownstone on Nineteenth Street between Fifth and Sixth avenues. Its many rooms afforded privacy to the whole family, whose members dressed fashionably and were constantly attended by servants. The children all went to private schools. Nearby lay Gramercy Park, America's equivalent to England's Bloomsbury Square, where Harriet Beecher Stowe, one of Frémont's admirers, lived, as did General William Tecumseh Sherman. Later the Frémonts, like the Roosevelts and other affluent New Yorkers, would move further uptown, to 924 Madison Avenue—commuting about the city in a carriage drawn by a pair of lively chestnut bays.

Frémont also bought a lovely upstate property near Tarrytown. Jessie called the place Pocaho, an Indian name. Its woods along the Hudson glowed a delicate green beneath the spring sun, and cattle grazed near the estate's rolling woodlands. Pocaho provided a grand summer retreat. To its campfires and picnics Jessie invited downstate friends as well as neighbors. She personally took over redecoration of its musty old mansion, filled with handmade furniture put together without a single nail. Pocaho's walls were lined with carved panels of oak, mahogany, and walnut. Alongside its broad, curving staircases, layered with the dust of ages, were rows of cracked rococo-framed mirrors.

During reconstruction of the house the general hated the noise of carpenters' hammers that filled Pocaho's echoing chambers. But like the rest of the family, he was taken with its setting. The estate's one hundred acres commanded a magnificent vista. Across the river there loomed up the cliff walls of the Palisades. From their front windows the Frémonts looked across Haverstra Bay, called the American Rhine, toward the Catskill Mountains.

At age fifty-two, Frémont still had sufficient funds to lead the dignified life that the world expected of public figures. Nellie Haskell, a friend who lived with the family in these years, described their life-style:

> The General was often away in the west on his railroad business, but when home, he usually read quietly or took evening walks with Mrs. Frémont or long rides

through the woods and along the post roads with the boys, Lily, and myself. He loved to listen to what he called "home-made music." He went occasionally to the theater when Mrs. Frémont asked him, which was seldom, because she knew he preferred to play chess or chat with the neighbors, the Phelpses, Schuylers, Aspinwalls or Beechers who dropped in often. As to formal dinners, he attended them only when Mrs. Frémont said: "You really must go this time." She attended many such functions when he was west on business, going to Washington for dinners and musicales. . . . But when Mr. Frémont was at home she tried to have only the sort of guests in the house agreeable to him.[1]

With the war over, everyone was talking about railroads. Collis Huntington and his partners had begun the Central Pacific line, which would move eastward from Sacramento, California's capital, across the Sierra Nevada to link up with the Union Pacific. Frémont's dreams of a national railroad system were finally being realized. How Senator Benton would have relished such times. Just as Frémont was about to get into the railroad craze, little did he and Jessie suspect that a national depression would imperil their affluence.

Frémont was approached by speculators who would plunge him into dubious projects. Only occasionally did he allow full family discussions of business matters at the round table of their Manhattan dining room or on the front porch at Pocaho. He showed little judgment in sifting through amazing fly-by-night schemes. As a result, Jessie spent weeks in Washington, where the Frémonts still kept a house on L Street, attempting to influence legislation on their behalf. Despite intermittent attacks of neuralgia, she lobbied for a variety of projects, including building of a railroad in the Catskills as well as seeking financial backers to produce naval torpedoes and acting as advocate of her husband's railroad plans.

There were now also public ceremonies to attend. In 1865, on the fifteenth anniversary of California's statehood, Frémont was enticed back to San Francisco, where he and General Vallejo led a parade down Market Street that was followed by a twenty-five-gun salute and an anniversary ball. Not all the events in which Frémont participated honored him alone. In 1868, Saint Louis erected a bronze monument to the memory of Senator Benton. Forty thousand people attended the unveiling on a May afternoon of that year. Only one person in that vast crowd was a blood relative of the great man. That was, of course, Jessie, who had been his favorite daughter. As she pulled the silk cord that loosened the Benton statue's wrappings, school children threw roses at the feet of her father's figure. A saluting train headed westward halted on a nearby track, its whistles blaring and its flags flying. Benton's left hand pointed toward the west; the words graven on the statue's pedestal read: "There is the East. There lies the road to India." Although Frémont occupied a place of honor on the platform, once more he was sidelined by Jessie's father. Between himself and the statue stood Jessie, matronly but still radiant, as if transfigured by the moving ceremony, still basking in the glory of her father.

In 1869 the Frémonts went to Copenhagen to attend the wedding of the future king and queen of Denmark. On this visit their daughter Lily's dresses were described as more chic than anything in the trousseau of the Princess Royal. Lily, who had a slight stutter, seemed none too secure about her father and mother, not quite knowing what to make of their gallivanting. She and the children were too often left alone in the company of governesses and other retainers. When the family returned from Europe, Lily wrote from Pocaho: "I'm in solitary possession of the house, Father being in Washington, Mother in the city, where she has been since Wednesday, giving some final sittings to Mr. Fagnani."[2]

As it was the fashion of high-society ladies to have their portraits painted, Jessie had commissioned Giuseppe Fagnani, an Italian painter working in New York, to produce a flattering portrait. In 1867, Fagnani, one of many foreign artists who fawned upon the rich, also painted Frémont in the uniform of a major general and holding a sword and scabbard. Recognized by all, he would stroll down Broadway, said a friend, "swinging along uptown like a man of twenty. The illusion of youth was further encouraged by the close-cropped hair, the form still trim, the elastic step, the rosy face, and the cheery buoyant manner when he spoke. He generally wore a business suit of light-colored plaid. Time and trial had not soured him. Though aging, this clear-eyed, agile man was the same stalwart Pathfinder whose footsteps so many men followed with enthusiasm."[3]

Behind this facade, all was not well, however. The presidential campaign and Civil War years had taken Frémont away from distant Las Mariposas. He had lost control of that property to Trenor Park, a Vermont lawyer, financier, and politician who became its manager from 1860 to 1863. One investor, the prominent John Parrott, considered Park a terrible supervisor. So did Frederick Billings, who still represented Frémont in California. Billings had sought to sell the Princeton Mine, a valuable property the riches of which were being improperly stripped by Park, who refused to give Billings monthly statements of the income from any of the Mariposas mines, streams, or pasturing sites. These Park rented out while charging Frémont 5 percent of the profits at a time when creditors demanded 2 percent a month in interest, all compounded.

As the estate's debts mounted, the list of investors grew longer and longer. Among the eastern *prominenti* who owned portions of Las Mariposas were Charles Gould, George Peabody, James Hoy, Thomas Drake, William S. Clark, Mark Brumagim, Nicholas Luning, and George Opdyke, Republican mayor of New York City. Having mortgaged the property to the hilt, in 1863 Frémont had turned over his remaining six-eighths interest to Morris Ketchum and James W. Pryor for $1.5 million, all of which he needed to retire its debts. Ketchum and other investors went on to earn millions of dollars from the estate. Though Billings had been Frémont's decent watchdog, he, too, profited from increasing numbers of Mariposas shares handed over to claimants in lieu of money owed.

Frémont continued to live in the East, remaining a trustee of the new Mariposa Mining Company. But he ultimately owned only five thousand dollars' worth of its stock, much less than other investors held. The company's stock began to be traded on the New York Stock Exchange on October 17, 1863. By December of the next year it would fall from thirty dollars to nineteen dollars per share.

In October 1863, Ketchum and Opdyke sent Frederick Law Olmsted to manage Las Mariposas with an annual salary of ten thousand dollars in gold. But the already famous landscape architect soon felt deceived by both Frémont and the owners of the company. By January 1865, the Bank of California refused to honor any Mariposa Company checks. Faced with years of mismanagement of both its property and its laborers, Olmsted wrote: "Here at Mariposa I stand in his [Frémont's] shoes and am paying his debts." In appraising Frémont's personal character, Olmsted claimed that there was "only one opinion—that is that he is a selfish, treacherous, unmitigated scoundrel. He is credited with but one manly virtue, courage or audacity [and] with but one talent, persuasiveness." Since Olmsted had arrived in California he had "not found a man speak well of [Frémont]. . . . He is universally despised, detested, execrated."[4]

Olmsted, along with Billings, had wanted to renew and upgrade mining operations at Las Mariposas, but, feeling defeated, he resigned his post as superintendent in April 1865 and returned eastward. Mayor Opdyke, who would be accused of defrauding the city of New York, was but one of a succession of slippery profiteers who milked the Mariposas estate, all because Frémont, sickened by so many financial and emotional reversals at Bear Valley, had refused to stay the course there. Yet his personal supervision was vital had he wished to hold on to the property. The sums of money spent there were huge, even by the standards of the day. In one year alone, to defend claims against him he had paid two hundred thousand dollars in legal expenses to David Dudley Field (later chief

Frémont was only sixty-one years old when this photograph was taken in 1874, but his haggard appearance is undoubtedly connected with the financial reversals he experienced during the seventies. (Reproduced by permission of the Huntington Library, San Marino, California; Album 188)

counsel to the crooks "Boss" Tweed, Jay Gould, and Jim Fisk). Ultimately, Field's fees ran to a half million dollars.

Leaving behind further involvements in Las Mariposas, Frémont next turned to railroading. He hoped thereby to recapture at least some of his losses. America's infatuation with the iron horse dated back to the 1850s and would become the basis of many new fortunes. In June 1863, while the Civil War was still raging, Frémont and a wealthy merchant, Samuel Hallett, planned a line to begin at the Missouri River and run westward through Kansas. They acquired control of the Leavenworth, Pawnee & Western Railroad, a company that existed only on paper. From offices on Beaver Street in New York City, Frémont and Hallett sought capital with which to fund expensive construction. The amounts required were massive—of the sort that we today associate with space-age technology. Frémont naively thought that old Washington contacts would help persuade Congress to back him in building a new national railroad system along his favorite route, the thirty-second parallel. To build such a road, one needed to know all the ins and outs of the 1850 Federal Railroad Act and subsequent complicated legislation that had granted over twenty million acres of public lands for railroads in ten western states. The railroad business had become a great land-grab enterprise quite beyond the general's expertise.

Frémont entered so many railroad schemes that it is difficult to keep them straight. In November 1865 he announced plans to buy the Southwest Pacific Railroad in Missouri, which he later merged with the Atlantic and Pacific. On June 1, 1866, he was accused by the San Francisco *Bulletin* of using this road purely as a land and township speculation: "It is rare," the paper asserted, "that a national fame ever rested on such an insubstantial foundation, or was ever acquired by the exercise of so little ability." Despite attracting such investors as Frederick Billings, Ed Beale, and Winston Churchill's grandfather, Leonard Jerome, Frémont built only twelve miles of track in one year. His track workers turned so violent that some were locked in a freight car and sent to Saint Louis lest they continue to destroy company property. On June 7, 1867, the governor of Missouri seized both railroads for non-payment of debt and ousted Frémont from the directorates of each. All these setbacks did not deter Frémont from dreaming that he could hook up various railroads, including the eastern division of the Union Pacific, to a rail network extending throughout the North American continent.

Foreign financial dalliances also continued to tempt Frémont. Undiscovered by biographers are his attempts during 1866 to build a Costa Rican railroad as well as another line across the Isthmus of Tehuantepec in southern Mexico. The Costa Rican road was to run from Puerto Limón on the Atlantic Coast to the Pacific. Frémont also imagined a railway net to connect with a transcontinental line at El Paso, Texas, with a spur hooking up at Guaymas in northwestern Mexico. His complex Costa Rican and Mexican projects were intertwined and required constant searching for enormous sums of money. At the Mexican legation in Washington he obtained from minister Matias Romero a tentative offer of two million dollars based upon his promise to raise another million dollars of venture capital. Frémont thought he could obtain Prussian financing. But Costa Rican Minister Esquivel Gutiérrez developed doubts about boasts that Frémont could subsidize any of his speculative ventures. The imposing Riggs National Bank labeled Frémont a "poor and visionary speculator with not very strict moral principles." Other bad publicity about his projects appeared in the *New York Herald*, ending hopes for a Costa Rican project.[5]

Although it was difficult to keep investors interested in his various railroad plans, in 1867 Frémont somehow bought the Memphis, El Paso & Pacific Company, a firm that had, however, constructed only five miles of road. It was a moribund corporation. Yet working out of a prestigious New York address, at 58 Wall Street, Frémont lobbied and received from the Texas legislature a grant of 18,200,000 acres of land—an area the size of a European principality. Against this new resource he advertised for sale some $10 million in bonds. None too scrupulous European agents sold $5,343,000 of these, mostly to French purchasers, misrepresenting their real value.

Frémont had muddled into another financial mess. His French agents sold bonds to land that simply did not exist. They banked 40 percent of the proceeds while promising 60 percent for actual building of the railroad. His brother-in-law, Baron Gauldrée Boileau, French consul general at New York, also floated Frémont's railroad bonds, using the French brokerage firm of Paradis et Compagnie to market bonds abroad. Boileau received $150,000 from Frémont for his work. His agents also promised the French government that one hundred locomotives and forty-five thousand tons of rails would be ordered in France and Belgium, hoping that such a large infusion of American orders into Europe would bolster his credit abroad.[6]

Frémont's French bankers produced false documents attesting that his railroad shares enjoyed a good market in the United States. They also claimed that he owned a continuous line from Memphis to San Diego and that the U.S. Congress had guaranteed payment of 6 percent interest on its construction bonds, another falsehood. Frémont, in Paris during 1869 to launch a railroad bond campaign, surely knew the false terms advertised by the company of which he was president.

By 1870, French authorities accused the Pathfinder of trying to sell 20 million francs' worth of fraudulent paper. Next he was tried in absentia for embezzling French citizens. His brother-in-law, Baron Boileau, was also indicted, and in 1873 Frémont received a sentence of five years in jail and a fine of 3,000 francs, which he never paid. Neither did he again return to France, a country that he and Jessie had so treasured. As usual, he blamed others for making false claims in his name, disowning any knowledge of misrepresentation.

In the midst of all this turmoil, the aging Lothario became involved in yet another furtive female relationship. This flirtation was with Vinnie Ream, later Mrs. Hoxie, a twenty-two-year-old American sculptress whom he had met in Paris. Frémont was drawn to the attractive Vinnie, who was already well known. (When she was but fifteen, Congress commissioned from her a statue of Lincoln.) His few surviving notes to her raise further suspicions that he again needed to go outside his marriage for sustenance and fulfillment, even that he had privately given up on the marriage. An 1869 letter refers to Vinnie as "my darling," while another reads, "What I have been writing to you looks like the letter of a business agent, but, although you may not see it, it is a love letter." Miss Ream sculpted a medallion of John Charles as well as a bust of Jessie and casts of their children's hands. He wrote about one of his visits to her: "You know what Richard said to Queen Ann—'Twas your beauty made me do it.' That's an Adamite way of putting the blame on the woman isn't it."[7]

On his visits to young Vinnie, who had settled in Washington, Frémont ran into an old enemy, Elihu Washburn, a former congressman and now American minister to France. Back in 1861, Washburn had made serious charges of fraud against General Frémont before the Committee on the Conduct of the War. It was Washburn who had sent back to the capital damaging advertisements and placards that Frémont's representatives had plastered all over Paris, and it was he who had also wired the secretary of state about these misrepresentations.

To help counter Washburn, who was after his hide, Frémont recruited the well-known congressman Ignatius Donnelly as his Washington lobbyist. But Donnelly's stinging attack on Washburn in the House of Representatives proved to be counterproductive. For a while personal accusations flew in both directions. Five members of the Washburn family were in Congress at one time or another. To cross any of them was foolish, even though Donnelly was chairman of the House Subcommittee on the Pacific Railroad. In the Senate, another enemy, James H. Howard of Michigan, used Washburn's reports from Europe as ammunition against granting Frémont's Memphis, El Paso & Pacific line a right-of-way through New Mexico and Arizona territories. As for Donnelly, although Frémont had promised him $50,000 in cash and $200,000 in railroad stock, the ambitious congressman ultimately received nothing. In fact, his brief association with Frémont's railroad problems blackened his already suspect reputation.[8]

Frémont had paid heavily for the puffery of Paradis et Compagnie. Among these claims was the patent untruth that the federal government stood behind Frémont's project in the same way that it had financed the Central Pacific and Union Pacific transcontinental lines. Frémont's testimony before Senator Howard's investigative committee filled a hundred printed pages. That body killed off further sales of his railroad bonds.[9] High construction costs and continuing difficulties over confirmation of land grants led Senator Howard's committee to authorize the building of a new line on the remnants of Frémont's failing railroad. To be called the Texas & Pacific, it would be constructed with full government backing, which Frémont had never achieved. In May 1872 all his Texas & Pacific franchises were assigned to Tom Scott's railroad interests. Fortunately, incorporation of this new line led to its assumption of responsibility for the defunct Memphis, El Paso, & Pacific. Scott and Grenville Dodge not only obtained congressional approval to build from Marshall, Texas, through El Paso to San Diego; they also gained rights to sixteen million acres of government land.[10]

Frémont, clearly out of his league, had let all these riches slip beyond his reach. The government did appoint him as "temporary receiver" of the new railroad line, a transitional post from which he drew a small salary for a few years while he oversaw the transfer of assets to the Texas & Pacific. But ultimately a federal judge replaced him with John A. C. Gray, who proceeded to collude with a dishonest magistrate, Judge Joseph Bradley, according to Frémont's son, Frank, to milk old Memphis, El Paso & Pacific accounts. At one point his father contemplated physical violence toward both of the knaves. Frank stated, "Only the wise counsel of my Mother prevented my Father shooting Gray."[11]

The family was laden with seemingly interminable debts. Jessie especially bemoaned the loans that they owed everyone in sight: "Tied up as we are by the French suits, this money has become imperatively needed," she complained. "I have sacrificed and exhausted my ready money [and] property in California. . . . The children too have given up theirs, and I am waiting the action of the court at San Francisco to sell a portion of their landed property. . . . I must keep within my clear resources."[12]

In 1872, Frémont had to sell their Pocaho retreat. Jessie hated placing that property on a real estate market that was severely depressed. She had brought up her children there and in New York City in an atmosphere of achievement and wealth. The boys had grown attached to the private school at Peekskill, which specialized in preparing pupils for West Point and Annapolis—to which they would both be admitted. Before falling upon hard times, she had written to Admiral Samuel Phillips Lee about getting her son Charley an appointment to the naval academy: "I am really peaceful and happy again, for in these stone walls I center the only remaining interests of my life."[13] Suddenly to dismantle a household filled with memories was like moving out the past. But at Jessie's "dear lovely Pocaho," the Frémonts had engaged in hospitality that they could not afford. Frequently invited there were the painter Albert Bierstadt, naturalist Louis Agassiz, and railroad tycoon Collis Huntington. Nellie Browne, who became like a daughter to the Frémonts, recalled those wonderful times: "Mr. Frémont had bought the Humboldt library after Humboldt's death. . . . Shelves ran to the ceiling, with a three-step ladder to reach the highest." She spoke of

> Mrs. Frémont's desire to have me fully appreciate the beauty of the typography and the hand-tooled binding. When we came to the Audubon books in color, she sat me on the floor, pointing out the very pictures that had absorbed her as a child in the Congressional Library. She told me of meeting Audubon with Humboldt in Washington. She . . . also showed me the precious collection of Napoleonic souvenirs . . . willed to her.[14]

As the national economic panic of 1873 rolled across the land, some five thousand major business firms collapsed, including the important Wall Street banking house of Jay Cooke & Company. Jessie, now battling process servers and court bailiffs, wrote to Nellie's new and rich husband that the tax collector was then at Pocaho's front door. State officials sought a levy on anything movable, "no matter whom it belongs to, even to one of the servants."[15] She begged Browne to help delay liens against Pocaho. Ultimately she had to part with virtually all her cherished acquisitions. Now made-over garments replaced silk and satin gowns. All her treasures had to be sold, including Wedgewood and Sèvres porcelains and even the children's horses.

No longer, either, would the Frémont carriages glide down Park Avenue. Their New York house on Nineteenth Street had to go, too, along with paintings of the West personally presented by artists Bierstadt and William Keith. The Frémonts, used to spending freely, had funded family extravagances by living on borrowed money or using up Jessie's inherited funds. She had personally financed the education of several young women admirers, including Nellie Browne.

The family had to make one more sacrifice of real estate: Bald Porcupine, a small island off the coast of Maine where they had a third residence. There had been so many good times at that vacation retreat, which guests could reach only by boat. From the island's tiny pier the ladies rode a donkey with a red Morocco sidesaddle to the Frémont house, the walls of which Jessie had decorated with Scottish tartan plaids in the fashionable style of Queen Victoria at Balmoral Castle, making everything as homespun and comfortable as possible. She was, however, tiring of building new nests for her progeny as fast as they were abandoned or destroyed. Much of Jessie's energy had gone toward trying to put together one home after another, about which her husband remained mute. On primitive Bald Porcupine Island, however, the general seemed truly able to relax, as when she described how "Frank and his Father are fencing with walking sticks all around me."[16]

Despite Jessie's attempts to encourage family unity, her children retained feelings of conflict about their father. Daughter Lily complained in a letter to the family doctor: "Father has the horrid old fashioned way of saying nice things when one isn't by to hear them. One knows he thinks them; still it's hard not to hear the actual words sometimes." Lily's brother Frank was more positive: "I would not call his disposition retiring but, rather, reserved," yet he was "overgenerous with his friends." His son continued: "As David Dudley Field [one of Frémont's many lawyers] told him once: 'General, if you keep trusting people and believing what they tell you, they will ruin you.'" Frank had other good recollections of his father:

> Hunting, except for food, he would not do, and always advised me never to kill except through necessity. He was always charitable and did much for people, but never permitted mention of it. In no sense holier than thou, instinctively he avoided the unclean, both mental and physical; and withal intensely human and understanding. . . . Dogs and horses, friends, world politics, the upbuilding of the West filled his life.

Frank believed that his father's years as an explorer had "unfitted him" for the rigidities of Victorian social life, with its late hours, all of which had no attraction.

For "nine o'clock found him ready to retire, while five in the morning found him awake."[17]

Immediately after selling both Pocaho and Bald Porcupine, the Frémonts moved into an ugly rented Manhattan brownstone at 924 Madison Avenue. Located near the corner of Seventy-seventh Street, this home was in what was then an undesirable area that Jessie called "poverty flats." Who was responsible for their humiliation? Frank again recalled: "One day when I was commenting upon the injustice of the government toward him in a certain case, he checked me by saying 'No, the United States and its government are all right. The fault lies in the fact that the conscience of the people is delegated to the members of Congress, and a delegated conscience never functions.' "[18]

Once again, Frémont refused to accept blame for his misfortunes. Whoever he this time chose to damn, the fact remained that huge sums of money had slipped through his fingers. Yet there is little evidence that he ever suffered remorse over his failure to pay his creditors, though his son alleged that he sought to do so. Whenever they, in turn, disappointed him, it was a different story. With his usual sense of privacy at work, he even failed to keep Jessie uninformed about some perilous investments.

She, to meet mounting debts, had to assume the role of breadwinner. Seeking to avoid sliding into poverty, she used her writing talents. While preparing articles for the *New York Ledger*, *Harper's*, *Will and Way*, and *Wide Awake* magazines, she established a connection with Robert Underwood Johnson, editor of *Century*, who paid her up to two hundred dollars per article. But most of her pieces brought in far less. John Charles thus had to rely upon "Gallant Jessie," as the family came to call her. It was not easy for a former hero to be rescued by his wife, who peddled her manuscripts with fervor and wrote into the night. Although her reveries today seemed rambling and diffused, Jessie's generation relished her stories, fashioned by lengthening tales that she told her own children. These writings, later called "a harmless pudding," are now all but forgotten.

Despite Jessie's efforts, the family had to move once again from uptown Manhattan to a small rented cottage on the Staten Island waterfront, which Jessie facetiously called "the Esplanade." A visitor who called on them there said: "They were prolonging the romance of half a century before. Mrs. Frémont was a staid-looking, matronly woman, with a remarkably strong face, resembling the portraits of her distinguished father." When the caller mentioned the general's travels, "he said, 'It sometimes seems like a dream. When I take a map and pass my finger over the states and great cities of the West, it seems impossible that I traveled through them before they had any population whatever—and such a little while ago! Every large city in the West was originally my camp.' "[19]

One of the ways in which Frémont hoped to recoup losses was to regain title to Black Point in San Francisco. Even before its expropriation during the

Civil War, gunnery practice at the site had become deafening. The cottage was so close to the fort "that when the men were ready to fire their Columbiads, they signalled us to open the windows to prevent the bursting of panes."[20] Having abandoned the place in 1861, Frémont had virtually forfeited his claims to Black Point, though he continued to press them with the government.

By 1878, as Frémont ended his speculative years, he had managed to lose several handsome fortunes as well as what was left of his financial reputation. Even America's Gilded Age rogue Jay Cooke did not trust Frémont, calling him "entirely unreliable in money matters." Cooke also said that "it injures anyone to have any connection with him." In 1870 Cooke wrote to his brother Henry that "it becomes pretty bad business to touch either Frémont or his bonds."[21]

Although he does not really belong in the company of such rascals as Cooke or Jay Gould, Frémont was indeed morally careless. Showing few restraints of conscience, he had never bothered to inform the public that claims made by his agents were false until he had in hand money raised by the sale of misleading debt instruments. From that practice came the charge that "loyalty to his own agents outweighed any normal resentment he should have had for their offensive conduct." Having "supported and defended their shady proceedings or their criminal acts, he was more loyal to men than to principles."[22]

Another charge was that he was "something of a vagrant—almost say a vagabond." He had, indeed, wandered "over vast, uninhabited areas." And "between a half and a third of his married life was spent drifting from home and drifting back again."[23] All this wandering resembled his participation in so many shaky enterprises. Yet when judged by the heady standards of the Gilded Age, from the end of the Civil War to the turn of the century, when fortunes were made and lost overnight, his speculative errors were common enough. But when the party ended, the mansions were gone and the money dissipated. ❖

Try as he might, the aging Pathfinder could never quite get the American West out of his heart. He avidly read everything he could find about what was happening to its great plains and mountains. It was a matter of pride, yet disconcerting, to learn that the regions he had once explored were increasingly furrowed by the farmer's plow. Between wheat fields, little and big towns alike were springing up alongside riverbanks where new railroad lines linked up these urban centers. The log hotels that once catered to buffalo hunters were giving way to red brick and sandstone. Stockades and dugouts were being replaced by Victorian gingerbread houses with fancy cornices and real plate glass windows. By the 1870s, tourists in parlor cars pulled by smoking diamond-stacked locomotives regularly crisscrossed the old trapper trails.

The romance of the West had begun to fade. The great herds of bison, numbering in the millions, that once roamed the plains, were decimated. Some of the brave men who, along with Frémont, had "tamed the West" were reduced to riding alongside Indians in theatrical extravaganzas like that of Buffalo Bill Cody.

In 1875, Frémont had managed to arrange for a train journey westward alone. As the locomotive chugged its sooty way through deep river gorges and rocky canyons toward the continental divide, the snows in the Rockies were visible outside his window. His mind wandered into the past, reconstructing scenes from his five expeditions. He thought of what it had meant to lead a train of horses and mules down a treacherous mountainside where steam engines now safely hauled their passengers.

His West had been displaced by one in which sportsmen sometimes took pot shots at Indians from the observation platforms of trains. How despicable it was that once proud tribes had been exiled into the deserts of Utah and Arizona. As he proceeded toward Salt Lake City, he wrote out in longhand a poem that was filled with regrets:

> *Written on Recrossing the Rocky Mountains*
> *in Winter After Many Years*
> Long years ago I wandered here,
> In the midsummer of the year,
> Life's summer too.

A score of horsemen here we rode,
The mountain world its glories showed,
    All fair to view

These scenes in glowing colors drest
Mirrored the life within my breast,
    Its world of hope.
The whispering woods and fragrant breeze
That stirred the grass in verdant seas,
    On billowy slope.

And glistening crag in sunlit sky,
Mid snowy clouds piled mountain high,
    Were joys to me.
My path was o'er the prairie wide,
Or here on grander mountain side,
    To choose all free.

The rose that waved in morning air,
And spread its dewy fragrance there
    In careless bloom
Gave to my heart its [   ] hue
O'er my glad life its color threw
    And sweet perfume

Now changed the scene and changed the eyes
That here once looked on glowing skies
    When summer smiled.
These riven trees and windswept plain
Now shew the winter's dread domain
    Its fury wild.

The rocks rise black from storm packed snow,
All checked the river's pleasant flow,
    Vanished the bloom.
These dreary wastes of frozen plain
Reflect my bosom's life again
    Now lonesome gloom.

The buoyant hopes and busy life
Have ended all in hateful strife
    And baffled aim.

The world's rude contact killed the rose,
No more its shining radiance shows,
        False roads to fame.

But here thick clouds the mountains hide
The dim horizon bleak and wide
        No pathway shews.
And rising gusts and darkening sky
Tell of the night that draweth nigh
        The brief day's close.

Where still some grand peaks mark the way
Touched by the light of parting day,
        And memory's sun,
Backward amid the twilight glow
Some lingering spots yet brightly show
        On roads hard won.[1]

Upon returning to the East Coast, Frémont unexpectedly received a piece of good fortune that would once more link him to the West. He was offered the territorial governorship of Idaho. But because his son Frank was ill with tuberculosis, he asked for Arizona instead, hoping for a better climate. His friend from West Virginia days, Carl Schurz, who had become secretary of the interior under President Rutherford B. Hayes, nominated Frémont for the latter post. But the Pathfinder had to work hard to win the Senate's confirmation. Old political enemies granted him few favors. In May 1878 he wrote to Zachariah Chandler, reminding that still-powerful politico of how, in 1864, he had stepped aside from the Republican presidential race. He now needed Chandler's help in marshaling support for his appointment. William Evarts, the secretary of state and an old foe, objected to consideration of Frémont as a territorial governor, stating: "General Frémont was an explorer, a statesman, and a soldier. His appointment as Governor of Arizona would draw a hundred thousand men to the territory at once." Evarts feared that all those admirers might even invade Mexico. Frémont was thus lucky to gain the backing of James G. Blaine as well as of Chandler, because his reputation for foolhardiness had lingered on.[2]

After months of waiting, the appointment was finally confirmed, and the Frémonts were soon on the way by rail toward a series of western accolades. At Chicago's Palmer House the Pathfinder spoke to "a group of millionaire railroad investors." About this meeting his daughter, Lily, wrote a friend: "It would give you thorough pleasure to see how father is brightening and freshening up as we widen the distance between us and New York. By the time we make Prescott, we think he will be quite himself again."[3] Mr. Palmer himself put the Frémonts up in his private hotel rooms and would not allow the general to pay the bill.

As they whistle-stopped their way toward San Francisco, dozens of admirers showed up at each train depot. Local delegations, carrying flowers and baskets of fine wines and whiskey, repeatedly asked Frémont's party to spend a night in their community. Dressed in a formal frock coat, and still not a compelling speaker, the general usually uttered a few patriotic words at trackside that seemed to content crowds gathered there to honor the old trail veteran. At Echo City, Utah, an old-timer who had heard that "our Pathfinder was at the station," came aboard, Lily recalled, "to tell Father how much he had used his original old survey maps, and how pleased he was to find how thoroughly he could always rely on them." When a snowstorm in the Rockies descended on their Pullman palace car, the general weathered it in total comfort. What a contrast, said Lily, to when "Father was *roi des montagnes* so long ago." As they approached the Great Basin one night, Jessie and John Charles looked out their train window near where one of his parties had crossed Bear River. For whatever reason, the moon that shimmered at them across the waters of the Great Salt Lake brought forth unrelated memories in him of how black gunpowder had once smelled near that very place.[4]

At Sacramento in California, Frémont succumbed to an invitation to leave the train when that state's governor, along with Frémont's old colleague Senator William Gwin, met the party. While visiting Sutter's Fort, which John Charles had once occupied by force, he and Jessie were treated like visiting royalty. Back in New York, Sutter, as president of the Associated Pioneers, had already given Frémont a reception, on August 1, 1878, at the Sturtevant Hotel before the general's departure for the Pacific Coast.

When the Frémonts entered San Francisco, Senators Cornelius Cole and F. F. Low headed yet another welcoming committee. At the Presidio its commanding general also met Frémont at his old Black Point property. Lily said her mother should have been the hostess at the residence that they still claimed.[5]

After their train reached Los Angeles, a marching band played "Hail the Hero" to memorialize Frémont's role in the Cahuenga Capitulation, the document that had ended California's participation in the Mexican War. Jessie was gratified by "the meeting between my Chief and his old scout Alexander Godey," who had defended Frémont against charges of immorality during the 1856 presidential campaign. She considered Godey one of a dwindling clutch of loyal adherents: "Next morning we went up on Fort Hill and viewed the emplacement and ruins of the demi-lune battery thrown up there to command the then little pueblo of Los Angeles. Then we went into the little Church of Our Lady of the Angels."[6]

A few days later, as Frémont moved his retinue toward the Arizona border, they encountered the brusque General William Tecumseh Sherman near Yuma. Sherman was hardly the person Frémont wanted to meet in the midst of the desert. Even Sherman's friends thought him irrational, and enemies called him insane. For his part, the supercilious West Pointer continued to have reservations about Frémont that dated from when they were young officers in California. Subalterns and the great alike did not escape Sherman's verbal fury. He even once wrote that Ulysses Grant "cannot make a speech with five sentences." Compared to Sherman, "the father of modern warfare," Frémont's military service was both pale and clouded.

Sherman, astride his stallion and puffing a cigar, warned Arizona's new governor that the 230 miles from Yuma to Prescott were "vile and well nigh impossible." He also told Jessie, whom he liked better than her husband: "Going over that road there are places where I shut my eyes and held my breath. You will cry and say your prayers." In order to make the desert crossing a bit more manageable to the women, he assigned three horse-drawn army ambulances painted in blue, with flapping canvas sides.

Before setting out for Prescott, Frémont's party spent several days at Yuma's military fort, which was located on a bluff above the muddy Colorado River. Upon leaving that place, Frémont obtained six strong mules to draw the wagons. The first two vans carried thirteen people, while a third hauled kegs of water, feed for animals, and tent equipment. The dust was so bad that the women were thickly veiled and swathed from head to foot; Jessie wore a dust-covered cape, with a chiffon scarf flying about her hair; her hands often clutched her head. The party could travel only thirty miles per day because of the scorching heat, blowing sand, and bone-breaking rocky trail. The trip took eight days. Jagged pink-colored peaks made scattered small settlements seem even more remote than they were. The group passed through vast empty spaces dotted only by outlying ranches and, occasionally, bedraggled Indian huts. They finally reached Prescott, as Jessie said, "speechless with fatigue" after viewing scores of bedraggled Indian pueblos made of adobe mud.

At Arizona's capital, Frémont was met by the outgoing governor, John Hoyt, and secretary of state, John Gosper, who rode with his group through streets draped with flags.[7] This parade was followed by a dinner dance, which gave Jessie a chance to show off a fashionable eastern gown. She spoke of such events as being second nature to her, while John Charles, never to the manor born, was not especially pleased by the need to shake so many hands.

Prescott, located on a mining and cattle frontier, had been named capital of Arizona Territory by President Lincoln. Situated below the Sierra Prieta, it was still an untamed place. Its Palace Bar Saloon was the biggest in the West. The unpaved streets were named for the Indians—Mojave, Apache, Yavapai—who, like its cedar forests, surrounded the town. The town was lashed by dust storms, but when the annual rains did come to Prescott, they melted away entire adobe dwellings.

The Frémonts had to be content with a four-room pine-planked house with warped, unfinished floorboards. Hardly a mansion fit for a governor, the place contained only a few pieces of scrappy furniture, but cost the Frémonts ninety dollars per month in rent. In its kitchen their cook, named Chung, dressed in traditional Chinese dress and pigtail, received forty dollars per month. All these expenses, much greater than equivalent ones on the East Coast, came out of the governor's $2,600 annual salary. Although the army provided a stable full of horses, the Frémonts had to pay for their hay at fifty dollars per ton. The family also had to forgo the luxury of a carriage, though they did bring along Mary, their Irish maid.

Jessie wrote eastern friends about the prohibitive price of canned goods, which had to be relied upon. Fresh fruits or vegetables were unavailable: "Though we are beautifully located, we are four hundred miles from a lemon, and if I were offered the choice of one of my beloved La Marque roses and a fat ripe tomato just off the vine, I should take the tomato." Even Thor, the family dog, found the earth so hard that they had to dig holes for his bones. Whenever he chased a rabbit into the brush, he would return covered with cactus needles; the dog tried to pull out the thorns with his mouth, but they lodged in his tongue. From wild Arizona, Jessie told correspondents that at Prescott "only six years ago they scalped people on this spot." But she was pleased that "now a fine brick school-house with a roll of two hundred scholars stands secure, where the Indians held rule. . . . I go every Friday [to the Prescott Free Academy] and give the upper class a history talk."[8]

Territorial governors were often political hacks imposed from without by Washington. Most proved to be easy to seduce for pecuniary gain, and Frémont was no exception. Collis P. Huntington, Washington lobbyist for the Southern Pacific Railroad and the principal member of its "Big Four," wrote to his partner David D. Colton on June 14, 1878: "Frémont has been appointed Governor of Arizona. I shall give him passes and I think it important that you see him on his arrival and see that he does not fall into the hands of BAD MEN. He is very friendly to us now."[9] The governor used Huntington's free railroad passes to full advantage.

Frémont also busied himself with Indians, mining law, and irrigation, putting forth an ambitious scheme for reclaiming the Arizona desert by creating an inland sea from the floodwaters of the Gulf of California. He believed that if the Colorado River could be backed up toward California's Salton Sink, these vapors would cool off the entire American Southwest, changing its arid climate. Such notions were not uncommon in the late nineteenth century, when it was believed that trees and standing bodies of water could coerce rain from passing clouds. Frémont went so far as to ask Mexico's President Porfirio Díaz to join in attempts to change the weather pattern along their parched borders. The visionary governor looked toward creating an agricultural paradise.

In addition to seeking new sources of water for Arizona, its governor ran up against an unassimilated population of Apaches, Navajos, and Hispanics. To the thin crust of Americans the Indians posed a constant threat; Anglos looked upon the natives as virtually subhuman. Although the federal government had stopped labeling tribes as "nations," there was still confusion regarding treaties covering land and water use. Some whites whispered that only the Indians at a treaty signing were really bound by its terms and that the influential Indians made it a point to miss these ceremonies. Frémont also had to deal with stubborn civilian and army agents while trying to follow the policy of President Hayes and Secretary of the Interior Schurz. The White House hoped to keep the fiercest Apaches concentrated at the desolate San Carlos Agency in southeastern Arizona, where the cavalry had herded them at gunpoint. As white anger toward Indians hardened, Frémont suggested a joint United States and Mexican campaign against the Apaches, with the aim of possibly exiling them to Baja California.

The Indian menace continued as occasional roving firebrands stole live-stock or attacked supply trains. The Chiricahua Apache chieftains Victorio and Geronimo also menaced white settlements, persistently eluding General George Crook's troops and the local militia, which Frémont had called out to protect settlers. In 1879 the governor suggested that the Pimas be removed from their ancestral lands to the Colorado River even though those Indians had never fired a shot against white men. Ultimately, the territorial legislature, embarrassed by the governor's plan, allocated two thousand dollars in order to send him east to lobby members of Congress for funds with which to resettle the Pimas in the Salt River valley near Phoenix.[10]

Although he was successful in the effort, Frémont lost his popularity in Arizona by lingering on in Washington for six months, during which he and Jessie recruited investors for personal mining and cattle raising speculations. Ordinarily the territory's residents remained largely indifferent to the comings and goings of their governors, but Frémont was too frequently absent from his post. Writing to President Hayes on May 27, 1879, he pleaded for more time out of the territory to arrange for a new branch of the U.S. Mint at Prescott. He also spoke of wanting to loosen local laws in order to attract new investors, but it was his own economic interests that remained paramount. The new administration of President Chester Arthur would show less forbearance toward his absenteeism as he sought to rebuild his sagging finances.

Jessie spoke of the bleak period during which her husband was in Washing-ton as a "solitary pull" during which she and her daughter virtually ran the governor's office. Although the family had come to depend upon Jessie's essays for income, the copying out of gubernatorial edicts disrupted her own writing projects. But, as usual, she also reveled in her husband's latest position and wrote

Nellie Haskell Browne: "Isn't it good to have the General in power again and supported?"[11]

For the most part, Jessie's sorrows remained private. But occasionally they caught her family by surprise. The barren desert had made her sad and moody. Jessie did not henceforth accompany John Charles on his travels throughout the territory. Instead, Lily regularly went with her father during inspection rides by buckboard wagon into the Arizona hinterland. On one occasion they returned to find Jessie lying on the floor of their house, dizzy from vertigo. She blamed it upon the mile-high atmosphere, with its scarcity of oxygen. But after ten months in Arizona, Jessie was no longer the complying army wife of earlier years. She suffered from what some called "the vapors," today's depression. In winter the bitterly cold mountain air of Prescott also bothered her. Jessie's ailments accompanied years of frontier frustration. Somehow, she had to get away.

General Sherman had warned Jessie when he met the Frémonts as they traveled toward Prescott: "I pity you. I pity you." This admonition had come from a battle-hardened warrior whose troops had ravaged Georgia. Sherman had been right. Arizona's roads led nowhere. Heat, rocks, and sagebrush held no inspiration for Jessie. After further mysterious fainting spells, Frémont sent her east while Lily agreed to remain as his secretary and to keep house for her father.

Jessie and her husband had spent half their married life apart. For three more years, except for his trips eastward, they were again not to live together— scarcely the life of a settled married woman. With John Charles so often out of their marriage, she seemed almost to be demystifying his charms. Their roles were reversing as she found new strengths in her own writings, which were to be done far from him. She would leave him and Lily behind to savor those dry winds of his beloved frontier. Momentarily she also left behind the role of nest-warmer, shadow, and stepping-stone.

By keeping personal expenses down, Jessie sent her daughter money for upkeep of the Prescott house. John Charles seemed not to miss her. His son Frank recalled that in those years, "My father's health was perfect. He thought nothing of riding 40 miles to examine a mine . . . then ride back the 40 miles to Prescott, making a three day trip of it."[12]

At a small cottage on Staten Island that Jessie called "the farm," she ground out stories, travel sketches, and juvenilia. In 1878, before going to Arizona, she had published *A Year of American Travel*. It would be followed by *Souvenirs of My Time* (1887) and *Far West Sketches* (1890). All of these works managed to feature her husband. In an article for the *Boston Psychical Society Journal* for December 1888 she confessed to an early premonition that he had died during his 1853–54 expedition.[13]

In October 1880 Frémont came back to Arizona for the last time. He stayed on for one more year, continuing to use his governorship to pursue gold and copper mining prospects. He was certainly no mining engineer, and he had little appreciation of either profit or loss in business. He and Arizona Supreme Court Justice Charles Silent rode throughout the territory in search of promising mineral sites.[14] In March 1881 the need to inspect these prospective investments played a part in Frémont's audacious, if temporary, moving of Arizona's capital to Tucson. Near that settlement he became interested in the promising Jerome copper mine. But he was unable to raise sufficient funds to extend its shafts. This lode later provided William Andrews Clark with the wealth that made him one of the copper kings of the West. While at Tucson, Frémont also signed an agreement to develop his far-fetched canal and irrigation scheme in northeastern Sonora. Although he was to be required to pay only five cents per acre for it (one hundred thousand dollars, later dropped to eighty thousand dollars) he could not possibly raise such sums. Furthermore, the Indian menace in northern Mexico was severe. Additional plans to develop coal mines and a rail system there reached another dead end, for level-headed financiers were quite uninterested in his blue-sky projects.[15]

Both John Charles and Lily ultimately found low-lying Tucson an unpleasant contrast to the high country around Prescott. During one winter cloudburst the rain melted down the walls of Tucson's adobe houses as if they were liquid gingerbread and molasses. Frémont spent little time in Tucson, leaving his daughter to cope alone. After Lily fell ill with typhoid fever, her father allowed her to join him and Jessie in the East. But this was only after his resignation of the governorship. Lily then found that prize possessions the family had stored at Morrell's warehouse in New York City had been lost when the building burned down. Among them were her treasured dolls and childhood memorabilia.[16]

In Arizona, Frémont was faulted for his weak leadership as governor. Secretary of the Interior Schurz, his old friend, tried to shield him. But the governor's continuing absences, bitterly criticized in the *Tombstone Epitaph* and Phoenix's *Salt River Herald*, were hard to explain, especially so when compared with the performance of General Lew Wallace, who not only ran nearby New Mexico efficiently but also was a popular governor steeped in Indian lore. Both men had served in the Mexican War and Civil War, but Wallace became renowned after publication in 1880 of his romantic novel *Ben Hur*. Like Frémont, Wallace was governor during exactly the same period of two and one-half years from 1878 to 1881. Finally, Wallace's skill in handling the bandit Billy the Kid made the New Mexican governor popular with the western press in a way that was never achieved by Frémont.[17]

Practically all of Frémont's plans for Arizona Territory went awry, partly because his own ventures became entwined with those ostensibly in the public's interest. When the territory's citizens learned that he sought a franchise to build a railroad running from Tucson to the Gulf of California, their indignation increased. Governor Frémont's failure to obtain federal funding for a home guard against the Apaches also made it virtually impossible for him to continue in office.

The governor's letter of resignation, dated October 11, 1881, may well have been requested by President Chester Arthur. John P. Clum, owner of the *Tucson Citizen,* had complained to the new interior secretary, Samuel Kirkwood, that Governor Frémont's frequent absences had encouraged lawlessness throughout half-wild Arizona.

When Frémont returned eastward, Jessie, was elated: "There is only one piece of news in the world today. The General is here. He tells me I am beautiful, but I tell him the truth. He looks young, rested, and as handsome as that day in '41 when I saw him swinging down the avenue in his uniform." Despite Jessie's devotion and loyalty, their marriage bore little relation to the happy picture she repeatedly presented to their friends. As she continued to be duped by her husband, Elizabeth Blair Lee complained about his transgressions in a letter to a mutual acquaintance:

> Mary Martin found out that Jessie Frémont was in N. York. She went to see her. Says she 'looks hungry.' They are so poor. . . . Mary says her infatuation about Frémont, his hold on her, is still in full force . . . called it 'Jessie's insanity,' for, she added, I can realize it to be a woman's duty to devote herself to her husband, maintain him, and do all she can to make him good and happy. But to allow him to gamble away his own & their children's bread over & over again . . . to do it that many times. And he too faithless even to pretend to live with her. . . . My idea of Jessie is that she belongs to him body & soul and he does with her as much as he pleases.[18]

As John Charles had evidently picked up another lady friend, all of the Blairs saw the Frémont marriage as a tattered union. Their friends believed that Jessie stayed in the marriage mostly out of fear. With her famous father long since gone, her husband was her only security in an age when divorce among Episcopalians was virtually unknown. Like Libbie Custer, she therefore accommodated his infidelities.

Though his wife may have been torn apart emotionally by his peccadillos, Frémont remained his outwardly composed self. Another description of him following his return from Arizona portrays him as "clear eyed and agile" as well as "one of the most attractive and best-defined of our historic personages. I frequently met him on Broadway, swinging along up town like a man of twenty. The illusion of youth was further encouraged by the [now] close-cropped hair, the form still trim, the elastic step, the rosy face, and the cheery, buoyant manner when he spoke. He generally wore a business suit of light-colored plaid. Time and trial had not soured him."[19]

Now that Frémont's political clout was gone, he and Jessie began to flatter public figures they had known, with no particular aim in mind. They both seemed to crave associations that reminded them of more fulfilling times. Jessie repeatedly thanked former President Hayes for appointing her husband governor, sending Hayes a hand-painted platter. John Charles also wrote regarding the deterioration of Mrs. Hayes's health.[20] Back in 1850, the Ohio town of Lower Sandusky had changed its name to Frémont, and it became the site of the Hayes Memorial Library, named after the president who gave Frémont his one last chance at public life. Jessie also enjoyed contact with former President Grant, who had no use for Frémont but liked her. At a reception he asked Jessie to stand near him: "You always seem to have something to say. Now my difficulty is to know what to say," she quoted him. When president, he had done various favors for her regarding transfer of personnel within the army and navy.

No one, formerly powerful or not, could extricate her husband from his latest Arizona losses. His son Frank said that his father had left too many details to men like Marshall O. Roberts, Tom Scott, John B. Gray, and Trenor O. Park, "who fed off his fortunes, and robbed him without compensation, but legally." Frank bitterly complained that "everything we had was sold," adding, "under the mistaken ideas prevalent in those days that a man should, when under financial disaster, relinquish all and everything to creditors, my Mother's separate properties, dating from the old California days, were all relinquished . . . and we went forward literally like picked chickens." Frank was especially bitter about Judge Silent, who had piqued his father's cupidity regarding alleged copper deposits at Verde, Arizona. Frank also observed: "In addition my father had unqualified faith in the future of Arizona as an agricultural state, and desired to have a channel cut from the Salton Sea to the ocean. . . . In the midst of trying to raise money for such an improbable project, Baring's Bank, his agents in London, failed and closed its doors. Meanwhile, Judge Silent became a rich man."[21] Frank chose to forget that his father once had a notorious reputation for not paying his own bills. To Frémont's credit, in these perilous later years he showed only steadfast dignity, uttering no complaints over their relative poverty.

Only occasionally did the general find such odd jobs as agent in Washington for Indians with land claims against the federal government. In that case, although he achieved power-of-attorney for the Cherokees regarding their Texas rights, he rather lazily assigned them to his old friend Nathaniel Banks for prosecution, which ended unsuccessfully.[22]

He also made one last desperate attempt to resuscitate his Mexican failures, still claiming four square leagues of land at Rancho San Juan del Río on the Yaqui River in Sonora. Although the Mexican government had once granted this property to an American owner back in 1857, Frémont, into the 1880s had no luck in obtaining clearance of his own title, in part because he could not afford bribes demanded by local Mexican officials. The Indian menace there had also not receded, impeding settlement of the land to which he vainly laid claim.[23]

In 1884, Jessie finally realized that her husband's fortunes showed no signs of revival. She urged him to accept one last invitation to travel to Michigan in order to bolster the presidential aspirations of Republican candidate James G. Blaine. But, in a mudslinging campaign linking him with corruption, Blaine lost the presidency to the Democratic candidate, Grover Cleveland. Both Frémont and Blaine occupied center stage only intermittently, and neither was really capable of shaping either the destiny of others or of himself, for that matter. ❖

Jessie sat at her desk each day working on her own writings. On the wall before her was the latest oil painting of her husband. She knew all too well that his days of glory were clearly over. But after nearly fifty years of married life, she still had to push his life forward. Uppermost in her list of priorities were his long-postponed memoirs. Because he had come to hate indoor work, she for years had assembled newspaper clippings, letters, and other memorabilia that might ease writing an overall account of his many deeds. Because he continued to chafe at poring over reams of yellowed correspondence, Jessie did everything she could to jar his fading memory. In 1886 she also insisted that they move back to Washington, if only temporarily, in order to obtain better access to public records.

At the capital they rented a house that overlooked the British legation, and Jessie converted its second floor into a sprawling work area. The *New York Evening Post* for September 7, 1886, described their quarters and daily routine:

> On the right of the bay-window is placed the General's table, surmounted by a tall set of pigeon-holes, where letters, notes and papers are kept. Opposite is Mrs. Frémont's table, a large plain affair, covered with green leather. The General dictates, and Mrs. Frémont writes down each word as it falls from his lips. Miss [Lily] Frémont, at the typewriter, transforms her mother's manuscript into neat, legible type. Here, they all work together, all day long. The rule of the house is to rise at seven, take a cup of tea, work from eight until twelve, when breakfast is taken. From one o'clock to six they forge ahead when they stop for the day and dinner is made. The copy is then sent out; in the morning, proof is received from the printer. General Frémont is now seventy-four years old, but looks scarce sixty. His hair, short beard, and moustache are white, but his brown eyes are clear and bright as stars. His complexion still has the ruddy glow of childhood.

Because Frémont had achieved prominence before most men had even begun their careers, his life's story seemed cumbersome to publishers. Finally, a Chicago firm, Belford Clarke & Co., agreed to print the memoirs, but only "if the General will erase all of the unessential details." To this he replied: "I will not write as speaking of myself." Instead, he maintained. "I will be speaking of another man." The memoirs thus became anything but animated and certainly not a life confession. In that book he actually threw dust in the eyes of future readers interested in a revelation of the inner man. His detachment from the events that he narrated made even dramatic descriptions ponderous. Yet Frémont hoped to rescue the family's precarious financial condition by these last writings. After all, life histories of both Grant and Sherman had been successful publishing ventures.

As the family soldiered on, preparing the memoirs, life in Washington proved disappointing. Most of the old landmarks had been obliterated, and many former friends had died. The family eventually decided to move to a little rented house along a muddy street on Staten Island, with which they had grown familiar. At this new location, during December 1884, they were visited by the philosopher Josiah Royce. Still young, and a rangy Harvard professor dressed in prototypical tweeds with pipe in hand, Royce had set about to write a history of California. During the process he came to suspect that Frémont had greatly exaggerated his role in its conquest from the Mexicans. Royce also encountered other peculiar blemishes in the Frémont record that puzzled him. His interview with both Frémonts would probably not have occurred if the general's nephew, William Carey Jones, formerly a college classmate of Royce, had not suspected that his uncle's controversial reputation needed some cleaning up.

That favor, however, Royce was not about to do, especially after he received cool and devious replies to his questions from the Frémonts. Royce's personal background contributed to the unflattering version of Frémont's activities that he ultimately prepared. Callow and himself opinionated, Royce was born in Grass Valley of pioneer parents who had taught Josiah to question the motives of money-grubbing exploiters of its minerals and forests.[1] To chop down majestic redwoods while calling such pursuits heroic was to turn history into myth. Royce believed that Frémont the despoiler was in fact deliberately rewriting the past.

During the summer of 1884, at Hubert Howe Bancroft's new research library in Berkeley, the young scholar had studied the official Larkin Papers, which suggested that Frémont had also repeatedly disobeyed orders during California's conquest. After his interview, Royce, in a letter to Henry Lebbeus Oak, Bancroft's assistant, described the Pathfinder's courteous but self-righteous attitude:

The General is well preserved, a pleasing old gentleman, quiet, cool, self-possessed, patient, willing to bear with objections of all sorts, but of course not too communicative. Mrs. F. is, I grieve to say, none the better for old age—very enthusiastic, garrulous, naively boastful, grandly elevated above the level of the historical in most that she either remembers or tells of the past. . . . I cross-questioned concerning F.'s motives . . . all little detestable incidents that Mrs. F. plainly regarded as worthy only of the attention of a very small-minded historian. I could get no access to documents.[2]

Both Royce and Oak high-mindedly saw Frémont's encouragement of the Bear Flag Revolt as "perverse romanticism" and a wrongful decision against California's duly constituted Mexican regime, even before any war had been declared.[3] Royce judged Frémont's past actions on ethical terms alone. The philosopher's reading of life adhered to the strictest moral and ethical principles. For Royce all judgments, including Frémont's past ones, expressed moral values. His philosophy was concerned with reconciling the existence of an all-knowing, merciless God. These omnipotent views were far from Frémont's thoughts or his record out West many years before.

Frémont continued to insist that he had entered the Mexican War in California with a uniquely independent status, possessing secret orders that diminished the roles of everyone else, especially that of Consul Thomas Oliver Larkin. The Pathfinder even denied that he possessed any directive to cooperate with Larkin, but Royce had actually found such instructions.[4] Facing the elderly man and his wife across a table, Royce had in his back pocket that "precious dispatch." He could hardly stay seated in his chair while listening to "these two historical characters demonstrate that this dispatch . . . was yet nonexistent, impossible, absurd, a fantastic bit of nonsense." Yet Royce perversely did not reveal that he had copied such a telltale document. Instead, he let Jessie rattle on about how her husband had merely followed her father's strategy because the views of President Polk and of Secretary of State Buchanan "were simply non-existent when he had his own plan to carry out."

Royce had hoped that the Pathfinder would agree with his reassessment of the California conquest. "But no; cordial he still was, dignified and charming as ever, and the good Jessie sat calm and sunny and benevolent in her easy chair; but alas, he lied, lied unmistakably, unmitigatedly, hopelessly." Royce came to see Frémont as an oversentimentalized hero and a military bully, and he "determined to explode the Frémont myth."[5]

Although Royce would go on to become a world-famous philosopher, there is a measure of naiveté mixed with shrewdness in his youthful assessment of the Pathfinder. He came away from the Frémonts complaining that they communicated with each other as if using an accursed "family cipher" that made them virtually impenetrable while employing a strategy to "throw up dust." Because they so twisted past events, he determined "to apply the thumb screw" to them.[6]

Royce's moralistic *Feud of Oakdale Flat* (1887), and his other writings as well, would indict California's unethical invaders, including Frémont.[7] In Royce's eyes, the general was not only an irresponsible military commander but a despoiler of a pioneer's Eden as well. The thirty-year-old critic also asserted that "friends and foes alike thus knew remarkably little of him, save that, for inexpressible reasons, they loved or hated him." This was because of "his peculiarly hidden and baffling character" while "the deep purpose" of his deeds and life "seemed always to have remained in reserve." Royce observed that, paradoxically, "the more you consulted him the fonder you were of him, and the less you were convinced by what he said. He added: "One may say that General Frémont possessed all the qualities of genius except ability." Too many persons had trusted him, "only to see Frémont repeatedly vanishing." He considered the Pathfinder "a creature escaped from a book, wandering about in a real world when he was made for dreamland." Royce disparagingly suggested that "an analysis of the very peculiar qualities that marked . . . General Frémont would doubtless be a charming task for a student of psychology." Royce, who had blackened Frémont's reputation more than any critic since General Kearny, learned, as many others had, that Frémont could not possibly admit less than past triumphs—and certainly not to an academic critic.[8]

Professor Royce had at least provided the Frémonts with a diversion from work on the memoirs, which continued sorely to tax John Charles until they were finally published in 1887 after being heavily edited by Jessie. Their 650 oversized pages were accompanied by her sketch of Senator Benton's life.[9] Unfortunately, the publishers overpriced the volume and advanced no funds, so the book produced no income whatsoever for the Frémonts. The poor sales were a result not only of its bulk, but also because of its stitching together of old reports. And because the memoirs concluded with 1847, the year of the court-martial, they failed to account for Frémont's later adventures.

During a severe eastern winter, John Charles fell ill with bronchitis and inflammation of the throat. For a time he could barely move. With no antibiotics available in those days, a physician prescribed flight to a warm climate. Because the Frémonts had no funds for such a journey, Jessie secretly contrived a means of escape. She sought an interview with the railroad magnate Collis P. Huntington. Though crafty and hard, this principal owner of the Southern Pacific line liked Jessie. Back in 1849 they had traveled together on the Panama route on the ship *Crescent City*. Later, Huntington had been a houseguest at Pocaho. He was also an unswerving admirer of the Pathfinder.

Huntington owned enough track to connect the north and south poles. He could travel from Newport News, Virginia, to San Francisco without ever riding on anyone else's rails. When he met with Jessie, he offered her a private railroad car for the trip to California. Her husband at first resisted this notion. She wrote:

> Here we were, lovers for forty-seven years, having our first lovers' quarrel! The General, thin and pale, sat frowning, staring out the window, answering my questions and protests with the exaggerated politeness I had often seen him use so effectively when angry with the boys. I prepared his favorite chicken broth; he barely touched it.... I was perfectly miserable, but whenever I looked at his sunken cheeks, I determined to see this thing through until the General refused to stir.

Finally he agreed to go, but only after Huntington personally came to their cottage with the letter of authorization in hand. "You forget," the magnate said "that our road goes over your buried campfires and climbs many a grade you jogged over on a mule. I think we rather owe you this."[10]

Frémont's pride thereby salved, he and Jessie took the two-week trip westward in Huntington's parlor car. On Christmas Eve of 1887 the elderly couple descended from the train at Los Angeles. Grateful to have escaped from a particularly harsh eastern winter, Jessie recalled: "We met the fresh yet soft air of the Pacific Ocean and entered a region of rich valleys and gentle hills with pastures and orchards and pretty farm houses." They hoped to move into one of these in Inglewood on the outskirts of the former pueblo. New streetcar lines radiated outward as far as the seashore. Beach trips past fields "with blossoming apricots, peaches and oranges, flanked by lovely green hills," did their morale a great deal of good: "We stay on the warm sea sand and come back with more new life."[11]

The Frémonts were fortunate to arrive in the midst of southern California's largest real estate boom, which made it possible for land promoters to provide them with housing in exchange for using their name in selling residential tracts. Jessie did not find this as demeaning as did her husband. He cringed when the *Los Angeles Times* for April 6, 1888, announced that they both had participated in a rail excursion to promote the sale of homesites to prospective buyers:

> Charming Inglewood, the future home of General and Mrs. Frémont, was the first station at which the train halted. Here ... will be built their pretty home in the midst of an orange grove and underneath the shade of olive and of palm. It is a beautiful spot the General has chosen as the home of his declining years. It is in keeping with the romance of his life ... where his own hand first unfurled the Stars and Stripes.

There is no evidence that the Frémonts ever stayed in such a house.

Despite the crisp newness of their surroundings, Jessie missed urban amenities, and before long she moved their household into central Los Angeles. There she cultivated new neighbors who were proud to live near the Frémonts. One of them recalled: "Her hair is quite thick and white, and altogether she and the General too are very dainty and delightful people. . . . It is difficult to imagine her over 70, as she must be. She says the General hates the word 'age' and has taught his little grandchildren to call him by his title, rather than Grandpa."[12]

The locals learned to recognize the slightly stooped, white-bearded man in a military cape who took morning walks. Jessie was happy to tell her eastern correspondents: "He is *serene* and sleeps and eats in his wholesome natural way. We . . . give him the bouillons and delicately broiled things he likes." With Huntington's help she temporarily had enough money to enjoy the services of both an Asian and a black hotel servant: "China holds the kitchen unmolested, and Africa the dining room," she wrote.[13]

Although no longer at the center of social or political life, the Frémonts were never fully private retirees. Invitations, even in distant California, still arrived with each mail, though the general continued to shun public celebrations. It must have been tiring to be dragged out by politicians every four years to utter a few banal words for the Republican party. Although he had been its first candidate, he repeatedly turned down such engagements. He wrote a Pasadena committee that sought to organize a banquet at that community's Raymond Hotel: "My returning health still demands some care." Later that spring the Frémonts did agree to be "the guests of the beautiful rich town of San Jose during its flower-fete." On that occasion a Mormon who had helped rescue the Pathfinder's 1853 expedition at Parowan burst through the crowd to pay his respects touchingly to Frémont.[14]

Jessie and John Charles were managing to ride out their retirement years with a measure of dignity. Although they enjoyed little financial protection, Jessie scraped together enough pin money to commission another oil painting of him. The young Gutzon Borglum, later renowned as the sculptor of Mount Rushmore's massive granite presidential figures, was then working in Los Angeles. Earlier, Borglum had done some illustrations for Jessie's books and articles. Only twenty-five, this son of Nebraska Danish immigrants produced a portrait in oils that Jessie called a "wonderfully true" likeness of her husband, as good as Thomas Hicks's earlier oil painting.[15]

In May 1888, Frémont agreed to take a small group into the mountains above the old Mariposas property. There, in a future national park, giant Sequoia trees had been named for him as well as for Generals Sherman and Grant. Jessie insisted upon a photographing session in front of "his tree." When they returned to Los Angeles, he again grew restless, pronouncing himself "*perfectly* well" fit for still more travel. California was no longer the thrilling place he had known

In May 1888 the Frémonts and their corpulent daughter, Lily, visited the General Frémont Tree in northern California. (Reproduced by permission of the Huntington Library, San Marino, California; Album 188)

during its conquest. Indeed, he saw Los Angeles as a kind of cemetery of the living, filling up with retired farmers from Iowa. But it would take him another year to get free of Jessie.[16]

Their marriage was now a tired exercise in domestic repetitiveness. John Charles had little left to say to Jessie, who was continuing to live out her roles of great senator's daughter, mother, marketable writer, and defender of her husband. But the childrearing years, largely Jessie's province, were long behind them. Coming out of a century when divorce was barely socially acceptable, it was not unusual, though burdensome, for such couples to remain married. Besides, the Frémonts could never have afforded to dwell apart, and he probably could not have lived permanently without Jessie nor she without him.

Jessie did enjoy retirement in California more than he did. She had grown stouter in the land of sunshine and oranges. To the poet Whittier she wrote from Los Angeles on November 19, 1889: "Here on this far shore where the serene climate gentles even hard memories, I seem to look back into another life, its strifes ended, only its results in good cherished."[17]

John Charles could conjure up no such cheeriness. In fact, he was becoming edgy in their California bungalow, where Jessie wished to keep him to herself. History had passed him by, and he found plenty of proofs that he had lived too long beyond the exciting decades of his explorations. Lately he had learned that several of his own mountain men were reduced to capturing bears for traveling circuses.

Though no longer young, Frémont retained a desire to relive his youthful adventures. But deep inside he knew that there would be no further expeditions, no easy flight from his overly solicitous wife. Though his former escape world was over, he had to try to get away, at least temporarily. He therefore managed two last trips to the East, concocting a story about complex investments that required immediate attention.

In truth, the only one of these financial involvements that remained was the remote Black Point claim. As he sought government reimbursement for that property it did not help that after 1882 the hated General Pope had become commander in chief of the army's Pacific Division. Frémont by 1890 valued his land at $42,000, with interest payable back to the year 1863. On his behalf three prominent southern Californians, M. H. Sherman, Charles Lummis, and Jonathan Slauson, urged a new friend, Senator Thomas Bard, to introduce compensatory legislation. Neither Frémont nor Jessie would live to see the results of this lobbying.

But Congress did restore the general to the army's retired list, because he had been able to produce evidence that, when he had been a major general in command of Missouri, he had given his salary to the president of the University of Saint Louis "to be distributed to sick and wounded soldiers."[18] Finally, his pension was approved by General Arthur MacArthur, the father of Douglas MacArthur, but Frémont would not live much longer to enjoy the remuneration.

During his second trip to Washington and New York, which he made ostensibly to salvage what was left of disparate resources, Frémont did not realize that he had left Jessie behind for the last time. She, trying to make the best of his going off again, told a friend that "the General's being away makes us feel the width of this huge continent," but "pretty soon now he can come back and we shall have a good companionable time writing up the Second Volume [of the memoirs]."[19] He had no such notions in mind. Before ill health finally struck him down, he savored visits with their two sons, Charley and Frank, both of whom had become military officers. The former, then on shore duty at the District of Columbia Navy Yard, would become an admiral, but Frank was to reach only the rank of major before being dismissed from the army for insubordination.[20]

In Washington, Frémont not only visited Charley, but also hoped to rub elbows again with some of the powerful men he had once known. But most of them were gone; others, among them Frederick Billings, who would die in the same year as Frémont, had faded from the scene. From California, Jessie also

In her old age, Jessie's mid-life obesity gave way to a gaunt visage. This photograph was taken at Los Angeles in 1888. (Reproduced by permission of the Huntington Library, San Marino, California; Album 188)

wrote that Alexis Godey, a fierce Frémont partisan, had died in Los Angeles at age seventy-one, leaving behind a beautiful twenty-year-old widow.[21]

On the East Coast, Frémont tried to contact the opera diva Adelina Patti, whom he had met in London years before and had heard sing at Los Angeles, where she had commanded a fee of ten thousand dollars, reputedly the largest ever paid a singer. Was his wish to see her again a vain search by a tired warrior for a final companionship, or simply a polite response to her letter of congratulation on his acquisition of a government pension? One of his last letters was to her. In New York, Frémont also met Katherine Tingley, a theosophist with a large following, who later established a utopian religious colony outside San Diego at a spot recommended by him.[22]

By mid-1890, John Charles had been away from California for almost a year. One day in July, having visited a Brooklyn gravesite as promised in a broiling sun, he returned, exhausted and lonely, to the Manhattan boarding house in which he was staying. He then wrote Jessie of his intention to return to Los Angeles, although he did not quite realize the gravity of his illness. On July 13 she would receive a fateful telegram from their son Charley which read: "Father is seriously ill." Jessie anxiously sent her daughter Lily down "to the telegraph station to learn more." A second dispatch arrived: "Father is dead. Charley." Jessie never again opened another telegram, for this one "seemed fairly to shrivel up my arm."[23]

From New York came a report from their old family physician, William Morton, who had diagnosed Frémont's last illness as enteritis culminating in peritonitis or a burst appendix. Charley quoted his father's final words: "If I keep this free of pain I can go home next week. 'Home' said the doctor (to test his mind), 'what do you call home?' With his eyes already closing, but with one pleased smile, the General said clearly: 'Why California of course.' And with the name which had been so long his guiding star, he spoke no more."

Charley informed his mother of having placed in the coffin a telegram from her that had arrived too late to be read by his father. He folded up the message and wrapped it around the miniature ivory of her that he had often carried on his expeditions, putting these items in the hands of the deceased. Charley reported that he looked "peaceful and quiet."[24]

Jessie did not have the means to travel east for the funeral. Thus, the figurine that she had first sent westward to him in 1845 with Kit Carson would have to suffice until she could once again lie beside her chief.

Frémont had finished his life much as he had begun it—in a series of hotel rooms, living among strangers and dying far from an established home and hearth. Back in California, when news of Frémont's death became public, those who had forgotten his name had to be reminded by the press that he had been born when James Madison was president and that he had received his first commission during Andrew Jackson's presidency. The *New York Tribune* reported on July 14, 1890, the day after his death, that the great explorer had died at 49 West 25th Street, stricken down by peritonitis and heat. He had met his end in a cheap rooming house located in a part of Manhattan that was going downhill. Once Frémont might have stayed at the Astor, but that time had long since passed.[25]

Charley refused to give out details about his father's last days, writing to his sister and mother: "He was not a man of parades and displays, and I have negatived all Grand Army and Society offers." None of these groups was in a position to "get up a fitting funeral," and "any other would be a mockery."[26]

Charley also reported that the old man had felt listless just before his death partly because of disagreements over an article he had finally completed for *Century Magazine*, entitled "Resume of Frémont's Expeditions" and illustrated by the talented Frederick Remington. The article was a distillation culled from the elephantine epic envisioned as the second volume of the memoirs. It would have to be published posthumously in March 1891. Frémont died knowing that Professor Royce's version of his exploits would appear in the same issue of *Century* with the title "Rough Times in Rough Places."[27]

Despite these last adversities, Frémont had recently told Frank that "he deeply regretted not being able to live another hundred years." For posterity he willed Frank a sword made by Tiffany featuring a bas relief of the general's profile studded with diamonds. The weapon had been presented by midwestern Germans who had limited its subscription list to ten cents per contributor. Also depicted on it was a relief of Truth thrusting another sword down the throat of a monster. ❖

Following her husband's death, Jessie and her daughter, both of whom remained in California, settled down to a life of further restricted income. After the memoirs proved to be such a financial flop, Lily had begun to take in typing to help with household expenses, while her mother continued to peddle occasional pieces to magazine publishers. For a time their future seemed especially precarious, because the government ceased to pay Frémont's pension. During the fall of 1890 the *Los Angeles Times* carried a headline entitled, "Aid for Mrs. Jessie Benton Frémont." The story read: "It becomes a painful duty to publicly announce that the distinguished daughter [of Senator Benton] and the widow of 'The Pathfinder' is in distressed circumstances financially. She is now living in Los Angeles with her daughter and is now seriously ill. The *Times* announces that contributions to date total $231.50."[1]

Eventually Senators Thomas Bard and Frank Flint obtained from Congress two thousand dollars for each year that Jessie outlived her husband. Despite this relief, she described her condition as "penniless." Although Jessie learned that John Charles's grave was "as untended as that of a pauper, overgrown with weeds and brambles," she was too poor to visit the site. She surmised that if only she could "get repayment for my property [Black Point], *then* I intend placing there a simple slab."[2] For Jessie was determined to see to it that her husband received every honor that the nation owed him.

Next to her father's passing, the death of John Charles was the greatest blow of her life, even beyond the loss of a child. She would spend her remaining years reliving every phase of his life. With the glow of his memory ever in mind, she moved inexorably into the past they had shared together, becoming chief guardian of his reputation.

In her efforts to make a hero of her husband, Jessie was aided by previously mentioned nineteenth-century notions concerning the role of heroes. These beliefs, which lingered on, were rooted in Thomas Carlyle's "Great Man" thesis, which involved a sentimental, almost lyrical, fascination with political figures such as Caesar and Napoleon, as well as mystifying personalities such as Byron and Nietzsche—all of whom "made history," as had Frémont. John Skirving, who fashioned the diorama that depicted Frémont's exploits in the West for the English public, had worked in the tradition of artists who featured the out-sized drama of society's leaders and whose huge canvases still litter the corridors of the Paris Louvre and other international galleries.

Among the nonpsychological factors that had helped Frémont rise to fame were the pressing needs of the nation he served. As expressed by the concept of Manifest Destiny, from the age of the Puritans to that of the cowboy a sense of national incompleteness had existed. An inflamed nationalism suggested that freedom could be found first in taming a continent threatened by foreign occupation along much of its Pacific shore and Northwest. Thoreau had said about all this: "Eastward I go only by force, but westward I go free." That freedom came to involve technology, specifically railroads, sorely needed to complete national expansion. Frémont thus had tapped a powerful sense of mission.

The Pathfinder's spectacular years of exploration would never have occurred without the support of powerful patrons committed to opening up and mapping the American West. While he made the most of these contacts, as we have also seen, he was propelled by his own needs to enter the wilderness—not only to explore it, but also to fill it with his own being. All the while his 1845 report alone had done as much to popularize the West as did Buffalo Bill a generation later—followed by the story writers Ned Buntline and Zane Grey.

Jessie not only shared in but also nurtured that process. Trying so hard to keep vital memories of his exploits alive, she continued to brook no criticism of him, defending her John Charles against all living foes. She even tried to anticipate the judgments of future historians. Jessie wanted him to remain "all National, American, and grandly unselfish."[3] As with other widows of famous men, she had to carry on his legend, to preserve the myth.

Day after day, year after year, her neighbors saw her sitting on her porch rocker. Weary, wrinkled, and shriveled, she surely thought back upon how life with John Charles had hardly been easy. Though she was outwardly undespairing, reality was not quite what she had imagined as a young wife. Yet she still overflowed with stories in which her husband always managed to be the hero. It was as if she was still hypnotically dominated by everything he had done. Vicariously, his every achievement had become hers as well. But defending his many escapades, personal and financial, had exhausted her energies and meager finances too. The only tangible hope, recovery of Black Point, involved an unending struggle. The place was still tenaciously occupied by the army's Pacific Department.[4]

The continuing attacks upon her late husband led Jessie to pull an ever longer bow in his defense, taking on as adversaries Nicolay and Hay, President Lincoln's former secretaries. Resentful of their version of Frémont's clashes with the president during the Civil War, she complained to Robert Underwood Johnson, *Century Magazine*'s editor, that she wanted no one to say that Lincoln *ever* needed to control the general. Jessie also deplored the recollections of William Tecumseh Sherman, whom she accused of bolstering his own self-image by deprecating Frémont in an autobiography. She labeled General Sherman "a man of selfish character devoid of principles and honor, not speaking the best of a fellow officer and a gentleman."[5]

Jessie Benton Frémont continued to portray her husband as victimized by his enemies, insisting that he was "as sweet as his will was strong." She tried to explain why he was perceived as self-centered and insensitive to others: "Retiring by nature, General Frémont's simple dignity, arising from a total lack of self-consciousness, was sometimes misinterpreted by casual observers for coldness and indifference—two qualities foreign to his nature. He was essentially modest."[6]

Their daughter also kept up the hero-making process by describing Frémont's wondrous feats. One of them was a spectacular eight-hundred-mile horseback ride from Los Angeles to Monterey and return that he and two companions had accomplished in eight days. They accomplished such speed by using three relays of unshod horses. Elizabeth maintained that no other man on earth could have accomplished such a feat. For her he was "The Jason of California."[7]

Frémont's son Frank also contributed to the legendry:

> There was a sharp division between the two sides of my father's character; the questing side, which was expressed in his explorations, and the human side, which was companionable, cheerful, and with a tendency to gaiety accounted for by his French forebears. . . . Though in no sense pharisaical, he instinctively avoided the unclean, both physical and moral; and with all this he was intensely human and understanding.[8]

Frank, genuinely fond of his father, considered that the outstanding quality of his character was simplicity:

> All ostentation and sham effects were not only foreign to his nature, but absolutely distasteful. He dressed plainly and preferred old garments, books, and old friends. . . . Horseback, walking, and fencing were his favorite exercises, and he excelled in them. Simple food, a glass of wine, claret or Matrai when he was tired. He never touched spirits, but did not assume to dictate to others. Indeed he carried this trait so far that he only *requested* my brother and myself not to drink or smoke, and told

me that he had no objection to so doing, but that on his explorations he had noted that his men seemed to suffer as much from the deprivation of tobacco as of food, so he desisted.[9]

Jessie and her three children portrayed Frémont as having never done a mortal wrong. Yet he had left her and Lily in such financial straits that on the July 4, 1891, the Women of California Club presented them with a "little red house on the corner of 28th and Hoover" in Los Angeles. This eight-room clapboard cottage was described daily to curious tourists by an electric tram conductor who took groups of them past the house. Those visitors who were lucky enough to get inside the bungalow sometimes found Jessie in its parlor, surrounded by memorabilia and admiringly sitting under Gutzon Borglum's painting of her husband.

Jessie had grown awkwardly deaf, and her voice had developed a curious crackle that accompanied shortness of breath. She confessed that she suffered from depression after she fell and broke her hip. After that she received few callers. But in 1900 she did make an exception when President William McKinley came to town. On that occasion he said: "I cannot stand in this presence without recalling those splendid pioneers of American civilization Kearny and Stockton and Frémont; and to that aged woman who shared with General Frémont in his early and late trials and triumphs, now residing in your beautiful city, I am sure you will all join with me in reverent and affectionate regard."[10]

After the president left, although she could no longer stand and was bone tired, she returned to work on a manuscript entitled "Great Events During the Life of Major General John C. Frémont." Intended as the second volume of his memoirs, this garrulous effort was to run 150,000 words in length, including massive unedited insertions of documents and letters. In 1891 she wrote about the project: "I have such fine offers, which will complete the General's work, make money for Lil, and give me a living object."[11] But this was not to be.

As the year 1902 drew to a close, Jessie became seriously ill. On Christmas eve she slipped into a coma, and two days later she was dead at the age of seventy-eight. She had asked to be buried alongside her husband at Piermont overlooking the Hudson, within sight of their beloved Pocaho. There they both rest atop Mount Nebo in a tomb that the state of New York erected in 1908 within Sparkhill's Rockland Cemetery. For decades to come the spot would be untended, weed-wild, and vandalized. In great contrast, after General Grant's death in 1885, he rated a national monument within New York City at Riverside Drive and 122d Street.[12]

Jessie left her daughter only five hundred dollars in cash and the little house that the ladies of Los Angeles had given her. The California Federation of Women's Clubs also tried to help Lily, who was close to sixty years old. Unfortu-

This photograph of Jessie Benton Frémont was taken at her Los Angeles home in 1892. Her husband had been dead for two years. Surrounded by treasured possessions, each day she continued to write at a tiny desk, until her own death ten years later in 1902. (Reproduced by permission of the Huntington Library, San Marino, California; Album 188)

nately her parents had died with their Black Point claims still unresolved. Senators Bard of California and Boies Penrose of Pennsylvania, as well as Charles Lummis, editor of the popular magazine *Out West*, all put pressure upon President Theodore Roosevelt to help Lily recover money for that property. Lummis, a Harvard classmate of Roosevelt, actually visited the White House on Lily's behalf.[13] But she, too, would go to her grave bereft of any government reimbursement. In

1912, Lily published her own recollections, which were even more lackluster than her father's memoirs. She also destroyed past correspondence that cast her father in a bad light. Jessie, like Sir Richard Burton's equally possessive wife, Isabel, had done the same.

In addition to Lily and her brothers, other stalwarts continued the Frémont legendry. For a few years annual celebrations of his birthday were held in California. On January 21, 1903, the Frémont Hotel in Los Angeles organized a dinner to honor his memory and entitled its printed program, "One of the Old Guard of Crusaders That Never Surrendered." Another celebratory inscription read, "He Wiped Out the American Desert." A third motto was subtitled, "The Hero Who Gave California to the Nation and Started Civilization in the West." Various groups gathered funds for a grave monument to honor the Frémonts to be located at Rockland Cemetery in Nyack, New York.[14]

Jessie Frémont, shortly before her death in 1902, with Horatio Nelson Rust, an Indian agent and later a nurseryman at Pasadena, California, on her right and Alfred H. Sellers, who had recently moved from Chicago to the southern part of California, on her left. (Reproduced by permission of Priscilla Roth Feigen, Rust's great-granddaughter)

In 1911 the eccentric western poet Joaquin Miller, who called himself "one of the closest friends of the Pathfinder," dedicated a bust of him at Oakland High School in California at a ceremony in which Governor Hiram Johnson and the president of the University of California, Benjamin Ide Wheeler, eulogized Frémont. Later, John D. Rockefeller, Sr., was to build a fountain in his memory on the Webb estate two miles north of Tarrytown on the Hudson, near where the family had spent so many happy hours.[15]

Frémont would also be remembered by other means. In comparison with his fellow explorers, he was honored by the number of places named for him. Although Sir Richard Burton opened up significant parts of Africa, there is no mountain, lake, river, island, city, or village that bears his name. More than one hundred places have been named for Frémont. There are Frémont counties in Colorado, Idaho, Iowa, and Wyoming as well as streets and towns named after him in California, Nebraska, and Ohio—in addition to the General Frémont Grove of trees in California's Santa Cruz Mountains, which he visited. Frémont Peak is in Wyoming, Frémont Springs in Nebraska, the Frémont Needle in Arizona, Frémont Pass in Colorado, Frémont River in Utah, and Frémont Glacier in the Cascade Range of Washington state.[16]

Despite these place names, the Pathfinder, having lived so haphazardly, left behind no identifiable homestead, unlike even his lesser known contemporaries. In Washington, Blair House is still across the street from the White House, and around the corner from Pennsylvania Avenue, alongside Lafayette Park, is the Beale family's Decatur House; both are national monuments. At Monterey, California, the Larkin House marks the residence of Consul Larkin. Near Woodstock, Vermont, the farm and residence of Frederick Billings have become a tourist attraction. But Frémont had shown himself unable to plant roots in any one place. It was as though each of his previous homesites had never existed, replaced only by legends of the past. ❖

An Appraisal of Personality

Our whole life is but a greater and longer childhood.—Benjamin Franklin.

Beneath John Charles Frémont's mild exterior there lay a bird of rare plumage. His outward appearance showed little sign of the destructive forces originating from within. While he was performing undeniable feats of endurance, the public Frémont became a well-known figure, and the private man stayed concealed from view.

Although Frémont was the opposite of shrewd, occasionally he displayed quite decent impulses. Courageous about the controversial slavery issue, he showed genuine concern for the plight of downtrodden slaves such as those he had seen when he was a boy in Charleston. Although he became popular among the abolitionists, he could never assume the role of Ralph Waldo Emerson's "representative man," by which that writer meant a forceful leader who would also live on in the minds of future generations.

But about one matter there was almost little question—that while out on the western trails, Frémont exhibited braveness, though some of his exploits verged upon foolhardiness. Yet he was not always a blustering adventurer. In fact, even while on his expeditions, some of Frémont's contemporaries used the terms *bland* and *gentlemanly* as well as *quiet* and *retiring* about him. But his superficial reticence was also accompanied by other labels attached to him, including "romantic visionary" and "a man unafraid." His great energy sometimes took the form of downright unruliness. Frémont's hunger for travel and excitement unsuited him for most employment. Ideally he should have possessed independent means of support. During too many of his dramatic episodes he confused others, exhibiting that mixture of panache and "contempt of danger" that, in the words of one observer, "proclaimed him a man to be obeyed under all circumstances." After he entered the national political arena, one of his major backers described him as "refined and dignified," but believed the country was fortunate that he had failed to become its president: "He was in no proper sense a statesman" but an "utter neuter gender in politics, according to that observer."[1]

The facade Frémont presented to the outer world was markedly at variance with his internal or unconscious self. Although significant disabilities appear to have dominated that inner persona, and partly determined his outer one, he does not, however, emerge as a wholly destructive personality. Nor was he a poisoner of all those whom he met. At times seen as a misfit, he was on some occasions more dupe than villain. Even his worst critics could hardly deny that he possessed remarkable talents as a cartographer and explorer.[2]

Because he proceeded to make his exploits seem more heroic than they actually were, the phrase "character is destiny" also seems applicable to him, for Frémont's illusions drove him to reach beyond his abilities. And because he trusted so few people, his controversial decisions were largely uncorrected by others. Sometimes his distrust of others was justified, for he too often chose helpers who let him down, encouraging risk taking with all its built-in dangers. But not all his associates were unworthy. Frederick Billings for a time gave him good advice.

No one, however, was quite able to operate on Frémont's particular emotional level. He could be both flamboyant and guarded. To such a distrustful survivor type, the display of some emotions can be a liability. Facing the outside world alone, he frequently arrived at crucial decisions by himself. Hence, he frequently arrived at crucial decisions alone. Yet, little evidence of loneliness ever seemed to surface in his personality. Fashioning a strange quilt of personal isolation, he developed a state of mind sometimes called "psychic numbness." In general, Frémont, like Lawrence of Arabia, showed considerable indifference to pain or pleasure. Accompanying these characteristics was a self-deception that hardly helped him to grow emotionally. His defenses against the world, in short, hid a defeating life-style that led to sudden, sometimes unpredictable failures whether in exploration, in politics, or in financial speculation. On these occasions he simply lacked insight into why things had gone awry.[3]

When still but a fledgling explorer, he had shown signs of instability while making decisions, some of which were crucial—as in the gamble he took running the rapids of the Platte River with a flimsy rubber boat. Later, in mid-career, his risk taking with women or with his disastrous financial gambits suggested a clear lack of self-control. He thrilled to danger rather than fearing it, like all true men of action. Ever the adventurer, he had to rove.[4]

As we have seen, especially when Frémont was out on the trail or, later, a general, his vacillations sometimes puzzled his contemporaries. During the fourth and fifth expeditions they could not understand his almost childish and arbitrary shifts of mood or inconsistent decisions. When Frémont later sought to describe his motivations during these adventures, he characterized all attempts as "hedged with obstacles which oppose my pen at every line."[5]

The Pathfinder was never able to discern the causes of his most outrageous errors or erratic exploits that ended in failure. Neither was he free to abandon unworkable personal defenses; nor could he accept responsibility for his excesses. He apparently felt that society should forgive him every personal transgression. Little guilt accompanied his acting out of frustration. During his entire lifetime one finds no real instance in which he even mentioned his own shortcomings. At his court-martial trial he pleaded "not guilty" to every charge, as he would throughout his later life, forever unable to accept being judged by others, especially older men.

Frémont thus repeatedly spoiled his successes. At times he seemed almost to move in a partial darkness, substituting glory-seeking excitations for enduring satisfactions. The five expeditions into the American West, so filled with high-pitched drama, served to disguise his inner nature. Life as an explorer allowed him to relieve personal anxieties by escapist flights from home and family instead of working through these frustrations. Impulsive behavior thus seems to have become a rickety cure-all for unresolved conflicts.[6]

While he allowed others to praise and explain away his disastrous acts, behind an even-toned voice and calm reserve lay a hauteur from which he projected envy onto real or imagined enemies. Every such emotional projection contains, as the psychoanalyst Melanie Klein has reminded us, a strong element of fantasy. A spirit of unreality, therefore, guided Frémont's turbulent life.[7] Some narcissists use adventurism to fuel "grandiosity, extreme self-centeredness, and a remarkable absence of interest and empathy for others." These traits differ from a healthy assertion of self-worth. For the narcissist "cannot live without an admiring audience." He has not the freedom to "stand alone or to glory in his individuality," and he overcomes insecurity "only by seeing his 'grandiose self' reflected in the attentions of others."[8]

Long ago Thucydides depicted the heroics of some ancient Greek chieftains as "daring beyond their power." Today as well we sometimes encounter so-called men of destiny for whom challenging any obstacle, natural or human, seems to be a primary goal. Such impulsiveness occasionally led Frémont to become ruthless when in a position of authority—even sacrificing his men, as during the dangerous winter crossings of California's Sierra Nevada and the Sangre de Cristo Range in southern Colorado and northern New Mexico.

During the Civil War, by keeping visitors waiting in the rain outside his command tent for long periods of time, he established his priority over whoever wanted to see him, regardless of their rank. If they did gain access to him, it would be on Frémont's terms. While patiently waiting outside, they were probably viewed, metaphorically, by him as saying: "You are worth waiting for. Indeed,

I must somehow see you." The bolstering effect upon Frémont's narcissism seems apparent.

The lives of such narcissists have deep roots, complicated by rumors and memories concerning what they *think* occurred during childhood. Their selective memory encourages a spectrum of unworkable resistances, denials, and projections. Because Frémont's formative years of childhood were obscured by long shadows, he fashioned an image of himself based in large measure upon fantasy. It seemed almost impossible for him to reconcile his troubled family heritage, the unspoken truths of which remained locked unconsciously within, with later realities. Furthermore, like other men of his pre-Freudian generation, he would have denied any assertion that he had a troubled past even if he had been offered a competent professional interpretation. Some individuals simply trowel over their psychological deficits and remain unable to feel them. Others become arrested at a stage when a severe early loss occurs. It may be helpful to cite a modern case, a part of which reads: "If the parent, or parents, had been lost when the patient was an adolescent, the patient was still, years later, living emotionally like an adolescent." Ambivalence, too—an indecisiveness which masks duplicitous feelings toward substitute authority figures who cross a person's path—can mark the reaction to early loss. In short, "the child needs the continuing relation with the parents in order to advance in his development."[9]

Bereft of two nurturing parents who could understand his needs, Frémont repeatedly, as we have seen, acted as though he wanted to validate his illegitimacy and lack of a complete family during childhood. Martha Wolfenstein and other child psychoanalysts, after studying hundreds of patients, have established the presence of unresolved bereavement stemming from loss of a parent in childhood. These modern clinicians have found that serious emotional impairment occurs throughout the lives of such patients.[10]

Recent findings regarding early separation and loss are thus crucial to understanding that later seemingly inexplicable conduct which often expresses a disguised repetition of early sadness. In such cases outbursts against authority are frequent. Also, persons who repeatedly place themselves in dangerous circumstances may be attempting to work their way back mentally to an unresolved conflict. But their fragmented sense of selfhood remains unable to consolidate achievements, leaving them vulnerable to imagined slights and offenses by others.

As we have seen, in all his writings Frémont never mentioned his father. Nor could he acknowledge that he was illegitimate or that his father died when the boy was only five years old. In fact, he wrote very little about his life before the age of sixteen. Indeed, his reminiscences have a peculiarly adolescent tone to them and appear to be those of a much younger man, one of little maturity, even of an incomplete person.

Before puberty, children who are unable to mourn may postpone grief or lose their capacities to relate closely to others. In some cases youngsters may cling to the idea that the parent will return. Or in other cases "the loss of the parent is denied and throughout their lives they remain arrested in relating to people."[11] The absent parent hence lingers on in memory as an idealized figure, while the rage of the child is directed outward toward others. Such persons, as children or adults, do not fully understand death, seeing it as abandonment, even betrayal. Whether tragedy actually occurred is less important than the "fictional screen memories" of the offspring. Freud believed "that neurotic symptoms were not related directly to actual events but to wishful phantasies, and that as far as neurosis was concerned, psychical reality was often more important than material reality."[12]

Today's psychoanalysts maintain that often it is the absence of support at a key moment of death, rather than the loss itself, that creates psychological impairments. For Frémont there followed an endless search for the "lost object." In the process he acted out his frustrations and anger over a hardly normal interruption of love caused by his father's death. There was probably little mourning of that vital and sudden void in Frémont's life. Today skilled analysts have inferred from studying many similar cases that children who fail to mourn the loss of a parent are generally not able to give up the search for an equivalent. Breakdowns in the parent-child relationship are usually followed by both anger and aggression. In order to avoid experiencing mental pain, the unconscious mind represses one's deepest hurts. These are sometimes substituted by fantasies of omnipotence—as if to repair early emotional deficits.

In their pursuit of "lost objects" there are some startling similarities between the lives of Frémont and Alexander Hamilton, who, like Frémont, lost a parent at an early age. Both men were born illegitimate, and each suffered estrangement from ordinary childhood. Hamilton, however, had the good fortune to be associated with a major and enduring surrogate figure, George Washington. For Frémont, there were no uncles, aunts, or extended family to provide early examples of how to carry on personal interactions with others. Until he met Senator Benton, those leaders who did take an interest in the young Frémont were transitory figures.

Both Frémont and Hamilton married into powerful families and used their connections when working outside regular avenues of advancement. Flouting authority, they attacked their competitors vehemently and placed blame for their indiscretions upon anyone other than themselves. Both were highly intelligent but sometimes impractical leaders; each was flawed by uncontrollable ambitions. Driven to demand his rightful place in the world, each found it difficult to compromise. To yield on matters of principle was intolerable and amounted to weakness itself.[13]

Frémont, like Hamilton, remained a loner. He was at his best when faced with natural instead of human obstacles. His charming shyness and benign demeanor were sorely tested whenever he was thwarted. Although he was usually able to conceal his anger, he gave way to indignation when others opposed even the most unworkable of his plans. Such classic "passive aggressive" behavior allowed him to appear affable while nursing animosity. His private letters to Jessie during the Civil War clearly show this disdain for and wish to control all superiors.

He could, furthermore, be callous of the opinions of others. Frémont's son Frank believed that his father's one great fault "was an indifference to what the general public might think." This insensitivity, he maintained, "left him a misunderstood figure." Frank was unknowingly describing strong childish emotions that his father, inwardly rebellious and stubborn to the end, retained throughout life. As we have seen, the philosopher Josiah Royce saw Frémont as a spoiled child whose "activities were so near the line between great deeds and charlatanism that it was difficult to distinguish the pose from the performance."[14]

Frémont's effrontery toward superiors was indirectly encouraged by his persuasive wife. In fact, some of his difficulties with older authority figures began about the time of their marriage. One critic asserted that "Frémont was caught between a powerful, domineering father-in-law and a wife with a will of iron who could carry a grudge for years.[15]

The editors of his papers concluded that "the documentary history of these two persons is but a single subject of study."[16] Jessie, ever uncritical of her husband, conferred a kind of sainthood upon him well before she became a widow. Her own fantasies about his perfection undoubtedly helped her to endure the turbulent, sometimes humiliating public life they lived. Although she herself was seldom criticized, she was called a virago, a nineteenth-century term of derision for a woman with masculine traits. Jessie cast herself in the role of rescuer of her husband, in which capacity she would go to any lengths to protect him. Even President Lincoln had to endure "General Jessie's" rebukes, calling her "quite a female politician." Only once did she allegedly confess to Frémont's weaknesses. This occurred when he was removed from his first Civil War command. Jessie was then supposed to have stated to Missouri's Governor Gustav Koerner: "Oh, if my husband had only been more positive! But he never did assert himself enough. That was his great fault."[17]

Both John Charles and Jessie engaged in little introspection. One result was that she, half mesmerized by him, was frequently torn between wanting her husband to remain active and a desire to keep him safely homebound. Despite her unshakable loyalty, and although she was a gallant wife, he never fully related to her or to anyone else. In the end the basic problems of character belonged to John Charles, not to Jessie.

Frémont's ambivalence regarding his wife was at least partly attributable to confusion about women in general. His mother, ever a shadowy figure in his life, may well have initially confused him about her escapades with his mysterious father—that adventurer who had torn her away from an unhappy marriage yet was a Gallic hero originally imprisoned in the West Indies by the British. This fantasized portrayal was dashingly foreign, but it provided little adult modeling by which the child after the age of five could either set or complete goals without conflict.

It is difficult to keep Frémont's career in balanced focus. His life pattern followed a sinuous path, bobbing, weaving, and twisting in response to perceived dangers. Despite his vainglorious and floundering rashness, which produced such turmoil, there were contemporaries who judged his life as successful. For them the many positions he held attested to the power he attained, as did his transient wealth. Yet his driven and restless biography reminds us of that cliché, "The enemy is within us." Although his struggles had at times stirred the nation he served, Frémont resembled Ishmael, the outcast son of the biblical Abraham. Their eternal quests, however grand, did not quiet their roving and tempestuous souls. ❖

Preface

1. Allan Nevins wrote the first modern biography, entitled *Frémont: The West's Greatest Adventurer*. Although his 1939 revision demoted Frémont from Pathfinder to Pathmarker, Nevins continued to praise him and greatly improved upon John Bigelow's earlier campaign biography, entitled *Memoir of Life and Public Services of John Charles Frémont*. Also important are Frémont's own *Memoirs of My Life* (cited hereafter as *Memoirs*). Another fulsome depiction of a hero is Herbert Bashford, *A Man Unafraid*. Frémont's harshest critic was the philosopher Josiah Royce; see his "Light on the Seizure of California," *Century Illustrated Monthly Magazine* 40 (Sept. 1890): 792–94, and Royce's "Frémont," *Atlantic Monthly* 26 (Oct. 1890): 548–56. Also critical was Cardinal L. Goodwin's *John Charles Frémont: An Explanation of His Career*. Ferol Egan's *Frémont, Explorer for a Restless Nation* deals mainly with Frémont's years of exploration. Michael Beahan's *John Frémont, California Bound* is pitched at the level of an adventure story, as is Hildegarde Hawthorne's *Born to Adventure: The Story of John Charles Frémont*. David Nevin's fictional *Dream West* (New York, 1984) was later produced as a misguided television drama. Finally, for a summary, see my Frémont article in *Encyclopaedia Britannica* 9:862–63.

2. *Memoirs*, 16.

3. Leon Edel, "The Art of Biography: The Figure under the Carpet," *New Republic*, Feb. 10, 1979, p. 26. Edel's *Writing Lives* (New York, 1984) puts forth the premise that the insights of psychoanalysis, used with prudence, must be a part of any searching biography.

4. A biographer of another quixotic hero, General Douglas MacArthur, points out, "Public action is always on one level inextricably linked to private needs," stressing "the historian's duty to lay bare concerns in order to encourage greater understanding and appreciation of the advantages and burdens of leadership in both those who assume its mantle, and those who follow." See Carol Morris Petillo, *Douglas MacArthur: Philippine Years* (Bloomington, Ind., 1981), 249. As political scientist Harold Lasswell averred in his *Psychopathology and Politics*, public leaders continually displace private motives and needs onto the public arena. Their outer shell masks an interior world.

5. As to the mythology surrounding Frémont, see Stephen Fender, *Plotting the Golden West*; David Wyatt, *The Fall Into Eden: Landscape and Imagination in California*; and Richard Slotkin, *The Fatal Environment* (New York, 1985), especially 198–207.

6. Among these sources are the published three volumes (plus two supplements and map portfolio) of *The Expeditions of John C. Frémont*, edited by Donald Jackson and Mary Lee Spence. Still unpublished is the second volume of his "autobiography," entitled "Great Events During the Life of Major General John C. Frémont" and mostly written posthumously by his wife and son Frank. Located at the Bancroft Library, Berkeley, California, this manuscript is as much her story as Frémont's. Some excellent new manuscripts and recently published reminiscences also throw light upon Frémont's character. An example is Leroy Hafen and Ann W. Hafen, eds., *Frémont's Fourth Expedition: A Documentary Account of the Disaster of 1848–1849*. Formerly unknown letters and diaries about Charles Preuss, Christopher "Kit" Carson,

Theodore Talbot, James Milligan, the Kern brothers, and other contemporaries continue to come to light.

Chapter 1. "The Glory of My Youth"

1. John Bigelow, *Memoir of the Life and Public Services of John Charles Frémont*, 20, 22; Donald Jackson and Mary Lee Spence, *The Expeditions of John C. Frémont* 1:xxiii–xxiv (hereafter cited as Jackson and Spence 1, but from vol. 2 onward, Spence and Jackson). See also "Professional Biography of Moncure Robinson," *William and Mary Quarterly* 2d ser., 1 (July 1921): 238; and *Tyler's Quarterly Historical and Geneological Magazine* 12 (1930–31): 261.

2. Quotation reprinted in Jackson and Spence 1:xxiii. See also *Richmond Enquirer*, July 12, 1811; "Richmond During the War of 1812," *Virginia Magazine of History and Biography* 7 (1899): 412; "The Randolph Manuscript," *Virginia Magazine of History and Biography* 17 (1909): 358; 22 (1914): 131; 32 (1924): 203; *Virginia Gazette and General Advertiser*, Oct. 9, 1796; *Journal, House of Delegates*, 1811–12, 29; *Virginia Calendar of State Papers* 2 and 3, passim; 5:128; 7:503; 8:320; 9:88; and Mary Stannard, *Richmond, Its People and Its Story* (Philadelphia, 1923), 55.

3. *Virginia Patriot*, July 11, 1811.

4. Consult R. G. Roy, "Le général Frémont," *Bulletin des Recherches Historiques* 31 (Nov. 1925): 477–78, and "Les ancêtres du Général Frémont," *Recherches Historiques* 4 (1897): 277–78, as well as *Bulletin des Recherches Historiques* 1 (1895): 189. Also see A. D. De Celles, "John Charles Frémont," *Bulletin des Recherches Historiques* 7 (1902): 360–61, and, "Louis-René Frémont," *Mid-America* 5 (Apr. 1934): 235–41. Today, Canadians include in guided tours of Québec what they call a view of "the house of General Frémont's father."

5. *Virginia Patriot*, July 26, Aug. 23, 1811; Jackson and Spence 1:xxii; Allan Nevins, *Frémont, Pathmarker of the West* (1939), 6.

6. Jackson and Spence 1:xxiii–xxiv.

7. Bigelow, *Memoir*, 22.

8. William M. Meigs, *The Life of Thomas Hart Benton*, 75–80; William N. Chambers, *Old Bullion Benton, Senator from the New West*, 51–52.

9. Roy, "Les ancêtres du General Frémont," 277–78. See also Roy's "Le Général Frémont, était-il Canadien français?" in *Les petites choses de notre histoire*, 164–68; Jackson and Spence 1:xvi; and Bigelow, *Memoir*, 17, 20.

10. Samuel M. Smucker, another early biographer, makes no mention of Anne Pryor being married previously to Pryor, but only that "in spite of opposition of the family of the young lady, the lovers were married." See Smucker, *Life of Frémont*, 6. Canadian writers R. G. Roy and A. D. De Celles falsely assert, as did Bigelow's presidential campaign biography (p. 21), that Louis René Frémont and Anne Beverly Whiting married, in either New York or Washington, on May 14, 1807.

11. John Galsworthy would write of Charleston's "Magnolia Plantation" that it was "a kind

of paradise" and that one could find nowhere else a place "so free and gracious, so lovely, wistful, so richly colored yet so ghost-like."

12. Quoted in an anonymously written campaign pamphlet, *Life of Col. Frémont* (New York, 1856), 2. Regarding a child's interaction with a depressed mother, see "Mourning and Melancholia," in *Standard Edition of the Complete Psychological Works of Sigmund Freud*, ed. James Strachey, 14:243; George H. Pollock, "Childhood Parent and Sibling Loss in Adult Patients," *Archives of General Psychiatry* 7 (1962): 295–305; Martha Wolfenstein, "Effects on Adults of Object Loss in the First Five Years," *Psychoanalytic Study of the Child* 21 (1966), 93–112; and John Bowlby, "Grief and Mourning in Infancy and Early Childhood," *Psychoanalytic Study of the Child* 15 (1960): 9–51.

13. Bigelow, *Memoir*, 21; *Republican Scrapbook* (Boston, 1856), 3; and Jackson and Spence 1:xxvi, n12, give more details of Frémont's early life.

14. Michael P. Johnson, "Planters and Patriarchy: Charleston, 1800–1860," *Journal of Southern History* 46 (Feb. 1980): 57.

15. G. Manigault to C. H. Manigualt, Dec. 7, 1808, quoted in Johnson, "Planters and Patriarchy," 49, 57. See also Philip D. Morgan, "Black Life in Eighteenth Century Charleston," *American Perspectives* 1 (1984): 187–232.

16. Charles W. Upham, *Life, Explorations and Public Service of John Charles Frémont*, 10, 16. Upham's biography appeared slightly before Bigelow's.

17. *Memoirs*, 20; Jackson and Spence 1:xxv.

18. Quoted in *Memoirs*, 19. See Allan Nevins Papers, Box 197, Columbia University, for correspondence regarding Frémont's confirmation as an Episcopalian. This became an important issue during the 1856 presidential campaign.

19. *Republican Scrapbook*, 21.

20. Cardinal L. Goodwin, *John Charles Frémont: An Explanation of His Career*, 7–8.

21. Ibid., and *Charleston News and Courier*, July 15, 1890.

22. Jackson and Spence 1:xxv; *Memoirs*, 19, 29–31.

23. *Memoirs*, 18–22.

24. Rev. I. S. J. Axson quoted in *Charleston News and Courier*, July 15, 1890; see also Rebecca Harding Davis, *Bits of Gossip*, 175–80.

25. *Memoirs*, 19.

26. Ibid.

27. Ibid., 18–22; see also Bigelow, *Memoir*, 17–20, and Smucker, *Life of Frémont*, 7.

28. Upham, *Life, Explorations and Public Service*, 9. Frémont contributed key phrases to this revelatory campaign biography, which has generally been overlooked.

29. For Frémont, trust would become a major issue. Erik Erikson has called basic family trust the foundation of healthy parent-child relationships. If it breaks down, loyalty crumbles. Security is undermined. Frémont had begun to erect a defensive scaffolding to take the place of what was missing. But the angry child can hardly express rage against an absent person. Such concepts are the subject of Erikson's *Identity and the Life Cycle*.

30. One of the tasks of adolescence is to consolidate an identity, to put together a sense of selfhood. When frustrated, Frémont seemed outwardly compliant, yet remained partly a child, not a complete adult. Frémont needed support, approval, and encouragement. But so early in his life, without a model against which to measure himself, he never quite learned when to rein himself in; nor would he easily take advice from others. See Heinz Kohut, *The Analysis of the Self* and *The Restoration of the Self*.

31. Frémont's very ambition would continually get in the way of his personal growth. He often faced decisions unrealistically, acting as though illusions were facts. One psychoanalyst has said that the "normal striving for power is born of strength," but the need to surpass one's

competitors at any cost is a reflection of "anxiety, hatred, and feelings of inferiority." An overwhelming need always to be "right," yet liked, makes such individuals vulnerable to flattery and poor advice, as well as impervious to criticism. A self-justifying Frémont became oblivious to the consequences of aggressivity toward others. Regarding such behavior, consult Karen Horney, *The Neurotic Personality of Our Time*, 80, 163.

Chapter 2. "He Is Loved, Respected, and Admired": Young Manhood

1. *Memoirs*, 22, 23.

2. Entry of Apr. 14, 1849, in Theodore H. Talbot, *The Journal of Theodore Talbot*, 81.

3. Ibid.

4. *Charleston News and Courier*, July 15, 1890.

5. Livingston's diary, printed in *Republican Scrapbook*, 21ff., also records Frémont's early opposition to slavery. Although the manuscript might have been back-dated to gain abolitionist votes for the presidency in 1856, it could have been quite honest. For more details regarding the 1837–38 expedition, see Jackson and Spence 1:xxix-xxx, 10, 123–24, 424.

6. Robert McKay to Richard Yeadon, Oct. 18, 1856, C-B 397, pt. 2, folder 1, Bancroft Library, Berkeley, Calif.

7. See Rebecca H. Davis, *Bits of Gossip*, 176; C. A. Guyer to J. N. Nicollet, Jan. 1, 1840, Lownes Collection, Brown University Library, cited in Pamela Herr, *Jessie Benton Frémont: American Woman of the Nineteenth Century*, 57.

8. McKay to Yeadon, Oct. 18, 1856, C-B 397, pt. 2, folder 1, Bancroft Library.

9. We must consider the possibility of political malevolence during an election year when the *Charleston Mercury* darkly alluded to the young Frémont as that "little naked, hungry charity boy of the streets of Charleston—the bastard son of a French fiddler, the ingrate citizen, the heartless traitor to the state of South Carolina." Quoted in *Saint Louis Leader*, Oct. 5, 1856; see also *Charleston Courier*, Oct. 27, 1856, and *Charleston Mercury*, Aug. 27, 1856.

10. See *Report Intended to Illustrate a Map of the Hydrographical Basin of the Upper Mississippi River, Made by J. N. Nicollet*, 28th Cong. 2d sess., 1843, H. Doc. 52 (Serial 464); and Lieutenant Frémont to Secretary of War Joel R. Poinsett, June 3, 1838, Poinsett Papers, Historical Society of Pennsylvania, Philadelphia. On Nicollet and this expedition, see Martha C. Bray, ed., *The Journals of Joseph N. Nicollet*; and Martha C. Bray and E. C. Bray, eds., *Joseph N. Nicollet on the Plains and Prairies* and *Joseph Nicollet and His Men*. Jackson and Spence 1:10, 12, 21, 38n, and 45 give further details regarding Frémont and Nicollet's close relationship.

11. At Saint Louis, Frémont also met Captain Robert E. Lee, an engineer making improvements on navigation of the Mississippi. Lee's polite helpfulness made a favorable impression upon him.

12. *Memoirs*, 51.

13. A member of the snapdragon family, the plant was *Mimulus glabratus frémontii*. Later *Frémontia*, a large flowering bush found in the California foothills, was named after him. For an account of plants collected by his explorations, see John Torrey's *Plantae Frémontianae; or, a Description of Plants Collected by Col. Frémont*, published by the Smithsonian Institution.

14. Jackson and Spence 1:xx–xxiv. Nina (Frances Cornelia Frémont), who may have, like her father and uncle, been illegitimate, married Henry M. Porter; see Spence and Jackson 3:282n.

15. Ibid., 1:11n. None of the Frémont biographers knew of his mother's second marriage.

16. Frémont occasionally confided in Poinsett by letter. While still in the field with Nicollet, he wrote on June 8, 1838, that "our party, 'tho small, is well armed, at least sufficiently so to secure us in the event of an accidental rencontre," by which he meant Indians. In a later

letter to Poinsett, however, he called them "not warlike." Consult J. C. Frémont to J. Poinsett, June 8, Sept. 5, 1838, Poinsett Papers, Library of Congress, Washington, D.C.; also see J. Fred Rippy, *Joel R. Poinsett, Versatile American*, passim.

17. See Harry Stack Sullivan, *The Interpersonal Theory of Psychiatry*.

18. Two modern sources on narcissism are Otto Kernberg, *Borderline Conditions and Pathological Narcissism* and Heinz Kohut, *Analysis of the Self*. See also Christopher Lasch, *Haven in a Heartless World: The Family Besieged*, 200n.

19. *Memoirs*, 22, 602.

20. Otto Rank, *The Myth of the Birth of the Hero*; and John Bakeless, *Lewis and Clark, Partners in Discovery* (New York, 1947), 386. Also suggestive of Frémont's psychological makeup are Erik Erikson, *Identity, Youth, and Crisis* and *Young Man Luther* (New York, 1958); Peter Blos's contribution to *Adolescent Psychiatry*, ed. S. Feinstein and P. Giovacchini (New York, 1977); Heinz Kohut, *The Restoration of the Self* (New York, 1977); and Nathan Leites, *The New Ego* (New York, 1977).

21. Frémont's ego strength was surely greater than that of Lewis, who returned to civilization a celebrated hero yet three years later committed suicide. The governorship of Louisiana forced him into the hated role of bureaucrat with a history of failed romance, alcoholism, and bankruptcy. See Howard I. Kushner, "The Suicide of Meriwether Lewis: A Psychoanalytic Inquiry," *William and Mary Quarterly* 38 (July 1981): 464–81, and *Self-Destruction in the Promised Land: A Psychocultural Biography of American Suicide*. On the other adventurers mentioned, see Richard A. Van Orman, *The Explorers*, 147. Regarding Stanley, see John Bierman, *Dark Safari: The Life Behind the Legend of Henry Morton Stanley* (New York, 1990).

22. H. H. Sibley, "Memoir of Jean N. Nicollet," *Minnesota Historical Society Collections* 1:190. A history of the corps is Frank N. Schubert's *Vanguard of Expansion: Army Engineers in the Trans-Mississippi West, 1819–1879*.

23. Quoted in John N. Wilford, *The Mapmakers*, 195.

Chapter 3. Enter the Bentons

1. See William N. Chambers, *Old Bullion Benton, Senator from the New West*; Elbert B. Smith, *Magnificent Missourian*, passim; and T. H. Benton, *Thirty Years' View* 1:468–69. A fighter of duels, Benton was a formidable opponent. In addition to the early tavern brawl with Andrew Jackson, he used knives, pistols, even clubs, to quell adversaries. In 1817 he killed one Charles Lucas in his second duel with the man.

2. Benton had another close family ally in Congress: Representative John B. Floyd, a relative of Mrs. Benton who would become governor of Virginia and President Buchanan's secretary of war.

3. "Recollection of J. B. Frémont," ca. 1894, MS. 51137, Huntington Library, San Marino, Calif. See the sketch in Elizabeth Ellet, *Queens of American Society: A Memoir of Mrs. Frémont*, 434.

4. J. B. Frémont, "Great Events During the Life of Major General John C. Frémont," manuscript, C-B 397, file labeled "Scraps," Bancroft Library, University of California, Berkeley.

5. J. J. Abert to J. C. Frémont, July 11, 1841, in ibid., 1:96–99.

6. J. N. Nicollet to J. C. Frémont, July 11, 1841, original in French, at University of Illinois Library, reproduced in Jackson and Spence 1:97–99.

7. The ceremony took place either in a parlor at Gadby's Hotel in Washington or at the home of Mrs. John J. Crittenden. We cannot be sure, because of the secrecy involved.

8. Quoted in Herr, *Jessie Benton Frémont*, 64.

9. Her father's many Washington activities are described in Jessie B. Frémont, *Souvenirs of My Time*, 88, 104–106, 135; see also J. B. Frémont to R. U. Johnson, Aug. 28, 1890, MS Reel 522, Huntington Library.

10. The fire destroyed Frémont's records; indeed, "all the letters . . . from 1842 to 1854, the last of the five expeditions, were lost," according to J. B. Frémont, *Souvenirs*, 145.

11. J. B. Frémont, "Great Events," 77, and *Souvenirs*, 170–71.

12. Charles Moody, "Here Was a Woman," *Out West*, 18 (Jan. 1903), 173.

13. An example of her concerns involved Alexis Ayot, a Canadian-born coureur de bois who had lost a leg from a gunshot wound while on Frémont's second expedition but had been refused government support because he was "not a soldier." Jessie went to Preston King, chairman of a congressional committee on pensions, and obtained a government pension for the destitute Ayot. Later she also took up the cause of a penniless and unknown writer, Bret Harte, trying to find him not only a publisher but also a government job. See her *Souvenirs*, 65, and Henry C. Merwin, *Life of Bret Harte*, 34–35.

14. Elizabeth Benton Frémont, *Recollections of Elizabeth Benton Frémont*, comp. I. T. Martin, 41, 61.

15. Elizabeth Custer's books, *Boots and Saddles* (1885), *Tenting on the Plains* (1887), and *Following the Guidon* (1890), resemble the "apologias" in Jessie's *Souvenirs* (1887) and *A Year of American Travel* (1878).

16. At West Point Custer, like Frémont at the College of Charleston, was reprimanded for repeated infractions of discipline; Custer's demerit book filled six pages. Like Frémont, he, too, was court-martialed. Although charming in their youth, both leaders were rebellious. Custer turned into a martinet, irrationally severe and unpopular. For both men a Byronic gallantry was overshadowed by untamed ambitions. Each would lead men into untenable situations. As head of the Seventh Cavalry, Custer once marched his unit 150 miles in fifty-five hours without a stop. Frémont's loss of men never came near the 264 soldiers sacrificed with Custer at the Little Big Horn. Both leaders, however, were determined to overcome all adversities, often at any cost. For a good overview of Custer's life, see Robert M. Utley, *Cavalier in Buckskin* (Norman, Okla., 1988). Also consult Charles K. Hofling, *Custer and the Little Big Horn: A Psychological Inquiry*, 76–83, for psychological data. Another army wife strongly protective of her husband's reputation was Julia Dent Grant. See *Personal Memoirs of Mrs. Ulysses S. Grant*, ed. John Y. Simon (Carbondale, Ill., 1967).

Chapter 4. "The Flower and the Rock": First Expedition

1. *Memoirs*, 603.

2. Jessie B. Frémont, *Souvenirs of My Time*, 137.

3. Ibid., 163.

4. *Memoirs*, 75.

5. Charles Preuss, *Exploring with Frémont: The Private Diaries of Charles Preuss*, trans. and ed. Erwin G. and Elisabeth K. Gudde, 3–4.

6. Regarding Delaware Charley's nose, see Spence and Jackson 2:96–97. Medical hazards are treated in George W. Read, "Diseases, Drugs, and Doctors on the Overland Trail . . . ," *Missouri Historical Review* 38 (April 1944): 260–76, and Raymond N. Doetsch, *Journey to the Green and Golden Land: The Epic of Survival on the Wagon Trail* (Port Washington, N.Y., 1976), as well as George Croh, *Gold Fever* (New York, 1966). Frémont's vouchers for medical and other supplies used on the trail appear in Jackson and Spence 1:42–46.

7. Consult Howard I. Kushner, "Biochemistsry, Suicide, and History," *Journal of Interdisciplinary History* 16 (Summer 1985): 69–85, and Kushner, "American Psychiatry and the Cause of Suicide," *Bulletin of the History of Medicine* 60 (1986): 36–57. Contrast John Unruh, *The*

Plains Across (Urbana, 1979), 156–200 with what Preuss, xxix, recorded secretly. Eventually Frémont allowed journals to be written. On the fourth expedition the men financed themselves, and he could really do no less.

8. As to diaries, a member of another expedition, Isaac Cooper, assumed the nom de plume of François des Montaignes and became a sharp critic. Cooper, a grouser whom Frémont had not allowed to go on to California, wrote secretely that he maintained a larder of luxuries denied to his men, and he also accused Frémont of filching supplies of pure water in order "to make good coffee." See François des Montaignes, *The Plains . . . ,* ed. N. A. Mower and Don Russell (Norman, 1972), xviii.

9. Claims and Acknowledgements of Payment of John C. Frémont, General Accounting Office, May 6, 1842, to May 8, 1843, National Archives, Washington, D.C.

10. *Memoirs*, 116, 164.

11. Ibid., 108, 112.

12. J. B. Frémont, *Souvenirs*, 202; *Memoirs*, 23, 119, 130; *Preuss*, 22.

13. *Memoirs*; Francis Grierson, *The Valley of the Shadows*, 261.

14. Regarding Carson, see J. C. Frémont, *Report of the Exploring Expedition to the Rocky Mountains in the Year 1842, and to Oregon and North California in the Years 1843–1844* (hereafter cited as *Report*, 1843), 16; William T. Sherman, *Memoirs*, 1:46–47; see also Thelma S. Guild and Harvey L. Carter, *Kit Carson: A Pattern for Heroes*.

15. Claims and Acknowledgements of Payment of John C. Frémont, General Accounting Office, May 6, 1842, to May 8, 1843, National Archives.

16. *Memoirs*, 481–82.

17. See plate 30 of Frémont's *Report* (1843). In contrast to Ludlow, Preuss is quoted in Jackson and Spence, 1:250n.

18. Preuss, *Exploring with Frémont*, 55.

19. Explanation of Account Vouchers, Oct. 31, 1842, Papers and Accounts of John C. Frémont, General Accounting Office, National Archives, Washington, D.C.

20. Nevins, *Frémont*, 109.

21. Preuss, *Exploring with Frémont*, 67.

22. *Memoirs*, 162.

23. For conflicting views of Frémont's purported writing processes, see Stephen Fender, *Plotting the Golden West: American Literature and the Rhetoric of the California Trail*, 173, and Clive Bush, *The Dream of Reason*, 223ff.

24. J. B. Frémont, "Great Events," 61–62.

25. Fender, *Plotting*, 16; *Report* (1843), 13, 16, 201.

26. *Memoirs*, 429, 485.

27. His *Report* of 1843 would have included photographs had he achieved success with the cumbersome daguerreotype cameras packed along on the first two expeditions.

Chapter 5. Axe and Arrow: On to California, the Second Expedition

1. Frémont's California expeditions are summarized in Andrew Rolle, *California: A History*, 4th ed. (Arlington Heights, Ill., 1987), 142–54; and Allan Nevins's *Narratives of Exploration and Adventure*.

2. President Tyler's son also complained that Benton constantly pressured his father's administration and that of President Polk to back the senator's expansionist dreams. See J. J. Abert to T. H. Benton, Mar. 10, 1843, in Jackson and Spence 1:159; regarding Tyler, see Rufus Rockwell Wilson, ed., *Uncollected Works of Abraham Lincoln* 1 (New York, 1948): 453.

3. Gilpin traveled with the party only as far as Fort Vancouver. He would become an

ardent propagandist for development of the West as a new Eden. Consult Thomas L. Karnes, *William Gilpin, Western Nationalist*, and Lawrence R. Murphy, *Lucien Bonaparte Maxwell, Napoleon of the Southwest*.

4. Quoted in Allan Nevins, *Frémont: Pathmarker of the West*, 133. Concerning the forbidden cannon, consult Donald Jackson, "The Myth of the Frémont Howitzer," *Bulletin of the Missouri Historical Society* 23 (Apr. 1967): 205–15; and Ernest Allen Lewis, *The Frémont Cannon: High Up and Far Back*.

5. Quoted in Alice Eyre, *The Famous Frémonts and Their America*, 98, which is a suspect source, however. In the *National Cyclopaedia of American Biography* 4 (New York, 1897) and *Century Illustrated Monthly Magazine* 41 (Apr. 1891): 766–71, Jessie explained how and why she withheld the order that would have sent Frémont back to Washington. See also John Charles Frémont's own sketch in that same volume, p. 270, and Jackson, "Myth of the Frémont Howitzer," 205–14.

6. J. J. Abert to T. H. Benton, July 10, 1843, and Abert to J. Pope, Oct. 24, 1851, quoted in William H. Goetzmann, *Army Exploration in the American West, 1803–1863*, 66–67. Abert had escalated the Topographical Corps, a separate entity from the Army Engineers, to national status.

7. Quoted in Nevins, *Narratives of Exploration*, 188. See *Memoirs*, 426, and *Journal of Lieut. J. W. Abert from Bent's Fort to Saint Louis in 1845* (Washington, D.C., 1846).

8. Joseph B. Chiles, *A Visit to California in 1841*, 20; George R. Stewart, *The California Trail: An Epic With Many Heroes*, 41. Another overlander whom Frémont met was a westering sportsman from Scotland, Sir William Stewart Drummond, accompanied by other thrill-seekers with personal servants.

9. In Frémont's *Memoirs* the story of the howitzer appears on pages 251–52, 272, 291, and 325–26.

10. T. H. Benton to J. C. Frémont, Mar. 20, 1843, MS. 23723, Huntington Library, San Marino, Calif.; Jackson and Spence 1:487; "The Reminiscences of Francis P. Frémont," Document, C-B 397, pt. 2, box 5, Bancroft Library, University of California, Berkeley.

11. *Memoirs*, 228; Charles Preuss, *Exploring with Frémont: The Private Diaries of Charles Preuss*, 196.

12. *Memoirs*, 170–72, 200.

13. *Memoirs*, 222.

14. Thomas S. Martin, "Narrative of John C. Frémont's Expedn. to California in 1845–6 and Subsequent Events in Cal. Down to 1853 . . . ," dictated to E. F. Murray for H. H. Bancroft, 1878, Bancroft Library. Bonneville overstayed a leave granted by the War Department for over two years while looking for the nonexistent Buenaventura. See Benjamin L. Bonneville, *The Adventures of Captain Bonneville*, ed. Edgeley Todd, xlii; *Memoirs*, 209, 415–16; and John L. Allan, "Pyramidal Height of Land: A Persistent Myth in the Exploration of Western Anglo-America," *International Geography* 1 (1972): 395ff.

15. *Memoirs*, 259; Gloria G. Cline, *Exploring the Great Basin*, 3, 32; J. C. Frémont, *Report of the Exploring Expedition to the Rocky Mountains in the Year 1842, and to Oregon and North California in the Years 1843–44*, 28th Cong., 2d sess., S. Doc. 174, 369.

16. *Memoirs*, 204, 285, 317; Nevins, *Narratives of Exploration*, 256n; Cline, *Exploring the Great Basin*, 3, 32.

17. Martin, "Narrative," 3–4.

18. J. R. L. Anderson, *The Ulysses Factor: The Exploring Instinct in Man*, 31, is suggestive. See Galen Rowell, *In the Throne Room of the Mountain Gods*, covering the role of stress. Also consult John Hunt, *The Conquest of Everest* (New York, 1954), and Walter L. Wilkins, "Group Behavior in Long Term Isolation," in *Psychological Stress: Issues in Research*, ed. Mortimer H.

Appley and Richard Trumbull, 278–88. Also consult Fred E. Fiedler, "Validation and Extension of the Contingency Model of Leadership Effectiveness," *Psychological Bulletin* 76 (Sept. 1981): 307–21.

19. Something like a "repetition compulsion" possibly resulted from the son's attempt to redress that earliest trauma (death of the father) over which he had no control. It resembles the "classical" psychoanalytic concept known as "repetition of a childhood trauma." Frémont, by reversing roles, tardily tried to master his abandonment, repeating ambivalently the damage done to him.

20. Preuss, *Exploring with Frémont*, 98.

21. Peter Burnett, "Recollections and Opinions of an Old Pioneer," *Oregon Historical Quarterly* 5 (1904): 86–88.

22. Ibid.

23. Again, he was the discoverer of neither place; in 1826, Peter Skene Ogden's Hudson's Bay Company trapping brigade was the first group to see these two bodies of water.

24. *Memoirs*, 88, 197, 228–29; Theodore Talbot, *Soldier in the West: Letters of Theodore Talbot . . . ,* ed. Robert V. Hine and Savoie Lottinville, 29.

25. Preuss, *Exploring with Frémont*, 86, 90.

26. *Memoirs*, 317–29. Carson's autobiography is in Harvey Carter, *"Dear Old Kit": The Historical Christopher Carson*, 89.

27. The Paiute Chief Truckee may have induced the Indian to join Frémont's party. See Edward S. Ellis, *The Life and Times of Christopher Carson, the Rocky Mountain Scout and Guide, with Reminiscences of Frémont's Exploring Expeditions . . . ,* 56, part of "Beadle's Dime Biographical Library."

28. J. C. Frémont, *Report of the Exploring Expedition*, 226.

29. Preuss, *Exploring with Frémont*, 108.

30. *Memoirs*, 343–44.

31. See ibid., 373, 409, and Preuss, *Exploring with Frémont*, 118, 127–28, 134. See also Frémont, *Report of the Exploring Expedition*, 251–65, and George D. Brewerton, "A Ride with Kit Carson Through the Great American Desert and the Rocky Mountains," *Harper's Monthly* 7 (1853): 315.

32. *Memoirs*, 345.

33. J. B. Frémont to J. C. Frémont, June 16, 1846, Spence and Jackson 2:150.

34. Frémont's second report, first printed as a Senate document and reprinted as a book in 1845, combined two far western tours. The third expedition would be described in his *Memoirs*. Frémont's *Report of the Exploring Expedition* and Captain Charles Wilkes's *Narrative of the United States Exploring Expedition* enjoyed great popularity, along with Richard Henry Dana's *Two Years Before the Mast* (1840) and Lansford Hastings's *Emigrants' Guide to Oregon and California* (1845). Eventually there were six United States and two British editions of Frémont's *Report of the Exploring Expedition*. Unfortunately, some of his field journals for the years 1842, 1843–44, and 1845–46 were destroyed in the fire at Senator Benton's home.

35. Compare John A. Hawgood, *America's Far Western Frontiers*, 18, 158, with Goetzmann, *Army Exploration*, 93, and William Goetzmann, *New Lands, New Men: America and the Second Great Age of Discovery*, 172.

36. Frémont billed the government $9,851.30, then a large sum, for production of his map. See Carl Wheat, *Mapping the Transmississippi West, 1540–1861* 2:194; J. B. Frémont, "The Origin of the Frémont Expeditions," *Century Illustrated Monthly Magazine* 41 (Mar. 1891): 766–71; and Jackson and Spence 1, map portfolio, 11–13.

37. Harry M. Majors, "Frémont in Oregon," *Northwest Discovery* 3 (Oct. 1982): 168. Frémont's work presaged a series of scientific expeditions culminating in the Pacific Railroad

surveys of 1853–55 and the great King-Wheeler and Hayden-Powell government surveys of the 1870s.

38. Joaquin [Cincinnatus Hiner] Miller, *Overland in a Covered Wagon*, ed. Sidney G. Firman, 42–3.

39. *Memoirs*, 419.

40. "The Reminiscences of Francis P. Frémont," Document, C-B 397, pt. 2, box 5, Bancroft Library: "Trees were to him sacred, and he would not let them be cut down on his property unless dead or dying." The explorer did not believe in trampling flowers or even killing snakes. "Traveling through the mountains on horseback I have noticed he would guide his horse so as to avoid crushing a flower or ant hill. All life had a significance for him." He once stated to his son rather mystically: "Any Indian knows that to kill a snake causelessly will bring rain and a wet camp." On this second expedition he had helplessly watched wolves tear apart a buffalo calf. Had his men not been dismounted, he would have ordered them to save the beleaguered yearling, for the calf had "friends" outside his herd. See Jackson and Spence 1:191.

41. Ernst Lewy, "Historical Charismatic Leaders," *Journal of Psychohistory* 6 (Winter 1979): 388; Bruce Mazlish, *The Revolutionary Ascetic*.

Chapter 6. "All That Was Chivalrous and Noble": The Third Expedition

1. J. J. Abert to J. C. Frémont, Feb. 12, 1845, in Jackson and Spence 1:396.

2. Quoted in Solomon N. Carvalho, *Incidents of Travel and Adventure*, 18.

3. Theodore Talbot to Mother, June 18, 1845, in Theodore Talbot, *Soldier in the West: Letters of Theodore Talbot . . .* , 19–20, 33.

4. E. Kern to R. Kern, dated "June 1845," quoted in David J. Weber, *Richard H. Kern: Expeditionary Artist in the Far Southwest, 1848–1853*, 18–19.

5. This occurred in 1830 when Carson was in the employ of the trapper Ewing Young. See Charles L. Camp, *Kit Carson in California* (San Francisco, 1922), 5, and Charles Preuss, *Exploring with Frémont: The Private Diaries of Charles Preuss*, 118, 128, 134.

6. See John A. Hawgood, *America's Far Western Frontiers*, 112. More than half a dozen Carson volumes are adulative, beginning with Charles Burdett's *Life of Kit Carson* (Philadelphia, 1890) and continuing through M. Morgan Estergreen's *Kit Carson: A Portrait in Courage* (Norman, Okla., 1962) to Harvey Carter, *"Dear Old Kit": The Historical Christopher Carson*, a new edition of Carson's own memoirs. Frémont's adulation of Carson is expressed in his *Memoirs*, 134.

7. T. H. Benton, *Thirty Years' View* 2:482.

8. *Memoirs*, 459, Kern to J. R. Bartlett, Mar. 14, 1851, Fort Sutter Papers, Huntington Library, San Marino, Calif.: *Missouri Reporter*, June 7, 1845 (in Folder 10, Dale Morgan Papers, Huntington Library). Regarding Frémont's stay in Monterey, see Susanna B. Dakin, *The Lives of William Hartnell*, 271. See also T. O. Larkin to Secretary of State, Mar. 6, 1846, National Archives, which describes Frémont's arrival at Monterey.

9. Manuel Castro, civil prefect of Monterey, should not be confused with José Castro, commandante general. See Neal Harlow, *California Conquered: War and Peace in the Pacific, 1846–1850*, 64; Allan Nevins, *Narratives of Exploration and Adventure*, 476n.

10. Ibid.

11. J. C. Frémont to José Dolores Pacheco, Feb. 21, 1846, cited in Spence and Jackson 2:68; T. O. Larkin to Secretary of State, Mar. 27, 1846, *The Larkin Papers: Personal, Business and Official Correspondence*, ed. George P. Hammond, 10:270, reports on the horse stealing episode.

12. J. C. Frémont to T. O. Larkin, Mar. 9, 1846; T. O. Larkin to "Any Commander," Mar.

9, 1846, *Larkin Papers* 4:243–45. On March 4, 1906, some local residents rode on horseback up the 3,171-foot mountain to launch Frémont Peak Day. In 1925 the Native Sons of the Golden West placed a plaque on the summit. By 1936 some 188 acres there were designated as Frémont Peak State Park. Because of the clear air and excellent visibility, the Frémont Peak Observatory Association also maintains a thirty-inch telescope at the site.

13. Bil [*sic*] Gilbert, *Westering Man: The Life of Joseph Walker*, 215–16, 312, is a sparsely documented popularization that cites an alleged 1876 interview with Walker in the *Napa County Reporter*.

14. Quoted in Carter, *"Dear Old Kit,"* 101. Reputedly, 175 natives were killed. Spence and Jackson 2:124 cites Sutter to Castro, May 13, 1846; also see Franklin Scott, "Peter Lassen, Danish Pioneer of California," *Southern California Quarterly* 63 (Summer 1981): 117–35.

15. *Memoirs*, 490.

16. *Memoirs*, 493–95; Carson "Autobiography" in Carter, *"Dear Old Kit,"* 105–106.

17. *Memoirs*, 517, 522; Britton Busch, ed., *Frémont's Private Navy: The 1846 Journal of Captain William Dane Phelps* (Glendale, Calif., 1987), 37.

18. *Memoirs*, 492–95; Camp, *Kit Carson*, 5.

19. J. C. Frémont to T. H. Benton, May 24, 1846, in *Memoirs*, 490–91, 499, and Frémont to Benton, Nov. 21, 1846, "Documents," *California Historical Society Quarterly* 5 (1926): 89–90.

20. Busch, *Frémont's Private Navy*, 37, and Cardinal L. Goodwin, *John Charles Frémont: An Explanation of His Career*, 260.

21. E. M. Kern to R. H. Kern, July 29, 1846, MS. 20649, Huntington Library.

22. Once war with Mexico broke out, Senator Benton wanted to head up the army's high command. Polk would have appointed him a general, but the regular army hierarchy—especially General Winfield Scott—opposed the idea, as did Secretary Buchanan. See T. H. Benton to J. Buchanan, Feb. 18, 1848, Pennsylvania Historical Society; and manuscript entitled "Mrs. J. C. Frémont's Statement Concerning Secret Affairs Relating to the Mexican War," Dec. 1884, Huntington Library, in which Jessie revealed that she and her sister translated and interpreted messages in Spanish from Buchanan's agents in Mexico. Power lay not with the secretary of state, she claimed, for "it was a moral impossibility that *any* move towards gaining California should have been made without my Father's knowledge." According to her, Benton and Frémont, not Larkin or any other official, controlled the destiny of California. See Werner M. Marti, *Messenger of Destiny: The California Adventures, 1846–1847, of Archibald H. Gillespie*, 68–69.

23. T. H. Benton to J. J. Abert, Apr. 23, 1847, Frémont Collection, Southwest Museum, Los Angeles.

24. *Memoirs*, 489.

25. Benton, *Thirty Years' View* 1:468–69. Originally, Frémont wanted a mission orchard purchased for him at Santa Clara or San Jose as well as a rancho. Paul Gates, "The Land Business of Thomas O. Larkin," *California Historical Society Quarterly* 54 (Winter 1975): 342, cites the *Alta California*, Jan. 6, 1848. See T. O. Larkin to R. B. Mason, Apr. 4, 1848, *Larkin Papers* 7:219.

Chapter 7. Bear Flag and Conquest

1. *Memoirs*, 536.

2. G. Bancroft to J. C. Frémont, Sept. 1886, in J. B. Frémont, "Great Events During the Life of Major General John C. Frémont," manuscript, C-B 397, file labeled "Scraps," Bancroft Library, University of California, Berkeley, 74–77.

3. J. C. Frémont to T. H. Benton, July 25, 1846 in Spence and Jackson 2:181.

4. Jessie's letter suggests that Gillespie's instructions were less explicit than Frémont

boasted. This scrap of evidence was written as the Mexican War was reaching its end. See *Memoirs*, 489–90; J. B. Frémont to J. Torrey, Mar. 21, 1847, in William H. Goetzmann, *Army Exploration in the American West, 1803–1863*, 122.

5. J. A. Sutter to J. Castro, May 13, 1846, "Documents," *California Historical Society Quarterly* 6 (1927): 82–83. Sutter also told Castro that Gillespie, who had come to California incognito, was more than a government courier to Frémont, possibly a spy.

6. Printed in George D. Lyman, *John Marsh, Pioneer*, 272.

7. J. C. Frémont to E. Kern, July 26, Oct. 7, 1846, Fort Sutter Papers, Huntington Library, San Marino, Calif.

8. E. M. Kern to R. H. Kern, July 29, 1846, MS. 20649, Huntington Library; William D. Phelps, *Fore and Aft; or, Leaves in the Life of an Old Sailor*, 22, 29.

9. Simeon Ide, *A Biographical Sketch of the Life of William B. Ide* (Claremont, N.H., 1880; repr. Oakland, Calif., 1944), 81–83, and Fred B. Rogers, *William Brown Ide, Bear Flagger*, 54.

10. T. Talbot to Sister, July 25, 1846, in Robert V. Hine and Savoie Lottinville, eds., *Soldier in the West: Letters of Theodore Talbot . . .* , 44, 46.

11. Ide, *Biographical Sketch*, 139; Rogers, *William Brown Ide*, 54. Regarding Frémont's much debated military role in California, see William H. Ellison, "San Juan to Cahuenga: The Experience of Frémont's Battalion," *Pacific Historical Review* 27 (May 1958): 245–61; and George Tays, "Frémont Had No Secret Instructions," *Pacific Historical Review* 9 (June 1940): 159–71. See also John A. Hawgood, "John C. Frémont and the Bear Flag Revolution, A Reappraisal," *Southern California Quarterly* 54 (Mar. 1962): 67–96; and Richard R. Stenberg, "Polk and Frémont, 1845–1846," *Pacific Historical Review* 7 (Sept. 1938): 211–27. Jessie Benton Frémont's *Souvenirs of My Time* and *Far West Sketches* are unreliable concerning the conquest era. She, like her husband, in his posthumous "The Conquest of California," *Century Illustrated Monthly Magazine* 41 (Apr. 1891), 917–28, and *Memoirs*, argues ex post facto, justifying his conduct.

12. Typically critical is Frederick Merk, *History of the Westward Movement* (New York, 1980), 358.

13. Mariano Guadalupe Vallejo, *Being a Brief Sketch . . . with His Address Before the Junta at Monterey in the Year 1846*, 3. Though humiliated, Vallejo, erect and dignified, later signed the constitution of 1849 as a delegate at Califonia's first constitutional convention.

14. Werner M. Marti, *Messenger of Destiny: The California Adventures, 1846–1847, of Archibald H. Gillespie*, 60. Allan Nevins, *Narratives of Exploration and Adventure*, 276, makes Carson the culprit. Thelma S. Guild and Harvey L. Carter, *Kit Carson: A Pattern for Heroes*, 155, 316n, put the blame for the murders on Frémont. His approval of such revenge would become an issue in the 1856 presidential campaign, when he was accused of fomenting a bloody atrocity.

15. Marti, *Messenger of Destiny*, 60; A. H. Gillespie Papers, Document 19, Department of Special Collections, UCLA Library. For further manuscript documentation, see also Spence and Jackson 2:186–87.

16. Marius Duvall, *A Navy Surgeon in California . . . the Journal of Marius Duvall*, ed. by Fred B. Rogers, 53–54.

17. Harvey Carter, *"Dear Old Kit": The Historical Christopher Carson*, 109–10.

18. Ide, *Biographical Sketch*, 45, 167.

19. Cardinal L. Goodwin, *John Charles Frémont: An Explanation of His Career*, 129, 132.

20. E. M. Kern to R. H. Kern, July 29, 1846, MS. 20649, Huntington Library; *Memoirs*, 521; Thomas S. Martin, *With Frémont to California and the Southwest, 1845–1849*, ed. Ferol Egan, 3, 12; Phelps, *Fore and Aft*, 39.

21. Alfred S. Waugh, *Travels in Search of the Elephant*, ed. John F. McDermott; Phelps,

Fore and Aft, 38; François des Montaignes, *The Plains . . .*, ed. N. A. Mower and Don Russell, 23. Concerning Frémont's height, one account describes him as only five feet two inches tall. His first biographer, John Bigelow, said that he was five feet nine inches in height and that he never shaved. Meanwhile, Jessie added yet another inch, making him five feet ten inches tall.

22. Phelps, *Fore and Aft*, 36.

23. J. B. Montgomery to W. B. Ide, June 16, 1846, in *Memoirs*, 524–25. See also Montgomery to W. A. Leidesdorff, June 20, 1846, Leidesdorff Papers, Huntington Library; and Joseph T. Downey, *The Cruise of the Portsmouth, 1845–1847*, ed. Howard Lamar, 128–29.

24. J. C. Frémont to J. B. Montgomery, June 16, 1846, "Documents," *California Historical Society Quarterly* 6 (1927): 275.

25. J. B. Montgomery to M. G. Vallejo (signed by W. A. Bartlett), June 15, 1846, *California Historical Society Quarterly* 1 (1922): 81; Montgomery to J. Castro, June 18, 1846, ibid. 2 (1923): 70; J. Castro to J. D. Sloat, July 9, 1846, "Documents," ibid. 7 (1928): 79.

26. *Memoirs*, 534.

27. Ibid.

28. Fred Walpole, *Four Years in the Pacific in Her Majesty's Ship Collingwood*, as quoted in *Memoirs*, 533; William A. Croffut, *An American Procession, 1835–1914*, 270; Theodore Talbot to Sister, July 25, 1846, quoted in Hine and Lottinville, *Soldiers in the West*, 46.

29. Journal of Clements R. Markham quoted in Fred B. Rogers, *Bear Flag Lieutenant: The Life Story of Henry L. Ford*, 23. See also K. Jack Bauer, *Surfboats and Horse Marines: U.S. Naval Operations in the Mexican War, 1846–48*, 158–59.

30. Louis McLane, *The Private Journal of Louis McLane, U.S.N. 1844–1848*, ed. Jay Monaghan, 104–105.

31. William H. Ellison, "San Juan to Cahuenga," *Pacific Historical Review* 27 (Aug. 1958): 247.

32. *Memoirs*, 600.

33. Quoted in Ellison, "San Juan to Cahuenga," 255.

34. For a good general history of California's conquest, consult Neal Harlow, *California Conquered: War and Peace on the Pacific, 1846–1850*.

Chapter 8. Frémont Versus Kearny and the Court-Martial

1. R. F. Stockton to S. W. Kearny, Dec. 23, 1846, in Spence and Jackson 2:243–45.

2. Marius Duvall, *A Navy Surgeon in California, 1846–47 . . . the Journal of Marius Duvall*, 95; S. W. Kearny to J. C. Frémont, Jan. 13, 1847, in Spence and Jackson 2:255.

3. S. W. Kearny to R. F. Stockton, Jan. 16, 1847, ibid.

4. J. C. Frémont to J. B. Frémont, Jan. 24, 1846, reprinted in *Memoirs*, 453; J. B. Frémont to J. C. Frémont, June 16, 1846, repr. in Spence and Jackson 2:148–49.

5. Duvall, *Navy Surgeon*, 93; William D. Phelps, *Fore and Aft; or, Leaves in the Life of an Old Sailor*, 57.

6. Diary entry July 31, 1856, quotes Benjamin D. Wilson, grandfather of General George S. Patton, in Edward O. C. Ord, *The City of the Angels . . .*, ed. Neal Harlow (San Marino, Calif., 1978), 24.

7. *Los Angeles Star*, Aug. 23, 1856.

8. *El Clamor Público*, Sept. 13, 1856. The credibility of charges that Frémont now showed himself to be a "tyrannical officer" and a "profligate man" are undermined by the political context in which they were hurled in the presidential election year 1856. *El Clamor Público*, a Los Angeles Republican newspaper, denied all these accusations as a debasement of local womanhood and of "the grand record of the conqueror of California for the United States."

9. A. Godey to J. W. Wheeler, Sept. 12, 1856, reprinted in Le Roy Hafen and Ann W. Hafen, eds., *Frémont's Fourth Expedition: A Documentary Account of the Disaster of 1848–1849*, 274–75.

10. John S. Griffin, *A Doctor Comes to California: The Diary of John S. Griffin, Assistant Surgeon With Kearny's Dragoons, 1845–1847*, 65–66; H. S. Turner, *The Original Journal of Henry Smith Turner . . .* , ed. Dwight L. Clark, 154; and H. S. Turner to Julia Turner, Feb. 22, 1847, Missouri Historical Society, St. Louis.

11. William T. Sherman, *Memoirs*, 24, 25.

12. Ibid., 27.

13. Mason's threat quoted in John Bigelow, *Memoir of the Life and Public Services of John C. Frémont*, 205; R. B. Mason to J. C. Frémont, Apr. 15, 1847, quoted in Bigelow, *Memoir*, 207.

14. Mason to Frémont, May 19, 1847, quoted in Bigelow, *Memoir*, 209.

15. J. Biddle to R. B. Mason, May 19, 1847, quoted in J. B. Frémont, "Great Events During the Life of Major General John C. Frémont," manuscript, C-B 397, file labeled "Scraps," Frémont Collection, Bancroft Library, University of California, Berkeley, 74–77; and Bigelow, *Memoirs*, 210. Mason considered the duel merely postponed. Jessie claimed that Frémont received a letter from Saint Louis during 1850 renewing the date of the challenge, but he "scorned this message," according to her. Mason died soon thereafter. He had a record of abusing subordinate officers, having gotten into a scrape with Jefferson Davis, who had him court-martialed.

16. Bigelow, *Memoir*, 210–13.

17. Ibid., 29.

18. Quoted in Hine and Lottinville, *Soldier in the West*, 58.

19. Quoted in Catherine Coffin Phillips, *Jessie Benton Frémont, a Woman Who Made History*, 120–21. Phillips's book contains invaluable data, but one must use her anecdotes with care. Like Irving Stone, in his unfortunate *Immortal Wife* (1944), Phillips manufactures conversations and mixes up chronology. But she did have access to manuscripts that have since disappeared.

20. James K. Polk, *Polk: The Diary of a President, 1845–1849*, ed. Allan Nevins, 221, 226.

21. "Letter from Stockton to Bancroft, Ciudad de Los Angeles, August 28, 1846," in *Proceedings of the Court Martial in the Trial of Lt. Col. Frémont*, 30th Cong., 1st. sess., Apr. 7, 1848, S. Exec. Doc. 33.

22. "Report of Secretary of War Marcy," in ibid., Dec. 5, 1846.

23. Polk, *Polk*, 103, 206–207, 227, 228, 244, 256, 275; Gerald Thompson, *Edward F. Beale and the American West*, 24.

24. Ibid., 275.

25. T. H. Benton to J. C. Frémont, Oct. 7, 8, 1847, Folders 41 and 51, Frémont Collection, Southwest Museum, Los Angeles (hereafter FCSM); T. H. Benton to J. C. Frémont, Oct. 7, 1847, in Spence and Jackson 2:404; *Washington Daily Union*, Sept. 1, 1847, Oct. 10, 1848.

26. Spence and Jackson 2 (*Supplement*): 326–27. Decades later, Frémont wrote out a scrap of evidence that indicated that relations among Kearny, Benton, and himself had not always been bitter. For thirty-three years before the trial, they had been social friends. Frémont always maintained that the general "should . . . as a brave man, have settled his quarrel with Stockton. Not devolved it upon me, and then charged me with disobedience to a superior officer because I declined to settle it in his favor." This 1886 scrap is in Folder 35, FCSM.

27. J. B. Frémont, "Great Events," 51–52. Quotation reproduced in Spence and Jackson 2:378–79.

28. J. B. Frémont, "Great Events," 55.

29. J. B. Frémont to James K. Polk, Sept. 21, 1847, in Spence and Jackson 2:388; Polk, *Polk*, 390.

30. W. L. Marcy to J. C. Frémont, Sept. 27, and Frémont's reply of Sept. 28, 1847, in Spence and Jackson 2:396–99; J. C. Frémont to A. Stearns, Oct. 26, 1847, Huntington Library, San Marino, Calif.

31. J. M. Perkins, attorney, to H. C. Harmon, government auditor, Dec. 2, 1880, Claims of California Volunteers, Papers and Accounts of John C. Frémont, 1847–1891, Microfilm MS. 401, Reel 3, National Archives, Washington, D.C. As late as 1880 a claimant, James Howe, who was then one hundred years old, was still seeking to collect back pay and allowance for rations. He planned to use the money for his burial. In 1919 (almost twenty years after Frémont's death) the widow of Jacob R. Snyder, once quartermaster of the California Battalion, sought a pension.

32. James Guthrie, Secretary of the Treasury, to Philip Clayton, government auditor, June 4, 1853, Claims of California Volunteers, Papers and Accounts of John C. Frémont, 1847–1891, Microfilm MS. 401, Reel 3, National Archives; J. C. Frémont to W. L. Marcy, May 19, 1848, in Spence 3:13. Frémont had incurred over $700,000 in debt while leading the California Battalion and as acting governor of California. In 1854 a $19,930 claim by Mariano Soberanes was watered down to $423 by a board of commissioners set up to examine such requests for reimbursement. Although the board had its own letterhead, with the name of John C. Frémont emblazoned across the top, its decisions were niggardly. The $423 allowed Soberanes, who claimed his rancho had been destroyed by Frémont's men, was to pay for fifteen horses and three bridles; the rest of the disputed items were listed as "supplies rendered."

33. J. C. Frémont to P. B. Reading, Oct. 26, 1847, in Spence and Jackson 2:445–48.

34. Justin H. Smith, *The War with Mexico*, 2:454.

35. Polk, *Polk*, 302–303.

36. Frémont, on Dec. 2, 1847, presented evidence to the court from which this quotation is taken. Reprinted in Spence and Jackson 2 (*Supplement*):172–73.

37. J. C. Frémont to Abel Stearns, Oct. 26, 1847, Huntington Library.

38. Testimony of Commodore Robert F. Stockton, Dec. 9, 1847, in Spence and Jackson 2 (*Supplement*): 197–98.

39. Frémont statement in ibid., 446.

40. Herald editorial quoted in Phillips, *Jessie Benton Frémont*, 125; J. C. Frémont to J. Buchanan, Mar. 7, 1848, Pennsylvania Historical Society, Philadelphia.

41. Factionalism in Washington influenced Frémont's court-martial proceedings and President Polk's judgment of him. The ranking officers in the army, Generals Scott and Taylor, though not academy products, enjoyed enormous power. Yet President Polk spent most of the war in jurisdictional disputes with his principal generals, although he was commander-in-chief. Polk, an exhausted chief executive, died only a few months after he left office. Strongly anti-Frémont is Dwight L. Clarke, *Stephen Watts Kearny: Soldier of the West*. Details of the California conquest embroglio are in *Proceedings of the Court Martial*, reprinted in Spence and Jackson 2 (*Supplement*). Also see Kenneth M. Johnson, *The Frémont Court Martial*.

42. S. Cool to D. H. Wright, Mar. 9, 1849, Aram Collection, Huntington Library.

43. Spence and Jackson 2:xliv; Thomas Kearny to Editor, *The Argonaut* (San Francisco), Feb. 14, 1931, 6; *Memoirs*, 602.

44. *Memoirs*, 602.

45. *National Intelligencer*, June 12, 14, 16, 19, 20, 1848; Bigelow, *Memoir* 347, 353; Spence and Jackson 2 (*Supplement*): xv–xvi.

46. *Memoirs*, 602.

47. T. H. Benton to J. Buchanan, Aug. 20, 1848, and Buchanan to J. C. Frémont, Aug. 29, 1848, reproduced in Spence 3:xxii, 47.

48. The court-martial stirred one historian to write: "The published report of this *cause celebre* reads like a novel, and it is remarkable that it has never been dramatized or filmed"

(Hawgood, *America's Far Western Frontiers*, 168n). For an angry repudiation of historians critical of Frémont, beginning with Hubert Howe Bancroft, see résumé in Ernest Wiltsee, *The Truth About Frémont: An Inquiry*.

Chapter 9. Battling Captain Wilkes

1. Daniel Henderson, *The Hidden Coasts*, 195–198. Like Frémont, Wilkes had been court-martialed (in 1847) for illegally punishing some of his men and reprimanded. In 1864, during the Civil War, he was again court-martialed for disobedience, disrespect, and insubordination. Consult Wilkes's *Narrative of the United States Exploring Expedition*.

2. *National Intelligencer*, May 15, June 9, 1848.

3. Ibid., June 10, 1848; Bigelow, *Memoir*, 339.

4. *National Intelligencer*, June 12, 14, 16, 19, 20, 1848; Bigelow, *Memoir*, 347, 353.

5. Wilkes, too, could be difficult. The Yale geologist James Dwight Dana, a member of his expedition, characterized Wilkes as "over-bearing and conceited." See Michael L. Smith, *Pacific Visions, California Scientists and the Environment, 1850–1915*, 15.

6. Henderson, *Hidden Coasts*, 198; J. C. Frémont to Lt. J. Alden, Aug. 11, 1848, Huntington Library, San Marino, Calif.

7. J. C. Frémont to J. Torrey, Nov. 1, 1847, in Spence and Jackson 2:455. Frémont wrote official reports of the 1842 (first) expedition to South Pass and the Wind River Mountains and of his 1843–44 (second) expedition to Oregon and Washington. He and Jessie worked on the report of the first expedition during the fall and winter of 1842–43, and it was published in 1843 as 30th Cong., 1st sess., S. Doc. 243. Both expeditions were combined in one report as 28th Cong., 2d sess., S. Doc. 174, in 1845. Frémont's *Geographical Memoir upon Upper California . . .* appeared as 30th Cong., 1st sess., S. Misc. Doc. 148 in 1848. In 1964, Allan Nevins and Dale L. Morgan edited a new edition (published in San Francisco). Frémont never wrote a full report of his third, fourth, or fifth expeditions. The *Geographical Memoir* explained the Frémont-Preuss map produced during the third expedition. Because reprints were made of these writings, the Frémont bibliography is a confused one. See also Spence 3:xxi, 3, 4, 16, 34–35, 572–607.

Chapter 10. Tragedy: The Fourth Expedition

1. Thomas S. Martin, *With Frémont to California and the Southwest, 1845–1849*, ed. Ferol Egan, 23; T. H. Benton to J. Buchanan, Aug. 20, 1848, in Spence 3:xxii; 30th Cong., 1st sess., S. Rep. 226 (Serial 512); *Congressional Globe*, 30th Cong., 1st sess., Aug. 5, 10, 1848.

2. E. Kern to M. K. Wolfe, Feb. 10, 1849, cited in Spence 3:xxiii; A. Cathcart to C. J. Colville, Nov. 17, 1848 in ibid., 67; R. Kern to "Dear Friend," Sept. 20, 1851, quoted in David J. Weber, *Richard H. Kern: Expeditionary Artist in the Far Southwest, 1848–1853*, 26. The Saint Louis merchants were Robert Campbell, O. D. Filley, and Thornson Grimsley. Dr. George Engelmann also gave financial support for "scientific investigations" but stayed on in Saint Louis.

3. J. B. Frémont, "Great Events During the Life of Major General John C. Frémont," manuscript, C-B 397, file labeled "Scraps," Frémont Collection, Bancroft Library, University of California, Berkeley, 70.

4. J. C. Frémont to T. H. Benton, Nov. 17, 1848, quoted in LeRoy Hafen and Ann W. Hafen, eds., *Frémont's Fourth Expedition: A Documentary Account of the Disaster of 1848–1849*, 76. This valuable compilation consists of diaries, letters, and reports of participants in the fourth expedition.

5. Ibid., passim, for Jessie's forebodings regarding this latest expedition.

6. A. Cathcart to C. J. Colville, Nov. 17, 1848, in Spence 3:68–69.

7. Quoted in Weber, *Kern*, 39; see also Janet Lecomte, *Pueblo, Hard-scrabble, Greenhorn: The Upper Arkansas, 1832–1856* (Norman, Okla., 1978), 218.

8. I am grateful to Professor David Weber for reworking the cartography of the fourth expedition, based upon Patricia Joy Richmond's unpublished manuscipt entitled "The Route of John C. Frémont's Expedition of 1848–49 into the San Luis Valley of the Colorado." In 1930, forest rangers found pieces of Frémont's equipment on Embargo Creek. Some have inferred that Williams deliberately misled him so that he would have to ditch his baggage, which Williams could later retrieve.

9. Godey's statement is in Hafen and Hafen, *Frémont's Fourth Expedition*. 269.

10. There appear to have been two versions of Kern's diary. The entry for Dec. 10, 1848, in the Huntington Library's manuscripts is different from that which emerged in 1856. The latter may have been altered in order to disparage Frémont during the presidential election that year, although Weber doubts this. See also Hafen and Hafen, *Frémont's Fourth Expedition*, 135–42.

11. Richard Kern quoted in Weber, *Kern*, 40; B. Kern to Joe, Feb. 20, 1849, cited in Hafen and Hafen, *Frémont's Fourth Expedition*, 5.

12. Martin, *With Frémont*, 46; a manuscript to which I have already referred is also reprinted in Hafen and Hafen, *Frémont's Fourth Expedition*, 135–42.

13. Martin, *With Frémont*, 47.

14. William Brandon, *The Men and the Mountain: Frémont's Fourth Expedition*, 244; Charles Preuss, *Exploring With Frémont: The Private Diaries of Charles Preuss*, trans. and ed. Erwin G. and Elizabeth K. Gudde, 149–52; Hafen and Hafen, *Frémont's Fourth Expedition*, 130.

15. Hafen and Hafen, *Frémont's Fourth Expedition*, 139, 256; Martin, *With Frémont*, 52–53; Thelma S. Guild and Harvey L. Carter, *Kit Carson: A Pattern For Heroes*, 183.

16. ALS. to "Joe at Taos," Feb. 20, 1849; and Micajah McGehee typescript, undated, in Library of Congress, Washington, D.C., both cited in Hafen and Hafen, *Frémont's Fourth Expedition*, 165, 255.

17. Quoted in Hafen and Hafen, *Frémont's Fourth Expedition*, 184–85.

18. J. C. Frémont to J. B. Frémont, Jan. 27, 1849, in Jessie B. Frémont, *A Year of American Travel*, 43, 45.

19. Hafen and Hafen, *Frémont's Fourth Expedition*, 261. The officer in charge at Taos was Benjamin Lloyd Beall.

20. Harvey Carter, *"Dear Old Kit": The Historical Christopher Carson*, 122.

21. Robert V. Hine, *Edward Kern and American Expansion*, ix. Also consult William Joseph Heffernan, *Edward M. Kern, Artist-Explorer*, 57–58.

22. Hafen and Hafen, *Frémont's Fourth Expedition*, 228.

23. "Extracts from the Journal of Lt. J. H. Simpson," July 23, 1849, Fort Sutter Papers, MS. 126, Huntington Library, San Marino, Calif. In 1856, when Frémont was running for the presidency, Simpson wrote to Edward Kern about divulging what they both knew concerning "Frémont's disaster above the Taos." J. H. Simpson to E. Kern, Aug. 14, 1856, Huntington Library. See Simpson's report, reprinted as *Navaho Expedition: Journal of a Military Reconnaissance . . .*, ed. Frank McNitt (Norman, Okla., 1964).

24. In 1851, "Bill Williams Mountain" in the San Juan Range was named by Richard Kern, cartographer on Captain Lorenzo Sitgreaves's expedition from Zuñi to the Colorado River and Fort Yuma. In the 1830s Williams had lived along the river that also bears his name. See Mary M. Gordon, ed., *Through Indian Country to California: John P. Sherburne's Diary of the Whipple Expedition, 1853–1854* (Stanford, 1988), 160n.

25. This paragraph is based upon J. B. Frémont's manuscript, "Great Events," 82–84; see

also Thomas H. Benton, *Thirty Years' View* 2:719, and Alpheus H. Favour, *Old Bill Williams, Mountain Man*, 167–211.

26. Antoine Leroux to R. H. Kern, Aug. 22, 1850, as well as manuscripts nos. 127–30, Apr. 10, 1849, to Aug. 22, 1850, Fort Sutter Papers, Huntington Library. Williams had been a missionary among the Osages, had married an Indian woman, and had bestowed upon himself the "degree of M.T. (Master Trapper)." See Carter, *"Dear Old Kit,"* 79–80, for a sketch of Williams.

27. E. Kern to Mary Wolfe, Feb. 1849, Huntington Library.

28. J. Kern to R. and E. Kern, May 30, 1850, MS. 20654, Huntington Library; C. King to J. Kern, May 14, 1850, cited in Weber, *Kern*, 324; Spence 3:26.

29. Simpson to R. Kern, May 11, 1852, Huntington Library.

30. A. Cathcart to C. J. Colville, Oct. 30, 1848, in Spence 3:66; Solomon N. Carvalho, *Incidents of Travel and Adventure in the Far West, with Col. Frémont's Last Expedition*, 17–18. See also Joan Sturhahn, *Carvalho: Artist, Photographer, Adventurer, Patriot*, for background.

31. Quoted in Hafen and Hafen, *Frémont's Fourth Expedition*, 274.

32. J. C. Frémont to J. B. Frémont, Feb. 6, 1849, printed in Charles W. Upham, *Life, Explorations and Public Service of John Charles Frémont*, 291.

33. Preuss, *Exploring With Frémont*, xxvi–xxvii.

34. J. Torrey to J. C. Frémont, July 1, 1848, in Spence 3:35.

35. Suggestive are R. E. Litman and N. Tabachnick, "Fatal One-Car Accidents," *Psychoanalytic Quarterly* 36 (1967): 248–59; N. Tabachnik, ed., "Comparative Psychiatric Study of Accidental and Suicidal Death," *Archives of General Psychiatry* 14 (1966): 60–68; Howard E. Wolin, "Grandiosity and Violence in the Kennedy Family," *Psychohistory Review* 103 (Winter 1979): 27–37.

Chapter 11. The Riches of Las Mariposas

1. Jessie Benton Frémont, *A Year of American Travel*, 14, 26–28, 30, 32–34, 39.

2. Preceding paragraphs are based upon "Reminiscence of Elizabeth Benton Frémont," manuscript, Bancroft Library, University of California, Berkeley. See also Jessie Benton Frémont, *Souvenirs of My Time*, 188.

3. Bayard Taylor, *Eldorado; or, Adventures in the Path of Empire*, 53; Catherine C. Phillips, *Jessie Benton Frémont, a Woman Who Made History*, 114.

4. Frémont's old enemy Sherman temporarily became a banker, catering to the needs of a growing San Francisco. In July 1847, Frémont hired Jacob W. Harlan to fence off sixteen lots that belonged to him and Commodores Sloat and Stockton. See Paul W. Gates, "The Frémont-Jones Scramble for California Land Claims," *Southern California Quarterly* 56 (Spring 1974): 29. Frémont's Alcatraz negotiations appear in 31st Cong., 2d sess., S. Exec. Doc. 18 (Serial 589), 3:21–22, and in *San Francisco Evening News*, Feb. 12, 1856. Also consult Spence 3:xxxiii–xxxiv.

5. Stearns had bought it in 1842 for only six thousand dollars; the purchase included nine hundred head of cattle, nearly one thousand sheep, and 240 horses. See J. C. Frémont to B. D. Wilson, June 1, Nov. 15, 1849, Box 14, Wilson Collection, Huntington Library, San Marino, Calif.; J. C. Frémont to P. de la Guerra, Dec. 18, 1851; and J. C. Frémont to A. Stearns, Apr. 24, 1851, Box 27, Dec. 12, 1851, Box 85, both in Stearns-Gaffey Collection, Huntington Library. See also Doris Wright, *A Yankee in Mexican California*, 101n; Lois Rather, *Jessie Frémont at Black Point*.

6. J. C. Frémont to P. B. Reading, Oct. 26, 1847, Box 286, RC Collection, California State Library, Sacramento. Las Pulgas was for sale for only two thousand dollars. Also consult Henry

R. Wagner, "Edward Bosque, Printer and Man of Affairs," *California Historical Society Quarterly* 21 (Dec. 1942): 325.

7. J. B. Frémont, *Year of American Travel*, 125; Elizabeth B. Frémont, *Recollections of Elizabeth Benton Frémont*, 27; J. B. Frémont, "Great Events During the Life of Major General John C. Frémont," manuscript, C-B 397, file labeled "Scraps," 101, Frémont Collection, Bancroft Library.

8. Quoted in Alice Eyre, *The Famous Frémonts and Their America*, 362; Spence and Jackson 2:204; C. Gregory Crampton, "The Opening of the Mariposa Mining Region, 1851–1859," Ph.D. diss., University of California, Berkeley, 1941; Jessie B. Frémont, *Mother Lode Narratives*, ed. S. Sargent.

9. *National Intelligencer*, Feb. 27, 1855; Gates, "Frémont-Jones Scramble," 27. Logan Hunton to J. C. Frémont, Nov. 13, 1861; Hunton to J. J. Crittenden, Nov. 14, 1861; T. L. Crittenden to J. C. Frémont, Dec. 23, 28, 1864; R. H. Crittenden, Dec. 24, 1864, all in Library of Congress, Washington, D.C. Regarding the Mariposas debts, Spence 3:xi cites sources in the Crittenden and Blair Papers in the Library of Congress; see also W. C. Jones, *John Charles Frémont, Appellant*, and Paul W. Gates, "Adjudication of Spanish-Mexican Land Claims in California," *Huntington Library Quarterly* 21 (May 1958): 213.

10. E. B. Frémont, *Recollections*, 27.

11. J. B. Frémont, *Year of American Travel*, 77, 84.

12. Ibid., 75–76.

Chapter 12. A Senator's Life Turns Sour

1. Richard A. Van Orman, *The Explorers*, 115.

2. E. B. Lee to S. B. Lee, Oct. 4, 1850, Blair Papers, Princeton University, N.J. Foote, later governor of Mississippi, was actually a Southern Unionist opposed to secession. He left both Frémont and Benton out of his memoirs, entitled *Casket of Reminiscences*, although he discussed his 1828, 1832, and 1837 duels in that book. Foote's offending remarks were published in *Speech . . . On the the Admission of California* (Washington, D.C., 1850). Also see John Bigelow, *Memoir of the Life and Public Service of John Charles Frémont*, 220.

3. *J. C. Frémont's Record* (New York, 1856), 10, an 1856 presidential campaign document; J. B. Frémont, "Great Events During the Life of Major General John C. Frémont," manuscript, C-B 397, file labeled "Scraps," Frémont Collection, Bancroft Library, University of California, Berkeley, 143; Bigelow, *Memoir*, 423–26. This incident was to be raised six years later in the heat of the 1856 presidential campaign. Senator Gwin's version of the episode is in "Memoirs of Hon. William M. Gwin," ed. W. H. Ellison, *California Historical Society Quarterly* 20 (March 1940): 20.

4. Only briefly did Frémont sit on the Congressional Committee of Public Lands, not the Judiciary Committee, which would create a commission to examine property rights in California. See his statement in "California Claims," 30th Cong., 1st sess., Feb. 23, 1848, S. Rep. 75, p. 16; his "To the People of California," *Alta California*, Dec. 24, 1850; and Hubert Howe Bancroft, *History of California* 7:518.

5. Cardinal L. Goodwin, *John Charles Frémont: An Explanation of His Career*, 189.

6. On January 19, 1850, during his absence from Washington, he sent a wagon to the San Jose state building, then California's state capitol. The driver hauled along from Monterey a trunk filled with a hundred books consigned to Peter Burnett, the first civilian governor. The legislature wanted to establish an official state library, and to ingratiate himself with that body Frémont made his books the first to be accessioned.

7. J. C. Frémont to A. Stearns, Dec. 1, 1850, Box 27, Stearns Manuscripts, and Frémont to

P. Dexter Tiffany, Sept. 12, 1850, Harbeck Collection, Huntington Library, San Marino, Calif.; J. B. Frémont to F. P. Blair, Aug. 15, 1851, in Spence 3:xxxix, 374.

8. Jones's claim was ultimately declared fraudulent by the Supreme Court of the United States despite the fact that he had written a definitive government report on California's disputed Mexican land claims. It was, incidentally, prepared after gold was discovered on Frémont's Mariposas claim. Consult John W. Dwinelle, *The Colonial History of San Francisco*, 82; *Alta California*, Apr. 2, 1850; June 8, 1854; *Sacramento Settlers and Miners Tribune*, Nov. 28, 1850.

9. John Tanner, Jr., and Gloria Lothrop, eds., "Don Juan Forster, Southern California Ranchero," *Southern California Quarterly* 52 (Sept. 1970): 210.

10. J. B. Frémont, *Mother Lode Narratives*, ed. S. Sargent, 79.

11. Richard Crouter and Andrew Rolle, "Edward Beale and the Indian Peace Commissioners in California," *Historical Society of Southern California Quarterly* 52 (June 1960): 107–31; C. Gregory Crampton, ed., *The Mariposa Indian War, 1850–1851: Diaries of Robert Eccleston*.

12. In 1856, as he contemplated running for the presidency, fearing adverse publicity, Frémont settled his cattle claims for $242,000. See the army document refusing his claims, signed by Colonels Richard B. Mason, J. L. Stevenson, and Captain J. L. Folsom, entitled "Copies of Papers Relating to Contract for 66 Head of Beef Cattle," Folsom Manuscripts, Bancroft Library; Gerald Thompson, *Edward F. Beale and the American West*, 46–53, 72; *Statutes at Large*, 33rd Cong., 1st sess.; Spence 3:xli-xlii, lxix. Frémont's own remaining drafts for the Indian cattle were eventually paid off with 10 percent interest. Consult *Baker* vs. *United States*, in *Court Claims Reports* 4 (Dec. 1868): 90, 201, 252–57.

13. J. B. Frémont to F. P. Blair, Jan. 31, Apr. 11, 1851, Blair-Lee Papers, Princeton University; J. C. Frémont to A. Stearns, Apr. 24, 1851, in Spence 3:229; J. C. Frémont to Stearns, Apr. 24, 1851, Stearns Papers, Huntington Library.

14. *Alta California*, Dec. 27, 1873; the title to Los Gentiles was not confirmed until the next year.

Chapter 13. New Fame Abroad and at Home

1. Baron Humboldt to J. C. Frémont, Oct. 7, 1850, printed in *Republican Scrapbook*, 19–20.

2. Regarding these artists, see William H. Goetzmann, *The West as Romantic Horizon*, and John C. Ewers, *Artists of the Old West*, passim.

3. Ray Billington, *Land of Savagery, Land of Promise: The European Image of the American Frontier in the Nineteenth Century* (New York, 1982), describes the European response to American exploration.

4. Quote from *Sartain's Union Magazine of Literature* (1850) is in Spence 3:495.

5. Emerson, who expressed afterthoughts about Frémont's morality, had also written that every scoundrel eventually becomes a hero. During the Civil War he called on Frémont after the general had been ousted from command of the West. Consult journal entries in Ralph Waldo Emerson, *Journals and Miscellaneous Notebooks*, ed. Linda Allardt and David W. Hill (Cambridge, Mass., 1960–82), 9:431; 11:23, 315; 13:456; 14:22; 15:191–92.

6. Quoted in Richard A. Van Orman, *The Explorers*, 109.

7. Mary Lee Spence, "David Hoffman: Frémont's Mariposa Agent in London," *Southern California Quarterly* 55 (Winter 1978): 383. Hoffman's inflated accounts of California's vast wealth remain stored in the British Museum entitled "To the British Public Respecting the Leasing Powers of David Hoffman, L.L.D., Regarding the Mariposa Estate." See also David Hoffman, *The Frémont Estate: An Address to the British Public Respecting Colonel Frémont's*

Leasing Powers to the Author from June, 1850 (London, 1851), and Hoffman's *California Frémont Estates and Gold Mines: Non-sale to Mr. T. D. Sargent* (London, 1852).

8. C. F. Mayer to D. Hoffman, Sept. 30, Oct. 10, 24, 1850, quoted in Spence, "David Hoffman," 385, 400.

9. Gordon Hendricks, *The Life and Work of Winslow Homer* (New York, 1979), 20, 29.

10. J. C. Frémont to T. H. Benton, Apr. 13, 1852, and Benton to D. Webster, May 14, 1852, in Spence 3:351; also manuscript scraps, Folder 69, Frémont Collection, Southwest Museum, Los Angeles, Calif. Both Frémont and Senator Benton still had enemies in the government who were smarting over the 1848 court-martial proceedings. Legislators emphasized the damage done by Frémont's troops as well as their stealing of private property. In the summer of 1853, Frémont met with the California Claims Board, and on March 3, 1854, the Senate passed Benton's measure. The House of Representatives then appointed three military officers to administer an appropriation of $168,000 to further consider Frémont's claims. There remained another $15,000, due to suppliers of the California Battalion, that the government never paid. Eventually the U.S. Treasury did honor a London court's verdict against Frémont for almost four thousand pounds sterling, with interest.

11. J. B. Frémont to E. B. Lee, Apr. 18, 1856, Blair-Lee Papers, Princeton University, N.J., quoted in Spence, "David Hoffman," 403. For more on the claims against Frémont, see A. H. Gillespie to A. Stearns, Mar. 9, 10, 1847, Stearns Manuscripts, Huntington Library, San Marino, Calif., and Oct. 15, 1848, entitled "Papers Relating to Damage Done By Troops of Stockton, Frémont, and Kearny in Los Angeles," Jan. 21, 1847, Stearns-Gaffey Collection, Box 73, Huntington Library. See also "Henry Dalton to Commissioners for Revision of Losses & Declaration of Stolen Property," May 31, 1847, Dalton Collection, Box 5, Huntington Library; *Congressional Globe*, 30th Cong., 1st sess., 561ff: *Senate Journal*, 30th Cong., 1st sess., (Serial 302), 299; R. B. Mason to J. D. Stevenson, Jan. 23, 1849, Special Collections, University of California, Los Angeles; J. C. Frémont to P. G. Washington, July 11, 1853, in Spence 3:374.

12. Hoffman to J. B. Frémont and J. B. Frémont to Hoffman, both dated Apr. 8, 1852, quoted in Spence, "David Hoffman," 395.

13. D. Hoffman to J. C. Frémont, Mar. 25, 1852, and Hoffman to J. B. Frémont, Apr. 8, 29, 1852, in Spence 3:338, 344, 349, 355.

14. Hoffman to Frémont, Nov. 25, 1851, quoted in Spence, "David Hoffman," 390, 401. See also Robert P. Hastings, "Rufus Allen Lockwood," *California Historical Society Quarterly* 34 (Sept. 1944): 244–47, 262–63, regarding title to Las Mariposas.

15. Spence, "David Hoffman," 380. After Hoffman's death in 1854, his wife sued Frémont in the New York Supreme Court to recover forty thousand dollars. The case was either dropped or settled out of court.

16. J. C. Frémont to C. F. Mayer, Oct. 12, 24, 1850, and Mayer to D. Hoffman, Oct. 14, Nov. 22, 1850, in Spence 3:207. Also see Mary Lee Spence, "George W. Wright: Politician, Lobbyist, Entrepreneur," *Pacific Historical Review* 63 (Aug. 1989): 348.

17. Franklin perished on his third expedition. In 1983 eight axes belonging to his venture into Arctic Canada were found. The next year, the bodies of members of that disastrous expedition were also located frozen in the Arctic permafrost. See John W. Lentz, "Clues to a Tragic Trek on Canada's Hood River," *National Geographic* 169 (Jan. 1986): 127–40.

18. According to Skirving, Frémont enjoyed annual rentals of seventy-five thousand dollars from his San Francisco town lots, for which he had paid very little. He had even— Skirving's brochure erroneously boasted—managed to buy Mission San Gabriel, in southern California, "for a few hundred dollars!" See Joseph E. Arrington, "Skirving's Moving Panorama: Colonel Frémont's Western Expeditions Pictorialized," *Oregon Historical Quarterly* 65 (June 1964): 133–72; and Spence, "David Hoffman," 384. Skirving's diorama was wound on rollers

and turned by hand machinery. This "movie" of its time required two hours to be viewed. The canvas on which it was painted stretched for half a mile in length. Skirving's "Biographical Sketch of Col. Frémont" (London, 1850) is in Huntington Library.

19. Dorothy P. Hulbert, ed., "The Trip to California: An Explanation Notice of the Panorama . . . at the Théâtre de Variétés, Paris, August 8, 1850," *Frontier and Midland* 14 (1934): 160–61, 168–69.

20. J. B. Frémont, "Great Events During the Life of Major General John C. Frémont," manuscript, C-B 397, file labeled "Scraps," 173–74, Frémont Collection, Bancroft Library, University of California, Berkeley.

21. Quote is from Elizabeth Ellet, *Queens of American Society: A Memoir of Mrs. Frémont*, 428. All this opulence in Paris and New York led Alice Eyre to entitle her book *The Famous Frémonts and Their America*. The latter source is untrustworthy, because it contains manufactured conversation, mixing fact with imagined dialogue.

22. This quotation is in Catherine C. Phillips, *Jessie Benton Frémont, a Woman Who Made History*, 191, which also fictitiously re-creates events. Frances Cornelia (Nina) Frémont married Major H. M. Porter, assistant provost marshal of New Orleans, on July 19, 1864. She traveled widely, including trips to London and Paris, according to a note dated May 1, 1861, in the Frémont Collection, Bancroft Library; see also John R. Howard, *Remembrance of Things Past . . .* , 84, and the *New Orleans True Delta*, July 30, 1864.

23. *Memoirs*, 21.

24. Quoted in Fawn Brodie, *The Devil Drives*, 4.

Chapter 14. Ardor Gone Astray: The Fifth Expedition

1. Documentation regarding Frémont's fifth expedition is in "Reports of Explorations and Surveys," 33rd Cong. 2d sess., H. Exec. Doc. 91 (Serials 791–800). The Beale and Heap letters are in Heap's *Central Route to the Pacific* (Philadelphia, 1854), reprinted in Le Roy Hafen, *The Far West and the Rockies: Historical Series, 1820–1875* (Glendale, Calif., 1961).

2. Details are in "Delaware Indians," 61st Cong., 1st. sess., S. Exec. Doc. 134, 6–9; Spence 3:382, 469.

3. Solomon N. Carvalho, *Incidents of Travel and Adventure in the Far West, with Col. Frémont's Last Expedition*. Regarding Gunnison, see his *Map of a Reconaissance . . .* (New York, 1852). See also Robert Taft, *Photography and the American Scene*, 262–64.

4. Taft, *Photography*, 29; Robert Taft, *Artists and Illustrators of the Old West, 1850–1900*, 15, 262–64, 273–74. Egglofstein was a partner in a Saint Louis surveying firm.

5. Quoted in John Bigelow, *Memoir of the Life and Public Service of John Charles Frémont*, 433, which reprints "Extracts from the Journal and Letters of S. N. Carvalho." Regarding Frémont's rheumatism, see Jessie Benton's "Great Events During the Life of Major General John C. Frémont," manuscript, C-B 397, file labeled "Scraps," 179ff., Frémont Collection, Bancroft Library, University of California, Berkeley.

6. Quoted in Joan Sturhahn, *Carvalho: Artist, Photographer, Adventurer, Patriot*, 77.

7. Regarding Bent's Fort, see Jackson W. Moore, Jr., *Bent's Old Fort: An Archeological Study*, and David Lavender, *Bent's Fort*.

8. David Miller and Mark Stegmaier, *James F. Milligan: His Journal of Frémont's Fifth Expedition, 1853–54* (Glendale, Calif., 1988), 75–96, 128, 136, 139, 187, provides a critical account of the fifth expedition, although Milligan was not actually present throughout it all.

9. Ibid., 438.

10. Carvalho, *Incidents of Travel*, 133.

11. ALS., dated Sept. 11, 1856, reprinted in Sturhahn, *Carvalho*, 129.

12. Bigelow, *Memoir*, 434.

13. Ibid., 440.

14. Ibid., 448, and Carvalho, *Incidents of Travel*, 101.

15. David Lavender, *Colorado River Country*, (Albuquerque, 1988), 56.

16. Bigelow, *Memoir*, 441.

17. Miller and Stegmaier, *James F. Milligan*, 202, gives an entirely different account of Fuller's death, making Frémont into a villain who left Fuller to freeze a night in a "single blanket." Yet Milligan is a suspect source.

18. J. C. Frémont to T. H. Benton, Feb. 9, 1854, printed in Bigelow, *Memoir*, 442.

19. *Daily Missouri Democrat* May 31, 1854, printed in Spence 3:lvii. William H. Palmer carried along a letter of credit from his brother Joseph of Palmer, Cook and Co., Frémont's San Francisco bankers. Exhausted, Carvalho and Eggloffstein made it to Salt Lake City, where they were offered employment by Lieutenant E. G. Beckwith. After Gunnison was murdered by Indians on October 26, 1853, he assumed command of the farthest northern government railroad survey to the Pacific.

20. Spence 3:478.

21. Eggloffstein's drawing appears as a colored lithograph in *Reports of Explorations and Surveys*, 33rd Cong., 2d sess., H. Exec. Doc. 91, vol. 2. His drawings were done for the Beckwith party after he reached Salt Lake City, and he became a major illustrator of the Pacific Railroad Reports and was also a member of the Ives survey of the Colorado River in 1858. See Taft, *Photography*, 262–64.

22. U.S. Senate, 33rd Cong., 1st sess., 1854, S. Misc. Doc. 67. The *National Intelligencer* article is in Bigelow, *Memoir*, 473–80.

23. Quoted in Bigelow, *Memoir*, 480; Frémont's first letter, dated "Parowan, Iron County, Utah Territory," Feb. 9, 1854, appeared in *National Intelligencer*, Apr. 11, 1854; another was printed in the same journal on June 15, 1854, and reprinted as 33rd Cong., 1st sess., 1854, S. Misc. Doc. 67.

24. When the official railroad surveys were completed in 1855, producing a series of volumes numbering eighty-five hundred pages, Frémont's fifth expedition stood entirely outside that effort. Although all the routes officially surveyed had proven practical, sectional bickering and the approach of the Civil War had long postponed selection of any railroad route.

25. Frémont's contributions to cartography were forgotten as his five expeditions were followed by scientific systematizers. Philanthropist George Peabody was to exhume superb fossil remains in regions that Frémont had traversed—Nebraska, Wyoming, Colorado, and California. Among other new explorers and anthropologists were John Wesley Powell, Adolph Bandelier, and Lewis Henry Morgan. After 1859, Morgan would extend his investigations of tribes on four trips to the Great Plains (see *The Nation*, Aug. 8, 1880). Had Frémont been trained differently, he might have written books similar to Morgan's *The American Beaver and His Works* (1868), *Systems of Consanguinity and Affinity in the Human Family* (1871), *Ancient Society* (1877), and *Houses and House of Life of the American Aborigines* (1881).

26. The Delawares returned to Saint Louis from New Orleans by steamboat, according to J. C. Frémont to G. Engelmann, May 7, 1854, cited in Spence 3:479.

Chapter 15. Toward the Presidency

1. Margaret Clapp, *Forgotten First Citizen: John Bigelow* (Boston, 1947), 104.

2. Other condemnatory pamphlets were *J. C. Frémont's Record* (New York, 1856): *Frémont's Romanism Established* (New York, 1856): *Frémont's "Principles" Exposed* (New York, 1856): *Infidelity and Abolitionism* (New York, 1856); *Black Republican an Imposter* (New York, 1856); and *Speech of the Hon. J. R. Thompson of New Jersey* (Washington, D.C., 1856).

3. J. B. Frémont, "Great Events During the Life of Major General John C. Frémont," manuscript, C-B 397, file labeled "Scraps," 199–200, Frémont Collection, Bancroft Library. Judge Ephraim Marsh, who had presided over the Know Nothing convention to nominate Fillmore, came to feel that support of either Buchanan or Fillmore would be to cast a vote for slavery. Marsh was disgusted that Fillmore had made a speech that "astounded the country in declaring that the election of Col. Frémont . . . would occasion a dissolution of the Union." See *Letter of Judge Ephraim Marsh of New Jersey, Who Presided at the Convention Which Nominated Millard Fillmore, Giving His Reasons for Supporting Col. J. C. Frémont* (New York, 1856), in British Museum, London; see also Fred Harvey Harrington, "Frémont and the North Americans," *American Historical Review* 64 (July 1939): 843.

4. *Los Angeles Star*, Aug. 23, 27, 30, Oct. 4, 1856.

5. T. O. Larkin to A. Hardy, Aug. 2, 1856, quoted in Thomas O. Larkin, *The Larkin Papers: Personal, Business and Official Correspondence* . . . , ed. George P. Hammond, 10, 290–91; and J. C. Frémont to Pioneer Society, Apr. 30, 1854, in Spence 3:478.

6. Quotations from G. Welles to F. P. Blair, Apr. 9, 1860, Blair Papers; G. Welles to P. King, Mar. 3, 1860, Welles Papers; King to Welles, Mar. 3, Apr. 9, 21, 1860, Box 18, Welles Papers; G. Wright to M. Blair, Mar. 12, 1861, Montgomery Blair Papers, all in Library of Congress, Washington, D.C.; F. Billings to T. W. Park, Jan. 14, Feb. 22, 1861, Park-McCullough House Archives, North Bennington, Vt. See also J. C. Frémont to R. Price, Mar. 31 (no year), Frémont Collection, Bancroft Library; John Niven to Andrew Rolle, May 13, 1983; Cardinal L. Goodwin, *John Charles Frémont: An Explanation of His Career*, 13, 41–42. Bigelow was not only Frémont's biographer, but also one of the founders of the Republican party.

7. J. H. Simpson to E. M. Kern, Aug. 14, 1856, MS. 20664, Huntington Library, San Marino, Calif.

8. Elizabeth Benton Frémont, *Recollections of Elizabeth Benton Frémont*, comp. I. T. Martin, 77; "The Reminiscences of Francis P. Frémont," Document, C-B 397, pt. 2, box 5, Bancroft Library.

9. *An Address By the Hon. Henry A. Wise, Delivered at Richmond Oct. 1856*, Huntington Library; Craig Simpson, *A Good Southerner: The Life of Henry A. Wise of Virginia*, 126, 131.

10. In addition to this title (Washington, D.C., 1856), see *Democratic Electoral Handbook* (Washington, D.C., 1856).

11. William A. Croffut, *An American Procession, 1835–1914*, 272; Le Roy Hafen and Ann W. Hafen, *Frémont's Fourth Expedition: A Documentary Account of the Disaster of 1848–1849*, 255–61.

12. Frederick S. Dellenbaugh, *Frémont and '49*, 460.

13. Clapp, *Forgotten First Citizen*, 104; Goodwin, *Frémont*, 204.

14. Another campaign publications was *The Republican Platform: The Lives of Frémont and Dayton, with Beautiful Steel Portraits of Each* (Boston, 1856). A biography for young people was Francis C. Woodworth's *The Young American's Life of Frémont*. For the English public, James Magoon published *The Life of J. C. Frémont, the Rocky Mountain Explorer* as part of "Beadles' American Sixpenny Biographies," popular in England. Also published in Britain was A. W. Greeley's "John Charles Frémont the Pathfinder," a chapter in Greeley's *Explorers and Travellers*, 212–39.

15. H. Greeley to Schuyler Colfax, May 16, 1856, quoted in Fred Harvey Harrington, *Fighting Politician: Major General N. P. Banks* (Philadelphia, 1948), 220.

16. Bronson Alcott, *The Journals of Bronson Alcott*, ed. Odell Shepard, 284.

17. Hon. Philip Dorsheimer to J. F. Donaldson, July 15, 1856, and "Extracts from Josiah Quincy's Address on the Nature and Power of the Slave States, and the Duties of the Free States," reprinted in *Republican Scrapbook*.

18. Quoted in Russel B. Nye, *Fettered Freedom* (East Lansing, Mich., 1949), 20.

19. All leaders, according to political scientist Harold Lasswell, shift unresolved personal anxieties onto groups and causes. Furthermore, the noise and hubub of campaign mobs and distractions of the crowd magnetize a leader's aura.

20. Houston quoted in Marsh, *Letter*, 4; T. Stevens to E. D. Gazzam, Aug. 7, 1856, quoted in Fawn Brodie, *Thaddeus Stevens, Scourge of the South* (New York, 1966), 344.

21. J. B. Frémont to E. B. Lee, Apr. 18, 1856, Blair Lee Papers, Princeton, N.J.; J. B. Frémont, "Great Events," 208. Jessie also bitterly complained of being dropped socially by Bigelow and E. D. Morgan, chairman of the Republican party, in J. B. Frémont to F. P. Blair, Jan. 8,. 1856, Blair Papers, Library of Congress.

22. Elbert B. Smith, *Magnificent Missourian: The Life of Thomas Hart Benton* (Philadelphia, 1958; repr., Westport, Conn., 1973), 316. Paradoxically, the *Daily Herald* of Marysville, Calif., for Aug, 31, 1856, claimed that in the Senate Frémont had voted with the South to deny money for clothing and feeding blacks who had escaped from a slave ship. The paper also reported that he had voted against abolishing slavery in the District of Columbia. Frémont did not bother to reply to such confusing charges.

23. Back during the Mexican War, Buchanan had praised Frémont in a printed broadside entitled "The Conqueror of California: Mr. Buchanan Endorses Frémont. . . . Deposition of the Sage of Wheatland in Favor of Colonel Frémont." The Republicans had reprinted this brochure, but no such publication could gain him the presidency.

24. John Bigelow, *Retrospections of an Active Life*, 1:145. Clapp, *Forgotten First Citizen*, 104, cites Bigelow's manuscript journal for July 14, 1890, New York Public Library. Frémont died the day before this entry was made.

25. Ruhl J. Bartlett, *Frémont and the Republican Party*, 1, 8–69, provides an excellent summary of the 1856 campaign. U. S. Grant to J. R. Grant, Sept. 23, 1859, *The Papers of Ulysses S. Grant* 1:350. See also William S. McFeely, *Grant: A Biography*, 69. As regards Grant, Frémont not only gave him his first major command in Missouri, but also spoke on his behalf among the midwestern Germans during Grant's 1868 presidential campaign. Grant was himself no marvel of personal integration—even compared to Frémont—subject as he was to bovine silences, splitting headaches under stress, bouts of alcoholism, and obstinacy.

26. Elizabeth B. Frémont, *Recollections of Elizabeth Benton Frémont*, comp. I. T. Martin, 80.

27. J. B. Frémont to E. B. Lee, May 4, 1857, Blair-Lee Papers, Princeton University, N.J.

28. California held a peculiar fascination for Jessie's circle of friends. While in the East, she had titillated an Englishwoman with a strange black chestnut and other articles sent from San Francisco by her brother-in-law William Carey Jones. See Amelia M. Murray, *Letters from the United States, Cuba and Canada* (New York, 1856), 173.

29. J. B. Frémont to J. C. Frémont, July 25, 29, 1857, Frémont Collection, Bancroft Library, contains the quotes in the previous two paragraphs.

30. J. B. Frémont to J. C. Frémont, Sept. 23, 1857, Frémont Collection, Bancroft Library.

31. J. B. Frémont to J. C. Frémont, July 24, 29, Sept. 23, 1857, Frémont Collection, Bancroft Library.

Chapter 16. Furor at Bear Valley and a European Affair

1. King worked for the California Geological Survey with W. H. Brewer and J. D. Whitney. See Folder B–4, Box 2, Clarence King Papers, Huntington Libary, San Marino, Calif. See also note 25 of this chapter, below, and *The Mariposas Estate* (London, 1861), a prospectus. Max Strobel, a mapmaker, produced a superb colored map of the property. See also "California

Scrapbook Number 28," with newspaper clippings regarding the tangled legal disputes about Las Mariposas, in the Huntington Library.

2. Not until October 1859, in *Biddle* vs. *Boggs* in *Proceedings of the Supreme Court of California*, 379, was Frémont's title finally settled. He ended up with nearly seven square miles, or 4,480 acres.

3. J. B. Frémont to F. P. Blair, July 16, Blair Papers, Princeton University, N.J.; A. Russell Buchanan, *David S. Terry of California, Dueling Judge*, 54, 85.

4. J. B. Frémont to F. P. Blair, July 2, 1859; J. B. Frémont to E. B. Lee, June 2, 1860, Blair Papers, Princeton.

5. John R. Howard, *Remembrance of Things Past . . .* , 87.

6. J. B. Frémont to E. B. Lee, Nov. 15, 1859, Blair Papers, Princeton.

7. J. B. Frémont to J. T. Fields, Dec. 15, 1862, Huntington Library.

8. J. C. Frémont to "Franky" Frémont, May 26, Nov. 28, 1862, and J. B. Frémont to J. T. Fields, Dec. 15, 1862, Huntington Library.

9. J. B. Frémont to F. P. Blair, May, 1858, Huntington Library.

10. E. B. Frémont to C. F. Lummis, Jan. 10, 1902, Huntington Library; Elizabeth B. Frémont, *Recollections of Elizabeth Benton Frémont*, 56, 72.

11. E. B. Frémont, *Recollections*, 88.

12. Howard, *Remembrance*, 87.

13. J. B. Frémont to F. P. Blair, July 16, 1858, Blair Papers, Princeton.

14. Jessie B. Frémont, *Far West Sketches*, 58; Howard, *Remembrance*, 87; E. B. Frémont, *Recollections*, 91–98.

15. Horace Greeley, *A Year of American Travel*.

16. Manuscript reminiscences of Joseph Kimball Darling, Film 65, Vermont Historical Society, Montpelier, Vt., 71–72.

17. Henry R. Wagner, "Edward Bosque, Printer and Man of Affairs," *California Historical Society Quarterly* 21 (Dec. 1942): 326; Jessie B. Frémont, *Mother Lode Narratives*, ed. Shirley Sargent, 16–17; J. B. Frémont to James T. Fields, Oct. 23, 1862, Huntington Library. Frémont's Mariposa "White House" burned to the ground long ago. The Oso Hotel was also destroyed by fire. A few buildings remain, the principal one being the courthouse, California's oldest. Entrances to the mining shafts are still visible. The original assay office, a brick structure, still stands. Frémont denuded the surrounding hills of timber as fuel for the furnaces of his stamp mills.

18. T. Jackson Lears, *No Place of Grace* (New York, 1981), 188.

19. J. C. Frémont to M. Blair, Jan. 7, 1857, July 4, 1858, Nov. 17, 1859, Feb. 26, 1861, Blair Papers, Library of Congress, Washington, D.C. Even in those years, Blair's representation of a client while acting as a federal judge was considered unprofessional, if not illegal. Blair, who became Lincoln's postmaster general, found it almost impossible to obtain payment of his fees from Frémont.

20. Newspaper accounts of Frémont's Mariposas troubles include *National Intelligencer*, Feb. 21, 24, 1852, Nov. 3, 1857, Aug. 21, 1858; *New York Weekly Tribune*, Aug. 14, 1858; *Mariposa Gazette*, Dec. 3, 1858; *Sacramento Union*, Dec. 7, 1858.

21. H. A. Wise to E. Everett, Feb. 1, 1851, Everett Papers, Massachusetts Historical Society, Boston.

22. *Daily Alta California*, Nov. 26, Dec. 5, 7, 24, 1859, provides a running commentary on *Biddle Boggs* vs. *Merced Mining Co.*

23. J. C. Frémont to Governor N. P. Banks (Mass.), Oct. 18, 1858; J. C. Frémont to G. B. Wright, Dec. 26, 1851, Huntington Library; *Daily Alta California*, Nov. 26, Dec. 5, Dec. 24, 1859; a full description of the Mariposas estate appeared Aug. 2–19, 1860.

24. J. B. Frémont, *Mother Lode Narratives*, 15.

25. These were renowned mining experts. Frémont also employed Frederic Claudel as assayist. J. Ross Browne, a U.S. commissioner examining mineral resources west of the Rocky Mountains, published a glowing sixty-five-page report, *The Mariposa Estate*. Howard, *Remembrance*, 76.

26. Correspondence regarding Frémont's infidelities includes G. Wright to M. Blair, Mar. 12, 1861, Box 38, Blair Papers, as well as P. King to G. Welles, Apr. 9, 21, 1860, and G. Welles to F. P. Blair, Sr., Apr. 9, 1860, Welles Papers, all in Library of Congress. I am also grateful to Professor Robin Winks for reference to correspondence from Frederick Billings to Trenor Park of Jan. 14 and 22 and Feb. 4, 6, 11, 14, 22, 27, 1861, at Park-McCullough House Archives, North Bennington, Vermont.

27. Moran had also met William Dayton, Frémont's presidential running mate in 1856, writing that he was "a fine commanding man. Intellectually, he would make a dozen of Frémont." See Sarah A. Wallace and Frances E. Gillespie, eds., *The Journal of Benjamin Moran* (Chicago, 1949), 1:788; 2:850.

28. G. Wright to M. Blair, Mar. 16, 1861, Box 38, Blair Papers, Library of Congress. A curious letter of Jessie's to the editor of *The Atlantic Monthly* reads: "I can't get along without seeing you & can't leave home." She wants him to come to her house in New York City: "The Genl. is in town every day & my letters come quickest simply addressed to me at New York." She continues: "You can brace yourself to an exciting & protracted sitting in which I shall want you to be satisfied but I must tell the truth." See J. B. Frémont to J. T. Fields, Oct. 8, 1862, Huntington Library.

29. Wagner, "Edward Bosque," 325–27.

30. In this suit Thurlow Weed charged Frémont with unscrupulous business practices. See *Weed vs. Opdyke: The Great Libel Case*, 7, 58–59, 61, 137, 148, 155.

31. Quotes from ibid. and J. B. Frémont, *Mother Lode Narratives*, 157. Despite its prominent visitors, Las Mariposas (seventy miles from Yosemite National Park by road and thirty miles by air) cannot boast even a plaque to mark the rancho's site.

Chapter 17. Civil War Showdown: A General Versus Lincoln

1. Quoted in J. C. Frémont to F. P. Blair, May 24, Aug. 5, 1861, Fields Collection, Huntington Library, San Marino, Calif. See also W. H. Seward to A. Lincoln, Dec. 25, 1860, Mar. 11, 1861, and Lincoln to Seward, Dec. 29, 1860, Mar. 11, 1861, in *The Collected Works of Abraham Lincoln*, ed. Roy P. Basler, 4:164, 281.

2. J. C. Frémont to F. P. Blair, May 24, Aug. 5, 1861, Fields Collection, Huntington Library; Cardinal L. Goodwin, *John Charles Frémont: An Explanation of His Career*, 211–13; Robert Murray, "The Frémont-Adams Contracts," *Journal of the West* 5 (Oct. 1966): 517–24; Allan Nevins, *Frémont: The West's Greatest Adventurer* 2: 475. Billings also bought supplies and horses in Canada.

3. Elizabeth B. Frémont, *Recollections of Elizabeth Benton Frémont*, comp. I. T. Martin, 118; J. B. Frémont, *Souvenirs of My Time*, 205–206. Only once, in 1878, did Frémont revisit the remnants of their property while en route to assume the governorship of Arizona. When Jessie and the children left San Francisco for New York by steamer on May 22, 1861, Beale leased Black Point from her. Along with the property he inherited Bret Harte, who had been living there as Jessie's guest. In 1863 the Frémont house would be demolished by the army, which erected a shore battery at Black Point to defend San Francisco Bay against Confederate raiders. The army had named this new post Fort Mason in honor of Colonel Richard B. Mason, whom Frémont had once challenged to a duel and who had become military governor of California. Mason was now long since dead.

4. James M. McPherson, *Ordeal By Fire* (New York, 1982), 156.

5. J. B. Frémont to D. Dix, in J. B. Frémont, "Great Events During the Life of Major General John C. Frémont," manuscript, C-B 397, pt. 1, file labeled "Scraps," Frémont Collection, Bancroft Library, University of California, Berkeley.

6. J. B. Frémont to M. Blair, July 28, 1861, Blair Papers, Library of Congress, Washington, D.C., and J. B. Frémont to W. H. Lamon, Oct 30, 1861, Huntington Library. The most fair-minded appraisal of Frémont's Missouri problems is by Robert L. Turkoly-Joczik in "Frémont and the Western Department," *Missouri Historical Review* 82 (July 1988): 359–67.

7. Allan Nevins, *The War for the Union* 1:314.

8. Billings purchased arms and supplies in Europe well before George F. L. Schyler arrived in Britain as the first official Union purchasing agent. See J. B. Frémont to M. Blair, July 25, 1861, quoted in W. F. Smith, "The Blairs and Frémont," *Missouri Historical Review* 23 (Jan. 1929): 222. These figures originate from correspondence at Park-McCullough House Archives, North Bennington, Vermont. Frémont sent Billings to Europe again in 1862 in search of wealthy German backers for his California properties as well as munitions.

9. Committee on the Conduct of the War, *Report*, Part 3, Jan. 17, 1862 (Washington, D.C.), 33–34, cited in Smith, "Blairs and Frémont," 218–19.

10. *National Intelligencer*, Aug. 20, 1861.

11. John R. Howard, *Remembrance of Things Past . . .*, 163; Nevins, *War for the Union* 1:317.

12. J. C. Frémont to F. Lieber, Aug. 5, 1861, Lieber Papers, Doc. 1477, Huntington Library.

13. Kern was to lose his commission as an "irregular" officer when Frémont lost the Missouri command. Pope went on to command the Army of Virginia and to confront Frémont once again, but he suffered defeat at the Second Battle of Manassas against Stonewall Jackson and Robert E. Lee. See Robert V. Hine, *Edward Kern and American Expansion*, 149–52, and Nevins, *War for the Union* 2:15.

14. Telegram, U. S. Grant to J. C. Frémont, Sept. 5, 1861, and Grant to C. de Arnaud, Nov. 30, 1861, in *The Papers of Ulysses S. Grant* 2:193, and 3:343–44n. See also Bruce Catton, *Grant Moves South* (Boston, 1960), 494; John C. Frémont, "In Command in Missouri," *Battles and Leaders of the Civil War*, ed. Robert Underwood Johnson and Clarence Clough Buel, 1:285, De Arnaud also wrote a book: *The Union and Its Ally, Russia* (Washington, 1890), 9–11, 30–31.

15. William Brotherhood is quoted in Frederick S. Dellenbaugh, *Frémont and '49*, 469. Regarding construction of the river boats, see Benjamin F. Cooling, *Forts Henry and Donelson*, 24–25. Regarding the sentries, see Nevins, *War for the Union* 2:314, which cites *New York Tribune*, Jan. 18, 1862; see also U.S. House of Representatives, *Report on the War*, 37th Cong., 3rd sess., Feb. 24, 1862, 198–209, 269–72; Howard, *Remembrance*, 140.

16. F. Lieber to C. Sumner, Nov. 29, 1961, Lieber Papers, Box 42, Huntington Library; Charles G. Halpine to Thurlow Weed, Oct. 17, 1861, and to H. Greeley, Oct. 18, 1861, Ford Collection, New York Public Library.

17. Grierson, *The Valley of the Shadows*, 233–34.

18. M. Blair to C. H. Ray, Nov. 17, 1861, Huntington Library.

19. John Schofield, *Forty-Six Years in the Army*, 42; Howard, *Remembrance*, 141–45. This was the home of the deceased Joshua B. Brant, who had been married to Jessie's cousin. Frémont, when young, had boarded with the Brants.

20. Smith, "Blairs and Frémont," 226; *Congressional Globe*, 37th Cong., 2d sess., 1862, 1121; Christopher Phillips, *Damned Yankee: The Life of General Nathaniel Lyon*, 236–39, 248; Kurt F. Leidecker, *Yankee Teacher: The Life of William Torrey Harris*, 202–203.

21. E. Smith, *Francis Preston Blair*, 298.

22. William S. McFeely, *Grant: A Biography*, 88–89; Kenneth P. Williams, *Lincoln Finds a General* 3:25, 37–42.

23. New York Weekly *Tribune*, Nov. 1, 1862; F. P. Blair's speech, printed in *Congressional Globe* (Washington, 1862), entitled "Frémont's Hundred Days in Missouri."

24. Lewis Wallace, *Lew Wallace: An Autobiography*, 327.

25. Ibid., 329. At the Battle of Shiloh, and elsewhere during his career, Wallace also could be personally difficult. But Frémont's refusal to see him resembled an occasion during the California conquest when, after being introduced to a man, Frémont looked at him coldly without bowing and passed on. "What kind of a man is this Frémont anyhow?" the confused stranger asked. See George W. Ames, "Horse Marines: California, 1846," *California Historical Society Quarterly* 18 (1939): 72–84.

26. John G. Nicolay and John Hay, *Abraham Lincoln: A History* (New York, 1890), 4:415.

27. J. B. Frémont, "Great Events."

28. Lincoln to J. B. Frémont, Sept. 12, 1861, in Basler, *Collected Works* 4:519.

29. Quoted in Ovando J. Hollister, *Life of Schuyler Colfax*, 183. Also see S. Colfax to J. Medill, Sept. 19, 1861, Huntington Library; Smith, *Francis Preston Blair*, 300.

30. Jessie Benton Frémont, *The Story of the Guard: A Chronicle of War*, 76–77, 85, 86–87, 94.

31. J. C. Frémont to J. B. Frémont, Oct. 18, 1861, reprinted in ibid., 92; regarding Morgan's profiteering at Frémont's expense, see H. C. Engelbrecht and F. C. Hanighen, *Merchants of Death*, 59–61.

32. J. C. Frémont to J. B. Frémont, Oct. 19, 1861, and letter to J. B. Frémont from "H," Nov. 1, 1861, reprinted in J. B. Frémont, *Story of the Guard*, 93–94, 188; J. C. Frémont to M. Blair, Aug. 9, 19, 21, 1861, Blair Papers, Princeton University, N.J.

33. Carol Morris Petillo, *Douglas MacArthur: Philippine Years* (Bloomington, Ind., 1981), xiii. Wartime leaders who refuse to bare their souls to superiors can become eccentric mavericks. Another example, from World War II, was General George S. Patton, who sometimes refused to coordinate field operations with other commanders.

34. J. B. Frémont to J. T. Fields, Jan. 19, 1862, and to A. A. Fields, May 29, 1862, Fields Collection, Huntington Library.

35. Alonzo Rothschild, *Lincoln, Master of Men*, 299, 300.

36. Basler, *Collected Works* 4:506.

37. Ibid., 507, 518.

38. Ibid.

39. Milton Rugoff, *The Beechers, an American Family in the Nineteenth Century*, 352, 382, 390, 448; Lincoln quoted in Rothschild, *Lincoln*, 300.

40. On Nov. 1, 1861, Lincoln did approve that part of Frémont's controversial order that instituted martial law; Nevins, *War for the Union* 2:278 and 3:362.

41. T. Harry Williams, *Lincoln and His Generals*, 37.

42. J. G. Randall, *Lincoln the President* 2:24; Paul M. Angle and Earl Schenck Miers, *The Living Lincoln* (New Brunswick, N.J., 1955), 433.

43. Anna Freud, *The Ego and the Mechanisms of Defense*, 51, suggests that such a defense "is first evolved in order to master some specific instinctual urge and so is associated with a particular phase of infantile development."

44. Nevins, *Frémont*, 520; Smith, "Blairs and Frémont," 214–60.

45. S. Chase to S. Cameron, Oct. 7, 1861, Huntington Library.

46. F. Blair to T. Dennison, Sept. 19, 1861, Blair Papers, Princeton University. Also in England, W. L. Dayton, Frémont's vice-presidential running mate in 1856, had drawn upon the federal treasury without authority to pay foreign contracts for munitions. On matters of supply,

see Fred A. Shannon, *The Organization and Administration of the Union Army, 1861–1865* (Cleveland, 1928).

47. Smith, "Blairs and Frémont," 256; F. Blair to M. Blair, Sept. 7, 1861, Blair Papers, Princeton University.

48. E. B. Lee to S. P. Lee, Oct. 7, 22, Blair Papers, Princeton University; M. Blair to A. Lincoln, Sept. 2, 1861, quoted in Smith, *Francis Preston Blair*, 456.

49. M. Blair to A. Lincoln, Sept. 2, 1861, quoted in Smith, *Francis Preston Blair,* 456.

50. E. B. Lee to S. P. Lee, Sept. 17, 1861, and two undated letters, F. Blair to F. P. Blair, all quoted in Smith, *Francis Preston Blair*, 300, 301, 456. The pro-Frémont newspapers claimed that Frank drank heavily, but Blair ultimately accepted appointment as a brigadier general, and after Frémont left Saint Louis, Blair returned there, raised his own army, and went on to help Grant at the Battle of Vicksburg. He subsequently would attain Frémont's rank of major general.

51. The details of the dismissal are in Basler, *Collected Works*, 4:562–63.

52. J. B. Frémont, *Souvenirs*, 195.

53. David P. Dyer, *Autobiography and Reminiscences* (Saint Louis, 1922), 92; Rothschild, *Lincoln*, 320.

54. McClellan had replaced doddering old Winfield Scott as general in command of all union forces. Because even Lincoln could not control him, Robert E. Lee was repeatedly saved by McClellan's caution. A more recent appraisal of Frémont by T. Harry Williams was that "Lincoln had sent a boy to do a man's work." Lincoln saw Frémont as an "attractive person, but a giddy and fumbling general, without the capacity to handle or learn by experience from his mistakes." Quotes from Frederick Maurice, *Statesmen and Soldiers of the Civil War*, 82; Williams, *Lincoln*, 37; Nevins, *Frémont*, 497.

55. Karl Marx, *America and the Civil War*, ed. Saul K. Padover (New York, 1972), 109–10.

56. J. G. Whittier, *Anti-Slavery Poems: Songs of Labor and Reform*, vol. 3 in *Collected Works*, 222.

57. Williams, *Lincoln*, 37; Nevins, *Frémont*, 497; Nevins, *War for the Union* 3:134, 160.

58. F. Lieber to C. Sumner, Jan. 12, 1862, Lieber Collection, Huntington Library.

59. Austin Crabbs, *Civil War Letters*, 1.

60. A. Hallock to J. Bell, Apr. 23, 1862, Bell Collection, Box 2, Huntington Library.

61. William Salter, *The Life of James W. Grimes*, 152–53.

62. Ibid., 155–56.

63. John F. Hume, *The Abolitionists*, 184.

64. Turkoly-Joczik, "Frémont and the Western Department," 367.

Chapter 18. Stonewall's Shenandoah

1. William A. Croffut, *An American Procession, 1835–1914*, 74.

2. Ibid.

3. Quoted in Stephen E. Ambrose, *Halleck, Lincoln's Chief of Staff* (Baton Rouge, 1962), 12.

4. Frederick Phisterer, *Statistical Record of the Armies of the United States* (New York, 1883), 24–54; Ambrose, *Halleck*, 11–14, 60, 117, 209; J. Fallon to H. W. Halleck, Mar. 24, 1863, Eldridge Collection, Box 18, Huntington Library, San Marino, Calif.

5. E. Smith, *Francis Preston Blair*, 297; F. P. Blair's speech, printed in *Congressional Globe* (Washington, 1862), entitled "Frémont's Hundred Days in Missouri," 15.

6. T. Weed to D. Davis, Mar. 15, 1864, Davis Papers, Illinois State Historical Library, Springfield, Ill.

7. Because the Union army offered freedom to blacks who enlisted, 178,000 served in units called United States Colored Troops. Championing the idea of a Negro command for Frémont was another radical political general, Nathaniel P. Banks, former speaker of the House of Representatives and once governor of Massachusetts who had backed Frémont in the 1856 campaign. But Lincoln had objections to "troops raised on any such special terms" and designated "to serve only under a particular commander." See Alonzo Rothschild, *Lincoln, Master of Men*, 322; and Joseph Glatthaar, *Forged in Battle: The Civil War Alliance of Black Soldiers and White Officers* (New York, 1989).

8. Quote is from U. S. Grant to E. Washburne, Mar. 22, 1862, Illinois State Historical Library; Van Buren Denslow, *Frémont and McClellan: Their Political and Military Careers Reviewed*, 7ff.

9. William Brotherhead, *General Frémont and the Injustice Done Him by Politicians and Envious Men*, 17, describes Frémont as "probably the most widely-known man of his age, not of royal birth, in the world," a leader who had won for his country "a province whose untold wealth repaid the cost incurred by Generals Taylor and Scott in conquering territory to be afterwards surrendered. As a man of science he has received the praises of Humboldt and, as popular hero, the applause of the people."

10. J. B. Frémont to F. Billings, Feb. 7, 1862, Park-McCullough House Archives, North Bennington, Vermont.

11. More than likely this was the same White whom George Wright accused of spreading the news about Frémont and Mrs. Corbett. For his quote, see H. White to C. H. Ray, May 28, 1862, Huntington Library; and Austin Crabbs, *Civil War Letters*, 25.

12. J. C. Frémont to C. Sumner, Dec. 14, 1863; J. C. Frémont to E. M. Stanton, Feb. 10, Dec. 14, 1862, cited in Benjamin P. Thomas and Harold M. Hyman, *Stanton: The Life and Times of Lincoln's Secretary of War*, 184.

13. Croffut, *American Procession*, 180.

14. Francis F. Wayland, ed., "Frémont's Pursuit of Jackson in the Shenandoah Valley: The Journal of Colonel Albert Tracy," *Virginia Magazine of History and Biography* 70 (Apr. 1962): 173–75.

15. Ibid., 181–83.

16. See Alf P. Mapp, Jr., *Frock Coats and Epaulets* (Boston, 1982), 298.

17. Croffut, *American Procession*, 185.

18. Wayland, Frémont's Pursuit," 341n; Mark Mayo Boatner, *The Civil War Dictionary* (New York, 1959), 3:210–11; E. B. Long, *The Civil War Day by Day* (Garden City, N.J., 1971), 224–25. Regarding deserters, see John Bowers, *Stonewall Jackson: Portrait of a Soldier*.

19. H. White to C. H. Ray, May 26, 1862, Huntington Library.

20. Allan Nevins, *The War for the Union* 2:125; J. C. Frémont to C. Schurz, Mar. 29, 1862, cited in Hans L. Trefousse, *Carl Schurz: A Biography*, 317. See also Trefousse, pp. 117–19, and Carl Schurz, *The Reminiscences of Carl Schurz, 1852–1863* (New York, 1907), 2:344.

21. J. C. Frémont to F. Frémont, n.d., Huntington Library, contains a footnote from John Charles to Jessie.

22. Quoted in Nevins, *Frémont*, 560.

23. Schurz, *Reminiscences* 2:343–44.

24. Lincoln quote is in a "special copy" of *Memoirs*, xiii, in the Huntington Library. Description is in John R. Howard, *Remembrance of Things Past . . .* , 82. Confederate quotes are from Terry L. Jones, *Lee's Tigers*, 71, 82–6, 91.

25. Croffut, *American Procession*, 169, 171.

26. John F. Hume, *The Abolitionists*, 185.

27. Howard, *Remembrance*, 159, 161, 168.

28. Wayland, "Frémont's Pursuit," 352–53.

29. Thomas and Hyman, *Stanton*, 264.

30. A. Lincoln to I. N. Arnold, May 26, 1863, in Roy Basler, *The Collected Works of Abraham Lincoln*, 6:230.

31. "Papers and Accounts of J. C. Frémont, May 23, 1876, Reel 3, MS. 401, and statement of J. J. Hopper, Head, Secret Service, June 28, 1862, National Archives, Washington, D.C.; "Letter of the Secretary of War," 1864, S. Exec. Doc. 5; *New York Tribune*, Mar. 18, 1863; A. Lincoln to E. M. Stanton, Mar. 7, 1863, in Basler, *Collected Works* 6:127.

32. See Robert Taft, *Photography and the American Scene*, 50. Only twelve portraits were actually published, all from daguerreotypes by Brady. Later, Frémont was dropped from select lists of generals such as that which appeared in *G.A.R. National Encampment* (Boston, 1904); consult Paul M. Angle and Earl S. Miers, eds., *The Living Lincoln* (New Brunswick, N.J., 1955), 542.

33. See chapter entitled " The Attempt to Burn New York" in David H. Bates, *Lincoln in the Telegraph Office*; Howard, *Remembrance*, 196. Also see "The Reminiscences of Francis P. Frémont," Document, C-B 397, pt. 2, box 5, p. 1, Bancroft Library, University of California, Berkeley.

Chapter 19. 1864: The Nonpresidency

1. F. Lieber to H. W. Halleck, Feb. 3, 1864, Lieber Papers, Huntington Library, San Marino, Calif.

2. *New York Weekly World*, Jan. 21, 1864.

3. Gustav Koerner, *Memoirs of Gustav Koerner*, 2 vols. (Cedar Rapids, Iowa, 1909), 2:432.

4. *New York Herald*, Aug. 20, 1863; *New York World*, Jan. 28, 1864.

5. *New York Herald*, June 5, 1864; Manuscript autobiography of Charles D. Drake, Missouri Historical Society, Saint Louis.

6. Henry A. Smythe to S. L. M. Barlow, n.d., Barlow Papers, Huntington Library.

7. Other *prominenti* included Henry Winter Davis, Zachariah Chandler, and Orestes Brownson

8. Quoted in Frederick S. Dellenbaugh, *Frémont and '49*, 470.

9. David Donald, *Charles Sumner and the Rights of Man* (New York, 1970), 165.

10. H. W. Halleck to F. Lieber, Mar. 18, June 2, 1864, Lieber Papers, Box 10, Huntington Library.

11. Sinclair Tousey to F. Lieber, Mar. 16, 1864, Box 65; F. Lieber to H. W. Halleck, June 4, 1864, Lieber Papers, Huntington Library.

12. T. J. Barnett to S. L. M. Barlow, Apr. 10, 1864, Barlow Papers, Huntington Library. Lincoln's fears, however, were eased when the Germans at the convention, who had supposedly been fanatically for Frémont, voted for Lincoln's nomination except for the delegates from Missouri, who proposed Grant as their candidate. With the war still raging, Lincoln knew that Grant could not possibly be spared to run for office. See Charles R. Wilson, "New Light on the Lincoln-Blair-Frémont Bargain of 1864," *American Historical Review* 62 (Oct. 1936): 71–78.

13. Wilson, "New Light," 75.

14. Barlow to Marble, New York, Aug. 24, 1864, Barlow Papers, Huntington Library; James G. Randall and Richard N. Current, *Lincoln the President: Last Full Measure* (New York, 1955), 229–30; Montgomery Blair to A. Lincoln, Dec. 18, 1862, quoted in Smith, *Francis Preston Blair*, 344–45; Douglas S. Freeman, *R. E. Lee* (New York, 1961 abridgement), 278.

15. McClellan to E. Wright, Mar. 19, 1864, McClellan Papers, Huntington Library.

16. McClellan to S. L. M. Barlow, Mar. 16, 1864, McClellan Papers, Library of Congress, Washington, D.C., quoted in William Starr Myers, *A Study in Personality: General George Brinton McClellan*, 444–47; McClellan to S. L. M. Barlow, Sept. 27, 1864, Barlow Papers, Huntington Library; Wilson, "New Light," 75.

17. *New York Nation*, Sept. 26, 1889.

18. "The American" was one of Hay's pseudonyms for Lincoln. Quoted from "Lincoln and Some Union Generals," comp. and ed. William Roscoe Thayer, *Harper's Weekly* (Dec. 1914).

19. A. T. Pickard, *Life and Letters of John Greenleaf Whittier* (Boston, 1907), 2:487.

Chapter 20. Muddled Financial Dreams

1. Quoted in Alice Eyre, *The Famous Frémonts and Their America*, 354.

2. Elizabeth B. Frémont, *Recollections of Elizabeth Benton Frémont*, 131; E. B. Frémont to N. H. Browne, June 8, 1870, Bancroft Library, University of California, Berkeley.

3. William A. Croffut, *An American Procession, 1835–1914*, 78.

4. F. L. Olmsted to F. Kapp, Apr. 6, 1864, quoted in *The Papers of Frederick Law Olmsted*, ed. Victoria P. Ranney, Gerard J. Rauluk, and Carolyn F. Hoffman, 5:220–21, 416.

5. In addition to reservations expressed by D. G. W. Riggs, the New York bankers Duncan and Sherman also did not want to do business with Frémont. Consult Matias Romero, *Correspondencia de la Legación Mexicana en Washington*, vols. 8–10, concerning contracts signed with Romero and General Sánchez Ochoa. Part of Romero's records have been translated in Thomas D. Schoonover, ed., *Mexican Lobby: Matias Romero in Washington*, 130–31. See also Schoonover's *Dollars over Dominion*, 260–62. The manuscript contract is "Nota de un contrato entre el Gral. Gaspar Sánchez Ochoa y el Gral, J. C. Frémont," signed at New York City, Feb. 2, 1866, in the González Ortega Papers, Bancroft Library. See also Fred A. Shannon, *The Organization and Administration of the Union Army*, (Cleveland, 1928), 58, and Robert W. Fraser. "The Ochoa Bond Negotiations of 1865–1867," *Pacific Historical Review* 11 (Dec. 1942): 401–15.

6. The Parisian agent Henri Probst had once supplied Emperor Maximilian's troops in Mexico. See Cardinal L. Goodwin, *John Charles Frémont: An Explanation of His Career*, 244. Craig Miner, *The St. Louis–San Francisco Transcontinental Railroad* (Wichita, Kans., 1972), 50–57.

7. See four undated letters (ca. 1869–70) of Frémont to Vinnie Ream and "Vinnie Ream's Journal Abroad" in Vinnie Ream Hoxie Family Papers, Library of Congress, Washington, D.C. See also Lorado Taft, *The History of American Sculpture* (New York, 1930), 212; Clara Clement, *Women in the Fine Arts* (Boston, 1904), 165; and Clara Clement and Laurence Hutton, *Artists in the Nineteenth Century and Their Works*, 202.

8. Martin Ridge, *Ignatius Donnelly: The Portrait of a Politician*, 124, 163; *Bulletin des Recherches Historiques* 8 (1902), 360–65.

9. See *Congressional Globe*, June 20–23, 1870; U.S. Senate, 41st Cong. 2d sess., 1870, S. Misc. Doc 96. French involvements of the Memphis, El Paso and Pacific Railroad are in U.S. Senate, 41st Cong. 2d sess., 1870, S. Misc. Doc. 121. In Washington, Nathaniel Banks sought to obtain the federal land grants that Frémont's French agents had promised in order to sell stock in his railroad, according to Fred Harvey Harrington, *Fighting Politician: Major General N. P. Banks*, 194.

10. Frémont's transcontinental railroad projects assumed different and confusing names. His venture with Hallett was originally the Kansas and Pacific, later the Memphis, El Paso and Pacific. At one point he projected a road to run from Norfolk, Virginia, westward to San Diego,

then north to San Francisco. He hoped to link the Memphis and Little Rock line with the San Diego and Fort Yuma, all to join together into one grand system that was never built. Regarding the Memphis and El Paso project, see *Congressional Globe*, June 20–23, 1870, and C. Vann Woodward, *Reunion and Reaction* (Boston, 1981), 70–71, 157–58.

11. "The Reminiscences of Francis P. Frémont," Document, C-B 397, pt. 2, box 5, Bancroft Library.

12. J. B. Frémont to S. L. M. Barlow, July 17, 1874, Barlow Papers, Box 91, Huntington Library, San Marino, Calif. For a time, Frémont was a Union Pacific executive. Although he brought legal action against the Union Pacific before the Supreme Court of New York, in 1864 he, along with Ulysses S. Grant and George Opdyke, appeared among the list of that railroad's incorporators. As of that year he claimed $225,000 for 14,490 shares of Union Pacific stock while acting as president of its eastern division. A yellowed letterhead confirms that he held that position. That firm never used construction money he advanced, but instead resold stock that he had trustingly allowed its executives to hold in his name. He sought reimbursement, but in 1867 his claim was "set aside and wholly annulled, with $10 costs." Frémont was lucky to sell these claims to his friend George Browne. This transaction, dated Nov. 26, 1877, is in C-B 397, pt. 1, folder 22, Bancroft Library. See *Frémont Plaintiff, in Supreme Court, City and County of New York* (Albany, 1864).

13. J. B. Frémont to S. P. Lee, Oct. 25, 1865, Blair-Lee Papers, Box 48, Princeton University, N.J.

14. Quoted in Catherine C. Phillips, *Jessie Benton Frémont, a Woman Who Made History*, 278. However, this is a questionable source.

15. Ibid., 293.

16. J. B. Frémont to Carey Jones, Aug. 22, 1870, MS. 28670, Huntington Library. Jones, Frémont's nephew, spent his career as a professor at the University of California, Berkeley.

17. E. B. Frémont to W. J. Morton, Feb. 15, 1877, C-B 391, p. 29, Bancroft Library; "Reminiscences of Francis P. Frémont," Document, C-B 397, pt. 2, box 5, pp. 5–8, Bancroft Library.

18. Ibid.

19. Croffut, *American Procession*, 269.

20. Elizabeth B. Frémont, *Recollections of Elizabeth Benton Frémont*, 118.

21. J. Cooke to H. Cooke, Mar. 1, 1870, in Ellis P. Oberholtzer, *Jay Cooke, Financier of the Civil War*, 2:97, 151, 174n.

22. Goodwin, *Frémont*, 260. Conversely, Allan Nevins too easily dismissed Goodwin's appraisals as deliberately hostile.

23. Quoted from Goodwin, *Frémont*, 259–60."Acting-out" involves the discharge of anxiety by overt behavior; see Burness E. Moore, ed., *A Glossary of Psychoanalytic Terms and Concepts* (New York, 1968), 16.

Chapter 21. Arizona Sunset

1. This holograph is in Folder 53, Frémont Collection, Southwest Museum, Los Angeles, Calif.

2. J. C. Frémont to Z. Chandler, May 28, 1878, Hayes Memorial Library, Frémont, Ohio; J. B. Frémont, "Great Events During the Life of Major General John C. Frémont," manuscript, C-B 397, pt. 1, file labeled "Scraps," Frémont Collection, Bancroft Library, University of California, Berkeley; Thomas A. McMullin and David Walker, *Biographical Dictionary of American Territorial Governors* (Westport, Conn., 1984), 35.

3. E. B. Frémont to W. J. Morton, Sept. 4, 12, 1878, C-B 391, p. 39, Bancroft Library.

4. Ibid., Sept. 12, 1878; this letter is a meaty sixteen-page document.

5. Ibid.

6. Catherine C. Phillips, *Jessie Benton Frémont, a Woman Who Made History*, 300.

7. The wooden-legged Gosper coveted the governorship but did not have the political clout to land the job.

8. J. B. Frémont, *Far West Sketches*, 204, quotes a letter of Nov. 21, 1878; Phillips, *Jessie Benton Frémont*, 300–301.

9. *The Colton Letters: Declaration of Huntington That Congressmen Are for Sale* (n.p., n.d.), 10.

10. The Chiricahua Apache chieftains Victorio and Geronimo menaced white settlements, persistently eluding General George Crook's troops.

11. Scraps in Frémont Collection, Bancroft Library; Phillips, *Jessie Benton Frémont*, 302.

12. "Reminiscences of Francis P. Frémont," Document, C-B 397, pt. 2, folder 5, Bancroft Library.

13. J. B. Frémont, "Great Events," 111. In an article for the *Boston Psychical Society Journal* for Dec. 1888, Jessie told of her early premonition that Frémont had died during his 1853 expedition.

14. J. C. Frémont to R. B. Hayes, May 27, 1874, Hayes Memorial Library, Frémont, Ohio; McMullin and Walker, *Biographical Directory of American Territorial Governors*, 36–37.

15. The mining agreement was in longhand, written by Frémont himself. See Santiago Avira to J. C. Frémont, June 21, 1881, William King Rogers Papers, Bancroft Library; J. C. Frémont to John Steven, Sept. 1, 1879, MS Reel 522, Huntington Library, San Marino, Calif. Geronimo in 1886 finally surrendered, and the Chiricahua Apaches were then removed to Florida.

16. Lily, Frémont's only surviving daughter, was becoming lonely and disappointed. Jessie had borne five children in all; two of them had died before their first year of life. Lily, though the firstborn, unlike her brothers was denied a proper education. Even her friendships had been cut off because of her father's sporadic political feuds. Among her confidantes had been Elizabeth (Lizzie) Blair, with whom she was once close. No great beauty, Lily came to be called "Tomboy Lily." She never married.

17. The *Salt River Herald* was the property of territorial secretary John J. Gosper, who performed much of the governor's work while Frémont was off selling mining stock. Another enemy was John P. Clum, a Republican who owned the *Tucson Citizen* and who resented Frémont's appointment of a Democrat, instead of Clum, as sheriff of Cochise County. See Bert M. Fireman, "Frémont's Arizona Adventure," *The American West* 1 (Winter 1964): 8–19; Elizabeth B. Frémont, *Recollections of Elizabeth Benton Frémont*, 135ff. Like Frémont, Wallace also invested private funds for mining (in the Sandia Mountains). As was the case with Frémont's projects, Wallace's ventures were a complete failure. His wife, Susan, like Jessie, hated the barren Southwest. Consult Oakah L. Jones, "Lew Wallace: Hoosier Governor of Territorial New Mexico," *New Mexico Historical Review* 60 (Apr. 1985): 148.

18. Scraps, Frémont Collection, Bancroft Library; Phillips, *Jessie Benton Frémont*, 305; E. B. Lee to S. P. Lee, July 21, 1883, Blair Papers, Princeton University, N.J.

19. Croffut, *American Procession*, 268.

20. J. C. Frémont to R. B. Hayes, June 24, 1889, Hayes Memorial Library.

21. "Reminiscences of Francis P. Frémont."

22. J. C. Frémont to N. Banks, Apr. 10, 1873, Banks Papers, Illinois Historical Library, Springfield.

23. Jessie wrote by hand long communications for Frémont to sign regarding Mexican claims, including J. C. Frémont to L. Zamarcona [Mexican minister to the United States], June 1, 1890, and J. C. Frémont to Don M. Ruelas [Mexican minister of foreign affairs], June 3, 1880,

as well as J. C. Frémont to Chairman of Mexican Claims Commission, June 10, 1880, all in Bancroft Library.

Chapter 22. "He Spoke No More"

1. Sarah Royce, *A Frontier Lady*, ed. R. H. Gabriel (New Haven, Conn., 1932), 3. Royce's iron-willed mother had toiled across the plains in an ox-drawn wagon, "guided only by the light of Frémont's *Travels*" as well as the King James version of the Bible and a book of John Milton's poetry, and had opened the first school in Grass Valley.

2. J. Royce to H. Oak, Dec. 9, 1884, C-B 386, Part 1, 3; J. B. Frémont, unpublished memoirs; J. C. Frémont, Jr., to J. B. Frémont, July 17, 1890, and to E. B. Frémont, all in Frémont Collection, Bancroft Library, University of California, Berkeley.

3. J. Royce to H. Oak, Apr. 14, 1885, ibid. Oak's still unpublished reminiscences question whether Frémont obeyed Secretary of the Navy George Bancroft's instructions or whether those of Secretary of State James Buchanan were instead observed: "If he disobeyed, he merits only the kind of fame that belongs to a successful filibuster or outlaw. If he deliberately gave false testimony about his orders he deserves the contempt of every honorable man." Consult eighteen letters by Royce to Oak from 1884 to 1915 in Huntington Library, San Marino, Calif. See also Royce's *California from the Conquest in 1845 to the Second Vigilance Committee in San Francisco: A Study of American Character*, and his "Frémont," *Atlantic Monthly* 26 (Oct. 1890): 548, as well as twenty-five-page manuscript essay entitled "Frémont and the Conquest of California," MS. 325, Huntington Library, and J. Royce, "Light on the Seizure of California," *Century Illustrated Monthly Magazine* 40 (Sept. 1890): 792–94.

4. Larkin, though not well educated, craftily held on to his wealth while the Frémont fortunes declined. The Frémonts called him a man of "imperfect education and small experience," boasting that it was Frémont alone who had played the important role in California's conquest. Consult John A. Hawgood, *First and Last Consul: Thomas Oliver Larkin and the Americanization of California*, 2d. ed. (Palo Alto, Calif., 1920): xxxvi; Harlan Hague and David J. Langum, *Thomas O. Larkin* (Norman, Okla., 1990).

5. John Clendenning, ed., *The Life and Thought of Josiah Royce*, 146. See also J. Royce to H. Oak, Dec. 9, 1884, Apr. 14, 1885, and similar letters that follow in John Clendenning, ed., *The Letters of Josiah Royce* (Chicago, 1970).

6. Clendennig, ed., *Life and Thought of Josiah Royce,* 155.

7. These writings included *California from the Conquest in 1846*, which was subtitled *A Study of American Character*. Royce, in a letter to Henry Oak, Aug. 8, 1885, in Clendenning, *Letters*, 170, privately called his own manuscript "Frémont's League with the Devil." But it was not a completely fair-minded treatment of a figure behind whose "charming and courtly manner" he saw "a deep purpose which seemed always to remain in reserve." For Royce had never experienced the need to make command decisions under difficult political and military circumstances. See also Clendenning, *Life and Thought*, 152.

8. J. Royce to H. Oak, Aug. 8, 1885, MS. 20137, Huntington Library; Royce, "Frémont," 548–50. Frémont's reply to these accusations would appear posthumously in the April 1891 issue of *Century Magazine*. He finally admitted knowing about Larkin's peaceful mission during the conquest, but he defended his role in backing the Bear Flaggers and called upon former Secretary of the Navy Bancroft as witness. As Bancroft alone had controlled the first military actions in California (which began as a naval operation), he let Frémont know that he was free to act as he wished. The latter's *Century* article implied that he had kept his instructions secret for forty years in order not to divulge Washington's contradictory designs upon Mexico. Frémont also left behind his own unpublished opinion of Professor Royce: "It seems easy to

men who have never filled important positions or had to make large decisions ... to sit in judgment on the actions of other men—and after the lapse of half a century." See J. C. Frémont to Mr. Whittemore, July 27, 1886, C-B 397, pt. 1, Bancroft Library. The Royce controversy continued beyond Frémont's death. See *The Nation* 52 (1891): 423–25, and *Century Illustrated Monthly Magazine* 41 (Apr. 1891): 917–28, as well as Clendenning, ed., *Life and Thought of Josiah Royce*, 189.

9. Determined to honor her father within her husband's memoirs, Jessie explained: "He *was* the West for a long time." See manuscript scrap dated 1887 on back of an envelope in Folder 44, Frémont Collection, Southwest Museum; William A. Croffut, *An American Procession, 1835–1914*, 61; Catherine C. Phillips, *Jessie Benton Frémont*, 340, and *Memoirs*, 485.

10. Quotes are from manuscript scraps in J. B. Frémont, "Great Events During the Life of Major General John C. Frémont," manuscript, C-B 397, pt. 1, in a file labeled "Scraps," Frémont Collection, Bancroft Library.

11. J. B. Frémont to C. D'Arnaud, Feb. 13, 1888, MS. 39958, Huntington Library.

12. Fragment of a letter from J. B. Green, ca. 1888, Huntington Library.

13. J. B. Frémont to J. B. Green, Mar. 21, 1888, Huntington Library.

14. J. C. Frémont to H. N. Rust, Jan. 16, 1888, Rust Collection, Huntington Library; Jessie B. Frémont, *Far West Sketches*, 40–41.

15. Borglum also did a bust of her. See J. B. Frémont to R. U. Johnson, Sept. 16, 1889, MS Reel 522, Huntington Library.

16. J. B. Frémont to J. B. Green, Mar. 21, 1888, Huntington Library.

17. Jessie could speak of being "established here" in Los Angeles, and of "many pleasant friends." See Phillips, *Jessie Benton Frémont*, 272.

18. Folder 2, Frémont Collection, Southwest Museum.

19. Manuscript scraps in J. B. Frémont, "Great Events."

20. Croffut, in *American Procession*, 66, oblivious to Frémont's French Canadian origins, describes both sons as "tall, black haired, black eyed, and 'bearded like a pard.'" And each, like their sister, showed strains of Gallic blood, the influence of their grandfather, the poor scholarly French gentleman who came to Virginia at the beginning of the century and found their grandmother in her teens." Frank Frémont's court-martial, like his father's many years before, was argued out in the national press. In 1908, President William Howard Taft approved the verdict. Frank, who had served briefly out West in Indian Territory, found employment with a munitions firm in Cuba. Also see Folder 2, Frémont Collection, Southwest Museum. John Charles, Jr., won laurels during the Spanish-American War as commander of the torpedo-boat *Porter*.

21. J. B. Frémont to J. C. Frémont, Jan. 22, 1889, Folder 41, Frémont Collection, Southwest Museum.

22. J. C. Frémont to Madame A. Patti, Apr. 24, 1890, MS Reel 522, Huntington Library. The colony was located where one of his favorite creatures had once come to his aid during California's conquest: "When he and his men had been lost in the enemy-infested hills, the flight of a bee directed his attention to the approach of a relief column." Following the "bee trail," he had emerged at the very spot he suggested to Madame Patti. The story, a garbled one, was associated in his aging mind with General Kearny's relief by Stockton after the Battle of San Pasqual near San Diego. The bee symbol was also embossed on Jessie's letterheads. And, of course, he had trapped a bee high atop the Rockies when ever so young. See Emmett Greenwalt, *California Utopia: Point Loma, 1897–1942* (Berkeley, Calif., 1955), 19.

23. J. B. Frémont, "Great Events."

24. Ibid., 1–2; J. C. Frémont, Jr., to J. B. Frémont, July 17, 1890, C-B 397, pt. 1, Bancroft Library.

25. London's *Daily Telegraph* for July 16, 1890, blandly described Frémont as "an eminent explorer before Mr. Gladstone was a conservative statesman. He was the first to traverse regions which were then unoccupied territories and which are not great centres of population." But the *Paris Herald* for July 13, 1890, recalled that he had presided over the birth of the Republican party, preparing the way for Lincoln's presidency.

26. J. C. Frémont, Jr., to E. B. Frémont, July 14, 1890, Bancroft Library.

27. Jessie had to edit her husband's remarks posthumously. Frémont's article, entitled "The Conquest of California," is in *Century Illustrated Monthly Magazine* 41 (Apr. 1891): 917–28. See also the pioneer John Bidwell's piece in the same issue on pp. 508–25 as well as Royce's colloquy on pp. 780–83 and J. C. Frémont to J. B. Frémont, July 11, 1890, Bancroft Library.

Chapter 23. Carrying on the Legend

1. Two days later the same paper reported that Congress, "in passing a pension bill for the benefit of Mrs. Frémont, has induced that eminent woman to promptly decline further private aids." She asked the *Los Angeles Times* to return three hundred dollars collected on her behalf (Sept. 24, 26, 1890).

2. J. B. Frémont to J. B. Colton, Jan. 16, 1902, Huntington Library, San Marino, Calif.

3. Frederick S. Dellenbaugh, *Frémont and '49*, 480.

4. J. R. Hawley to H. N. Rust, July 29, 1890, MS. 1016, and W. S. Melick to H. N Rust, MS. 1017, Rust Collection, Huntington Library. Rust, a Pasadena nurseryman, became a close friend of Jessie.

5. J. B. Frémont to R. U. Johnson, Apr. 7, 1890, MS Reel 522, Huntington Library; scrap on back of envelope in Folder 45, Frémont Collection, Southwest Museum, Los Angeles, Calif. Hay had become secretary of state.

6. J. B. Frémont, "Great Events During the Life of Major General John C. Frémont," manuscript, C-B 397, pt. 1, file labeled "Scraps," Frémont Collection, Bancroft Library, University of California, Berkeley.

7. Elizabeth B. Frémont, *Recollections of Elizabeth Benton Frémont*, 28–30, is a description reproduced in Jeremiah Lynch, *A Senator of the Fifties* (San Francisco, 1911), 15–17. In 1879, Jeanne Carr extolled this same ride "over ridges, down gorges, around bluffs, and through gloomy defiles" (MS. 91, Huntington Library).

8. Alice Eyre, *The Famous Frémonts and Their America*, 346–47.

9. "Reminiscences of Francis P. Frémont," Document, C-B 397, pt. 2, folder 5, Bancroft Library.

10. T. R. Bard, "Paper Relating to the Claim of Mrs. Frémont," 57th Cong., 1st sess., Dec. 12, 1901, Doc. 61, p. 1.

11. J. B. Frémont to Nellie Browne, Jan. 27, 1891, Bancroft Library; J. B. Frémont to R. U. Johnson, Oct. 1, 1890, MS Reel 522, Huntington Library.

12. Not until Nov. 22, 1894, was Frémont's body—originally buried at Trinity Church in New York—interred near a future monument site. On that occasion Nelson Miles, the army's senior general, represented that service, while Captain John Charles Frémont, Jr., born Apr. 19, 1851, was the navy's spokesman. But fund-raising lagged for years. Not until 1908 did New York Governor Charles Evans Hughes gain an appropriation from the legislature to construct the actual monument. The popular General Daniel Sickles, who had lost a leg in the Civil War, headed up that state's monuments commission, created to erect memorials to the dead of that war.

13. Although the Frémonts had paid forty-one thousand dollars for that site in 1860, the federal government never conceded that their land was even private property. As of 1892,

twelve separate House and Senate committees had investigated their Black Point claim. Lummis recorded in his diary: "T. R. calls me on the whole lot. Talks about Frémont, has file and will do all he can." Roosevelt then reported that compensation for Black Point was in the hands of a recalcitrant Congress, some of whose Southern members remembered that Frémont had sought to free slaves everywhere his army marched during the Civil War. See C. F. Lummis to B. Penrose, and to T. R. Bard, Jan. 5, 1903, Folders 95–97, Frémont Collection, Southwest Museum; B. Colton to T. Roosevelt, Jan. 11, 1902, Huntington Library. Caroline Severance, a prominent clubwoman, was also among the circle of Los Angeles friends who had sought to aid Frémont's heirs. For Lummis's magazine, *Land of Sunshine*, Jessie had written "California and Frémont" (4 [Dec. 1895]): 3–14). He reciprocated by printing Charles Moody's "Here Was a Woman," *Out West* 4 (Feb. 1903): 185. Also see obituaries of Benton Frémont, a grandson, in *San Francisco Examiner*, Oct. 9, 1960; *Fresno Bee*, Oct. 12, 1960. After "95 years of government red tape," the legacy was still unpaid. Upon Benton Frémont's death in 1960, the property was appraised at $2.3 million, but Benton died a pauper.

14. After 1932, vandals stole two howitzers mounted on this edifice as well as the Great Seal of the State of New York. Finally, in 1989 the monument was restored and rededicated. See *Rockland [N.Y.] Journal News*, May 19, 1989.

15. Folder 16, Frémont Collection, Southwest Museum. Joaquin Miller wrote a poem, "Frémont," in *Out West* 4 (Dec. 1895): 185; see also, Dudley Gordon, *Charles F. Lummis, Crusader in Corduroy* (Los Angeles, 1972), 300; "Reminiscences of Francis P. Frémont."

16. Harry M. Majors, *Exploring Washington* (Holland, Mich., 1975), passim. Among flora and fauna are a Frémont pine, cottonwood, and squirrel. The Frémontodendron, or California Glory hybrid, produces a beautiful yellow flower. The General Frémont redwood tree was also named for him. After its dedication in 1888, postcards of it grew popular. California's Frémont County became Yolo County. The town of Frémont, founded in 1846, disappeared by 1864. Frémont Canyon became Sierra Canyon. The peak in San Benito County where he raised the American flag over California on March 6, 1846, is now called Gabilan Peak. Frémont Pass, north of Los Angeles, is today's San Fernando Pass. Still in existence are a Frémont township in Alameda County, California, and a Frémont State Park. In 1881, Frémont and his daughter occupied Casa del Governador, one of Tucson's oldest adobes, now a branch museum of the Arizona Historical Society.

Chapter 24. Ghosts of the Past: An Appraisal of Personality

1. Alfred S. Waugh, *Travels in Search of the Elephant*, ed. John F. McDermott, 15; John Bigelow, *Retrospections of an Active Life* 1:142.

2. Metaphorically, the poet T. S. Eliot has suggested about the process of exploring:

> We shall not cease from exploration,
> And the end of all exploring
> Will be to arrive where we started.

The motivations of "heroic" characters are discussed in Philip Slater, *The Pursuit of Loneliness*; David Winter, *The Power Motive*; and David McClelland, *Power: The Inner Experience*. See also Philip Slater, *Footholds*, and his *The Glory of Hera: Greek Mythology and the Greek Family*, as well as Hugh Berrington, "The Fiery Chariot: British Prime Ministers and the Search for Love," *British Journal of Political Science* 4 (1974): 345–69; and Lucille Iremonger, *Fiery Chariot: A Study of British Prime Ministers and the Search for Love.*

3. This phenomenon has been described by the psychiatrist Robert J. Lifton in his *The*

Life of the Self (New York, 1983) and *Thought Reform and the Psychology of Totalism* (Chapel Hill, 1989).

4. Because the loss of a parent does not necessarily lead to neurosis, some suggest that the "tough-mindedness" of leaders has a genetic instead of a psychoanalytic base. Lloyd Etheredge identified a predisposition among American diplomats prone to use military force as do military men. See his *A World of Men: The Private Sources of American Foreign Policy* (Cambridge, Mass., 1978), as well as Christopher Lasch, *Haven in a Heartless World: The Family Besieged*, and Erik Erikson, "Identity and the Life Cycle," *Psychological Issues* 1 (1959): 110–13. A popularization of Erikson's life-cycle concepts is Daniel J. Levinson, *The Seasons of a Man's Life*. See also Peter Blos, "The Epigenesis of the Adult Neurosis," *Psychoanalytic Study of the Child* 17 (1972): 111; Gregory Rochlin, *Man's Aggression: The Defense of the Self*; and M. L. Rutter, "Relationships between Child and Adult Psychiatric Disorders," *Acta Psychiatrica Scandinavia* 48 (1972): 3–21, as well as L. N. Robbins, "Follow-up Studies Investigating Childhood Disorders," in *Psychiatric Epidemiology*, ed. E. H. Ware and J. K. Wing, 29–68.

5. *Memoirs*, 67.

6. The concept of impulse, or a sudden unstoppable drive to act, was first described by Sigmund Freud; later, Franz Alexander saw such behavior as virtually uncontrollable. See his *Our Age of Unreason: A Study of Irrational Forces in Social Life*; he believed that "chronic achievers" are often persons who experience hidden guilt for having unconsciously usurped their father's role.

7. Klein called the process "projective identification." See also Alfred Adler, *The Practice and Theory of Individual Psychology*, and Robert J. Brugger, ed., *Ourselves and Our Past: Psychological Approaches to American History*.

8. Christopher Lasch, *The Culture of Narcissism*, is a useful popularization. Regarding grandiosity, see Heinz Kohut, *The Analysis of the Self*; Otto Kernberg, *Borderline Conditions and Pathological Narcissism*, 228; and Kohut, "Thoughts on Narcissism and Narcissistic Rage," *Psychoanalytic Study of the Child* 17 (1972): 205–36; as well as Freud's "On Narcissism," in *Standard Edition of the Complete Psychological Works of Sigmund Freud* 14:67ff., and Otto Kernberg, "Factors in the Psychoanalytic Treatment of Narcissistic Personalities," *Journal of the American Psychoanalytic Association* 18 (1969): 51–85.

9. Martha Wolfenstein, "How Is Mourning Possible?" *Psychoanalytic Study of the Child* 21 (1966): 107–108, 112; see also Helen Deutsch, "Absence of Grief," in *Neuroses and Character Types*, 226–36; J. Fleming and S. Altschul, "Activation of Mourning and Growth Through Psychoanalysis," *International Journal of Psychoanalysis* 24 (1969): 419–31; and Martha Wolfenstein, "Loss, Rage, and Repetition," *Psychoanalytic Study of the Child* 24 (1969): 433.

10. See Martha Wolfenstein, "Effects on Adults of Object Loss in the First Five Years," *Journal of the American Psychoanalytic Association* 24 (1976): 659–68. The literature concerning vulnerability that stems from childhood is immense.

11. Christoph Heinicke, "Parental Deprivation in Early Childhood: A Predisposition to Later Depression," in *Separation and Depression*, ed. P. Scott and E. C. Senay (Washington, D.C., 1973), 148. Also see Margaret Mahler, "On the First Three Sub-Phases of the Separation-Individuation Process," *International Journal of Psychoanalysis* 53 (1972): 333–38; and "The Invulnerable Child," discussion group headed by E. James Anthony, Association for Child Psychoanalysis, Princeton, N.J., Mar. 25, 1983, reported in *Bulletin of the, Southern California Psychoanalytic Institute*, Fall 1983: 26.

12. Sigmund Freud, *An Autobiographical Study* (1925), included in *Standard Edition of the Complete Psychological Works of Sigmund Freud* 20:34. A similar situation sometimes exists in the business world, when economic realities matter less than the *perception* of those realities. Many professional historians have been glacially slow to grasp such concepts.

13. See Jacob Cooke, *Alexander Hamilton*. James T. Flexner, *The Young Hamilton*, is heavily psychoanalytic. See also Wolfenstein, "Effects on Adults of Object Loss."

14. "Reminiscences of Francis P. Frémont," Document, C-B 397, pt. 2, folder 5, Bancroft Library; Josiah Royce, "Frémont," *Atlantic Monthly* 26 (Oct. 1890), 548ff.

15. Kenneth M. Johnson, *The Frémont Court Martial*, 78–79.

16. Jackson and Spence 1:xxxvi.

17. Both quotes from Carl Sandburg, *Abraham Lincoln: The War Years*, 4 vols. (New York, 1939), 1:344, 350. Unfortunately, Sandburg does not document quotations; hence, the source of these is untraced.

Manuscripts

Correspondence by and regarding Frémont's many activities is spread throughout dozens of depositories, private and governmental. It is impossible to list all of these many items, some of which are fragmentary, running from excellent to hopeless in usefulness. References to key collections, however, are cited in the notes for this book, as are most sources used.

Among the best of sources are the large Blair and Lee family collections at the Library of Congress in Washington D.C. There also are the Gideon Welles, Joel R. Poinsett, Edwin D. Morgan, W. A. Croffut, Vinnie Ream Hoxie, and Charles Wilkes collections. Stored there as well is the manuscript diary of Micajah McGehee, who participated in the unfortunate fourth expedition. At the National Archives in that city are also numerous Frémont manuscript materials, including government mustering-out claims and pay records pertaining to his expeditions and Civil War service. Examples are "Papers and Accounts of J. C. Frémont, May 23, 1876," and "Statement of J. J. Hopper, Head, Secret Service, June 28, 1862," Reel 3, Manuscript 401.

At the Bancroft Library, University of California, Berkeley, there is a Frémont Collection containing a fragmentary text for a second projected volume of Frémont's memoirs. Prepared by his wife and son Francis, this long manuscript, entitled "Great Events During the Life of Major General John C. Frémont," was never published. See there likewise "The Reminiscences of Francis P. Frémont" and family letters, including fragments of a memoir by Jessie Frémont. Also at the Bancroft are the papers of Thomas Oliver Larkin, which are noted under "Printed Manuscript Material" (below in this bibliography), and the Gonzalez Ortega Papers, which document certain Arizona mining and cattle operations. Historian Hubert Howe Bancroft compiled, as well, a valuable array of "Pioneer Notes," which remain at the library that he founded. Among these, the Peter H. Burnett, Joseph Folsom, and Joseph Chiles papers contain information concerning Frémont. Of particular use is the reminiscence of Thomas Salathiel Martin, one of the Pathfinder's companions, entitled "Narrative of John C. Frémont's Expedition in California in 1845–1846 . . ." (Cal. MS. D. 122). Also notable are the recollections of William F. Swasey (Cal. MS. D. 200) and John Fowler's "The Bear Flag Revolt in California, 1846" (Cal. MS. D. 83), as well as William Hargrave's "California in 1846."

There are also Frémont Papers at the Southwest Museum in Los Angeles, as well as at the Huntington Library, San Marino, California. The latter institution possesses Jessie's manuscript entitled "Secret Affairs Relating to the Mexican War" as well as the Fort Sutter Papers, which shed light upon Frémont's relationship with the Kern brothers, his cartographers and artists. Also at the Huntington I used the William A. Leidesdorff, Abel Stearns-Gaffey, Henry Dalton, and Harbeck collections regarding the early American period in California as well as the small Copley Collection on microfilm (the originals are in La Jolla, California). Also at the Huntington is "Claims of California Volunteers, Papers and Accounts of John C. Frémont, Dec. 2, 1880," Manuscript 401, Microfilm Reel 3 (original destroyed), written by J. M. Perkins, attorney, to H. C. Harmon, government auditor. The Huntington Library also houses the S. L. M. Barlow Papers, whose twenty-nine thousand manuscripts contain scattered material regarding Frémont's involvement in the 1856 and 1864 presidential campaigns, his Civil War years, and his economic ventures. See also the Huntington's Francis Lieber Papers and its James T. Field Manuscripts; the latter touch upon Jessie Frémont's publishing activities. The letters of Josiah Royce at the Huntington cast a unique light on that renowned philosopher's bitterness toward Frémont.

The extensive Blair-Lee Collections at Princeton University in New Jersey and the Frederick Billings Papers at Park-McCullough House in North Bennington, Vermont, were also useful. The Billings manuscripts contain data regarding management of the Mariposas estate as well as information concerning Civil War procurement of arms and other supplies for Frémont. The Allan Nevins Papers at Columbia University in New York City and a second collection of his at the Huntington Library yielded mostly background material.

Numerous theses and dissertations that concern Frémont also exist. One of them concerns his Mariposas operations: C. Gregory Crampton's "The Opening of the Mariposa Mining Region," Ph.D. dissertation, University of California, Berkeley, 1941.

Finally, the RC Collection at the California State Library in Sacramento contains Frémont papers concerning land purchases. Similarly, the Special Collections Department at the University of California at Los Angeles houses miscellaneous Frémont materials, as do the Davis Papers Illinois State Historical Society and the Rutherford B. Hayes Presidential Center, Fremont, Ohio.

Printed Manuscript Material

Rare documents concerning the battle between Frémont's runaway mother and her legitimate husband were reprinted in the *Richmond Enquirer*, *Virginia Patriot*, *Virginia Gazette*, and other early-nineteenth-century southern newspapers. They are cited in the Notes for chapter 1. The early diary of Robert F. Livingston was printed in *Republican Scrapbook*, New York, 1856; a copy of it is in the Occidental College Library at Los Angeles. John Bigelow's *Life of John Charles Frémont* (see below) includes important manuscripts involving Frémont's controversial birth, Commodore Robert F. Stockton and the conquest of California, battles with the rival explorer Charles Wilkes, and Frémont's court-martial trial as well as correspondence he sent to such newspapers as the *National Intelligencer*. For an example of how Frémont communicated effectively through the press, see his statement "To the People of California" in the *San Francisco Alta California*, December 24, 1850. Henry S. Turner, in *Letters of Capt. Henry S. Turner on the Kearny-Frémont Controversy* (Los Angeles, 1958), also throws light on the bitter court-martial proceedings.

Documents relating to Frémont's five expeditions have been collected in three volumes (with two supplements and a map portfolio) by Donald Jackson and Mary Lee Spence in *The Expeditions of John C. Frémont* (Urbana, Ill.); volume 1, ed. Jackson and Spence, is *Travels from 1838 to 1844* (1970); volume 2, ed. Spence and Jackson, is *The Bear Flag Revolt and the Court Martial* (1973); and volume 3, ed. Spence, is *Travels from 1848 to 1854* (1984). *Proceedings of the Court Martial in the Trial of Lieut. Col. Frémont*, originally printed in

Washington in 1848, has been republished by Spence and Jackson as their supplement to volume 2. Frémont's *Report of the Exploring Expedition to the Rocky Mountains in the Year 1842, and to Oregon and North California in the Years 1843–44* appeared originally as S. Doc. 174, 28th Cong., 2d sess., Washington, D.C., 1845. Various editions of that report were printed, one in Germany and others in England and Ireland. A handy version of Frémont's report has recently been published by the Smithsonian Institution (1988). Also Frémont's *Geographical Memoir upon Upper California . . .* , reprinted from the 1848 edition, was edited by Allan Nevins and Dale Morgan in San Francisco in 1964.

In recent times other important manuscripts have been printed, including *Soldier in the West: Letters of Theodore Talbot . . .* , edited by Robert V. Hine and Savoie Lottinville (Norman, Okla., 1972); Talbot was on Frémont's second and third expeditions. Documents regarding the fourth expedition are in *Frémont's Fourth Expedition: A Documentary Account of the Disaster of 1848–1849*, edited by Le Roy and Ann W. Hafen (Glendale, Calif., 1960); it reproduces formerly unknown manuscripts of Charles Preuss, Christopher "Kit" Carson, Theodore Talbot, James Milligan, the Kern brothers, and other companions of Frémont. The first portion of the fifth expedition is chronicled in a recently discovered diary printed under the title *James F. Milligan: His Journal of Frémont's Fifth Expedition, 1853–1854*, edited by Mark Stegmaier and David Miller (Glendale, Calif., 1988). The correspondence of an important contemporary, Thomas O. Larkin, has been printed as *The Larkin Papers: Personal, Business and Official Correspondence . . .* , in ten volumes, with index; it is edited by George P. Hammond and was published in Berkeley in 1951–68. Similarly, volume 5 of *The Papers of Frederick Law Olmsted*, subtitled *The California Frontier*, is invaluable regarding Olmsted's supervision of Las Mariposas. The Olmsted papers are edited by Victoria P. Ranney, Gerald J. Rauluk, and Carolyn F. Hoffman, in five volumes to date, and published in Baltimore in 1990.

Frémont's relations with Abraham Lincoln are recorded in *The Collected Works of Abraham Lincoln*, nine volumes edited by Roy Basler (New Brunswick, N.J., 1953). Francis F. Wayland has edited "The Journal of Colonel Albert Tracy, March–July, 1862," another recently discovered source, under the title "Frémont's Pursuit of Jackson in the Shenandoah Valley"; the article appear in *Virginia Magazine of History* 70 (April, 1962): 165–93, 332–35. Tracy was Frémont's military aide there and earlier in Missouri.

Other Printed Materials

Not every reference in the Notes appears in the following list, which includes contemporary newspaper accounts and legal documents.

Abert, James W. *Through the Country of the Comanche Indians in the Fall of the Year 1845*. San Francisco, 1970.
———. *Notes of a Military Reconnaissance. . . .* Washington, D.C., 1848.
Abert, John J. *Report of Col. John J. Abert and Col. James Kearney. . . .* Washington, D.C., 1831.
Adler, Alfred. *The Practice and Theory of Individual Psychology*. London, 1927.
Alcott, Bronson. *The Journals of Bronson Alcott*. Ed. Odell Shepard. Boston, 1938.
Alexander, Franz. *Our Age of Unreason: A Study of Irrational Forces in Social Life*. Philadelphia, 1942.
Allen, John L. *Passage Through the Garden: Lewis and Clark and the Image of the American Northwest*. Urbana, Ill., 1975.
———. "Pyramidal Height of Land: A Persistent Myth in the Exploration of Western Anglo-America." *International Geography* 1 (1972): 395–407.

Ames, George W. "Horse Marines: California, 1846." *California Historical Society Quarterly* 18 (Winter 1939): 72–84.

Anderson, J. R. L. *The Ulysses Factor: The Exploring Instinct in Man*. London, 1970.

Arrington, Joseph E. "Skirving's Moving Panorama: Colonel Frémont's Western Expeditions Pictorialized." *Oregon Historical Quarterly* 65 (June 1964): 133–72.

Bancroft, Hubert H. *California Pioneer Register and Index, 1542–1848*. In Bancroft's *History of California*. 7 vols. San Francisco, 1884–90.

Bartlett, Ruhl J. *Frémont and the Republican Party*. Columbus, Ohio, 1930.

Bashford, Herbert. *A Man Unafraid*. San Francisco, 1927.

Bates, Davis H. "The Attempt to Burn New York." In *Lincoln in the Telegraph Office*. New York, 1861.

Battles and Leaders of the Civil War. 4 vols. Ed. Robert U. Johnson. New York, 1887–88.

Bauer, K. Jack. *Surfboats and Horse Marines: U.S. Naval Operations in the Mexican War, 1846–48*. Annapolis, Md., 1969.

Bayard, Samuel. *A Sketch of the Life of Com. Robert F. Stockton . . . and Extracts from the Defence of Col. J. C. Frémont. . . .* New York, 1856.

Beahan, Michael. *John Frémont, California Bound*. New York, 1982.

Benton, Thomas H. *Thirty Years' View, or a History of the Working of the American Government for Thirty Years from 1820 to 1850*. 2 vols. New York, 1854–56.

Berrington, Hugh. "The Fiery Chariot: British Prime Ministers and the Search for Love." *British Journal of Political Science* 4 (1974): 345–69.

Bidwell, John. "Frémont in the Conquest of California." *Century Illustrated Monthly Magazine* 41 (March, 1891): 470–517. Reprinted as *In California Before the Gold Rush*. Ed. Lindley Bynum. San Francisco, 1948.

Bierman, John. *The Life Behind the Legend of Henry Morton Stanley*. New York, 1990.

Bigelow, John. *Memoir of the Life and Public Services of John Charles Frémont*. New York, 1856.

———. *Retrospections of an Active Life*. 5 vols. New York, 1909–13.

Blair, Francis P. *Frémont's Hundred Days in Missouri: Speech of F. P. Blair, Jr*. Washington, D.C., 1862.

Blos, Peter. "The Epigenesis of the Adult Neurosis." *Psychoanalytic Study of the Child* 17 (1972): 11–26.

Bonneville, Benjamin L. *The Adventures of Captain Bonneville*. Ed. Edgeley Todd. Norman, Okla., 1961.

Bowers, John. *Stonewall Jackson: Portrait of a Soldier*. Morrow, Calif., 1989.

Bowlby, John. "Grief and Mourning in Infancy and Early Childhood." *Psychoanalytic Study of the Child* 15 (1960): 9–51.

Brandon, William. *The Men and the Mountain: Frémont's Fourth Expedition*. New York: 1955.

Bray, Martha C., and E. C. Bray. *Joseph Nicollet and His Men*. Philadelphia, 1980.

———. *Joseph N. Nicollet on the Plains and Prairies*. Saint Paul, Minn., 1976.

Briggs, Carl, and Clyde F. Trudell. *Quarterdeck and Saddlehorn: The Story of Edward F. Beale, 1822–1893*. Glendale, Calif., 1983.

Brodie, Fawn. *The Devil Drives*. New York, 1967.

Brotherhead, William. *General Frémont and the Injustice Done Him By Politicians and Envious Men*. Philadelphia, 1862.

Browne, John R. *The Mariposa Estate*. San Francisco, 1868.

Brugger, Robert J. *Ourselves and Our Past: Psychological Approaches to American History*. Baltimore, 1981.

Buchanan, A. Russell. *David S. Terry of California, Dueling Judge*. San Marino, Calif., 1956.

Burnett, Peter H. "Recollections and Opinions of an Old Pioneer." Reprint of 1880 original in *Oregon Historical Quarterly* 5 (1904): 86–88.

Bush, Clive. *The Dream of Reason*. New York, 1977.

California Scrapbook Number 28. San Francisco newspaper clippings (1858–59) regarding legal dispute over Almaden and Mariposa mines in Huntington Library, San Marino, Calif.

Camp, Charles L., ed. "The Frémont Episode." *California Historical Society Quarterly* 1–9 (1922–29): 178 in vol. 1 and *passim*.

Carter, Harvey L. *"Dear Old Kit": The Historical Christopher Carson*. Norman, Okla., 1968.

Carvalho, Solomon N. *Incidents of Travel and Adventure in the Far West, with Col. Frémont's Last Expedition*. Ed. Bertram Wallace Korn. New York, 1857; reprint, 1954.

Chambers, William N. *Old Bullion Benton, Senator of the New West*. Boston, 1956.

Chaplin, Jeremiah. *Grant: Words of Our Hero*. Boston, 1886.

Chiles, Joseph. *A Visit to California in 1841*. Ed. George R. Stewart. Berkeley, Calif., 1970.

Clarke, Dwight L. *Stephen Watts Kearny: Soldier of the West*. Norman, Okla., 1961.

Clement, Clara, and Laurence Hutton. *Artists in the Nineteenth Century and Their Works*. Boston, 1894.

Clendenning, John. *The Life and Thought of Josiah Royce*. Madison, Wis., 1985.

Cline, Gloria G. *Exploring the Great Basin*. Norman, Okla., 1963.

Colfax, Schuyler. *Frémont's Hundred Days in Missouri: A Speech in Reply to Mr. Blair*. Washington, D.C., 1862.

Cooke, Jacob. *Alexander Hamilton*. New York, 1982.

Cooling, Benjamin F. *Forts Henry and Donelson*. Knoxville, Ky., 1987.

Crabbs, Austin. *Civil War Letters*. Denver, 1982.

Crampton, C. Gregory, ed. *The Mariposa Indian War, 1850–1851: Diaries of Robert Eccleston*. Salt Lake City, 1957.

Croffut, William A. *An American Procession, 1835–1914*. Boston, 1931.

Crouter, Richard, and Andrew Rolle. "Edward Beale and the Indian Peace Commissioners in California." *Southern California Quarterly* 52 (June 1960): 107–31.

Dakin, Susanna B. *The Lives of William Hartnell*. Stanford, 1949.

Davis, Rebecca H. *Bits of Gossip*. Boston, 1904.

De Celles, A. D. "John Charles Frémont." *Bulletin des Recherches Historiques* 7 (1902): 360–61.

———. "Louis-René Frémont." *Mid-America* 5 (April 1934): 235–41

Dellenbaugh, Frederick S. *Frémont and '49*. New York, 1914.

Denslow, Van Buren. *Frémont and McClellan: Their Political and Military Careers Reviewed*. Yonkers, N.Y., 1862.

Deutsch, Helen. "Absence of Grief." In *Neurosis and Character Types*. New York, 1965.

Doetsch, Raymond N. *Journey to the Green and Golden Land: The Epic of Survival on the Overland Trail*. Port Washington, N.Y., 1876.

Downey, Joseph T. *The Cruise of the Portsmouth, 1845–1847*. Ed. Howard Lamar. New Haven, 1958.

Duvall, Marius. *A Navy Surgeon in California, 1846–47 . . . the Journal of Marius Duvall*. Ed. Fred B. Rogers. San Francisco, 1957.

Dwinelle, John W. *The Colonial History of San Francisco*. San Francisco, 1866.

Eaton, John. *Grant, Lincoln, and the Freedmen. . . .* New York, 1907.

Egan, Ferol. *Frémont, Explorer for a Restless Nation*. New York, 1977.

Ellet, Elizabeth. *Queens of American Society: A Memoir of Mrs. Frémont*. New York, 1867.

Ellis, Edward S. *The Life and Times of Christopher Carson, the Rocky Mountain Scout and Guide, with Reminiscences of Frémont's Exploring Expeditions. . . .* New York, 1861.

Ellison, William H. "San Juan to Cahuenga: The Experience of Frémont's Battalion." *Pacific Historical Review* 27 (Aug. 1958): 245–61.

Engelbrecht, H. C., and F. C. Hanighen. *Merchants of Death*. New York, 1934.

Erikson, Erik. *Identity and the Life Cycle*. New York, 1980.

———. *Identity, Youth, and Crisis*. New York, 1968.

Ewers, John C. *Artists of the Old West*. New York, 1965.

Eyre, Alice. *The Famous Frémonts and Their America*. Santa Ana, Calif., 1948. Rev. ed., Boston, 1961.

Favour, Alpheus H. *Old Bill Williams, Mountain Man*. Norman, Okla., 1962.

Fender, Stephen. *Plotting the Golden West: American Literature and the Rhetoric of the California Trail*. Cambridge, Mass., 1981.

Fiedler, Fred E. "Validation and Extension of the Contingency Model of Leadership Effectiveness." *Psychological Bulletin* 76 (Sept. 1981): 307–21.

Fireman, Bert M. "Frémont's Arizona Adventure." *American West* 1 (Winter 1964): 8–19.

Fleming, J., and S. Altschul. "Activation of Mourning and Growth Through Psychoanalysis." *International Journal of Psychoanalysis* 24 (1969): 419–31.

Flexner, James T. *The Young Hamilton*. Boston, 1978.

Foote, Henry S. *Speech . . . on Admission of California*. Washington, D.C., 1850.

———. *Casket of Reminiscences*. Washington, D.C., 1874.

Fraser, Robert W. "The Ochoa Bond Negotiations of 1865–1867." *Pacific Historical Review* 11 (Dec. 1942): 401–15.

Frémont, Elizabeth B. *Recollections of Elizabeth Benton Frémont*. Comp. I. T. Martin. New York, 1912.

Frémont, Jessie B. " California and Frémont." *Land of Sunshine* 4 (Dec.1895): 3–14

———. *Far West Sketches*. New York, 1890.

———. *Mother Lode Narratives*. Ed. Shirley Sargent. Ashland, Ore., 1970.

———. "The Origin of the Frémont Expeditions." *Century Illustrated Monthly Magazine* 41 (Mar. 1891): 766–71.

———. *Souvenirs of My Time*. Boston, 1887.

———. *The Story of the Guard: A Chronicle of War*. Boston, 1863.

———. *A Year of American Travel*. New York, 1878; reprint, San Francisco, 1960.

Frémont, John C. "The Conquest of California." *Century Illustrated Monthly Magazine* 41 (Apr. 1891): 917–28. Posthumously published.

———. "In Command in Missouri." In *Battles and Leaders of the Civil War*. Vol. 1. Ed. Robert U. Johnson and Clarence C. Buel. 4 vols. New York, 1887.

———. *Memoirs of My Life*. Chicago, 1887.

Frémont, Louis-René. "Documents Concerning. . . ." *Mid-America* 16, n.s. 5 (1934): 235–41.

Freud, Anna. *The Ego and the Mechanisms of Defense*. Rev. ed., New York, 1966.

Freud, Sigmund. "Mourning and Melancholia." In *Standard Edition of the Complete Psychological Works of Sigmund Freud*. Vol. 14. Ed. James Strachey. London, 1957.

———. "On Narcissism." In *Standard Edition of the Complete Psychological Works of Sigmund Freud*. Vol. 14. Ed. James Strachey. London, 1957.

Friis, Herman R. "The Role of the United States Topographical Engineers in Compiling a Cartographic Image of the Plains Region." In *Images of the Plains.* Ed. Brian W. Blouet and Merlin P. Lawson. Lincoln, Nebr., 1975.

Gates, Paul W. "Adjudication of Spanish-Mexican Land Claims in California." *Huntington Library Quarterly* 21 (May 1958): 213–36.

———. "The Frémont-Jones Scramble for California Land Claims." *Southern California Quarterly* 56 (Spring, 1974): 13–44.

Gilbert, Bil [*sic*]. *Westering Man: The Life of Joseph Walker.* New York, 1983.

Goetzmann, William H. *Army Exploration in the American West, 1803–1863.* New Haven, Conn., 1959.

———. *Exploration and Empire: The Explorer and the Scientist in the Winning of the American West.* New York, 1966.

———. *New Lands, New Men: America and the Second Great Age of Discovery.* New York, 1986.

———. *The West as Romantic Horizon.* Omaha, Nebr., 1981.

Goodwin, Cardinal L. *John Charles Frémont: An Explanation of His Career.* Palo Alto, Calif., 1930.

Grant, Ulysses S. *The Papers of Ulysses S. Grant.* 3 vols. Carbondale, Ill., 1967.

Greeley, A. W. "John Charles Frémont the Pathfinder." In *Explorers and Travellers.* London, 1894.

Greeley, Horace. *An Overland Journey from New York to San Francisco in the Summer of 1859.* San Francisco, 1860.

———. *A Year of American Travel.* New York, 1860.

Grierson, Francis. *The Valley of the Shadows.* New York, 1909.

Griffin, John S. *The Doctor Comes to California: The Diary of John S. Griffin, Assistant Surgeon With Kearny's Dragoons, 1845–1847.* San Francisco, 1943.

Groh, George. *Gold Fever.* New York, 1966.

Guild, Thelma S., and Harvey L. Carter. *Kit Carson: A Pattern for Heroes.* Lincoln, Nebr., 1984.

Gunnison, John W. *Map of a Reconnaissance Between Fort Leavenworth on the Missouri River and the Great Salt Lake in the Territory of Utah.* New York:1852.

Gwin, William M. "Memoirs of Hon. William M. Gwin." Ed. W. H. Ellison. *California Historical Society Quarterly* 20 (Mar. 1940): 1–26.

Hague, Harlan, and David J. Langum. *Thomas O. Larkin: A Life of Patriotism and Profit in Old California.* Norman, Okla., 1990.

Harlow, Neal. *California Conquered: War and Peace on the Pacific, 1846–1850.* Berkeley, Calif., 1982.

Harrington, Fred H. "Frémont and the North Americans." *American Historical Review* 54 (July 1939): 842–48.

Hastings, Lansford W. *The Emigrants' Guide to Oregon and California.* Cincinnati:1845. Reprint, New York, 1969.

Hawgood, John A. *America's Far Western Frontiers.* New York, 1967.

———. "John C. Frémont and the Bear Flag Revolution: A Reappraisal." *Southern California Quarterly* 44 (June 1962): 67–96.

Hawthorne, Hildegarde. *Born to Adventure: The Story of John Charles Frémont.* New York, 1947.

Heffernan, William J. *Edward M. Kern, Artist-Explorer.* Bakersfield, Calif., 1953.

Henderson, Daniel. *The Hidden Coasts.* Westport, Conn., 1953.

Herr, Pamela. *Jessie Benton Frémont: American Woman of the Nineteenth Century*. New York, 1987.

Hine, Robert V. *Edward Kern and American Expansion*. New Haven, 1962.

Hofling, Charles K. *Custer and the Little Big Horn: A Psychological Inquiry*. Detroit, 1981.

Hollister, Ovando J. *Life of Schuyler Colfax*. New York, 1886.

Horney, Karen. *The Neurotic Personality of Our Time*. New York, 1927.

Howard, John R. *Remembrance of Things Past.* . . . New York, 1925.

Hulbert, Dorothy. "The Trip to California: An Explanation Notice of the Panorama . . . at the Théâtre de Variétés, Paris, August 8, 1850." *Frontier and Midland* 14 (1934): 160–61, 168–69.

Hume, John F. *The Abolitionists*. New York, 1905.

Hussey, John A. "The Origin of the Gillespie Mission." *California Historical Society Quarterly* 18 (Mar. 1940): 32–63.

Hyman, Harold M. *Stanton: The Life and Times of Lincoln's Secretary of War*. New York, 1962.

Ide, Simeon. *A Biographical Sketch of the Life of William B. Ide*. Claremont, N.H., 1880. Reprint, Oakland, Calif., 1944.

Iremonger, Lucille. *Fiery Chariot: A Study of British Prime Ministers and the Search for Love*. London, 1970.

Jackson, Donald. "The Myth of the Frémont Howitzer." *Bulletin of the Missouri Historical Society* 23 (Apr. 1967): 205–14.

Johnson, Kenneth M. *The Frémont Court Martial*. Los Angeles, 1968.

Johnson, Michael P. "Planters and Patriarchy: Charleston, 1800–1860." *Journal of Southern History* 46 (Feb. 1980): 45–72.

Jones, Oakah L. "Lew Wallace: Hoosier Governor of Territorial New Mexico." *New Mexico Historical Review* 60 (Apr. 1985): 129–58.

Jones, Terry L. *Lee's Tigers*. Baton Rouge, La., 1987.

Jones, William C., Jr. *The First Phase of the Winning of California*. San Francisco, 1887.

Jones, William C., Sr. *John Charles Frémont, Appellant* [to Supreme Court of the United States]. Washington, D.C., 1855.

Karnes, Thomas L. *William Gilpin, Western Nationalist*. Austin, Texas, 1970.

Kearny, Thomas. "Concerning Frémont." *The Argonaut* (Feb. 15, 1931): 6.

Kernberg, Otto. *Borderline Conditions and Pathological Narcissism*. New York, 1975.

———. "Factors in the Psychoanalytic Treatment of Narcissistic Personalities." *Journal of the American Psychoanalytic Association* 18 (1969): 419–31.

Kohut, Heinz. *The Analysis of the Self*. New York, 1971.

———. *The Restoration of the Self*. New York, 1977.

———. "Thoughts on Narcissism and Narcissistic Rage." *Psychoanalytic Study of the Child* 17 (1972): 205–36.

Kushner, Howard. "Biochemistry, Suicide, and History." *Journal of Interdisciplinary History* 16 (Summer 1985): 69–85.

———. "The Suicide of Meriwether Lewis: A Psychoanalytic Inquiry." *William and Mary Quarterly* 38 (July 1981): 464–81.

———. *Self-Destruction in the Promised Land: A Psychocultural Biography of American Suicide*. New Brunswick, N.J., 1984.

Lasch, Christopher. *The Culture of Narcissism*. New York, 1978.

———. *Haven in a Heartless World: The Family Besieged*. New York, 1977.

Lasswell, Harold. *Psychopathology and Politics*. Chicago, 1977.

Lavender, David. *Bent's Fort*. New York, 1954.

Leidecker, Kurt F. *Yankee Teacher: The Life of William Torrey Harris*. New York, 1946.

Levinson, Daniel J. *The Seasons of a Man's Life*. New York, 1978.

Lewis, Ernest A. *The Frémont Cannon: High Up and Far Back*. Glendale, Calif., 1981.

Lewy, Ernst. "Historical Charismatic Leaders." *Journal of Psychohistory* 6 (Winter 1979): 388–91.

Lifton, Robert J. *The Life of the Self*. New York, 1983.

———. *Thought Reform and the Psychology of Totalism*. Chapel Hill, N.C., 1989.

Lummis, Charles F. "Whittier and Frémont." *Out West* 18 (Mar. 1903): 336.

Lyman, George D. *John Marsh, Pioneer*. New York, 1930.

McClelland, David. *Power: The Inner Experience*. New York, 1975.

McFeely, William S. *Grant: A Biography*. New York, 1981.

McGehee, Micajah. "Rough Times in Rough Places." *Century Illustrated Monthly Magazine* 41 (Mar. 1891): 771–80.

McLane, Louis. *The Private Journal of Louis McLane, U.S.N. 1844–1848*. Ed. Jay Monaghan. Los Angeles, 1971.

McNeil, Samuel. *McNeil's Travels in 1849. . . .* Columbus, Ohio, 1850.

Magoon, James. *The Life of J. C. Frémont, the Rocky Mountain Explorer*. London, 1862.

Mahler, Margaret. "On the First Three Sub-phases of the Separation-Individuation Process." *International Journal of Psychoanalysis* 53 (1972): 333–38.

Majors, Harry M. "Frémont in Oregon." *Northwest Discovery* 3 (Oct. 1982): 168–88.

Marti, Werner. *Messenger of Destiny: The California Adventures, 1846–1847, of Archibald H. Gillespie*. San Francisco, 1960.

Martin, Thomas S. *With Frémont to California and the Southwest, 1845–1849*. Ed. Ferol Egan. Ashland, Ore., 1975.

Maurice, Frederick. *Statesmen and Soldiers of the Civil War*. Boston, 1926.

Mazlish, Bruce. *The Revolutionary Ascetic*. New York, 1977.

Meigs, William M. *The Life of Thomas Hart Benton*. Philadelphia, 1904.

Merwin, Henry C. *Life of Bret Harte*. Boston, 1911.

Miller, Joaquin [Cincinnatus Hiner]. "Frémont." *Out West* 4 (Dec. 1895): 185.

———. *Overland in a Covered Wagon*. Ed. Sidney G. Firman. New York, 1930.

Miner, H. Craig. *The St. Louis-San Francisco Transcontinental Railroad: The Thirty-fifth Parallel Project, 1853–1890*.Lawrence, Kans., 1972.

Montaignes, François des [pseudonym of Isaac Cooper]. *The Plains. . . .* Ed. N. A. Mower and Don Russell. Norman, Okla., 1972.

Moody, Charles A. "Here Was a Woman." *Out West* 18 (Jan. 1903): 169–86.

Moore, Jackson W., Jr. *Bent's Old Fort: An Archeological Study*. Denver, 1973.

Morgan, Philip D. "Black Life in Eighteenth Century Charleston." *American Perspectives* 1 (1984): 187–232.

Murphy, Lawrence R. *Lucien Bonaparte Maxwell, Napoleon of the Southwest*. Norman, Okla., 1983.

Murray, Robert. "The Frémont-Adams Contracts." *Journal of the West* 5 (Oct. 1966): 517–24.

Myers, William S. *A Study in Personality: General George Brinton McClellan*. New York, 1934.

Nevins, Allan. *Frémont: The West's Greatest Adventurer*. 2 vols. New York, 1928. Rev.ed., New York, 1939, 1955, 1961, under title *Frémont: Pathmarker of the West*.

———. *Narratives of Exploration and Adventure*. New York, 1956.

————. *The War for the Union.* 4 vols. New York, 1959–71.

Nicollet, Joseph N. *The Journals of Joseph N. Nicollet.* Ed. Martha C. Bray. Saint Paul, Minn., 1970.

Oberholtzer, Ellis P. *Jay Cooke, Financier of the Civil War.* Philadelphia, 1907.

Peacock, Virginia. *American Belles of the Nineteenth Century.* Philadelphia, 1901.

Phelps, William D. *Alta California, 1840–1842: The Journal and Observations of William Dane Phelps, Master of the Ship* Alert. Ed. Britton Busch. Glendale, Calif., 1987.

————. *Fore and Aft; or, Leaves in the Life of an Old Sailor.* Boston, 1871.

Phillips, Catherine C. *Jessie Benton Frémont, a Woman Who Made History.* San Francisco, 1935.

Phillips, Christopher. *Damned Yankee: The Life of General Nathaniel Lyon.* Columbia, Mo., 1990.

Polk, James K. *Polk: The Diary of a President, 1845–1849.* Ed. Allan Nevins. New York, 1968.

Pollock, George H. "Childhood, Parent and Sibling Loss in Adult Patients." *Archives of General Psychiatry* 7 (1962): 295–305.

Preuss, Charles. *Exploring with Frémont: The Private Diaries of Charles Preuss.* Trans. and ed. Erwin G. and Elizabeth K. Gudde. Norman, Okla., 1958.

Randall, James G. *Lincoln the President.* 2 vols. New York, 1946.

Rank, Otto. *The Myth of the Birth of the Hero.* New York, 1941.

Rather, Lois, *Jessie Frémont at Black Point.* Oakland, 1974.

Read, George W. "Diseases, Drugs, and Doctors on the Overland Trail. ..." *Missouri Historical Review* 38 (Apr. 1944): 260–76.

Ridge, Martin. *Ignatius Donnelly: The Portrait of a Politician.* Chicago, 1962.

Rippy, J. Fred. *Joel R. Poinsett, Versatile American.* Durham, N.C., 1935.

Robbins, L. N. "Follow-up Studies Investigating Childhood Disorders." *Psychiatric Epidemiology.* Ed. E. H. Ware and J. K. Wing. New York, 1970.

Rochlin, Gregory. *Man's Aggression: The Defense of the Self.* Boston, 1973.

Rogers, Fred B. *William Brown Ide, Bear Flagger.* San Francisco, 1962.

————. *Bear Flag Lieutenant: The Life Story of Henry L. Ford.* San Francisco, 1961.

Rolle, Andrew. "Exploring an Explorer: Psychohistory and John Charles Frémont." *Pacific Historical Review* 51 (May 1982): 131–63.

————. "Frémont." *Encyclopaedia Britannica.* Vol. 9 (1967): 862–63.

Romero, Matias. *Correspondencia de la Legación Mexicana en Washington.* 10 vols. Mexico City, 1870.

Rothschild, Alonzo. *Lincoln, Master of Men.* Boston, 1906.

Rowell, Galen. *In the Throne Room of the Mountain Gods.* San Francisco, 1977.

Roy, R. G. "Le général Frémont." *Bulletin des Recherches Historiques* 31 (Nov. 1925): 477–78.

————. "Le général Frémont, était-il Canadien français?" In *Les petites choses de notre histoire.* Quebec, 1922.

————. "Les ancêtres du Général Frémont." *Recherches Historiques* 4 (1897): 277–78.

Royce, Josiah. *California from the Conquest in 1846 to the Second Vigilance Committee in San Francisco: A Study of American Character.* New York, 1886. Reprint, New York, 1948.

————. "Frémont." *Atlantic Monthly* 26 (Oct. 1890): 548ff.

————. *The Letters of Josiah Royce.* Ed. John Clendenning. Chicago, 1970.

————. "Light on the Seizure of California." *Century Illustrated Monthly Magazine* 40 (Sept. 1890): 792–94.

————. "Montgomery and Frémont: New Documents on the Bear Flag Affair." *Century Illustrated Monthly Magazine* 41 (Mar. 1891): 780–83.

Rugoff, Milton. *The Beechers, an American Family in the Nineteenth Century.* New York, 1981.

Rutter, M. L. "Relationships Between Child and Adult Psychiatric Disorders." *Acta Psychiatrica Scandinavia* 48 (1972): 3–21.

Salter, William. *The Life of James W. Grimes.* New York, 1876.

Schofield, John M. *Forty-Six Years in the Army.* New York, 1897.

Schoonover, Thomas D. *Dollars over Dominion.* Baton Rouge, La., 1978.

————. *Mexican Lobby: Matias Romero in Washington.* Lexington, Ky., 1986.

Schubert, Frank N. *Vanguard of Expansion: Army Engineers in the Trans-Mississippi West, 1819-1879.* Washington, D.C., 1981.

Schurz, Carl. *The Reminiscences of . . . , 1852–1863.* 2 vols. New York, 1907.

Sherman, William T. *Memoirs.* Reprint, Bloomington, Ind., 1957.

Shore, Miles F. "Biography in the 1980s." *Journal of Interdisciplinary History* 12 (Summer 1981): 89–113.

Sibley, H. H. "Memoir of Jean N. Nicollet." In *Minnesota Historical Society Collections.* Vol. 1. Saint Paul, Minn., 1872.

Simpson, Craig. *A Good Southerner: The Life of Henry A. Wise of Virginia.* Chapel Hill, N.C., 1985.

Simpson, James H. *Journal of a Military Reconnaissance . . . Made in 1849.* Philadelphia, 1852.

Slater, Philip. *Footholds.* New York, 1977.

————. *The Glory of Hera: Greek Mythology and the Greek Family.* Boston, 1971.

————. *The Pursuit of Loneliness.* New York, 1970.

Slotkin, Richard. *The Fatal Environment: The Myth of the Frontier.* New York, 1985.

Smith, Elbert B. *Francis Preston Blair.* New York: 1980.

————. *Magnificent Missourian: The Life of Thomas Hart Benton.* Philadelphia, 1958. Reprint, Westport, Conn., 1973.

Smith, Justin H. *The War with Mexico.* 2 vols. New York, 1919.

Smith, Michael L. *Pacific Visions: California Scientists and the Environment, 1850–1915.* New Haven, 1987.

Smith, William E. "The Blairs and Frémont." *Missouri Historical Review* 23 (Jan. 1929): 214–60.

————. *The Francis Preston Blair Family in Politics.* 2 vols. New York, 1933.

Smucker, Samuel M. *The Life of John Charles Frémont.* New York, 1856.

Spence, Mary L. "David Hoffman: Frémont's Mariposa Agent in London." *Southern California Quarterly* 60 (Winter 1978): 379–403.

————. "The Frémonts and Utah." *Utah Historical Quarterly* 44 (Summer 1976): 286–302.

————. "George W. Wright: Politician, Lobbyist, Entrepreneur." *Historical Review* 58 (Aug. 1989): 345–59.

————. "Jessie Benton Frémont: First Lady of Arizona." *Journal of Arizona History* 24 (Spring 1983): 55–72.

Steckmesser, K. L. *The Western Hero in History and Legend.* Norman, Okla., 1965.

Stenberg, Richard R. "Polk and Frémont, 1845–1846." *Pacific Historical Review* 7 (Sept. 1938): 211–27.

Stewart, George R. *The California Trail: An Epic with Many Heroes.* New York, 1962.

Strobel, Max. *Las Mariposas.* New York, 1861.

Sturhahn, Joan. *Carvalho: Artist, Photographer, Adventurer, Patriot*. Merrick, N.Y., 1976.

Sullivan, Harry S. *The Interpersonal Theory of Psychiatry*. New York, 1953.

Taft, Robert. *Artists and Illustrators of the Old West, 1850–1900*. New York, 1953.

———. *Photography and the American Scene*. New York, 1938.

Talbot, Theodore. *The Journal of Theodore Talbot*. Ed. Charles H. Carey. Portland, Ore., 1931.

Tanner, John, Jr., and Gloria Lothrop, eds. "Don Juan Forster, Southern California Ranchero." *Southern California Quarterly* 52 (Sept. 1970): 195–230.

Taylor, Bayard. *Eldorado; or, Adventures in the Path of Empire*. Reprint, New York, 1949.

Tays, George. "Frémont Had No Secret Instructions." *Pacific Historical Review* 9 (June 1940): 159–71.

Thomas, Benjamin P., and Harold Hyman. *Stanton: The Life and Times of Lincoln's Secretary of War*. New York, 1962.

Thompson, Gerald. *Edward F. Beale and the American West*. Albuquerque, N.M., 1983.

Torrey, John. *Plantae Frémontianae; or, a Description of Plants Collected by Col. Frémont*. Washington, D.C., 1854.

Tracy, Albert. "Frémont's Pursuit of Jackson in the Shenandoah Valley: The Journal of Colonel Albert Tracy." Ed. Francis F. Wayland. *Virginia Magazine of History and Biography* 70 (Apr. 1962): 173–75.

Trefousse, Hans L. *Carl Schurz: A Biography*. Nashville, Tenn., 1982.

Turkoly-Joczik, Robert L. "Frémont and the Western Department." *Missouri Historical Review* 82 (July 1988): 363–85.

Turner, Henry S. *The Original Journal of Henry Smith Turner. . . .* Ed. Dwight L. Clark. Norman, Okla., 1967.

Unruh, John. *The Plains Across: The Overland Emigrants and the Trans-Mississippi West, 1840–1860*. Urbana, Ill., 1979.

Upham, Charles W. *Life, Explorations and Public Service of John Charles Frémont*. Boston, 1856.

Vallejo, Mariano G. *Being a Brief Sketch . . . with His Address Before the Junta at Monterey in the Year 1846*. San Francisco, 1927.

———. *Release from Fort Sutter*. San Francisco, 1937.

Van Orman, Richard A. *The Explorers*. Albuquerque, N.M., 1984.

Wagner, Henry R. "Edward Bosque, Printer and Man of Affairs." *California Historical Society Quarterly* 21 (Dec. 1942): 325–40.

Wallace, J. *Abandoned by Lincoln: A Military Biography of General John Pope*. Urbana, Ill., 1990.

Wallace, Lewis. *Lew Wallace: An Autobiography*. New York, 1906.

Waugh, Alfred S. *Travels in Search of the Elephant*. Ed. John F. McDermott. Saint Louis, 1951.

Weber, David J. *Richard H. Kern: Expeditionary Artist in the Far Southwest, 1848–1853*. Albuquerque, N.M., 1985.

Weed vs. Opdyke: The Great Libel Case. New York, 1865.

Wheat, Carl. *Mapping the Transmississippi West, 1540–1861*. 5 vols. San Francisco, 1957–63.

Whittier, J. G. *Anti-Slavery Poems: Songs of Labor and Reform*, vol. 3 in *Collected Works*. Cambridge, Mass., 1888.

Wilford, John N. *The Mapmakers*. New York, 1981.

Wilkes, Charles. *Narrative of the United States Exploring Expedition*. 5 vols. and atlas. Washington, 1844.

Wilkins, Walter L. "Group Behavior in Long Term Isolation." In *Psychological Stress: Issues in Research*. Ed. Mortimer H. Appley and Richard Trumbull. New York, 1967.

Williams, Kenneth P. *Lincoln Finds a General*. 3 vols. New York, 1949–59.

Williams, T. Harry. *Lincoln and His Generals*. New York, 1952.

Wilson, Charles R. "New Light on the Lincoln-Blair-Frémont Bargain of 1864." *American Historical Review* 62 (Oct. 1936): 71–78.

Wiltsee, Ernest. *The Truth About Frémont: An Inquiry*. San Francisco, 1936.

Winter, David. *The Power Motive*. New York, 1973.

Wise, W. H. A. *Los Gringos; or, An Inside View of Mexico and California*. Reprint, New York, 1949.

Wolfenstein, Martha. "Effects on Adults of Object Loss in the First Five Years." *Psychoanalytic Study of the Child* (New York, 1966), 21:93–112.

———. "How is Mourning Possible?" *Psychoanalytic Study of the Child* (New York, 1966), 21:107–108, 112.

———. "Loss, Rage, and Repetition." *Psychoanalytic Study of the Child* (New York, 1969), 21:433.

Wolin, Howard E. "Grandiosity and Violence in the Kennedy Family." *Psychohistory Review* 8 (Winter 1979): 27–37.

Woodworth, Francis C. *The Young American's Life of Frémont*. New York, 1856.

Wright, Doris. *A Yankee in Mexican California*. Santa Barbara, Calif., 1977.

Wyatt, David. *The Fall into Eden: Landscape and the Imagination in California*. New York, 1986.